Curriculum Research and Development in Action

By the same author

An Introduction to Curriculum Research
and Development

Curriculum Research and Development in Action

edited by

Lawrence Stenhouse
Professor of Education,
Centre for Applied Research in Education,
University of East Anglia

HEINEMANN EDUCATIONAL BOOKS

Heinemann Educational Books Ltd
22 Bedford Square, London WC1B 3HH

LONDON EDINBURGH MELBOURNE AUCKLAND
HONG KONG SINGAPORE KUALA LUMPUR NEW DEHLI
IBADAN NAIROBI JOHANNESBURG
EXETER (NH) KINGSTON PORT OF SPAIN

First published 1980

British Library Cataloguing in Publication Data
Curriculum research and development in action.
    1. Universities and colleges – Great Britain
    – Curricula – Case studies
    I. Stenhouse, Lawrence
    378. 1′99′0941   LB2362.G7
ISBN 0–435–80852–4 (cased)
        0–435–80853–2 (paper)

Printed in Great Britain by
Richard Clay (The Chaucer Press)
Bungay, Suffolk

Contents

Acknowledgements

The editor and publishers wish to thank the following for permission to reproduce copyright material on the pages indicated:

Cambridge University Press for the extract from A. G. Howson (ed.), *Developments in Mathematical Education* (Proceedings of the Second International Congress on Mathematical Education) (p. 37).

Education Development Center, Inc., Newton, Mass., for Table 15.1 (p. 219) and extracts (pp. 218 and 220) from Hanley *et al., Curiosity, Competence, Community – An Evaluation of Man: A Course of Study*.

Education for Teaching for extracts from J. Elliot and C. Adelman, 'Reflecting Where the Action Is: the Design of the Ford Teaching Project' (p. 233).

Evans/Methuen Educational for extracts from the Schools Council Working Paper No. 26: *Education Through the Use of Materials* (pp. 151 and 152).

The Controller, Her Majesty's Stationery Office, for extracts from Schools Council Working Paper No. 2: *Raising the School Leaving Age: a Co-operative Programme of Research and Development* (pp. 140–41).

Holmes McDougall for extracts from *A New Look at History*, Schools Council Project History 13–16 (p. 183).

Macmillan Education for extracts from D. Tawney (ed.), *Evaluation in Curriculum Development: Twelve Case Studies* (Schools Council Research Studies) (p. 89).

The Nuffield Foundation for the extract from its 9th Annual Report (p. 81).

Schools Council Publications for the extracts from the Schools Council Working Paper No. 1: *Science for the Young School Leaver* (p. 82) and from D. Shemilt, *On Observing Experiments and Anticipating Reality: the Evaluation of History 13–16*, (draft material) (p. 186–7).

Teaching History for extracts from D. Sylvester, 'First Views from the Bridge' in issue no. 3, 10, 433 (pp. 182–3 and p. 185).

1 Introduction

This book is intended as a companion to my *Introduction to Curriculum Research and Development* (Stenhouse, 1975); but the two are not inseparable companions. Together they are intended to sustain a curriculum course in which both the practice of the students and that of the curriculum projects can be illuminated by theory and provide a grounding for it. The first thought behind the present volume was to provide a framework for a study of the practice of large-scale curriculum research and development. Each student in a seminar group of up to fourteen in number should be able to undertake a study in some depth of a particular project or enterprise using the relevant chapter in this book as a starting point, and *An Introduction to Curriculum Research and Development* as a source book for theoretical issues.

However, some of those who have seen the manuscript have remarked that the book presents through brief case studies a portrait in a landscape of the English curriculum development movement which is particularly associated with the Nuffield Foundation and the Schools Council. This suggests that it may interest the general reader seeking information about a major feature of education over the last fifteen years, and that it can provide the overseas educationist with an introduction to the practice – and by inference to the assumptions – of curriculum research and development in England. He should be warned that while Wales, and to a lesser extent Scotland, have been involved in some of this work, he would do well not to generalise his conclusions to either country without attempting verification. Each has a distinctive character and intellectual tradition; and Scotland has an almost wholly independent educational system.

The choice of topics in this book is worth an introductory comment. The opening chapter by Jean Rudduck describes the work of one of the English subject associations, the National Association for the Teaching of English (NATE). These teacher groups have been of great importance in shaping curriculum, especially since the Second World War. NATE has been a powerful influence on the Schools Council English Committee and has stimulated the setting up of projects, while its annual conferences have been important in generating and reviewing ideas. In general, teachers' subject associations have been major elements in the scene of any project. The subject projects have found them important in consultation, support and dissemination. Those projects, like the Humanities Project or Project Technology, which cut across subject boundaries and hence across those of subject associations, have missed this support and have often had to struggle against the opposition of the associations. Subject associations are an important aspect of the landscape in which projects must be set.

Wilfred Flemming's account of the Schools Mathematics Project (SMP) introduces the curriculum movement with an untypical, but instructive, example. SMP is unique among the projects in that it started from an informal – almost domestic – group of mathematicians teaching in schools and university who secured financial support from industry rather than from a foundation or the Schools Council. It testifies, too, to the potential strength of leads coming, as this one did, from the public school sector, whose high status and success in providing access to higher education make it a reference point for many state schools. It is interesting and important that this project secured a financial independence by the sales of materials which provided a basis for the continuity for which its director, Bryan Thwaites, argues in his comment.

Primary French, which is reviewed by Ralph Fletcher, introduces not only the Nuffield Foundation, but also the local education authorities (LEAs) and Her Majesty's Inspectorate (HMI). Rather typically the Nuffield Foundation noticed that there might be a job to be done and looked around for allies in the system who might collaborate in doing it.

The HMI role, to which we are introduced here, is difficult to document and is not adequately treated in this book. While there is no doubt of their influence, researchers are not allowed access to the documents of the Inspectorate. Moreover, it is not clear that the important HMI influence at conferences and on visits to LEAs and schools is likely to be documented at all. Their support or opposition is of considerable importance, but it is often a matter of 'a word in the right ear'.

Again, LEA policies are of crucial importance. Indeed, there is evidence from some curriculum projects that LEA organisation and attitude may be crucial for success or failure in their area, and the Humanities Curriculum Project and later Geography for the Young School Leaver based their dissemination strategies firmly on LEAs. The reader should not underestimate the importance of LEA initiatives and influence, and should note that the concentration of this book on curriculum projects mutes the LEA role. Another book could be written about curriculum development and innovation in LEAs.

Primary French also introduces the theme of systematic evaluation studies with Clare Burstall's controversial *Primary French in the Balance* (Burstall *et al.* 1974). The Schools Council, having commissioned a statement on evaluation from Stephen Wiseman and Douglas Pidgeon, did not accept the resulting study for publication, and it was published as *Curriculum Evaluation* by the National Foundation for Educational Research in 1970. The line taken in that book was that inherited from experimental psychology, sometimes called the psycho-statistical paradigm. It has been critically attacked in *Beyond the Numbers Game* (Hamilton, Parlett, MacDonald, Jenkins and King, 1977) and its failure to provide summative evaluation data in its application in the United States is reported by Walker and Schaffarzick in an article in the *Review of Educational Research* (1974).

The subsequent story of educational evaluation in England and Wales is interesting. My own interpretation is that a number of projects – of which I think the Humanities Curriculum Project was the first – produced proposals for their own evaluations. Some persuasion was initially required to get the Schools Council to fund such evaluations, but in the end it was readily willing to do so provided the resources allocated were not too great. American experience suggests that, if you give the research community its head, your evaluation investment may be as large as – or even larger than – your investment in development. Some of these Schools Council evaluations are reviewed in a publication in the Council's Research Series, *Evaluation in Curriculum Development: Twelve Case Studies* (Schools Council, 1973); and the use of 'in' rather than 'of' in the title suggests a resolution to keep evaluation in a developmental – perhaps even a 'formative' – role.

However, there was another aspect of the power of evaluation. As I interpret it, the Schools Council was generally hostile to the designation of curriculum development as a professional area: that is, it did not encourage directors to undertake successive development projects or to regard themselves as career curriculum specialists. This was associated with its general policy of seconding teachers to staff curriculum development teams.

But it did come to recognise the professional identity of evaluators and, in alliance with the Schools Council's research team, the evaluators were able to establish a relatively durable group, which met for a series of conferences. It was from this group that the *Twelve Case Studies* and Tawney's *Curriculum Evaluation Today: Trends and Implications* (1975) were produced. Supplemented by Hamilton's *Curriculum Evaluation* (1976), these provide for the student of evaluation a good general account of the situation in Britain.

By the end of the first three chapters of this book we have been introduced to the main protagonists of curriculum development other than the Schools Council itself. They are: the teachers' associations, the teachers, the universities, HMI, the examining boards, the local education authorities, the educational research community as represented by the evaluators, and the Nuffield Foundation.

The fourth chapter, by Rob Walker, provides a portrait of one of the Nuffield Science Projects, and an interesting one, since it heralded the large fundings associated with the raising of the school leaving age, being directed at the ordinary citizen in the secondary school. In its strategies it represented the maturity of the Nuffield pattern both in its style – find the right person and back him – and in its organisation of writing and trials. It was the project to which the Nuffield Foundation directed me for briefing when I took up the directorship of the Humanities Project.

Rob Walker also contributes an account of Project Technology, politically perhaps the most complex of all the projects. Although this was a Schools Council project, there is a lot of Nuffield style about it – the hands of Geoffrey Caston and Joslyn Owen at the Schools Council? There is a sense in which Project Technology, in its aim to build out and consolidate a movement, was the first dissemination project. From the first it wanted its message to take precedence over materials, and it represented first and foremost an attitude towards science and technical work, a true fusion of them in a concept of technology which brought up to date the practical application of scientific thinking which was earlier represented by such nineteenth century figures as Kelvin.

Science 5–13 by contrast was both rooted in schools and of all projects most influenced by formative evaluation. John Elliott's account draws heavily on interview and documents the desire to follow up Nuffield Junior Science, which had failed to take in the system (see Wastnedge 1972), with a curricular expression of similar ideas which gave more support to teachers. A principal means towards this was clarifying objectives and this in turn provided a classic niche and a strong influence for the evaluator (Wynne Harlen). Both in its books for teachers and in its materials, Science 5–13 is an exemplar of the objectives approach to curriculum expressed through a mature flexibility which overcomes many of the problems encountered by this approach pursued with doctrinaire confidence.

The Humanities Curriculum Project, reviewed here by Alasdair Aston, was another bridge between the Nuffield tradition and that of the Schools Council. The lack of subject base in this and the Keele Integrated Studies Project had an interesting side effect: the senior staff of both were educationists rather than teachers of subjects. Hence, perhaps, the Humanities Project's interest in the modulation of teaching strategy to raise and explore the problem of the authority relationship between teachers and adolescents. Probably no other project has been so productive of debate about methods. And although – or rather perhaps because – the rejection by the project of the objectives model left no ready-made niche for the evaluator, its evaluation by Benny MacDonald greatly influenced subsequent theory.

The Design and Craft Project, though perhaps it did not attract such general interest as the Humanities Project, had more in common with it than at first meets the eye; for it sought in the craft area to make skill subordinate to judgement and hence encountered a good many problems of teaching method and spirit. And, as Tom Dodd notes, it provided a means of expression for its director's view of the relationship of education and society. Like the Humanities

Curriculum Project, it was in a social sense an emancipatory project, eager to increase the powers of the man in the street.

History 13–16 and Geography for the Young School Leaver are second generation projects and reasonably representative of the Schools Council in full flight. Ivor Goodson's account of History 13–16 catches the keenly felt need for development in both of these subject areas, subject as they apparently were to inroads from integrated studies, as well as to the vagaries of option systems in schools. It is clear that a crucial issue in the History project is its judgement that history as a study is not amenable to the development of a conceptually based curriculum. The result is a project which emphasises historical method both in traditional and in radical contexts. There is a sense in which this has been a modest project, though recent large grants for dissemination are likely to amplify its voice.

By contrast Geography for the Young School Leaver (which incidentally shares with the Humanities Project the characteristic of being originally funded on a College of Education) is the contemporary extrovert among projects. It started with a resolution to disseminate vigorously and in terms of adoption it is the most successful of all Schools Council projects. A great majority of schools in England and Wales have taken it up. Carl Parsons has rightly emphasised this planning and design component which has led to the project's mass acceptability. Its materials are not only well produced but also raise in principle problems of teaching method similar to those in the Humanities Project while providing a kindlier support for the teacher who finds these problems difficult to resolve.

In his chapter on Mathematics Applicable Raymond Heritage provides an account of a second-generation mathematics project sponsored by the Schools Council. This project, directed by C. Ormell, is concerned with mathematics for sixth-formers who are not specialising in the subject. This niche has given it something of the freedom of the young-school-leaver projects and the older target population has also been an advantage. The result is that the project has been able to pursue a line which is controversial both in respect of its underlying philosophy of knowledge and in its educational practice. It has been innovatory too in response to the problems it has posed itself: for example, in using sealed 'hints' in examination which offer candidates help in exchange for a marks forfeit, thereby overcoming the steep gradient of disadvantage when a candidate in a mathematics examination gets 'stuck'.

The remaining chapters document the British dissemination of an American project (not too common a situation), an example of the Scottish tradition of curriculum development, and finally a project which has given attention to problems of teaching which were thrown into relief by the curriculum development movement.

The British dissemination of MAN: a Course of Study is racily and controversially described by David Jenkins. The curriculum is of particular interest as an expression in classroom materials and teachers' handbooks of a particular view of teaching which has an alternative expression in Jerome Bruner's books, *The Process of Education* (1960) and *Towards a Theory of Instruction* (1966). It is thus a curriculum which may reasonably be criticised by well-articulated criteria. It falls short, but remains in the view of those disseminating it in Britain, much the best practical expression of the problems and possibilities of discovery-based teaching in academic subject areas. Jenkins is ambivalent about this, unsure apparently whether the disseminators have made a break-through as a result of a well-taken pass or are off-side.

Sally Brown's account of Scottish Integrated Science points up the different pattern of curriculum development in Scotland where in a more centralised system the Inspectorate has been much more influential and where Scottish Education Department policy, the examination system and the committee-style development have been in step. But it is by no means clear that the classroom teacher has been able to keep up with their powerful march. Moreover, Scotland has not made a large investment in materials production like that of the Schools Council and the strains of part-time writing are sometimes evident.

Finally, Elizabeth Adams gives us a picture of the Ford T Project, a virtuoso collaboration between teachers and researchers to explore the problems and logics of inquiry – and discovery – teaching. This project, in which John Elliott, formerly of the Humanities Project, and Clem Adelman, formerly of the Chelsea Science Centre, worked together made considerable progress with the teaching method problem which had been thrown into relief by the curriculum development movement.

It is our hope that taken together these studies in the practice of curriculum research and development will provide a framework which the student can fill out both by further study of the projects dealt with briefly here and by study of other projects and curricular initiatives in which he may be interested. To support him in the latter enterprise, I close this introduction with the guideline which, as editor, I sent to the contributors to this volume.

Guide for contributors

The following should be covered – or touched on – in the case of each project:

1. Did the project have a prehistory, before the director and staff were appointed?
2. How much freedom did the director/staff have on appointment and how did they use it?
3. Did the project have aims (as opposed to teaching aims)? Did it spell these out? Was it reform, research, development, experiment?
4. Did the project deal in teaching aims? If so how did it deal with them?
5. Was there any discernable 'design' – experimental design or development model? Was it expressed or implicit or even unconscious? To what extent did it leave space for the responsive?

6. Did the project produce materials? Willingly or under pressure? For teachers or pupils or both? Did it test them? In what sense?
7. Was the publisher an important influence?
8. Did the project produce research reports, books, articles, etc? If so, what are they like?
9. Was there an evaluation? Was it in any sense independent of the project? What did it evaluate? Did it publish its reports? How were they received?
10. Was there a consultative or steering committee? Who was on it? Was it influential – through discussion, constraints or support?
11. Was there any plan of dissemination? If so, what was its aim, what was its pattern of organisation?
12. Did the project arouse criticism or hostility? If so, what were the grounds?
13. How did the project react to such criticisms; and what was its defence against them?
14. Was the project given credit or praise by teachers or press? If so, on what grounds?
15. How do these grounds relate to what the project says about itself?
16. What is the situation at present?
17. What do you regard as the main strengths and weaknesses of the project?
18. Provide a bibliography of:
    (a) Teaching materials produced by project
    (b) Handbooks etc. produced by the project
    (c) Periodicals or journals produced by project (even if ceased)
    (d) Articles or papers or books about the project

2   The National Association for the Teaching of English

Basic information

Status   Subject Association.

Membership   Currently about 3,500. Members are drawn from all levels of the education system. Current subscription: ordinary member £6.00 per year, student member £3.00 per year.

Office   10b Thornhill Road, Edgerton, Huddersfield, HD3 3AU.

Secretary   Until 1978, Anthony Adams, lecturer, Department of Education, Cambridge University.
1978–79 Lewis Smith, York and District Education Centre.

Established   1963.

Concerns   'To improve the teaching of English at all levels of education; to provide a forum for discussion, experiment and research in all matters which touch on the teaching of the language and its literature; to foster international cooperation on all matters of interest to English teachers; to provide a national, authoritative voice on all aspects of education which concern English.'

Research and development interests   NATE has been involved with a number of research and development projects in association with the Schools Council and other funding agencies. These have included a study of the use of the class reader, language and the disadvantaged child, English in the primary school, the use of the educational visitor at the pre-school stage. NATE has been instrumental in the foundation of language policies across the curriculum. It has also concerned itself with public examinations in English.

Origins and growth of the Association

George Allen, Her Majesty's Staff Inspector for English, was at one of the last meetings of the English Panel of the Secondary Schools Examination Council, which he chaired. It was late 1962 and the Examination Council was soon to be disbanded to make way for the Schools Council for Curriculum and Examinations. 'It was time', George Allen said, 'that there was a national association for English Teachers'. Denys Thompson, a member of the panel and editor of the journal *The Use of English* took the initiative and brought in, to help with the negotiations, Boris Ford, then Director of the Institute of Education at Sheffield, who, according to a letter in the NATE archive (19 December 1962), was thought of as 'an excellent organiser who knows everyone'.

A London Association for the Teaching of English, LATE, had been established some years before and there were also in existence some local Use of English groups. All these came together, in 1963 to form the National Association for the Teaching of English (NATE). A meeting was arranged on 4 April, in London, for the co-ordinators of these local groups: 'My clear recollection is that it was a difficult meeting, steered with great skill and patience by the chairman'. The chairman was Boris Ford. (Thompson, letter, 8 June 1968, NATE archive).

An extract from the minutes of this first meeting documents the early concerns and aspirations:

> The objectives of an Association of teachers of English should be to promote livelier and better teaching of English. It will be the responsibility of members themselves to determine, by discussing in local groups and at national conferences, the detailed meaning to be attached to this generalised statement.
> In the early stages, at least, its interpretation must be catholic and non-partisan.

The structure of the Association should be federal, allowing for the affiliation of existing groups of English teachers; provision should also be made for individual membership.

The role of the Association would be:

(i)   To suggest, stimulate and co-ordinate the discussion of particular topics ... [The three mentioned were text books, the CSE examination and LEA expenditure on books.]
(ii) To collect and disseminate information about, for instance, examination syllabuses, new teaching approaches, relevant research.
(iii) To arrange an annual conference ...
(iv) To represent teachers of English at a National Level, and where necessary to act as a pressure group.   (NATE archive)

An inaugural conference was planned for September 1963 and Boris Ford wrote to all Directors of Institutes (NATE archive) asking each to contribute £25 to sponsor the conference. He also wrote to the Calouste Gulbenkian Foundation for a grant and Whitehead recalls, in his chairman's address to the fifth annual conference, NATE's gratitude to the Foundation which had 'acted as a kindly godfather to the Association during its difficult opening years'. (Whitehead 1967, p. 4) One hundred residential and thirty non-residential places were booked in London for the inaugural conference – the places to be offered on a representational basis. Professor Randolf Quirk was one of the invited speakers and he was 'exceedingly enthusiastic; indeed he is so keen to launch the Association that he is prepared to fly back from holiday to join the conference' (letter, 10 May 1963, NATE archive). The conference succeeded and NATE was a reality.

In 1964 the first edition of the NATE journal appeared and the first of the NATE annual conferences was held. The significance of the conference was acknowledged by the robust presence of Sir Edward Boyle, Secretary of State for Education, who gave the opening address. In it, he said this:

> It looks as though in the new [Schools] Council, teachers will be in an absolute majority, and this I welcome unreservedly. Certainly in English, as in other subjects, the Schools Council offers us a new chance to see that the curriculum comes first and the examinations second; only so will freedom of the curriculum be a reality ... Its work will not be easy but it will be easier if the subject associations also play their part... That's why I welcome so warmly your new and vigorous association. It will and must provide a focusing point for professional opinions about all that has to do with teaching of English at all stages. (*Bulletin*, 1, 2, 1964)

The first number of the NATE quarterly *Bulletin* 'consisted of 18 pages and had a print order of 1,000 copies' (Editorial, *English in Education*, Summer 1973). Boris Ford had questioned the wisdom of launching another English journal (NATE archive) but a need was felt. An editorial in the second issue of the *Bulletin* explained that whereas *The Use of English*, which was edited by Denys Thompson, presented 'articles by *individuals* describing good classroom practice, one of the strengths of NATE lies in its groups and the work they can do in study projects, researches and surveys; and the *Bulletin* will publish the results of these and in general reflect group activity.' In 1967 the title of the NATE *Bulletin* became *English in Education*.

Membership and structure

By April 1964 NATE had 1,000 members and 40 branches. By 1966 there were 3,500 members and 60 branches. By 1968, membership stood at 4,000; 30 branches were active, 19 were about to be launched, and several had failed to report and were presumed lost. A NATE officer 'confessed that the processes by which a study-group comes to life and thrives remain mysterious'. (ABM minutes). In 1977 there were over 3,000 members, 34 branches and 7 corporate members, including LATE, which had retained its identity as an independent association. Clearly, one reason why members leave is the rise in subscription, and one reason why branches die is the growing local activity of other agencies, such as teachers' centres.

A consistent trend throughout NATE's life-time has been the much higher number of secondary than primary school teachers who are attracted to take out membership. (See, for instance, Table 29, p. 371 in *A Language for Life*, the Bullock Report 1975.)

NATE's structure has changed only in detail since its inception in 1963. The governing body of NATE, the Council, is appointed at the business meeting of the Annual Conference. There are twelve elected members of Council, six co-opted members and a representative from each of the NATE branches. A number of invited representatives also attend. In addition to Council there is an Executive Committee, a Finances and General Purposes Committee, a Publications Committee and three sub-committees: the 16+ and Examinations

Committee; the Primary Committee; and the Pre-School Committee. The Council meets, as do most of the committees, three times a year. The meetings of the Council are now open to all NATE members who may attend as observers.

The NATE Honorary Officers are chairman, vice-chairman and the past chairman; secretary and two assistant secretaries; treasurer; membership secretary; conference officer; publications editor. Other administrative roles are the Newsletter editor, the advisory officer and the NATE office manager. At one time there was also a publicity officer, and a secretary of studies whose responsibility was to co-ordinate and stimulate branch activity. Until 1974, when NATE made some financial economies, honoraria were paid to the treasurer, editor, secretary and assistant secretaries, but now only the office manager and her part-time secretaries, at present working from privately owned premises in Huddersfield, receive payment.

NATE's financial resources are its membership subscriptions, royalties from sales, and any profit from its large-scale annual conferences. A recurrent lament in the minutes of the ABMs is that 'The desires of NATE still outstrip the resources of time and money available' (April 1970). Until recently, branches received 25 per cent of the income from subscriptions. When the membership fee was £4 this meant that every branch received £1 per member. When the subscription was recently increased to £6 branches continued to receive only £1 per member, and branch leaders were encouraged to make claims on the central fund for special activities, projects or events. The treasurer's estimates for 1977–78 were:

Income (excluding conference profit):	£17,023
Expenditure:	£15,669

The influence of NATE

How does one begin to assess the influence of NATE on teachers of English and on policy makers (whether examining boards, publishers, head-teachers, or LEAs) whose decisions affect the work of teachers of English?

It is tempting to look at membership figures as an indication of NATE's potential for influence but although the Association regularly reminds itself that 'increased membership is the first necessity if we are to strengthen our voice', the officers are aware, and frequently say, that the magnitude of NATE's influence cannot be deduced from the formal membership:

... the influence of the Association is much more widespread than the size of its membership on paper would suggest; ... our publications certainly find their way into the hands of teachers who are not in any way known to the Association. The same is true of branch meetings, many of which are open to non-members also. The effect of NATE as a body permeating the teaching of English is difficult to define but certainly exists, and it seems to us that there has been a measurable change in the climate of opinion about English teaching in the last ten years – for which the Association must take much of the credit   (Secretary's report, ABM minutes, 1973)

Joslyn Owen, former Joint Secretary of the Schools Council and now a Chief Education Officer, supports this view of NATEs influence:

> ... the most successful associations in England have so far been the Association for Science Education, the National Association for the Teaching of English and a small group of associations which centre their interests on school mathematics. In each of these a marked awareness has been visible from the mid-1960s and earlier about the challenge of curriculum reform.   (Owen 1973, 112)

Owen mentions one feature which impressed him particularly: '... in mathematics and in English the associations themselves have initiated important development work on a national scale, sometimes with – but more often without – the support of public funds.'

(Owen 1973, 113)

Let us look first, then, at NATE's funded and unfunded work in curriculum development.

NATE'S FUNDED PROJECTS

In 1967, the Calouste Gulbenkian Foundation awarded NATE a grant of £8,250 for three projects concerned with the improvement of English teaching. (Whitehead 1967, 4). The first was designed to examine English in the primary schools in the light of the Plowden Report. The second was a user-survey of the teaching of prose literature with pupils in the 11–16 age range. A NATE research officer was appointed to gather and process the data for this project which was under the overall supervision of Frank Whitehead. The third activity was an international conference held in the summer of 1968 on the teaching of English to disadvantaged children. All three projects issued publicly available materials of some kind (see bibliography). The third activity had two additional outcomes. The original conference, 'The Language of Failure Conference', led to the setting up of a NATE subcommittee 'The Language of Failure' committee. This committee supported Ethel Seaman in initiating and co-ordinating a home visiting project known as the Norwich Feasibility Study (1972–75) – which was described in the Bullock Report (1975):

> One particularly encouraging initiative came from a group of Norwich teachers who planned it in association with NATE. The teachers [with the permission of the Norwich Education Committee and under the guidance of John Nicholls of the English Department of Keswick Hall College of Education] volunteered to make monthly visits to families with a number of children, one of whom was between eighteen months and two years. The teachers worked with parents and aimed to help them increase the range of linguistic opportunity for their children.   (5.16)

In 1975 the Language of Failure committee was replaced by the Pre-School committee with responsibility for continuing to work for the Association in pre-school language development. Through it, NATE takes account of early home influences, the pre-school playgroup movement and child minders as well as local authority provision such as day nurseries and nursery schools. This committee also seeks to keep in touch with current language development of the very young as well as explorations of alternative strategies for encouraging this.

But at least one member of NATE was disappointed that the Association was not playing a more prominent role in large-scale curriculum development activity such as that currently being funded by the Schools Council and the Nuffield Foundation. In 1972, John Dixon, a leading figure in NATE and a former chairman of the English Committee of the Schools Council, included the following passage in a paper prepared for the final plenary session of the annual conference:

> Over each of the past five years there have been at least two or three national curriculum projects to attract a school or department – Breakthrough [to Literacy], Language in Use, the Humanities [Curriculum Project], Children as Readers. Only one of these has been run by NATE, and we must ask ourselves – why?
>
> (Dixon 1972, 72)

The answer is complex, and is partly about the difficulty of distinguishing NATE projects from projects directed by NATE members. Children as Readers was formally set up as a NATE project. It had a total grant of £18,109 and was directed by Douglas Barnes from 1968–70, and then by Jeremy Mulford from 1970–73. The project failed to produce a major publication: the Schools Council, which funded the project, chose not to make use of the final report. Indeed, publication may not have been regarded by members of the project team as the most appropriate way to disseminate the work of the project. As early as 1968 Mulford had written this passage in a NATE Newsletter (August edition): 'Although we should like eventually to publish, we are keeping firmly in mind that teachers are joining primarily to sharpen their own awareness of what they are doing.'

The form of the project ensured a degree of dissemination through teacher involvement: the project was organised by a voluntary panel of teachers who worked in their spare time on exploring the role of literature in the curriculum of primary and secondary pupils. Anthony Adams, the NATE Secretary stressed the importance of the structure of the project:

> We set up groups of teachers supported by the project team, doing curriculum development on a local, in-service, teachers' centre based programme as opposed to the centre-periphery model of curriculum development which had been very much the model up to that time. I would suspect that we were among the first to get this sort of thing off the ground. It would be very difficult to document, but it was a very important development. The real value of the project has been the work done with teachers.
>
> (Interview, December 1977)

The projects described above, three sponsored by the Gulbenkian Foundation and one by the Schools Council, were all proposals for which NATE, as a body, had been responsible, but there were other projects not officially associated with NATE but where there were enough NATE links to make the projects' paternity ambiguous.

Six Schools Council projects exhibit, with NATE, cross-membership of personnel and some common ground in the development of ideas. The Written Language of 11–18 Year-Olds (1966–71; £33,517) was directed by James Britton, a former chairman of NATE. The dissemination phase of this project was conceived as a separate enterprise and was directed by Nancy Martin (1971–76; £68,426). Nancy Martin, also a prominent figure in NATE, followed closely the model that has come to be associated with NATE: the main dissemination activity was conducted through the meetings of teacher groups, sometimes, but not always, based on existing NATE branch memberships. Pat D'Arcy, current chairman of NATE, directed the Review of Post-war Research and Experiments in Method in the Teaching of Reading (1967–70; £2,600). The late Connie Rosen directed Language Development in the Primary School (1969–72; £11,500). Andrew Wilkinson directed the project on Oracy (1967–72; £16,000). Frank Whitehead directed the project on Children's Reading Habits (1969–74; £25,137). John Dixon is responsible for the project English 16–19 (1975–79; £77,000). What is interesting is that this list of project directors reads like a *Who's Who* for NATE. The plot thickens when one probes further and finds that many of the names (Britton, Martin, the Rosens) would also figure in the *Who's Who* for LATE.

It is perhaps the research and development work of the LATE group, especially their exploration of the idea of 'language across the curriculum', that has been most widely acclaimed; and given the opportunities which the project teams have taken to express their ideas in editions of the NATE journal and to present them to teachers at NATE conferences, this identification with NATE is not surprising. Anthony Adams sums up the complexity of the relationships:

> [The idea of] Language across the curriculum began as a discussion document produced by LATE and first reached public notice ·at the NATE conference at Reading (in 1971) and from then onwards 'language across the curriculum' got off the ground. That coincided with the chairmanship of Jimmy Britton – and that led to his inclusion in the Bullock Committee. It would be quite wrong to argue that Jimmy's ideas owe anything to NATE. They have been formulated over twenty to thirty years of thinking. But, without a doubt, Jimmy's influence in both LATE and NATE has been central in establishing the idea, not just nationally but internationally, and has led to what some think is a slightly dangerous, over-ready acceptance of the Britton-Martin model of language ... It has become the NATE orthodoxy and it is very difficult to hear any NATE speaker open his mouth on a public platform – including myself, I must confess – without using this model. Jimmy's thinking has been so involved with NATE for so long, and with so many people knowing him well as a friend, and talking with him ... (Interview, December 1977)

It is reasonable to suggest that these six projects have offered a real potential for curriculum re-thinking to teachers of English; but it is also reasonable to suggest that many of the innovative ideas which were being explored in the projects were ideas that NATE journal readers, branch members and conference-goers would recognise as NATE ideas, partly because NATE was a generative force and partly because it was an obvious dissemination outlet for ideas that had been developed by its members. In the monopoly of curriculum ideas, the NATE/non-NATE tangle is extraordinarily difficult to unravel.

BRANCH ACTIVITY

NATE's branches were seen by the founders of NATE and by subsequent NATE Councils as existing to undertake local projects. These projects are necessarily limited in scope but their products, whether discussion papers, teaching materials or accounts of experience, are often made available to other NATE members. The products include such things as a broadsheet on 'Folk Song in English Lessons' produced by the Bristol branch, a thirteen-page commentary on aspects of teaching practice in English produced by the Sheffield branch; a set of audio-tapes, with commentaries of children talking, produced by the Staffordshire branch and referred to in the Bullock Report (1975, 5.13). In addition, NATE branches have sounded local opinion and gathered local data from which central committees have constructed official NATE submissions – to the Bullock Committee, for instance – and branches are now being invited to engage in curriculum planning exercises as a follow-up to the publication of the Bullock Report. The activities of NATE branches are, in the main, confined to NATE members, although many hold open meetings and charge a small admission fee.

ANNUAL CONFERENCES

Each year the NATE annual conference attracts 400 participants, despite recent cut-backs in LEA expenditure on in-service courses. The development of the NATE conference has been impressive. Over the years, a conventional structure in which focus is provided by eminent speakers has given way to a workshop approach in which group activities – 'commissions' as NATE calls them – are the core. The process of playing down the plenary address in order to highlight the work of the commissions was so far advanced in 1975 that the Newsletter editor commented on the singular challenge to the visiting lecturer 'who had the death spot at the only plenary session'. Anthony Adams, the NATE secretary, discusses the potential of the NATE commissions:

> The commission is a working group – about 25–30 people operating really as a small research and in-service training team. It could be that they would bring materials with them that they would then exchange and discuss together; it could be that they would look at videotape and discuss ways in which you could analyse pupil language in the classroom. It is essentially an in-service training conference at the most sensitive level of the phrase in-service training. It's been teacher education in terms of teacher involvement ... we find that a remarkable number of teachers can work this way.
>
> (Interview, December 1977)

Adams went on to suggest that whereas many conferences, by their structure, force participants into a passive acceptance of 'knowledge about', the NATE conferences try to build 'knowledge of' and this knowledge can only come 'from being involved in a working context where you take over ideas and make them part of yourself through working with them'.

But annual conferences which build a strong tradition tend to attract – and probably depend on for the continuity of their tradition – a set of 'regulars'.

The direct influence of the annual conferences on the practice and thinking of English teachers is, therefore, limited to the minority of members who attend. At first, members who did not attend were able to gain something through the second-order experience of reading the conference report. Now, however, the absence of formal lectures and the dominance of the commissions (at the 1977 conference there were 14 different commissions) presents a challenge. No longer can reportage be achieved through the convention of reproducing the transcripts of the talks, and the dynamic values of the group activities can be 'but palely reflected in print at a later stage'. (*English in Education*, Editorial, 1, 2, 1967) Reports of the annual conferences, therefore, are no longer compiled.

The international conferences which NATE has been involved in, alongside sister organisations from the USA, Canada, and now Australia, have tended to appoint a conference reporter whose task it is to offer a distillation of the conference experience shaped around issues which might stimulate discussion and experiment among teachers who have not attended the conferences. The documents, although rooted in a particular experience, have to stand as independent publications. Among these, *Growth through English*, the account of the 'Dartmouth Seminar' held in 1966 and run jointly by NATE and the parallel American Association has, according to Anthony Adams, 'been highly influential on both sides of the Atlantic'. (Adams 1976, 11). One mark of the book's influence is that it was reprinted in 1975. Another is the sharpness of the criticism which Whitehead articulates in an article printed in 1976. His main two concerns are with the over-simple models of English on which the book is premised (the 'skills' model, the 'cultural heritage' model and the 'personal growth' model) and the over-broad definition of literature which, Whitehead claims, has done a disservice to teachers by assimilating 'pupils' stories and poems (the literature of the classroom) to the mature products of real authors'. (Whitehead 1976, 13).

In addition to the annual conferences and the occasional international conferences, NATE's committees have also organised conferences. For instance, the Primary Committee holds a regular summer school and the 1977 meeting was on the theme 'Developing a Reading Programme'.

The NATE network

NATE has not only been potentially influential in its direct contact with teachers through conferences, branch meetings, project activities and publications, but it has increasingly gained momentum as a political force, in this way building a potential for indirect influence on the manner and content of teaching. The 'voice of NATE' – almost a catch phrase in the secretary's annual reports – has undoubtedly achieved, over the years, a firmer tone.

In the area of examinations, NATE has sufficient prestige for it to be represented on the English panels of some examining boards, and NATE has, on its own initiative, organised two one-day meetings for representatives of both

GCE and CSE boards 'Ten years ago it would have been a confrontation', said the secretary, reporting NATE's achievement. NATE has sent representatives to the Schools Council Working Party considering CEE feasibility studies and has made its own contribution to the set of documents prepared for the Council on the N and F examinations.

NATE has been formally invited to make submissions to the Plowden, James and Bullock Committees and also to respond to a memorandum on the attainment of school leavers put out by the House of Commons Expenditure Committee (NATE ABM minute, 6 April 1977). NATE was represented at four of the eight regional conferences organised by the Secretary of State for Education as contributions to 'the Great Debate', and, because NATE did not have an opportunity to make a formal oral contribution to the Great Debate, the Association sent an Open Letter to the Minister 'stressing the fundamental role of language in learning'. (Newsletter, Summer 1977).

NATE has also given serious thought to its relationships with local educaation authorities. In 1972 it initiated an enquiry into the number of specialist English advisers. The results showed a total of 27 appointments, but by 1977 the total number had increased to 70, and of these, 57 had joined a new Association which was set up as a result of discussions with NATE – the Association of English Advisers. The NATE secretary, himself a former English adviser, represents NATE at the Association's meetings. Later, in 1975, NATE held a one-day conference on 'In-Service Work in English'. The 70 participants were nearly all advisers and the NATE Newsletter editor commented: 'At least one person in virtually every local authority in the country has now heard of NATE'.

NATE has built up lateral support for its interests through its joint initiative with ASE (Association for Science Education) in setting up COSTA, a consortium of subject teaching associations. In both 1971 and 1977 NATE formally invited members of other subject associations to its annual conference to consider the implications, in particular, of the idea of 'language across the curriculum'.

NATE has also been watchful about liaison with other countries. In 1974 the secretary reported the strengthening of links with Scotland and in 1975 a West of Scotland Association for Teachers of English was established. 'On a wider geographical front', said the secretary in 1977, 'we have continued to cement relationships with our fellow associations in Canada, Australia and the United States'. James Britton has now negotiated cross-membership of all these associations and is launching an international Newsletter.

It is not surprising, given NATE's scrupulous concern to strengthen its position through such alliances, that the secretary singled out for comment as a development of note during his period of office 'the establishing of NATE as a very strong political force in teacher education'. He added that he and the current DES Staff Inspector for English probably had between them 'the biggest networks in the field of English'. (Adams interview, 1977).

Identity and policy

In 1967, Frank Whitehead, as chairman of NATE, reiterated the principles of openness which, in his view, NATE stood for:

> We need to keep before us the idea of an open society which welcomes into its membership every teacher of good will, however inexperienced or hesitant; a society too in which everyone will feel able to contribute to the ongoing discussions his own experience and indeed his own doubts. For we must certainly avoid at any time giving the impression that we are dominated by any particular faction, fashion or clique.
> (Whitehead 1967, 6)

Such an ideal is not easily preserved, for once the novelty of a new association has worn off, people join because they see, or want to see, the association as standing for a particular set of values rather than offering a diverse set of opportunities. Whitehead himself, looking back over thirteen years of NATE, concludes that NATE 'was a much more broadly based organisation than it has since become'. (Whitehead 1976, 11).

There is evidence to suggest that outsiders certainly tend to perceive NATE as standing for a particular policy in relation to English teaching. For instance, the authors of *Language and Reading among Under-achievers* (Moseleys 1977) are aware of 'a small body of opinion which is constantly stressing the importance of English for self-expression rather than communication' and which leaves school children without the basic language skills that might enable them to live adequately in the world of work. The charge is laid at NATE's feet: 'Looking at books which stress the teaching of these personal and imaginative aspects of language, one becomes aware that many of the authors are influential members of the National Association for the Teaching of English' (13).

As the Newsletter editor suggests, people like to keep their mythologies and to some outsiders, NATE is the Land of the Language Men, and its social landscape is graced – or marred – by the airy Commune of the Creative Writers. Anthony Adams cuts through the speculation with a straight-forward and balanced comment:

> We have taken the view, based on research – but not our own – that you don't learn language skills in isolation, and that it is through an engagement with expressive language in the first instance that the technical skills develop at a later stage. It's wrong to suggest that NATE has been promoting a particular lobby exclusively ... but I think certain people have become associated with certain kinds of attitude towards language and *they* tend to be associated in the public mind with NATE at the present time'.
> (Interview, December 1977)

In short, as can happen with a curriculum development project, in the absence of explicit statements of policy, people become vulnerable to personalities and attribute the thinking of these charismatic figures to the organisation as a whole.

A teacher of English who came to London just over a year ago to be head of department in a large comprehensive school bears out this impression:

> Many of the most vocal members of NATE tend to be members of the London Association for the Teaching of English. What NATE seems to have done is to have

taken the words of James Britton and Harold Rosen and given them the validity of a gospel of theory and practice ... I think this is far less prevalent in the provinces where members of NATE come less directly into contact with the London Institute of Education and various well-known writers associated with it.

(Interview, January 1978)

Nevertheless, the teacher acknowledges the contribution that NATE has made to the 'reassessment of the individual in the classroom' and to 'increasing understanding of the importance of reading in all its modes'. What he reacted to, with some hostility, was the almost inevitable assurance that NATE generated among its close members in its early heyday, an assurance that is probably borne of exhilaration with new ideas. But this coterie confidence, he added, is on the decline:

Many teachers of English are now rethinking their own positions independently of the strong voices that have held sway in the staffs of London schools particularly. I hope the day of the teacher who is certain that his practices are right has gone, and that a measure of healthy uncertainty is with us again. I'm against any system of English which remains unchallenged.

On the inside of NATE, the debate has a different complexion. Whereas Whitehead (who seems to have moved on to the periphery) sees NATE as narrowing its concerns and thereby distorting the profile of English, others see it as merely struggling to keep pace with the times. Hodgson, in an unpublished PhD thesis (1975, ch. 13), documents this shift. He argues that there has been a change of identity since 1963 when NATE was born 'as the child of a liberal human consciousness fashioned ... by a morally committed, critically aware group of largely Cambridge English School/London Institute inspired teachers ...' Then, he suggests, NATE was concerned with the centrality of literature and with resistance to the more stultifying effects of examinations. In recent years, a new social awareness has developed among NATE members, and some have moved towards a pedagogy 'which would take into account the cultural present of the average and the 'less able' child. It would express itself through the personal growth model of English rather than through the skills model or the cultural heritage model, both of which imply a transmission process that binds knowledge, teacher and pupil into a more traditional and more hierarchical set of relationships. Hodgson claims that the first signs of this move were events at the International Conference on the Teaching of English organised jointly by NATE and their American counterpart, NCTE, at York in 1971. A breakaway group – mainly members of LATE, it seems – set up an unscheduled commission, the now notorious Commission 7, and made 'the first overtly political statement heard at a NATE conference' (Hodgson 1975, 444). They asked whether their aims, set out in a NATE Newsletter (Barrs et al. 1971) 'could be accomplished in undemocratic and authoritarian structures, where the aims and assumptions of other teachers and of the institution as a whole are not always in sympathy'. They added: 'Should not a body of English teachers like NATE be prepared to draw specific social and political conclusions from its present position of commitment?' What the breakaway group was calling for was a stronger political platform within NATE.

Several months later, the following paragraph appeared in the NATE Newsletter (January 1972): 'NATE is at the crossroads . . . The organisation has reached a point in history when it will grow and gain true significance or when its membership will dwindle and its efforts prove limited. Which do you want?'

The central challenge of 1971 has still not been definitively answered and there seem to have been, since then, a number of smaller, and slightly different crises of identity. At the extraordinary meeting of Council in 1972, called to discuss policy issues, two constituencies of members were identified: the radicals, who urged NATE to adopt a more positive and agressive position, and the pragmatists, who complained that NATE had given insufficient help with the teaching of reading and spelling, with the handling of O-level texts, and with improved methods of testing. Four years later, in 1976, a discussion paper prepared for a meeting of Council (15 April) urged NATE to choose between two competing images, and the crisis of identity was focused once again: 'The small articulate body of a radical nature, with strong policies which might alienate many teachers – or the larger, more diffuse, more democratic one which necessarily must have policies which are less explicit.' (NATE Archive).

It is interesting to note, however, that Bill Spouge, NATE secretary in 1972, said in an interview (Hodgson 1975, footnote 447) that in his opinion, the majority of the people who attended the 1972 extraordinary meeting of NATE 'did so in order to preserve NATE as they knew it'. Moreover, the response of the Birmingham branch – one of the largest and most active – to the set of policy issues discussed by Council in 1976 was similarly cautious:

> NATE's policy need not consist of overt public statements of aims and opinion. The policy of such an Association will become clear from its publications, its statements on issues as they arise, the support it gives to some groups and ideas, its opposition to other groups and ideas, and so on. It is clear already that NATE opposes all pressures on the teaching of English towards a narrow and rigid conformity . . . but it must avoid giving the impression that it stands for a different kind of conformity.
>
> (Minutes)

So, for the present, the dualities remain in tension and NATE seems able to survive by tolerating its own ambiguities. It is strengthening its foothold in the political arena while at the same time avoiding an identity as an exclusively political force.

One wonders how Walter Raleigh, turn-of-the-century man of letters, would have responded to NATE, given his urbane chastisement of the activist tendencies of the English Association, which was established almost sixty years earlier than NATE:

> I am sorry to see it has gone on the warpath. They all do; either to smash something else or to bully someone else into doing what they were associated to do. A society must either drink or publish; if it does neither it becomes the happy hunting ground of cantankerous people who have all their afternoons to spare.   (In Boas 1956, 45)

Conclusion

The task remains of assessing NATE's influence on curriculum development and I shall, on principle, avoid it. I can suggest a *potential* for influence; I cannot comment on the *actual* influence of NATE.

As John Dixon pointed out (1972, 74), changes in the teaching of English have depended on changes in organisation, and changes in organisation have depended on changes in forms of assessment, and changes in forms of assessment reflect changes of view about what is to be achieved by pupils and teacher. NATE has tried to operate at many levels and its activities amount to a considerable potential for change within the mesh of principles and practice that constitute the curriculum.

The fact that prominent members of NATE also belong to LATE, publish books in their own name, or direct projects in their own name makes it difficult to isolate and trace the actual influence of NATE. NATE has become part of the culture of English teaching. Even those who feel ambivalent about NATE are inclined to be fair in acknowledging its immense achievement in stimulating new thinking and practice. This ambivalence is nicely caught by a drama teacher from a London comprehensive – and he shall have the last word:

I took down from my bookshelf some of the books that seem to sum up NATE. James Britton's *Language and Learning*: that book had a tremendous influence on me. It introduced me to names I'd never heard of before, ideas I'd never heard of before. Shortly after that, *Language, the Learner and the School* (Barnes *et al.*) – that was a smashing bit of work. Another one that influenced me greatly was John Dixon's *Growth through English*. And another – I was in my first year of teaching – was *Language in Context*, NATE's evidence submitted to the Bullock Committee.

I have a whole set of NATE journals. Some of them look very dated now, but there's a continuity running through them all. I remember in my very first post finding, in a stock cupboard, back numbers of NATE journals, and asking if I could borrow them to study. The same names kept cropping up and I was beginning to see that this was a definite school of thought – a model of language in the classroom being put forward.

That, in a way, sums up what NATE is to me, but it's simplified because it's all been praise, and some of my feelings are criticisms.

There's something cliqueish about NATE. Over and over again I, as a drama teacher, have tried to make contact with teachers in an English department that was very NATE oriented, but they were so into their own thing. They seemed to share a common language. Part of my ill-feeling, I suppose, was being left out.

And then there is the way they write about classroom interaction. They seem so intent on showing us the child in the act of learning through language that they don't give the teacher much help. Pages of transcript, but where, how, when, and in what role to slide into the kids' work – that is where NATE lets us down.

A large, vital organisation is able to contain within it its own criticism. The tremendous thing about NATE is that it *can* criticise itself. (At this point the teacher reads a passage from an article by Harold Rosen, which was printed in the NATE journal, Spring 1975). 'Perhaps in the necessary emphasis we have given to personal growth, language for personal development, and literature as an intensely personal exploration, we have made English sound like the greatest egotrip invented, and we have forgotten that when working class children have responded to our teaching, then it is either because we have lured them into a world of private experience and cushioned individualism or because we have seen them as socially constituted human beings who can draw sustenance for their imagination from their own world and its values, from parents, grand-parents and neighbours.'

There isn't such a thing really as 'NATE thinking'. There are people with broadly similar values who interpret those values in different ways. So many diverse currents operate in NATE that the ground swell can sometimes even seem to be working against the top splash.

ANTHONY ADAMS

NATE: A Response

As I recently retired from the secretaryship of NATE, this seems an opportune moment for me to comment upon Jean Rudduck's account. I think that the picture presented here is one that is not at all far from the truth. It was generally in my own annual reports to the Conference that the 'almost-a-catch-phrase "the voice of NATE"' occured and I would want to emphasise my own conviction that, as the only organised body that can speak for English teachers, NATE has an important and continuing role to play. It is no accident that, in these days of 'Great Debates' on education and in a society in which an increasingly instrumental view is being taken of the purposes of education, there are more new NATE branches coming into existence than I ever remember before. Problems in the last two years have been many: disputes with CSE and O-Level Boards, attempted censorship of classroom materials, the almost universal (and often mindless) cry of 'back to basics', fundamental uncertainty about what the role of the teacher of English actually is.

Threatened with seeing the real achievements in curriculum development in their subject in the last fifteen years (much of which has come about through the work Jean Rudduck describes and in the books of Whitehead, Dixon, Creber, Britton and Adams – all active NATE members) collapsing because of intolerable pressures being brought to bear upon them from outside, many teachers of English are seeking to form a pressure group of their own to ensure that *their* professionalism has some influence on what is happening. Weekly I am invited to address meetings throughout the country on this theme (often with the title 'The Challenge to English Teachers Today') and weekly I find large and responsive audiences who have turned out to hear me, not because of my own work such as it is, but because I am secretary of the Association. In the present malaise there is no doubt that the need for a strong and united body of teachers of English, with political muscle, is more than ever apparent.

This has certainly been my aim and policy as secretary of the Association. But it would be a pity if what are often internal debates about 'role' and emphasis received too much attention from those outside. (Frank Whitehead, incidentally, is still a very active member of his local branch.) It is true that there are strong differences of opinion between James Britton and Frank Whitehead about the role of language in education (see *The Use of English* (Spring 1978, 29, 2) for a clear expression of this) but there are important areas of agreement also. And in providing 'a meeting point for all those who teach English' NATE seeks to enable such debate to go forward: it has always (in my view rightly) been opposed to a 'party line' on English teaching. Where we do stand firm however is the conviction that this debate is the professional province and responsibility of English teachers whose voice must be both articulate and heard.

Finally I would also want to emphasise more than Jean Rudduck has done the international role of the Association. As secretary, I have attended meetings in this country and North America of the International Steering Committee on the teaching of English and it is interesting to note how many of our current concerns are reflected in the North American experience also. I hope that the international membership scheme that is only just beginning to get off the ground will gather momentum and that we shall have the opportunity of continuing the transatlantic dialogue that was begun at Dartmouth. There is no doubt that the cross-fertilisation of ideas that took place there has influenced practice as well as theory on both sides of the Atlantic and I suspect the influence has been a very positive one. I hope that we shall see more international exchange on the teaching of English (of persons as well as ideas) and that we shall cease to think in too limited and parochial a way about mother tongue teaching in this country.

There is much that remains to be done. Even as I write these words letters lie on my desk about new phases in our own development, links with the United Kingdom Reading Association, with the Open University, concerns for education in a multi-cultural society, sexism in literature and education – all matters discussed at the 1978 Annual Conference. The role of NATE will undoubtedly broaden in the next ten years. Looking back on what has been achieved since 1963 I think that we have a good deal about which to be proud and pleased, though I hope not complacent at the same time.

3 The School Mathematics Project

Basic information

Beginnings The heads of mathematics of four public schools together with Bryan Thwaites, then Professor of Theoretical Mechanics in the University of Southampton, initiated the School Mathematics Project (SMP) in 1961 as a semi-private experimental venture. The intention was to reform the teaching of mathematics in the four schools to reflect modern developments in the subject and its wider usage, and to encourage other schools to do the same. The production of new GCE O- and A-level syllabuses acceptable to the universities was to be undertaken together with associated text books and teachers' guides. Four state grammar schools joined in to form the central group of schools responsible for shaping policy. Some two years later, the number of participating schools increased to 41.

Support The University of Southampton provided accommodation for the project within its Department of Mathematics and appointed a lecturer funded from external sources to assist Professor Thwaites. Supporting non-academic staff also were appointed. During the first few years, the financial support from industry and other sources was between £5,000 and £10,000 per annum. The project gained rapidly in momentum. By 1966, it had become clear that the role of the project was longer term and wider than originally envisaged. SMP was legally constituted a charitable trust in August 1967, with Dr. Bryan Thwaites, by then Principal of Westfield College, University of London, chairman of the Board of Trustees. The project now exists as a voluntary, fully independent, self-supporting organisation whose annual expenditure runs into five figures. It is self-dedicated to curriculum development and research in mathematical education.

Production timetable The first experimental text, called *Book T*, for transition from the traditional O-level to the new projected course at the 13+ stage, was produced cooperatively by some 7 school teachers and the university editor, for use and testing in the schools in 1962–63. Modification and re-testing in 1963–64 led to a third version which was published by Cambridge University Press in July 1964. Meanwhile, an experimental draft of the continuation book for 14+ pupils, T4, had been written in time for the first SMP GCE O-level examination to be held in July 1964, with the Oxford and Cambridge Examinations Board acting as coordinator on behalf of the GCE Examining Boards. *Book T4* was published in June 1965.

   The production of all SMP textbooks followed the same pattern: they were written by school teachers and published only after classroom trials and subsequent revision.

An experimental draft of the first book of a new projected five-year O-level course was ready for use by the grammar school 11+ pupils at the start of the session 1963–64. The completed sereis, *Books 1–5*, was written and published in stages over a period of some five years to 1969.

The first SMP A-level examination came in July, 1966, two years after the first O-level. Publication of the four A-level texts was completed by September, 1968, and of the Further Mathematics series, by 1971. The services of an advisory group of five university mathematicians were available to the teachers involved in the preparation of the materials. Before the syllabuses were drawn up, a questionnaire was issued to all university mathematics departments to ascertain their views on sixth form mathematics.

A modified version of *Books 1–5*, the lettered series, *Books A–H*, intended to be suitable for a CSE examination, was begun in 1966 and completed in stages by 1972. Three supplementary books, *X*, *Y* and *Z*, bringing the series to O-level standard, were published, one each year during 1972–74. *Books A–D* were subsequently issued in card form, *Cards I and II*, to facilitate the use of individualised and group learning techniques, and to extend the range of pupils with whom the material could be used.

The preparation of a primary and middle school series, SMP 7–13, a new venture for the project, was begun at a conference of interested persons held in April 1972. *Units 1 and 2* of the series, consisting of pupils' workcards and booklets, were published in March 1977, together with answer books, pupil's record sheet, assessment tests and teachers' handbook. The six unit series is to be completed by 1980. New versions of the A-level and Additional Mathematics syllabuses, permitting the use of non-programmable electronic calculators, came into operation in 1977.

Following an enquiry to the O-level schools, arrangements have been made for there to be two O-level syllabuses from 1977. The present 'non-calculator' syllabus will continue and an alternative 'calculator' syllabus has been drawn up. Teaching materials for the latter are in preparation.

An outline for possible N and F syllabuses and examinations has been prepared.

Evaluation   Evaluation has been formative, relying on the subjective impressions of teachers using the trial materials and, later, the published texts.

Growth of interest

Table 3.1

Year (Summer)	1964	1965	1966	1967	1968	1969	1970	1975	1977
No. of O-level candidates	919	1,848	3,526	6,642	10,980	12,879	20,100	54,015	62,691*

*Some 20 per cent of the national entry.

The numbers of A-level candidates in 1975 and 1977 were respectively 5926 and 7024, the latter being about 10 per cent of the national entry.

The influence of the project has almost certainly been greater than these figures suggest. For example, when the CSE and other GCE examining boards instituted their own examinations in modern mathematics, the pattern had already been set by the SMP. More than half the schools in the country are said to be making some use of the SMP materials.

Headquarters   The SMP office is at Westfield College, Kidderpore Avenue, London NW 3 7ST.

Full time staff   Mr. John Hersee (Executive Director, appointed 1 January 1976), Dr. Alan T. Rogerson (Research Director), Mr. John Ling (Team Leader, SMP 11–16, appointed 1 September 1977), Mrs. Shirley Berry (Secretary).

Project teams   Over ten working groups are currently functioning. Over one hundred teachers have been or are currently involved in writing materials.

Course materials   A substantial body of classroom materials with teacher's guides has been produced in the attempt to provide for the mathematical and examinational needs of school pupils of various abilities from the age of seven upwards. There is also a guide for parents, a series of handbooks dealing with specific topics, and texts which look ahead to university mathematics. Eight English language and five foreign language editions of some of the courses are available or in preparation. Production continues and full details may be obtained from the publishers.

Publishers   Cambridge University Press, PO Box 110, Cambridge CB2 3RL.

Materials in preparation   A two-year O-level self-tuition course in conjunction with the National Extension College. Remedial cards for the 11–13 very slow learners. Materials for a course for one-year sixth form pupils. Supplementary material in revision of the Further Mathematics texts.

Plans for further materials   A fundamental review of the SMP provision for the 11–16 age range is being carried out, bearing in mind the possibility of a common system of examination at 16+ and the changing educational scene.

A computing-in-mathematics group is investigating the implications for teaching of the electronic calculator and computer.

Teacher support   Assistance to individual teachers is given on request by the members of the executive staff, the editors, authors and revisers of the various texts.

Residential teacher training conferences are arranged as required. Attendances over the past five years have totalled over 2,500 at some six to eight conferences per annum.

Other support   The School Mathematics Project has given general help to the cause of mathematical education. For example, a joint Mathematical Association/SMP committee organises the National Mathematics Contest held in March each year which is open to persons under the age of 20 who have not proceeded to higher education. The contest is the first of a series of competitions to select a team of eight, sponsored by the SMP, to represent the UK in an International Mathematical Olympiad.

Background influences: developments in the USA

Amongst British projects in mathematical education, the SMP stands in a class of its own if only for its size and the range of its activity. Its remarkable growth is indicative of the support and approval it has received but there has been fundamental criticism of the type of course it has provided. This account of the SMP and its contribution centres on its O-level and main school courses.

The movement for modernising the teaching of mathematics by introducing concepts from the 'new mathematics' was becoming world-wide in the early 1960s. (Meder 1957, Smithies 1963). Considerable impetus came from developments in the USA following the launching of the first Russian sputnik in October 1957. Some six months later, the School Mathematics Study Group (SMSG) was in being. It was national in scope and funded from government sources to an amount of four million dollars during the first four years of its existence (Wooton 1965).

The SMSG course, determined by university mathematicians, presented mathematics as a series of logical structures. A rigorous deductive development based on the notion of set made mathematics appear remote-from-reality, self-generating and self-contained. Morris Kline (1966) pointed out also that too little attention had been given to pedagogical considerations and that teachers were insufficiently prepared for the change. In view of the social pressures in operation, mathematical applications were oddly neglected in the new course.

At the time, SMSG seemed generally to make good sense. Technology cannot advance without mathematics, and the US government had taken the advice of mathematicians. But it consulted pure mathematicians and they have tended to be inward-looking in relation to their subject this century following the discovery of non-Euclidean geometry around 1830 which directed their attention more particularly to structure, rigour and formal developments within mathematics. SMSG was certainly short on application, seeming to reflect G. H. Hardy's words, 'If he is consistent, a man of the mathematical school washes his hands of applications.' (Coulson 1973).

Other American projects adopted similar approaches to the SMSG (Thornton 1963; Nacome 1975; Sherman 1977) in particular, the Educational Services Incorporated African Mathematics Program (1961–70), funded to an amount of $3\frac{1}{4}$ million dollars, which produced complete courses for African primary and secondary school pupils and teachers-in-training. Its materials, or adaptations therefrom, were used by 2,000,000 primary, 200,000 secondary school pupils and 60,000 students-in-training. (Entebbe Mathematics Series 1971). The UNESCO Mathematics Project for the Arab States, launched in Cairo in 1969, came under the same influences. (UNESCO 1969a, 1969b, 1970–71).

Progress in Britain: the contribution of SMP

Teachers in Britain took longer than in the US to decide the school implications of modern mathematics. A feature of the educational system in England and Wales is that before curriculum change can be effected, teachers have to be convinced of its desirability. Innovation tends to come about slowly by a piecemeal process through the influence of textbook writers, teacher-educators, research workers and such agencies as the Mathematical Association, the Association of Teachers of Mathematics, LEAs and the Department of Education and Science.

The pressure to reform school courses built up gradually. (Rollett 1963, Pitt 1963). There were informed teachers who resisted, unconvinced of the advantages of modern mathematics for the classroom. The terminology seemed likely to hinder rather than help the learning process. (Goodstein 1962). The majority of teachers probably knew very little about the 'new mathematics' since the universities only began to modernise their undergraduate courses during the 1950s. Thus existing teachers were faced with the need to relearn their subject. Feelings of uneasiness, even apprehension, existed. A course of lectures by professors of mathematics from various universities at the University of Leicester in 1952 attracted unusually large audiences of teachers who seemed to be hearing about most of the topics for the first time. The position of mathematics staffs in the teacher-education institutions was similar.

The OEEC conference in Royaumont in 1959, (OEEC 1961), following a survey of the status of mathematics in member states, brought the need in Europe into sharp focus and several modern mathematics school projects were started in Britain during the 1960s. (Mathematical Association 1968). The SMP was one of the first off the mark. Professor Thwaites' involvement in school mathematical education became well-known if only because of the Southampton Mathematical Conference. (Thwaites 1961a, 62) and his inaugural lecture at Southampton in 1961 in which he drew forceful attention to the dire shortage of mathematics teachers which had reached crisis proportions. (Thwaites 1961b).

Widespread concern had already resulted in an upsurge of activity in mathematical education. For example, A. P. Rollett had convened the Whitelands conference of teacher-educators in 1955 and, as a result, the Mathematics Section of ATCDE was re-formed. E. E. Biggs was beginning her work in the primary schools. There was the Oxford Mathematical Conference in 1957 for teachers and users of mathematics to which the origins of the SMP have been ascribed. (Oxford Mathematical Conference 1957).

These activities were essentially exercises in personal and public relationships and a sense of mission was in evidence. The SMP was set up in this climate. The management of its affairs was outstandingly able (Clarke 1973).[1] Its immense programme was carried through on time. Institutions and people of standing were involved. The project rose rapidly to a unique position of strength, independence and influence whence it could challenge accepted positions. It received the widest publicity through its publications and its programme of lectures and conferences, the draft materials were readily available and an increasing measure of teacher-confidence was established.

Secondary schools were being offered a system of modern mathematical education – a continuous course from 11+ to 18+ with its own examinations including a single-subject A-level agreed by the universities, an advisory service and in-service training facilities. The materials captured the spirit, joy and fascination of modern professional mathematics and their presentation was polished. There was openness in the approach, humour, and a place for learning by discovery. In keeping with British practice, mathematical applications were not neglected, a wider range being introduced than in traditional courses. The materials took us nearer to the position 'where, in fine, all the branches of elementary mathematics, pure and applied, theoretical and experimental, are comingled at appropriate times, so that the mind sees and uses its mathematical conceptions and processes as a beautiful well-ordered and powerful whole, instead of a thing of shreds and patches.' (Branford 1908).

Teachers, many of whom were dissatisfied with existing practice, had gradually come to feel that the change to modern courses had to come and would be irreversible. The SMP materials were very well received (see, for example, Sturgess 1971). Perhaps the main contribution of the project has been to the personal re-education and support of established teachers including those involved in the writing, thereby facilitating the national acceptance of the need for syllabus reform. The textbooks presented mathematics in a form which could be widely understood and so helped to put teachers in the position to make valid judgements on the new courses.

Controversy in mathematical education

On the other hand, the modern conceptual trend in school mathematics met with resistance from the start (Hammersley 1968, Lyness 1969) and a firm reaction to the new syllabuses has since set in. The call for 'back to basics' in the USA has become sufficiently strong for it to have been countered at the third International Congress on Mathematical Education (1976) in two papers. (Hilton 1976).

In this country, it is said that modern mathematics courses place undue emphasis on pattern and structure to the neglect of the techniques and processes required by users of the subject and, in particular, that SMP pupils do not acquire the skills in arithmetic, algebra and analysis which are needed in other school subjects and industry. (*Maths in School 1975–76; Bulletin,* Institute of Mathematics and its Applications 1969–76; *Times Educational Supplement* 1974–76. *Int. J. Maths. Ed. Sc. Tech.* 1975–77). A policy of continuously reviewing its syllabuses has allowed SMP to respond. There were three major revisions of its courses during the first ten years. The A-level and Further Mathematics courses are continuing to be revised (Rogerson 1975) and materials containing manipulatory exercises supplementary to the O-level courses have been produced. But the controversy continues.

The issues are not resolved by questioning SMP teachers, their pupils, students-in-training or university teachers of mathematics. Some are keenly enthusiastic, some non-committal and others hostile.

What is clear is that standards of numeracy amongst school leavers have declined (Lindsay 1975; Parliamentary Committee 1978), the shortage of qualified teachers of mathematics in the schools continues, (Kerr 1977; Ollerenshaw 1977), and there has been a serious drop in the number of students opting for the subject at university (Griffiths 1975; McLane 1975).

Yet there has been progress (see Howson 1978). University departments and colleges of education, some of which were without mathematics lecturers twenty years ago, are now well staffed. The provision for in-service training has improved. Primary arithmetic, which was narrowly focussed on computation for instrumental purposes, has been enlivened by the introduction of a wide range of mathematical ideas coherently presented and there is more understanding about how children learn. Classrooms are happier places and children's attitudes to mathematics have consequently improved. Many teachers have been conspicuously successful using the newer methods. Despite such gains, the high expectations which accompanied the immense activity in the various fields of mathematical education during the 50s and 60s have not been fulfilled.

Various forces in our society have undoubtedly combined to delay the progress of mass education in recent years. The alleged decline has not been confined to one subject and it would be 'facile to attribute present low standards to a deterioration brought about by something called "modern" mathematics' (HMI 1977). Those who produced the SMP syllabuses were breaking new ground at the time with little previous experience to guide them. Their experimental venture, initially involving a small number of schools, became large scale and, in consequence, served as a focus for the dialogue on the place of modern mathematics in schools.

Towards an evaluation of SMP

CURRICULUM METHODS

The collection of director's reports serves as a main source of information about the SMP and its early development(Thwaites 1972a). In these, we find, 'of over-riding importance to us ... is that the syllabuses and the associated teaching methods should be developed as the practical outcome of teaching experience, rather than as a result of theoretical discussion round committee tables' (6). The syllabuses are 'an amalgam, though most carefully alloyed, of their [teachers'] own interests, preferences and prejudices which, in turn, have been moulded by their schools' traditions and characters' (7).

The recognition in practice by the SMP of the professional role of the teacher as the main arbiter, if not always the architect, of the curriculum, which is in keeping with the traditions of the Mathematical Association, must be counted as a major reason for the pedagogical quality and wide acceptance by schools of the course materials (see Howson 1974, 1975).

As the director's reports imply, practical experience rather than curriculum theory has been the guide. No attempt appears to have been made to set out the course objectives in detailed behavioural terms and, though the materials were tried out in schools, no summative evaluation has been carried out. To break down course objectives into minute detail, as some curriculum theorists have advocated, is hardly feasible in this subject and the creative element in mathematics learning often arises spontaneously. Mathematics teachers have tended to the distrustful of curriculum theory. In view of the long history of reform in the teaching of their subject, they are inclined to agree with Herbert M. Kliebard (1975) who, in reference to the a-historical perspective of curriculum theory, writes, 'Issues tend to arise *de novo*, usually in the form of a bandwagon, then quickly disappear in a cloud of dust. The field in general is characterised by an uncritical propensity for novelty and change rather than funded knowledge or a dialogue across generations.'

In fact, the general principles underlying the SMP course as set out in the director's reports are capable of various interpretations for classroom purposes. Looking back, it seems that, if the principles had been stated more comprehensively and in some specific detail with a view to eventual evaluation, maybe teachers would have been better helped, especially those unable to attend training conferences.

The SMP group of people seem not to have made advance preparation for the possible overall assessment of their projected materials. They could hardly have anticipated the extent of the project's development and impact and, in any case, one can well believe that they were so carried along by an optimistic, enthusiastic conviction of the rightness of what they were doing, the magnitude, interest and challenge of the task, the wide following they attracted, and their intention to revise their materials regularly in the light of classroom experience, that the thought of objective evaluation did not at first cross their minds. Each revision of the materials necessitated some form of evaluation and the project teams continued 'to rely on the subjective impressions of the classroom situation' (Thwaites 1972a, 98). 'We have to admit that no progress has been made during the year [1965–66] with the problems of assessing, in any absolute sense, the educational merits of the new curriculum' (115). Objective evaluation is discussed on two pages with special reference to its complexity. The suggestion is twice made that some national authority should undertake comprehensive, independent assessments of projects and their products. A specific proposal to the Schools Council was considered early in 1971 but it was felt that teachers would not find the results of evaluation of individual projects helpful in present circumstances.

The large number of variables in any educational situation, including subjective factors which do not lend themselves to measurement, makes research difficult to conduct and can render its findings inconclusive. Any curriculum project must rest on a set of values and function from a position of informed faith and belief. The SMP is no exception and evidently has proceeded largely on this basis. Curriculum innovation usually originates in the intuitive, experimental gropings of teachers and educational research follows as an instrument of validation.

In attempting to assess the worth of the SMP materials account must be taken of the needs and conditions then and now, the extensive dialogue, any independent evaluations, and any other relevant considerations. (Parlett and

Hamilton 1972). More evidence is needed, in particular, on the performance of ex-SMP students at university in their first and subsequent years when reading mathematics or another subject which requires mathematics.

The SMP materials were written by teachers for the use of teachers. The reader may care to consider the extent to which the publisher's sales figures – by January 1978, for example, 300,000 and 690,000 copies respectively of *Books I* and *A* including overseas sales – may be taken to reflect the soundness of the course, and so serve as a form of summative evaluation. The materials of some modern mathematics courses prepared during the 1960s have ceased publication.

It is appropriate to our study of SMP methods as a curriculum development project to note that, in common with other projects, some of its intentions – in this case, invariably fine intentions – have not fully been achieved, as the following examples indicate:

1. The director's personal conviction is 'that SMP (and other similar experiments) are only in the foothills of the mountainous changes in mathematical syllabuses which tower ahead' (Thwaites 1972a, 7). An SMP organisation 'with built-in mechanisms for evolution' is looked for. No special validity is claimed for the SMP syllabus which is but one of many possible and variety of syllabus is said to be desirable. It is not desirable that the 'SMP offerings should degenerate into a new classroom dogma'. Yet, despite the efforts taken to prevent it happening there are indications that, 'SMP maths' became a dogma for some people though, for obvious reasons, not to the same extent as 'Fletcher maths' in the primary schools.

2. 'The cardinal feature of the SMP is that it is a free association of school teachers of mathematics who have a common interest in improving the teaching of mathematics ... It is independent of all governmental and other official bodies; this not only gives the SMP valuable freedom in the conduct of its research but also ensures that there is no pressure on schools to adopt SMP materials against their will' (Thwaites 1972a, 195). At least one teacher considers he did not teach the SMP course from free choice but as a result of indoctrination. '... perish the thought that a mere teacher should dare to question the views of university professors, educational researchers *and* book publishers, who said they *must* change their thinking on mathematics in schools. ... I had been 'brainwashed' into thinking tradition is a dirty word. Today ... I see what an absolute fool I have been' (Hodgkinson 1976).

3. 'The project cannot possibly claim to know all the answers and yet in this extraordinary *laissez faire* system of English education the probability is emerging that what began as a private experimental scheme will be adopted before its results are fully assessed, by large numbers of the country's schools'. (p. 16, 1962–63 Report in Thwaites 1972a). This may

be a penetrating comment on the process of change in education but it also reflects a failure in intention. Initially, knowledge and experience of ordinary state schools may have been lacking. In any case, in the exciting, complex situation which existed, with the need for action paramount and so much at stake it must have been difficult to temper enthusiasm with reason in the application of professional safeguards. It is not clear that the results of the 'private experimental scheme' ever were 'fully assessed'.

4. The existence of a tendency towards weakness in arithmetical and algebraic skills amongst SMP students which the publication of the supplementary manipulatory exercises in 1977 seems to confirm, is an example of failure in an intention which seems not to have been stated explicitly.

The reader may care to consider the implications of these examples. How far do they reflect deficiencies in the English system of education and teacher-training, in individual schools and teachers? Where does the responsibility lie? To whom is an independent organisation operating within the state system accountable?

THE COURSE

Content and method

The invention of non-Euclidean geometries and of algebras other than the classical algebra are amongst the developments which, in a sense, changed the character of mathematics, giving it a different basis and an extended content. This is why the gap, which the SMP proposed to close had opened up between school and university mathematics.

The new SMP syllabuses departed radically from established practice, firmly and effectively confronting the situation. The O-level and main school materials introduce a variety of concepts and topics taken to varying depths, including the notions of set, mapping, group, vector, matrix and some topological ideas together with linear programming, transformation geometry (introducing motion into the subject), computers and programming, probability and statistics. Topics such as relation, function and number-systems are linked with the concept of set which is basic in the course and serves as a main unifying idea. The accent is on conceptual learning as is seen clearly in the treatment of area.

The standard method of teaching school mathematics is to move from topic to topic as often as is necessary to maintain interest, returning to the topics from time to time for consolidation and extension purposes. (IAAM 1957; NCTM 1953). Pupils easily forget what they have learnt and frequent revision is necessary. Learning thus proceeds spirally in a hit or miss, but directed, manner which more or less ensures that the necessary concepts, techniques and processes are learnt sufficiently well for examination purposes. If the order of the textbook treatment is not to the teacher's liking, no matter. With average competence, he does not have to follow it slavishly.

The SMP textbooks apparently take these teaching procedures for granted. The course progresses from topic to topic in lively fashion and there is natural development as in the emergence of matrices. The teacher will have to know what he wants to get from the course for his pupils in order to lay the emphasis correctly and organise the revision. More revision exercises would have been an advantage. The treatment generally seems more superficial than in a traditional course presumably because of the increased syllabus content. Learning must inevitably be more thinly spread. It is easy to understand how pupils may not be acquiring the arithmetical and algebraic skills considered requisite by users of mathematics. The supplementary manipulatory exercise materials will be helpful and they will serve to draw the teacher's attention to the need. But the problem of the time factor must remain as the course is so full.

An issue of principle is involved, for, as appears in the director's 1962–63 report (19, 20), '... we have constantly tried to shift the emphasis towards mathematical ideas and away from manipulative techniques. Considerable facility in manipulation is, of course, required by pupils who are hoping to become mathematicians, physicists or engineers, but it is the opinion of those in the project that the acquisition of these techniques is best left until the post O-level stage ... This will also free the pupil who stops at O-level from much unnecessary learning.' 'At O-level, then, we seek to convey something of the nature of various algebraic concepts rather than convey a definite body of knowledge.' (17). This view is maintained in the SMP pamphlet *Manipulative Skills in Mathematics* (1974). 'The syllabus has been constructed with the pupil who will do no mathematics beyond O-level primarily in mind' (16).

The course is thus intended to be an end in itself at that stage. The traditional stress on techniques is clearly to be avoided, but there exists the alternative possibility of shifting the emphasis too far in the direction of understanding high-level ideas and not facing the nitty-gritty of mathematics learning. Acquiring knowledge, skills and habits of thought as the outcome of sustained effort and the due practice is a 'way of life' in mathematics, not only for utilitarian reasons, but as a means of deepening understanding. The student who does not suitably meet this 'way of life' for himself can only arrive at a diminished view of the subject. Teachers generally find that the 'bite' of mathematics is more likely to lead to commitment than butterfly learning by itself, however pleasant.

Has the emphasis in the SMP course moved too far in the direction of mathematical ideas? This may be the case, as is indicated by the findings of M. Preston (1972) in an investigation into affective behaviour in CSE mathematics using a sample of 699 SMP, 116 Scottish Mathematics Group (SMG), 83 Midland Mathematics Experiments (MME) and 73 Westminster pupils. He identifies three factors of affective behaviour defined respectively as: (a) tending to see mathematics as an algorithmic, mechanical, somewhat stereotyped subject; (b) tending to see mathematics in an open-ended, intuitive heuristic setting; and (c) representing commitment, interest and willingness to work at mathematics. 'The results of pupils taking the SMP course do seem significantly different from the norm. The level of Factor B mean scores indicates these pupils see mathematics in a wider context of applications, that they have a more strongly developed sense of intuition and their approach to problems allows greater flexibility. The disappointing values emerging from Table 7 [the table of scores including those for Factor C] is the level of commitment and interest for the SMP pupils' (49, 67). The lower mean score was significant at the 1 per cent level. Preston also finds that 'the cognitive skill of a student is indirectly related to his score on the algorithmic scale and directly related to his interest and commitment' (45).

The SMP O-level course is examined by two papers, each of $2\frac{1}{2}$ hours duration. Paper 1 consists of two sections, one containing short-answer questions and the other objective type questions. In Paper II, section A questions are easier than those in section B which score about two-thirds of the marks. Candidates are allowed the use of tables which include comprehensive lists of formula and definitions. Since the examination can exercise a determining influence on the teaching, the reader may wish to consult some past papers.

Evolutionary or revolutionary change

It is clear from the textbooks that SMP has endeavoured to bring about a liberation in the secondary mathematics classroom equivalent to that which has been achieved in the teaching of the subject in some infant and junior schools. The project's strategy for effecting innovation has rightly been two-pronged because to have employed traditional methods in the teaching of modern mathematics would have defeated the educational purpose of the exercise. This suggests that the effective introduction of modern mathematics courses may be a more complicated business than it appears at first sight, especially in developing countries. The double transformation required must challenge the most knowledgeable and experienced teacher and its general implementation take years of continuing trial and experiment in constantly changing circumstances. If this is the case, there is a strong argument for evolutionary rather than revolutionary change. Yet the latter is needed if we are to keep pace with developments. This is the dilemma which the SMP has had to face.

Perhaps classroom mathematics should evolve from and be integrated with the traditional. Abrupt breaks with tradition, as in the skills versus ideas dichotomy, are to be avoided. Discarding Euclid's development in favour of transformation geometry, admirable though the SMP treatment of the latter is, both in its own right and as a focus of integration, could be another case in point. In its zeal, SMP may have been partially defeating its own purposes by adopting policies which are too radical.

A similar note of caution was sounded recently by Rene Thom (1973) when he spoke of genetic constraints he believes to be operative in the learning of mathematics.

> There is always a stage of necessary apprenticeship, genetic constraints to respect, in order to learn to walk, to speak, to read, to write, and it does not seem as if progress in psychology has been able to modify in any way the normal calendar which governs the acquisition of such knowledge. This is why one can legitimately ask whether the same kind of constraints are not operating in the learning of mathematics. If this is the case, then the hope of arriving, by means of a general reorganisation of curricula or methods, at an accelerated awareness of the great theories of contemporary mathematics, could well prove illusory ... This is why it is not obvious that an advancement in recent knowledge must, of necessity, be reflected in syllabuses, especially at the elementary and secondary levels.

In the second of two articles, A. J. Malpas (1974) investigates the SMP claim that *Books A* to *H* are suitable for all pupils excepting those in the fourth quartile of the intelligence range. This he does by examining the cognitive demands of the books in relation to pupils 'in the middle 50 per cent of the intelligence range', using a Piagetian yardstick. The results indicate that a majority of these pupils may be expected to experience considerable difficulty with a substantial part of the work in the third and fourth years, and all the books from D onwards are likely to make severe demands on them. The work is 'within the intellectual compass of probably an average to good O-level-bound group.' This suggests that the SMP may have been in error in its view that the same basic type of course in modern mathematics can be modified by simplifying the language, using a card system to facilitate individual learning, and the like, so as to be suitable for three quarters of the school population.

The treatment of number

The director of the SMP writes 'that this first English experiment in cooperative mathematical teaching has not been as radical, so far, as some of the larger experiments in the USA and in Europe.' (Thwaites 1972a, 44) Though we have suggested, in effect, that the SMP experiment may already have been too radical for school pupils, teachers and employers, it may be pointed out that having gone so far in that direction, to have moved slightly further would have enabled a distinctly more satisfying treatment of number to be undertaken.

The *Teacher's Guide* for *Book 1* states that 'directed numbers traditionally cause many difficulties and are often as much misunderstood by the teacher as the pupil' (139). The SMP textbooks provide evidence for this in that they mix directed number with natural number. In *Book 4*, 198, we find '... the counting numbers, that is, the positive whole numbers, together with zero ... The union of the set of counting numbers with their inverses and zero under addition is a new set of numbers called *integers*. This set is the set of "directed" whole numbers' (*sic*). But the counting numbers do not have inverses; otherwise there would be no need to invent directed numbers.

In *Book 1* (chapters 1 and 2), number is introduced as counting number and the accent is on the ordinal concept. Cardinals are taken for granted as in:

Pick out from the following questions the one whose answer is in a counting number:

(a)   If 5 men eat 4 loaves each, how many loaves are needed?
(b)   If 18 loaves are divided equally between 6 men, how many does each man get?
(c)   How many loaves are left if 4 loaves are eaten from a batch of 20?
(d)   If 3 loaves are divided equally between 4 children, how much does each child get?

Directed numbers are introduced in chapter 12. 'Corresponding to every counting number (for example, 3), we associate a *negative shift number* (3 paces back) and a *positive shift number* (3 paces forward)'. These are termed negative three ($^-3$) and positive three ($^+3$) respectively and 'calculating rules' for the new 'numbers' are derived. Later in the chapter appears: 'So far in this chapter, care has been taken to distinguish between the counting and the positive numbers. However, it will be clear by now that the positive numbers, when added and subtracted, behave just like the counting numbers. This means that there should be no confusion if we leave out the $+$ sign. We shall therefore write 3 instead of $+3$' (205). By the time *Book 4* is reached, the counting numbers and the positive integers are mentally equated and the current misconception of the number concept extension process is fully apparent. To have entitled chapter 12 'Negative Numbers' instead of 'Directed Numbers', the title used in the lettered series, giving the impression that the negative integers are numbers in a class apart, different in type from the positive integers, prepares the way for the misconception.

In the circumstances, would it not have been better to have approached number as the property of a set in *Book 1*, Chapter 2, bringing in notions of correspondence and equivalence to explain ordering and counting? The integers could then have been discussed as an extension of the number concept in illustration of an important aspect of the way mathematical thinking proceeds.

Mathematical applications

In the first of his two articles, Malpas (1974) investigates the objectives of the SMP main course. He finds that 73 of the 93 chapters of *Books A* to *H* make 'substantial reference to the external world', about half being concerned with abstracting mathematical concepts and developing the languages, and two-fifths with applying the mathematics so learnt. The complete mathematical modelling process involves deriving from a verbalisation of the real situation under investigation a pictorial diagram leading to a symbolic representation (the abstraction/language aspect) followed by the same steps in reverse (the application aspect) (see Figure 3.1). (For an earlier account of the Modelling Cycle, see Ormell 1973a.)

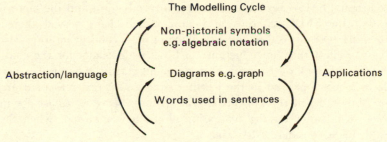

Figure 3.1

Pupils like to apply their knowledge as soon as it is acquired, and for learning to be well-motivated and effective, the abstraction/application cycle should be completed in toto. In only 9.5 per cent of the 73 chapters does this happen. The majority deal only with half the cycle, usually abstraction/language in the earlier chapters and application much later. It is inferred from this pattern that 'it was abstraction and not the situation which really interested the authors'. Pupils would probably sense this and their interest could be diminished.

This raises a basic issue in the teaching of mathematics. The claim, often heard in the classroom, that mathematics is useful on account of its wide applicability in the real world, may be accepted by the student on the teacher's authority but it is not usually borne out in his immediate personal experience. Much of what he learns lacks apparent relevance, and therefore, meaning, unless he generally enjoys mathematics for its own sake when problems of motivation do not arise. Otherwise, the concrete examples the student is called upon to work do not have sufficient interest of themselves to hold him. There is usually a degree of artificiality about them and they are used only to give practice in the working of the appropriate mathematical rule, or so it seems; but when the mathematics has been learnt, what is it for? Various writers have suggested or implied that the teaching of mathematics is in difficulty at this point. (Niss 1977; Kendall 1977; Lighthill 1972). (See also chapter 13, 'The Sixth Form Mathematics Curriculum Project'.)

LOOKING AHEAD

Extensive and rapid change has been a salient feature of the educational scene during the fifteen years which have passed since the SMP courses were thought out. A period of stimulating expansion has given way to one of retrenchment. Increasing emphasis is being placed on public accountability and the utilitarian purposes of schooling. There has been little time for adaptation and teachers of mathematics are still learning how to deal with their subject in a modern setting. Further changes seem undesirable but there is no standing still. The director of the SMP stated in 1972 that he hoped 'to see all existing books torn up, burnt or otherwise disposed of by 1985 at the latest'. (Thwaites 1972b)

The original SMSG texts are no longer in production and the fact must be faced that the SMP materials may now largely have served their initial classroom purposes. It is time to be thinking of the second-generation series and how best to effect their introduction: an SMP team leader for the courses for 11–16 year-olds took over his duties in September 1977. The present materials will have to be appraised in the existing situation in order to plan any new course. Maybe the method of this appraisal would serve as a basis for making provision in advance for the evaluation of the new materials when the time comes, if this is considered desirable.

Modern mathematics courses in schools tend to reflect the viewpoint of the pure mathematician in being oriented towards the subject and its structure. A crisis of meaning arises for some students, and the user of mathematics is severely critical of the orientation. Would it be possible to redress the balance by injecting into existing courses exercises suitable for the development of the understanding and translation skills which successful modelling requires? Maybe, but probably not with the SMP course which is more or less wedded to the outlook in question and already full. An alternative also to be considered is the production of a course with a different main emphasis, one in which the accent is on applicability, realistic modelling and the relevant mathematical knowledge.

The world we live in is both Euclidean and Newtonian for all workaday, scientific and technological purposes, and well within the limits of accuracy possible in measurement. Does this imply a reconceptualisation of the nature of mathematics for the purposes of the envisaged re-centred course, away from the formalist towards a Platonic view? (Thom 1970. See also Ormell 1973b). What would be the content of the course? One would expect the unifying terms, 'set', 'mapping' and 'relation', to be introduced in order to further understanding and assist explanation, but how many such notions would be considered helpful and necessary? We are told by Jerome S. Bruner in his *Process of Education* that the way to ensure that a student's learning is both remembered and of use to him in the future is to communicate an understanding of the fundamental structure of the subject being studied, together with any implied habits and skills. Would it be sufficient to stress the elementary patterns of sequential development in mathematics – number to counting to addition to multiplication? Or would it be desirable also to link number with sets and explain cardinals, ordinals, numerals, the commutative, associative and distributive laws, the extension of the number concept . . . ? Would the course be less or more suited to the future purposes of any potential mathematician? The demands it would make would be different but no less exacting.

The reader will wish to make up his own mind on the various issues in curriculum development and mathematical education which have been raised in relation to the SMP and its materials. Perhaps one may be allowed to suggest that yesterday's challenge to the SMP has been effectively met and is now over except in the field of in-service training where the need continues unabated.

One of the present challenges is to devise trial courses for the 11–16 age group, deriving in part from stated theoretical principles. They must be suitable for classroom and teacher use, place due emphasis on structural learning and eliminate the dichotomy between mathematics and its applications. Such courses could have the advantage of being less radical in their mathematical approach but more searching, in real terms, of understanding and competence. They could also be sufficiently different and demanding as to hold the teacher's interest and help maintain the trend for development in mathematical education.

Any new SMP courses will doubtless be built on the primary and middle school series, SMP 7–13, of which the first units appeared in March 1977. They were produced by practising teachers and tested in schools before publication in accordance with the standard practice of the SMP. A card system is used and, according to the publishers, 'the very able, average and less able children are well catered for'. A reviewer writes:

> The handbook states ... that there is not much new mathematics to be found in it. This disclaimer is somewhat coy as many topics are enhanced by the introduction of such ideas as sets, the laws of commutativity and distribution, Caley tables, equivalence, mapping, number line, ordering and bases other than denary. There is no doubt that the course emphasizes most of all the need for a firm foundation for work on number, and practice in computational skills, measurement and shape. Perhaps in the present educational climate, the course is being published at an opportune time.
>
> (Foster 1977)

A new USA programme, *Developing Mathematical Processes*, takes up a position closely similar to that of the SMP 7–13 course both in teaching approach and the introduction of modern terminology. (Moser 1970–76). The new version of the USA series, *Modern School Mathematics: Structure and Use*, (Duncan 1978), however, does not even use the word 'set', presumably reflecting the strength of the reaction of the elementary school teacher against the 'new math'.

In the SMP director's reports, it is stated (Thwaites 1972a, 115) that many of the new texts seem 'to have brought about, almost inevitably (as it now seems), a change of heart and of approach on the part of teachers who are now refashioning their teaching methods so as to sharpen their pupils' imagination, intuition and curiosity'. The mention of these possibilities serves as a timely reminder of the valuable intrinsic elements in mathematical education that transform the subject in its learning and teaching yet do not have obvious connection with the utilitarian ends for which the community is currently calling. 'To be educated is not to have arrived at a destination. It is to travel with a different point of view', (Peters 1963).

BRYAN THWAITES

SMP: A Response

Of all the critiques of the work of the SMP which have appeared from time to time, Wilfred Flemming's is the most sensitive and perceptive, and I greatly appreciate it. Certainly his analysis will help the SMP to examine its mechanisms and future objectives more effectively, and to identify its own strengths and weaknesses.[1] Given, then, that there is nothing in the account with which I take serious issue, all that I need do is to add one or two glosses which may further interest the reader.

Looking back over the last quarter-century, I am inclined to make the bold claim that it was the SMP which successfully established, for the first time, a definitive methodology of curriculum development. This methodology had five ingredients, all of them indispensable: authorship by experienced practising teachers, repeated pre-publication testing of draft materials in the classroom, GCE and CSE examinations to correspond to the courses, in-service training for teachers, and a continuing service for teachers. Permeating these ingredients is the additional idea of assessment of the pupil's materials; Wilfred Flemming interestingly observes that the SMP felt that subjective assessment of this kind is probably more valuable than the attempts at objective assessment which have been made elsewhere.

The SMPs methodology, then, set new standards for curriculum development and the reader may care to assess the projects described in this volume according to these standards, and to correlate his assessments with the quality of influence exerted by the projects.

Beyond that, and beyond its astonishing and sometimes slightly terrifying impact on mathematical education all over the world, what else might be deduced from the SMP's experience? Perhaps the deepest impression left on me by the recent period of extraordinary change is the long time-scale inherent in education in general and in curriculum development in particular. (The knowledge picked up by a young teacher in 1978 may be imparted at the end of his career and used around the year 2050!) In these circumstances, I dare say that the typical 'research project' funded for a short fixed term is virtually useless: there has to be almost limitless follow-up if a project seeks to have any but a trivial and ephemeral impact. It is for this reason that the affairs of the School Mathematics Project have been directed in such a way as to ensure that, for practical purposes, it has an indefinite life.

Finally, I cannot resist the temptation to offer a strictly personal view which, I know, is not universally shared. If only by virtue of the large numbers of academics who have become involved in curriculum development for schools, there has emerged the idea that mathematical education is a discipline in its own right which should carry with it all the conventional panoply of chairs, of journals, of international conferences and so on. I doubt whether this idea is either justified or valid. Education is ultimately manifested in the relationship between the individual teacher and the individual pupil, and I do not believe that the relationship is subject to the rigorous analysis which is a necessary characteristic of an academic discipline. Everything rests, in the end, on the personal qualities of the individual teacher and hardly anything else matters.

Notes

1. It may be noted that the SMP clearly carries the impress of Dr. Thwaites' personal views on education as they appear in his article 'Visions of greatness or the defence of values in education', *IMA Bulletin* 12, 10, 300–304 1976. From the start, the organisation was set on maintaining a position of independence, a 'position unencumbered by existing interests and independent of existing organisations'. At one stage, a grant of £30,000 from the Schools Council was refused. The position taken up by the SMP must have made for tension and conflict as may be gleaned from the Director's reports. Hidden in the process of curriculum development are personal, social, political and other beliefs and values whose effects do not lend themselves to ready assessment, either from within or without a project, to confound the theorist.

2. This was my reaction to an earlier version of Flemming's article which was considerably longer than that now published. The shortened version seems to lay greater emphasis on the original ideas of the SMP than is now relevant; from it, readers may obtain the impression that there is some fixed and unchanging view of school mathematics which essentially characterises the SMP. On the contrary, the SMP evolves inexorably and, in so doing, adjusts its attitudes to the current scene.

4 Nuffield O-Level Chemistry[1]

Basic information

Sponsor   Nuffield Foundation.

Grant   Initially, £250,000 for the three O-level projects (Chemistry, Physics, Biology); subsequently approximately £100,000 more was allocated to them.

Location   Nuffield Lodge, Regents Park, London NW1 4RS.

Period of development   September 1962–August 1965. Publication: summer 1966.

Designated pupils   Above average ability, 11–16 year olds, in grammar schools and O-level classes in other establishments.

Organiser   H. F. Halliwell. Former chemistry teacher; head of science; headmaster; lecturer in education and in chemistry, University College of North Staffordshire, Keele; former chief examiner in chemistry, Northern Ireland. Member of SMA chemistry panel, 1957–62.

Project team   Teachers with experience in maintained (grammar and comprehensive) and independent schools and a technical college. Two members were seconded from Shell International, Ltd. The initial nucleus of four were all members of the SMA chemistry panel. With the advice of the Consultative Committee, they thrashed out the basic framework for the project in the first two to three months. Additional members were added as new needs arose. The number was determined by the range of resources, examinations and experimental work. Each took responsbility for one publication. With Nuffield foundation personnel, they liaised with all other groups involved, such as examining bodies, instrument-makers, etc, and with other project teams; prepared materials for school trials, collected and responded to feedback, revised materials; collected and tested experiments, checking on safety; addressed meetings and conferences, ran and participated in teachers' courses, dealt with visitors and requests for information from overseas. There was considerable devolution of responsibility within the team and those engaged in trials.

Trials   'Pilot' trials: autumn 1963. Twelve schools, mainly first and second year pupils.
  'Extended' trials: January–June 1964. 73 schools.
  'Main' trials: 1964/65. 56 schools.

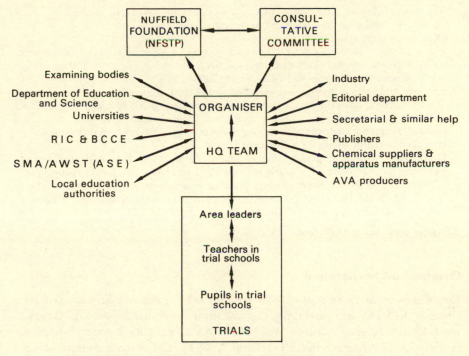

Figure 4.1 People and groups involved in development.

Trials covered a wide geographical range and all types of school, in England, Wales and Northern Ireland. Altogether approximately 4,000 pupils.

Materials Materials are aimed primarily at the teacher; there are supplementary materials for pupils, but no pupils' textbook.

Also teaching aids. Fuller details are given in the bibliography. Published by Longman Group and Penguin Education.

Revision Research for the revision was undertaken under the direction of Dr. R. B. Ingle during 1970–1971. The major changes have been:
i. the preparation of an alternative Sample Scheme;
ii. revision of content in accordance with conceptual levels of pupils, to eliminate those parts found to be 'very difficult';
iii. the addition of a pupils' textbook.

Cost The cost of the original materials is no longer applicable, since revised materials are now appearing. Apart from resources, the chief needs are chemicals and 'not very complicated glassware'. A few items of special equipment are recommended.

A complete set of *one copy* of each publication in the revised version will cost approximately £60.

Dissemination
Media Annual HFSTP Progress Reports published 1962–66.
Occasional NFSTP Newsletters, 1965–70.

The Annual Report of the Nuffield Foundation from 1961 onwards gave information, as did articles in scientifically-orientated journals.
Occasional press releases.
Films: *Chemistry by Investigation* (ICI) and *Exploring Chemistry* (Unilever) were designed to help teachers put the proposals into effective use.
TV programmes: *Teaching Nuffield Chemistry*, BBC, 1968.
Lectures and talks at meetings of relevant professional associations.
Trials   Geographical distribution aided dissemination, as did specially-created 'area committees' and the 'continuation group' from 1965 onwards.
Courses   Loughborough conference, August/September, 1964–for trials teachers, who then acted as tutors for subsequent courses.
Department of Education and Science, Schools Council and local education authorities ran series of courses for teachers from 1966 onwards; The Royal Institute of Chemistry included 'Nuffield' matters in its annual conferences and summer schools from 1962; in the late 1960s Science Teachers' Centres were established in many university departments and colleges of education.

Adaptations and translations   Numerous.

Origins and background

Established formally in April 1962, the Nuffield Foundation Science Teaching Project (NFSTP) was essentially the evolutionary outcome of many years of work by the Science Masters' Assocation (SMA) and, to a lesser extent, the Association of Women Science Teachers (AWST). The two associations merged in 1963 to form the Association for Science Education (ASE). The necessary impetus, however, came primarily from the changed economic, political and ideological climate of the late nineteen fifties and early sixties, and in particular from

1. a belief in the central importance of scientific and technological advance for the economy, for national defence, prestige and welfare;
2. continuing economic crises;
3. the 'Cold War', and revelations about Soviet scientific and technological manpower and progress; and
4. continuing manpower shortages, anxieties and confusions.

Within this context, widespread concern was being expressed about the nature and quality of science education at all levels.

Throughout the twentieth century, scientific knowledge had been growing extremely rapidly in both bulk and sophisticaton, with the result that, by the 1950s, science syllabuses – which had changed relatively little – were overloaded with outdated and socially irrelevant material. Universities complained about their 'illiterate' student intake. School science teachers voiced strong discontent over the 'science' that they were having to teach on the prescription of examination syllabuses. Not only did these syllabuses lack any modern orientation, but they were so overloaded that didactic teaching was seemingly unavoidable. By putting a premium on the accumulation of information rather than on the development of conceptual structure and understanding, examinations also encouraged rote learning. In addition time-table allocations in science, laboratories, equipment and technical assistance were all seen as totally inadequate. Discontent was aggravated by the fact that nationally-funded curriculum development projects were under way in America, under the direction of very eminent scientists. The discipline-orientation of these projects reflected much contemporary educational writing and it also legitimated the century-long arguments for 'inquiry' methods, for 'teaching the pursuit of science'. Science curriculum reform was going on nearer home, too, in Scotland.

Such was the climate of concern by the late fifties that quite extravagant claims for science education could be made. For example, Jacob Bronowski appears to have raised few eyebrows in 1958 when he told a British Association audience: 'We must saturate the schools with science ... The scientists are inheriting, they are conquering the earth, and if you do not speak their uncouth language, then you will sink to the level of the native yokels when the Normans overran England.' (Bronowski 1958, 306).

Similarly, C. P. Snow's *Two Cultures* lectures (Snow 1959) were widely approved and quoted in spite of their rather limited educational perspective of a dichotomous 'literacy' and 'numeracy', and the controversy sparked off by Leavis probably did much to ensure a very wide hearing.

Perhaps the most striking manifestation of the new climate was the changed attitude of industry to school science. In 1949 industrial involvement in school science was minimal. In 1955 a total of 141 industrial firms sponsored the establishment and deployment of the *Industrial Fund* (IFASES 1963) which, between then and 1963, provided £$3\frac{1}{4}$ million – far more than the entire outlay on the Nuffield Foundation Science Teaching Project – for building and equipping science laboratories in independent and direct grant schools: a quite remarkable example of pressure group action. (On its inception, the Minister of Education undertook to parallel the venture in maintained schools, but other claims upon the educational purse of the nation took precedence.)

In this same climate two other series of events were taking place quite independently. On the one hand the Nuffield Foundation was moving steadily in the direction of support for curriculum change. On the other, special 'panels' of the SMA/AWST Science and Education Committee had been preparing new and updated syllabuses and teaching notes for O- and A-level physics, chemistry and biology. Their work was based on the SMA's 1957 *Policy Statement* (SMA 1957), which was also under revision. This was no new-style exercise on the part of the science teachers: they had been doing it for close on thirty years. This time, however, the changes they were advocating involved both content and approach. It grew steadily more clear that, if the desired changes were to be realised, teachers would need considerable help in the form of detailed teachers' guides and other books, visual aids and in-service courses. Public examinations, too, would need to be brought into line with new, wider objectives. So far the work had been entirely voluntary and spare-time, but the new demands were quite beyond the associations' resources of time, manpower and money. So soaked were they in the climate that they had helped to create, that the science teachers believed that the money would be quite readily forthcoming from government sources. Government, however, was uninterested in school science before the 'technological revolution' of the Labour Party's election platform in 1963/64 and the teachers were warned that there was little prospect of support. At this precise point, the partly fortuitous conjunction of time, place, circumstance and persons united their interests with those of the Nuffield Foundation. The outcome was the Nuffield Foundation Science Teaching Project.

Aims and rationale of the NFSTP

Early Nuffield projects aimed at reforming school science by providing the *means* to change in the form of centrally-produced curriculum development projects, designed 'for teachers by teachers', and consisting of co-ordinated sets of tested resource materials for use by individual teachers in 'any way they wish'. At the heart of the NFSTP lay a belief that, in an area of such uncertainty and so many unknowns, the only thing to do was to get together some of the 'best teachers' they could locate and 'give them the opportunity to recall systematically how they went about teaching science' (Waring 1975, 252). The model for development was action research. In it, the new approach was to be defined and exemplified in draft materials produced by central teams, which would then be tested in schools following careful briefing of trials teachers to ensure that they understood the underlying ethos. Feedback from the trials would be used to modify, replace and generally improve the materials before publication. In the longer term revisions would become necessary and provision was to be made for it, but the ultimate aim was to encourage continuing innovation by teachers in individual classrooms.

The starting-point was at O-level but, from the outset, there was a firm (and documented) commitment to the extension of the work to cater for all age and ability ranges. The decision to start with the top 25 per cent of pupils was made on the grounds that:

1. SMA/AWST O- and A- level syllabuses published in 1961 had been well received and were generally regarded as ready for full-scale development;
2. choosing O instead of A-Level would net future non-scientists as well as future scientists, and thereby 'help to bridge the *Two Cultures* gap';
3. curriculum development on this scale was an entirely new venture in Britain and Nuffield Foundation personnel felt that, because of its experimental nature, they were entitled to go in at the point at which they believed most could be learned;
4. public examinations *can* be a means to relatively quick change if they can be geared to the achievement of a project's objectives, and be seen to be so geared.
(Waring 1975, 247–54)

For the first two years of the NFSTP, administration and co-ordination as a whole rested with Dr. Leslie Farrar-Brown (Director of the Nuffield

Foundation) and his assistant directors. By 1964, however, the number of projects was increasing steadily and co-ordination was becoming onerous on top of normal duties. In addition much negotiation and decision-making lay ahead in relation to examinations, apparatus and equipment, visual aids, publication and teachers' in-service courses, and Dr. Farrar-Brown's retirement was imminent. A new post, that of co-ordinator, was therefore created and John Maddox, Science Correspondent of the Guardian, appointed.

O-level chemistry project personnel

THE CONSULTATIVE COMMITTEE

The Chairman, Professor (later Sir) Ronald Nyholm, FRS, of University College, London, was appointed first, and then the organiser of the project, H. F. Halliwell. Nyholm was an eminent scientist and a man of considerable influence and, in consultation with Halliwell and others, he built up a Committee consisting of a number of university scientists and representatives from scientific professional institutions, the Ministry of Education, the ASE, industry, and different types of school. In Nyholm's view, the Committee's task was to supply expert advice on the handling of modern ideas and on their translation into a chemistry course for pupils in different types of school, to ensure liaison with universities and to provide legitimation. Meetings were held some four or five times a year at first; less often later. At them, detailed proposals from the team were discussed and amended by mutual agreement. In essence, however, the team was left to develop the project in its own way.

THE ORGANISER

As soon as the Consultative Committee chairman had been appointed, consultations began with the Royal Institute of Chemistry and the newly-formed British Committee on Chemical Education in the search for an organiser. H.F. Halliwell was invited to meet Nyholm and then, on the latter's strong recommendation, he took part in an 'informal discussion' at Nuffield Lodge. An offer of an appointment was made, and steps were taken to secure Halliwell's secondment from 15 September 1962.

A former chemistry teacher, head of science and then headmaster, Halliwell was lecturing in education and in chemistry at Keele. He had been chief examiner in chemistry in Northern Ireland in the nineteen fifties and, during that period, had helped to devise science curricula for the new secondary intermediate schools and courses for their teachers. This experience had enabled him to develop and test many of the ideas that later formed part of the Nuffield Chemistry Project with pupils of average and below average ability (and therefore less able than his Nuffield client population). Halliwell had also been a member of the SMA Chemistry Panel from 1957 to 1962.

THE HEADQUARTERS TEAM

Halliwell's first concern was to have, as deputy organiser, E. H. Coulson, Chairman of the SMA Chemistry Panel, an extremely active member of numerous SMA and Royal Institute of Chemistry (RIC) committees over twenty or more years, a chief examiner in chemistry and a grammar school teacher of very high standing. Halliwell had been given complete autonomy over his choice of team, but he always discussed his choice with others, so now he and Coulson invited two other members of the Chemistry Panel to join them, and secured their secondment. Of these four initiating members of the team three had, between them, over ninety years of successful teaching and they had published both books and articles. The fourth was, intentionally, a younger man. Later on other team members were added. In contrast to biology and physics, the numerical constitution of the chemistry team was determined by jobs to be done, that is, by the range of resources and by such tasks as examinations and experiments. Temporary working parties helped with the collection and preparation of materials for the *Handbook for Teachers* and with the collection and testing of experiments. As a matter of deliberate policy, team members continued to teach, part-time, in their schools.

This method of choosing a team had both strengths and weaknesses. On the one hand, their attitudes, beliefs and opinions were already known to the organiser. Once Halliwell had been appointed to produce what was, after all, *a* course (not *the definitive* course), it was natural for him to invite people he already knew, with whom he, and others, could work. This may, in fact, have been a very important factor in the delicate situation of negotiation and compromise that makes up the tissue of development work. On the other hand it automatically excluded many other able teachers who might have been even more effective, and choice via an open interview situation is normally less likely to arouse resentment and hostility.

THE ORGANISER AS LEADER

A deliberate policy of first establishing basic consensus and then devolving responsibility and encouraging individuality, was carried right through the organisational network of the project. Halliwell saw it as his responsibility to define, firstly, the framework in terms of ultimate aims; secondly, the means to their achievement; and thirdly, the basic pattern of organisation and administration within the project. In continuing dialogue with Coulson, he produced four *Memoranda* between September and early December 1962. These identified and discussed the major decision-making areas:

1. the three-year programme of activities;
2. the need for a common treatment of overlapping topics in biology, chemistry and physics;
3. the problem of examinations and of the need to experiment with new-type questions and methods;

4. the characteristics of a 'modern approach to chemistry' and hence the aims of the project;
5. their implications for classroom practice;
6. the range of resources needed to try to help the teacher meet the aims and cope with the problems.

These important and fundamental documents are of considerable interest because, as an explicit and comprehensive 'platform', they provided the basis for all future discussion and for all development work. In addition they represent a distillation of knowledge and experience and a breadth of perspective that derived from many years of successful teaching.

This framework having been established, responsibility for production and testing of resources could be assumed by individual team members. They started by producing documents of intent for group discussion, and these provided the foundation for their individual work. General consensus was sought and usually achieved in an essentially co-operative and non-authoritarian climate. Where controversy remained (and at times it was strong) and compromise could not be reached, Halliwell had to make – and did make – the decision. Nevertheless, it is clear that team members believe that their contribution was, indeed, a personal one. There is, too, a strong recollection by all of considerable enthusiasm and commitment, and of unflagging support from organiser and deputy.

Devolution of responsibility extended to the trials, Twelve 'area leaders' were selected on grounds of personal qualities and geographical distribution, and each was made responsible for local organisation. Each chose his own team of trials teachers and acted as an intermediary in organising and advising them and in providing and relaying feedback to headquarters.

Translation of a framework of ideas into a project

ENDS AND MEANS

The revised SMA/AWST policy statement provided the starting point for development. Like all policy statements, however, it had to be interpreted and made explicit in order to define the project's intentions and the proposed means for their realisation in schools. Two statements, in particular, were important in defining the project's aims:

> Present scientific illiteracy is in part due to a lack of factual knowledge, but is much more the result of a lack of understanding of the basic nature and aims of science . . .
> (SMA/AWST 1961, 4)

> Science should be recognised – and taught – as a major human activity, which explores the realm of human experience, maps it methodically but also imaginatively, and, by disciplined speculation, creates a coherent system of knowledge.
> (SMA/AWST 1961, 5)

A stepwise and systematic clarification of the team's interpretation of these statements provided the project's aims, which were based on what 'being scientific means to a scientist'. The fundamental aim was to provide experience that would enable pupils:

1. to know when and how to be 'scientific', that is, to be able to discriminate between problems that can and that cannot be solved by a scientific approach, and how to go about it when appropriate;
2. to build up a body of knowledge of the 'alchemy of stuffs' and some understanding of scientific explanation in terms of a model. Pupils should be able critically to distinguish between facts, patterns of facts and speculative generalisations;
3. to become aware of science as both 'process' and 'product' and of the relationship between them;
4. to be aware that one product of science is power – for good or bad – over the environment;
5. to be aware of chemistry as the activity of men and women, now and in the past, all over the world;
6. to experience such satisfaction as would 'ensure the further development of critical and appreciative attitudes towards scientific affairs', whatever their future careers.

(Memorandum II, 2–3 in Waring 1975 443–46)

The experiences to be provided, therefore, should afford pupils opportunities for creative thinking, for engaging in the planning of experiments to discipline their speculations and for learning the necessary manipulative skills. The approach was fundamentally dependent upon the interplay between the 'bench, and the blackboard of the mind' (that is, between actuality and imaginative thinking) that, for Halliwell, characterises 'being scientific'.

'FLEXIBILITY WITHIN A FRAMEWORK': THE NUFFIELD CHEMISTRY SYLLABUS

'Being scientific' was the means to the project's ends, and it was possible to frame an examination syllabus in these terms. Whereas traditional chemistry syllabuses deal with lists of concepts and of specific materials, the Nuffield O-level Chemistry syllabus did not name a single chemical: it was entirely in terms of what pupils should develop the ability to *do*, that is, of *chemistry as process*. This was summarised under four headings:

1. knowing how to get new materials from those available;
2. looking for patterns in the behaviour of substances;
3. using explanatory concepts and models and knowing how to check theory by observation and experiment;
4. associating energy changes with material changes.

The basic materials chosen by individual teachers to illustrate these activities should build up a conception of *chemistry as product*, and it should be possible for teachers to vary these to suit their own and their pupils' needs and interests. Overall, a good deal of traditional material would be used, but less traditional areas would also have to be included.

For full understanding, Halliwell urged, the study of chemistry must be set in its human and social context. This meant providing examples of 'excited and exciting minds, of the flash of genius', and developing the ability to see chemistry as an addition to a 'body of experience which vastly affects our lives and the development of our sense of values'. The social context of chemistry was to be seen as something more than its direct applications (*Memorandum* IV, 4–5 in Waring 1975, 459).

A fundamental aim was 'understanding' but, Halliwell argued, it was important to appreciate that full understanding could only be achieved over time, that it would grow in richness and precision from the first vague conceptions to a final critical awareness, and that, inevitably, pupils of different ability would develop such understanding to different extents by the ends of the course. The best methods of trying to ensure understanding by pupils of differing abilities and interests would, he warned, still have to be worked out.

THE DEVELOPMENTAL MODEL

O-level Chemistry used a developmental model that has a long history going back at least as far as Rousseau: namely, that the abilities of pupils develop in discernable stages, of which three were seen to have relevance for the project. (This model owes nothing to Piaget, although comparison is interesting.)

> *Stage I* (ages eleven and twelve approximately) was a time for 'doing experiments' (which must, however, form a coherent foundation of experience for Stage II), for acquiring basic practical techniques and skills and for starting the training in disciplining speculation – at this stage, speculation about what was happening.
> *Stage II* (ages thirteen to fourteen) was a time for turning attention to explanation in terms of particulate models. These should be developed only when they could be *used*. Practical work should now be slanted more to testing ideas and should be accompanied by a more marked concern with the energy changes involved.
> *Stage III* would be characterised by the developing and ripening of experience of the interplay of fact and imagination.   (*Memorandum* IV, 2 in Waring 1975, 455–56)

Development of the resources materials

A fundamental aim of the Chemistry project was to provide maximum flexibility within this basic framework and so to avoid the development of just another orthodoxy. Choice of material to illustrate chemistry as product was one way of providing variety and flexibility. To help teachers plan their pathways through the syllabus, the team intended to indicate a number of possible routes in outline in the *Introduction and Guide*. In the event, it took far longer than they had expected to reach agreement on the single scheme necessary for the trials, however, and this intention had to be shelved while team members worked on outline teaching schemes and lesson summaries (including practical work), based on this 'sample scheme'. Once trials started, teachers' continuing requests for ever more detailed notes produced such a mass of material, that the 'sample scheme' had to be collected into two, previously unanticipated, extra volumes – the *Basic Course* and the *Options*. This vastly increased pressure on time and it partially defeated the intention of flexibility, because it did much to consolidate any tendency to view the resources as a course, a view compounded by examination questions that became closely linked to its content. Another outcome was that no alternative 'sample schemes' were produced for Stage II.

Pupils' materials were also planned with flexibility in mind. It was his concern to avoid producing a 'new orthodoxy' that had decided Halliwell not to provide a pupils' textbook – so easily seen as a single authoritative source of information – and the team steadfastly resisted pressures for one. *Laboratory Instruction Sheets* were kept to the minimum in number and in detail, and other pupil material consisted of a *Book of Data* and a collection of *Background Books*. Thus the resources were designed very largely for the teacher, emphasising the importance of his role in developing schemes for his pupils.

The trials

Three sets of trials were held. Their purpose was

1. to test the feasibility and practicability in the classroom of new ideas;
2. to test whether or not the suggested approach could be transmitted to and put into operation by a range of teachers of varying experience and expertise;
3. to obtain essential feedback for rewriting, so as to increase the effectiveness and applicability of the materials and to make them as acceptable as possible to teachers;
4. to help in dissemination by involving teachers in a range of schools, across the country.

Briefing sessions, consisting of lectures and discussions were held before the 'pilot' and 'extended' trials. Before the 'main' trials, however, two, week-long conferences were held at Loughborough College of Advanced Technology. Here, the chemistry team put the emphasis on a workshop approach in which most of the time was spent in exploration of the practical work in the way that pupils would, it was hoped, experience it. The Loughborough Conference was also seen as a means of establishing a pattern for future in-service courses, and of training tutors to run courses in this 'workshop' spirit. It was also an important source of feedback. For many teachers, it was something of a revelation: 'I came away – this is not an exaggeration – thinking about chemistry in an entirely new light.' (Harding 1975, 16.13).

The administrative organisation and devolution of responsibility has already been described. Teachers sent weekly reports on standard forms to their area leader, each of whom summarised them and added his own comments in a single, monthly report to headquarters. All weekly film loop reports accompanied these summaries. Area Leaders met their teachers regularly, and also had meetings in London about once a term. Material for the *Handbook for Teachers* was sent out in duplicate to all participants. Feedback here involved the return of one copy, altered as each teacher saw fit. This eased some of the load at Headquarters, and it increased the teachers' sense of involvement.

The major criticisms of the materials during trials were that too little time had been allocated to topics and that certain topics were 'too difficult' at this level. By extending the time allotted to Stage I, and by adjusting Stage II and III accordingly, the problem of time appeared to be largely overcome. It also meant that pupils were older when they began to meet the topics that were causing most difficulty, and area leaders agreed that this should alleviate the difficulties, although they pointed out that pupils' mathematical weakness was likely to continue to be a great handicap.

Constraints on development

The one formidable constraint was lack of time. Not only was there the unanticipated pressure for considerably more detailing of materials, but, since these were the first projects to be carried out on any scale, all administrative arrangements had to be planned from scratch. So had all negotiations and agreements with publishers, with instrument-makers and scientific suppliers, with producers of audio-visual material, with Ministry officials, professional institutions and examining bodies. Considerable interest in the NFSTP had been aroused, and there were numerous letters, callers and overseas visitors to be dealt with. Later on there were requests for talks, and there were courses to be organised and run. All this was additional to the development work itself and to the analysis and use of feedback. At times, especially in the final year, the pressure became almost intolerable.

Apart from this, however, there does not appear to have been any strong sense of constraint. Finance, Halliwell recalls, was no problem. The Nuffield Foundation was 'very generous'; he had budgeted carefully and he kept within this, except for the additional sums made necessary by the continuing expansion of the exercise. All requests were readily acceded to. Secretarial and administrative help were adjusted to changing needs, and accommodation was adequate. Trials teachers were enthusiastic and very willing, with few exceptions. There is no doubt that the early projects benefited greatly from the 'Hawthorne effect', although it must necessarily have affected the reliability of feedback.

Examinations

It was essential that all forms of assessment, particularly public examinations, be in keeping with the project's objectives, and this required the active co-operation of the Secondary School Examinations Council, the Curriculum Study Group and Ministry of Education and the Examination Boards. (In 1964 the Schools Council replaced the first two bodies). This was needed to get agreement on an unconventional and intentionally flexible syllabus; to try to ensure that the emphasis was on the assessment of intellectual skills, that is, on what pupils could *do*; to get agreement on the wider range of objectives; to explore available instruments of assessment and to develop their appropriate and effective use in what would be 'new-style' examinations, which must be seen to be of comparable reliability and validity; and to provide assurances to pupils, parents and schools that trials and, later on, adoption of the syllabus, would not jeopardise pupils' chances of examination success. The NFSTP also aimed to get a more significant role for the teacher, eventually, in public examinations that were internally-assessed and externally-moderated, although not much progress was made (or attempted) at this stage.

Apart from the negotiations and the collaborative experiments with the Boards, aims had to be converted into examination specifications (*Introduction and Guide*, 1966, 124), trial examinations had to be devised, administered and analysed. New techniques, such as multiple choice, structured, and open-ended essay questions had been developed elsewhere, but the Nuffield teams had to develop their own test items from scratch (no easy task) and test them for reliability and validity as instruments for detecting the abilities specified in the objectives. Expert help was available and it was used.

Dissemination

Dissemination occurred both informally, through the large number of people associated with the project, and formally. Though valuable in itself, there is a strong risk of distortion in informal communication, and distorted impressions are very difficult to change. Yet the work going on was tentative and experimental and it was considered necessary to protect it from over-critical scrutiny, at least in the early stages. Though a fair amount of information actually went out formally it was, for some considerable time, deliberately unspecific about both content and approach and, inevitably, criticism about 'secrecy' and a 'private party' were voiced in 1964. (*Times Educational Supplement* (1964) 249 and 569). By that autumn, however, the main body of each project was taking shape and so a good deal of information was made available via journals and talks and, especially, the annual meeting of the ASE. In 1965, a *NFSTP Newsletter* was added to the annual Progress Report. A 'continuation group' was set up in 1965 to sustain communication channels and iron out problems between the time that the team disbanded in the summer of 1965 and publication a year later. Continuity at local level was provided for by the establishment of 'area committees'. Some of these flourished for years; others fell away gradually; some did not even get off the ground. Much undoubtedly depended upon the initiative of individuals.

Exhibitions of apparatus and equipment at courses and, especially, at each annual meeting of the ASE provided yet another communication channel, as did advertisements and catalogues. Pre-publication drafts of the materials were sent out to a number of individuals and to university science departments with a request for comments upon content and approach. Science departments were also asked to show the materials to students in the hope of arousing greater interest in science teaching as a career.

Shortly before the work of the Chemistry team ended, a film was made with the help of Unilever. Called *Exploring Chemistry*, it showed the approach in action in a laboratory in a totally unscripted situation. The film was widely acclaimed and received international awards. A second film, *Chemistry by Investigation*, followed, with help from ICI. Both have been widely used in pre- and in-service training. In 1966 plans were made for a television series. Five programmes on *Teaching Nuffield Chemistry* were shown on BBC television on two separate occasions in 1968. They, too, aroused much interest.

Publishers produced prospectuses in 1966 and, in 1967, books were on display at the National Book League's exhibition. The publications themselves would, clearly, form the major communication channels, along with in-service and pre-service courses for teachers.

Six large-scale 'tutor-training' conferences, financed by Schools Council and local education authorities and run by Nuffield Foundation personnel, were held by the three O-level projects in January 1966, two for each subject. Tutors trained at them then helped to run 70 courses for teachers during that summer. In addition, a variety of courses was offered by the Department of Education and Science (this replaced the Ministry of Education in 1964) although, in accordance with the official policy of neutrality among the Inspectorate, Nuffield projects were discussed along with other approaches at most of these. After considerable initial interest, however, attendance at courses was poor enough to give rise to some concern. In addition to these courses, the Royal Institute of Chemistry had given the materials much publicity over the years, and this was consolidated by the subsequent establishment of science teachers' centres in university departments and colleges of education.

Reception

The materials were published in 1966 and were welcomed by reviewers as a 'radical but restrained swing to modernity'. (*New Scientist* 1966, 5–6). Dissenting voices were heard, but these were largely those of a few established teachers whose personal philosophy of science education differed from that of the project. (Bradley 1967; Fowles 1968, for example). According to the Curriculum

Diffusion Research Project (Kelly 1975) the projects have been widely welcomed and used. There has been some concern, however, that many teachers (and researchers) have tended to treat the materials as courses rather than resources, that is, as 'packages', a negation of the fundamental intention of encouraging flexibility and of avoiding the creation of a new orthodoxy.

Adoption offers a measure of 'success', as do sales. Even here, difficulties arise, for when it is resources that are being considered, what constitutes 'success' – full or partial use? With or without the special examination? With or without the approach advocated? Not all users enter pupils for the special examination and there may be as many outside this group as inside it whose use of materials would be at least recognisably in line with that advocated. Few conclusions can be drawn from figures, then, without knowing how the materials are being used in classroom and laboratory. Even here there are risks, since a focus on teacher-effectiveness in terms of the fairly narrow range of activities defined by a project may obscure other aspects of classroom interaction of equal or greater importance in relation to outcomes. It is hardly surprising, then, that such post-project evaluation as has been carried out has revealed little about the relation between pupil outcomes and the project, since causal relationships cannot be drawn without a great deal of knowledge about the intervening component of classroom interaction.

To date, Nuffield Chemistry has been translated into many foreign languages and is in use in a considerable number of foreign countries, with or without significant alteration. This, too, is a measure of success, although Halliwell has some reservation about the process: ... answers to the problems we have in mind will be different in different countries ... no scheme is likely to have universal application – therefore each community, while learning from the efforts of others, must base its proposals clearly on its own needs and in its own perspectives ... (Halliwell 1972, 353–4).

Evaluation

'Formative' evaluation was confined very largely to the subjective judgements of trials teachers, who were necessarily assumed to be teaching the course in an appropriate way (they were chosen on this basis, although it was never tested); a confidential report, also subjective, produced by HMIs in September, 1964; and the drawing of inferences from examination reports. In the case of the teachers' judgements, the project was set up to provide tested resources in a limited period of time. The focus was therefore on the 'rightness' of the materials, and this left room for much variation in terms of what constituted a 'successful' lesson in the eyes of teachers. In the case of examination reports, those working on the examinations focused their attention very much on the development of viable new-type examinations, rather than on the achievement of desirable outcomes by pupils, although some disturbing indications that all was not well in some classrooms were, indeed, picked up. In any case, examinations cover only a limited range of mainly cognitive outcomes and the availability and effectiveness of instruments defines very closely what is actually assessed. HMIs were, in general, impressed by what they saw in trial chemistry classrooms, although they suggested that girls might be having 'special difficulties'.

No official post-project evaluation study was carried out, although a study of attitudes was sponsored but not commissioned by the Nuffield Foundation in 1966 (Meyer 1970). A Schools Council survey in 1968 (Schools Council 1969) and the Curriculum Diffusion Research Project (Kelly 1975) at Chelsea College, looked at adoption, and, in the latter case, communication channels and the factors affecting decision-making. Eggleston's work, which attempts to lift the lid off the 'black box' of the classroom is still in an early stage (Eggleston *et al.* 1976). Apart from these studies, none of which has been uniquely concerned with O-level chemistry, evaluation since 1966 has been left to individual, usually small-scale, studies of very variable quality. Few have recognised the dangers of drawing conclusions about causal relationships (between use of materials and pupil achievement) without thorough investigation of what teachers have actually been doing in lessons (and not only in pupils' science lessons).

At the same time, in-service courses have not been evaluated, so that little is known about teachers' take-away perceptions. Harding (Harding 1975, chapter 16) explored Nuffield-using teachers' perceptions of the approach and revealed the existence of a disquieting amount of uncertainty and woolly thinking, reminiscent of that found by Herron (Herron 1971). Eggleston, in turn, concluded that a 'considerable dissonance exists between the aims of curriculum developers and related classroom practice'. Yet this is not really surprising. In the first place, much confusion has resulted from the tendency (exhibited by researchers as well as teachers) to treat the materials as packages, which teachers must 'get right'. In the second place, there is considerable evidence (see, for instance, McKinley *et al.* 1975) to show that good teaching cannot be generalised to others in this way and that, however beautifully and meticulously worked-out a scheme may be, it may not automatically represent a solution to individual teachers' classroom problems. The more detailed it becomes, the greater the possibility that it will stifle innovation in classrooms as teachers struggle to use it within their own particular context of constraints and facilitators.

Nevertheless, it is extremely important to set these early projects in their context of time and place and to judge them in terms of what they were intended to be – a first approximation to the goal of providing flexible resources for professional use by teachers – and not in terms of the failings of the wider educational system.

In his review in *Nature* in 1966 (Hartwell 1966), Hartwell drew attention to a major underlying assumption and to the need to put it to rigorous test. This was the assumption that teaching 'process' and 'product' can and does make possible, *per se*, the development of particular skills and states of mind and of the interrelationships between them that constitute the discipline's 'way of knowing'. Yet even today this has hardly been questioned in science education, let alone explored. Nor is it at all certain that desirable change in school science should take place within this context.

ERNEST COULSON

Nuffield O-Level Chemistry: A Response

Professor Frank Halliwell is at present on a lengthy tour abroad but I am sure that he would wish me, as his deputy in the headquarters team of the Nuffield O-level Chemistry Project, to add a few words to Dr. Mary Waring's admirably accurate and comprehensive contribution to this book.

As Dr. Waring has made clear, the impetus for the reform of existing syllabuses in the three main branches of science came from practising teachers, expressed through the committees and panels of the Science Masters' Association and the Association of Woman Science Teachers. This school science teacher domination of curriculum development was carried into the detailed work of the Nuffield projects in that members of the headquarters teams were largely recruited from practising teachers. This is a point of some importance and does in fact place Great Britain in a special position in the field of educational development. In most other countries new curricula are imposed from above, often being produced mainly by teachers in establishments of higher education or by government officials. Both from the viewpoints of possible acceptance and of suitability to the pupils for whom new courses are designed, this 'grass roots' origin is of crucial significance. It is most encouraging that the Schools Council, which was formed after the Nuffield projects commenced operations, is similarly oriented towards practising teacher opinion, and that the Association for Science Education (formed by the amalgamation of the SMA and AWST) is playing an increasingly important part in the general direction of science education in schools.

During the past fifteen years much has been said and written about learning theories and evaluation techniques. Neither area of study had reached prominence in 1962, when the headquarters team of the Nuffield O-level Chemistry Project began work. I think it likely that one or two team members might have heard of Piaget, but am sure that none of us knew about Bloom's *Taxonomy of Educational Objectives*. In fact, the small group responsible for planning and implementing assessment methods invented independently a version of the Bloom classification of abilities to be tested. Preoccupied as we were with approach and method, with assessment, and, increasingly, with content, we had neither the time nor the necessary expertise to do other than use a system of school trials to test whether the course material produced was both teachable and intelligible to the age and ability ranges for which it was designed, and whether an assessment procedure could be devised that encouraged those qualities of manipulative ability and thought which the course sought to develop in pupils. It is my personal opinion that it is not feasible or desirable to attempt to conduct an exercise in curriculum development, and a complete and rigorous evaluation of the product at the same time. The strain on both teachers and pupils would be excessive and unwarranted. The full impact and effectiveness of a new learning programme can only be assessed after it has been used in schools for at least five years. Even then the results of evaluation exercises must be treated with caution, whether they are favourable or unfavourable. Already reaction against Piagetian theory is growing rapidly[1] – it may well be that its status in learning theory will turn out to be akin to that of the phlogiston theory in the development of chemical theory.

I have no doubt that one of the great strengths of the Nuffield projects is that they have no powers of compulsion whatsoever. Those of us involved with the chemistry project could only, in effect, say to other teachers 'Here is a learning scheme in chemistry which has excited us, we hope that you will be attracted to it also; perhaps to use it as it is – as a course, perhaps to use parts of it as components of a different scheme of your own devising – as a source.' There is, of course, a third, equally valid reaction: the decision to have nothing to do with the scheme because the teacher concerned has a totally different approach to teaching the subject. The chemistry scheme has attracted all three responses, and I would not have it otherwise: the personality of the teacher is a factor of prime importance in how and what he teaches. There is evidence, however, that the majority of chemistry teachers has been influenced in some way by the Nuffield ideas. Some indication of their more or less complete adoption is given by the numbers of candidates entering for the special Nuffield chemistry examinations. At O-level, starting from 167 candidates in 1965, there are now (1978) 20,127 candidates; the corresponding figures for the A-level examination are 214 in 1968 and 8,008 in 1978. In both cases the numbers are still rising.

When the three original science projects teams began to operate, in 1962, they were told by the then Director of the Nuffield Foundation, Dr. Leslie Farrar-Brown, that their goal was 'to produce a spring-board and not a terminus'. The revision exercise for the O-level chemistry materials, to which Dr. Waring has referred, provides a subsidiary spring-board on the same foundations, again with the invaluable aid of a large number of practising chemistry teachers.

Notes

1. The information in this chapter is drawn from detailed accounts in Waring, 1975, and Waring, 1978. Many people contributed to these works and full acknowledgement is made in them, but I should like to express my appreciation once again. In particular, the Nuffield Foundation, Frank Halliwell and Ernest Coulson have been unstinting in their encouragement and help.

2. See, for example, a brief but excellent article by E. W. Jerkons, *Educ. Chem.*, 1978, 15, 85.

5 Primary French Project

Basic information

There were three projects, separately financed and organised but working in close liaison:

(i) *The Primary French Pilot Scheme*, set up in 1963 by the Ministry of Education under the aegis of its Curriculum Study Group. In 1964 it became the responsibility of the Schools Council which administered the scheme in collaboration with the LEAs involved and the HM Inspectorate until its termination in 1974–75;

(ii) *The Primary French Materials Project*, an integral part of the Foreign Languages Teaching Materials Project established in 1963 by the Nuffield Foundation. Its purpose was the production of French teaching materials for pupils aged from 8 to 13 for use in the Pilot Scheme. Ultimately it engaged in the production of teaching materials in German, Russian and Spanish for the same age range. Progressively taken over by the Schools Council with an extension of responsibilities to cover the age range 13–16 in all languages. It was wound up in 1974 and replaced by the Language Materials Development Unit of the Languages Teaching Centre at the University of York.

(iii) *The Primary French Evaluation Project*, undertaken by the National Foundation for Educational Research whose longitudinal study of the pupils involved in the Pilot Scheme ran from 1964 to 1974.

Sponsors Sponsored jointly by the Nuffield Foundation and the Schools Council from 1962–75. Nuffield participation ceased in 1967.

Grant	Nuffield Foundation	£360,000	
	Schools Council	£892,000	In the main this was for the production of teaching materials. The Schools Council contribution also covered the production of materials in the other three languages.
	Schools Council	£87,250	For the evaluation project
	DES	£110,000	
	Schools Council	£21,000	For the dissemination project
	Total	£1,470,250	

N.B. These monies did not cover the very large sums spent on teacher training, purchase of teaching materials and hardware by the LEAs.

Location 1963–67 mainly in accommodation provided by the University of Leeds. 1967–74 in University of York accommodation at Micklegate House. The Language Materials Development Unit has now succeeded it at the same site.
Address: University of York, Micklegate House, Micklegate York. Tel: York 27844

Designated pupils Age range initially 8–13 and finally 8–16.

Project Team
Directors:

	Professor A. Spicer	to December 1969
	Mr. D. Rowlands	to December 1972
	Mr. D. Rix	to December 1973
	Mrs. S. Honor	to December 1974

French section organisers:

Mr. D. Grant	to September 1966	Primary
Mr. M. Buckby	1966–68	Primary–Secondary
Mr. N. Patrick	1966–69	Secondary
Mr. M. Buckby	1966–73	Secondary
Mrs. S. Honor	1973–74	Secondary

Organisers of other language sections:

German	Mr. A. Peck
Russian	Mr. D. Rix
Spanish	Mr. D. Rowlands
	Mr. R. Clark from 1970

Trials The earliest French materials were tried out in 50 volunteer primary schools in England, Scotland and the Channel Islands between January and July 1964. Subsequently craft materials were mainly pre-tested in the pilot scheme and associated area schools and then revised for publication.

Materials There are three main categories:
  (i) occasional papers on matters connected with linguistic research, published by the Nuffield Foundation;
  (ii) language courses for use in schools:

French	*En Avant* (8–13)	
	A Votre Avis (13–16)	
German	*Vorwärts* (11–16, or with abridged initial stages 13–16)	
Spanish	*Adelante* (11–16, or with abridged initial stages 13–16)	
Russian	*Vperyod!* (11–16)	

Published by E. J. Arnold and Macmillan Education
  (iii) ancillary publications concerned with teaching method, published variously by the Nuffield, Foundation, E. J. Arnold and the Language Materials Development Unit.
For further details of all of these, see the Bibliography.

Background

It is widely considered that Wilder Penfield, the Canadian neurologist, laid the foundations for an early start for language learning through his work on the effects of brain damage. He and his colleague concluded that the years before the age of ten are the time when the brain can most readily acquire new speech. Possibly as a consequence there followed various education experiments: in

1961 Sweden introduced the teaching of English from the age of 10; from 1962 certain cities in Italy taught English to primary children after school hours; there was a Berlin project in 1964 when English was taught to a restricted number of primary children and in the same year Austria experimented with English for nine year-olds (Stern 1969, chapter 10). Prior to 1962 the British official attitude was not enthusiastic, as is evidenced by Ministry of Education pamphlet 29 on *Modern Languages*, which made only passing comment on the possibility of the primary teaching of French. This is in contrast with feeling in the USA where as early as 1953 the Office of Education had organised a conference entitled: 'Should languages be tackled at elementary school level?' The answer was a positive one and Foreign Languages in the Elementary School (FLES) was set up (Durette 1972).

Nevertheless by 1964 a British experiment was to be launched which rivalled any in its scope and thoroughness. The mainspring was the Nuffield Foundation, whose director at this time was Leslie Farrer-Brown. In a personal statement, as yet unpublished, he gives the following background. On 7 December 1959 he held a meeting with eight language teaching experts. They were concerned at the fact that 'very few children who studied French for five years could at the age of 16 converse in French, read a French book or write a letter which a French person might understand.' It was generally agreed at the meeting that what was lacking was motivation in the pupil. Farrer-Brown then conceived the idea that, as 'the younger a child is when it starts to learn a second language, the better', it might be feasible for primary children 'to devote almost all of their time to French in the sense that they would not only have lessons in the French language, but would do the bulk of their other lessons in French'. The aim would be that they would then be able to speak the language when they arrived at secondary stage. This concept was accorded only limited support by the rest of the group.

Little more was done about the idea until two or three months later when Farrer-Brown was introduced to Professor Jeffares of the English Department of Leeds University. He told Jeffares of his suggestion and the latter arranged a meeting with George Taylor (Director of Education for Leeds) and Alec Clegg (Director of Education for the West Riding). Farrer-Brown spoke to them of the possibility of an early start for second language learning and told them that his trustees had agreed to finance such a venture. Within a few days Taylor had found a suitable school and teacher (Mrs. Kellerman) and a visit had been organised to St. Cloud to gain an insight into the latest pedagogical advances in language teaching. (At St. Cloud was located the *Centre de Recherche et d'Etude pour la Diffusion du Français* CREDIF). The resulting educational experiment was so successful that in 1962 it was extended to another six schools. At this stage one of the languages being taught was in fact Italian (Kellerman 1964).

It should be noted in passing that the Nuffield Foundation was concurrently involved in another experiment with three primary schools in East Ham, where French was being taught under normal class conditions using the normal teacher. In East Ham the project was under the direction of S. R. Ingram. It is of interest and consequence that Mr. Ingram was perhaps the country's leading exponent of the TAVOR system of French language teaching. TAVOR, originally devised as a way of teaching the language to American occupational forces attached to SHAPE, was one of the first courses to use film strip and synchronised tape. It was possibly because of the shifting of the burden of teaching from teacher to machine that it was deemed possible to allow non-specialists to cope with this highly specialist subject at primary level.

The dichotomy between the Leeds and East Ham approaches is very significant and this '*querelle des spécialistes et des non-spécialistes*' has yet to be resolved. Both of these systems were financially supported by the Nuffield Foundation: at Leeds it was to the tune of £1,500.

As a consequence of the success of these intial projects the Foundation decided to disseminate its experiences and in May 1962 in association with the Leeds Education Committee it organised a conference of interested Directors of Education, HM Inspectors of schools and some others to study the work being done in schools in Leeds and to consider possible developments. As a result the Foundation set aside £100,000 (ultimately increased to £360,000) for such developments. It was envisaged that action would be needed in four main fields: 'production of teaching resources; development of teacher training; revision of examinations and fundamental linguistic research' (Farrer-Brown, unpublished personal account).

The Ministry of Education's acceptance of the Foundation's proposals had a larger background than the success of the Leeds and East Ham experiments. In the Annan Report on *The Teaching of Russian* (1962) for example, the authors suggested that a sensible way of making room in the time-table for Russian would be to start the teaching of French at the age of nine and then at secondary level to diminish the time allocated to French in favour of Russian. Again, in 1962, the UNESCO Institute for Education in Hamburg had convened a meeting of international experts to consider the primary school teaching of language (UNESCO 1962). Yet another crucial matter in the eyes of the Ministry was the alleged 'opening of the floodgates' which occurred as a result of the success of the Leeds experiment (Rowlands 1972). Facts are here difficult to establish. There is for example a wide variation between the 5,000 schools suggested by Stern in his *Languages and the Young School Child* (1969, 18) and the more modest figure arrived at by Lazaro of 280 schools. (Lazaro 1963). Yet in 1964 a further survey by the newly established Schools Council speaks of 2,500 schools involved in the teaching of primary French. Nevertheless, whatever the actual figures were, it is very probable that Ministerial support for an extension of the Leeds experiment was largely occasioned by the need to control the inflationary situation which that experiment had inspired. The Lazaro Report itself had shown the urgency of such a move by stating that of the 144 teachers of French involved in the survey one third only had acceptable teaching techniques, one third had formal language qualifications and half of the classes were being badly taught and showed poor achievement.

Launching of primary French

On 13 March 1963 the Minister of Education announced the launching of the Primary French Pilot Scheme by means of which all pupils in certain schools were to be taught French from the age of eight in order to discover 'whether it would be feasible and educationally desirable to extend the teaching of a foreign language to pupils who represented a wider range of age and ability than those to whom foreign languages had been traditionally taught.' (Burstall 1974).

The tasks which had to be undertaken were now fairly clear. They were:

1. The selection of appropriate schools and their organisation into areas.
2. The training of semi-specialist teachers.
3. The dissemination of information on progress.
4. The preparation of a body of French teaching materials to cover the 8–13 age groups.
5. The carrying out of research which would help in the production of these materials and which might guide the way to new teaching techniques.
6. The investigation of new ways of continuous assessment leading to changes at O-level.
7. The setting up of an impartial and disinterested evaluation of the project.
8. The provision of teaching materials in the so-called minority languages (German, Spanish and Russian) for the age group 11–16, aimed at a broad ability band.

This last task would seem to indicate that one of the fundamental aims of the pilot scheme was indeed to facilitate the growth of these subjects in accordance with the suggestion made in the Annan Report.

Because two major and usually independent bodies were concerned, the Ministry of Education and the Nuffield Foundation, the execution of these tasks was entrusted to a somewhat complex structure of committees or working parties. As A. Spicer, the first organiser of the newly formed Nuffield Foreign Language Teaching Materials Project, said in his address to the Second (1966) Hamburg Conference, 'the whole scheme marked the beginning of a new form of enterprise between the Ministry and an independent organisation.' Additionally, of course, there was need for representation of, and constant consultation with, the large number of bodies who had dealings with primary and secondary schools such as LEAs, training colleges, universities, heads and teachers, professional associations, HMIs and Nuffield itself. The interrelating structure and individual responsibilities of the committees will probably not be generally known until the thirty years moratorium on the publication of the minutes of such meetings has elapsed.

The committees were as follows:

1. The Ministry's Curriculum Study Group (forerunner of the Schools Council).

2. A sub-committee of the latter, known as Sub-Committee A, composed of four HMIs, three co-opted teachers and chaired by George Taylor, Chief Education Officer of Leeds. This would have been the principal policy-making group.

3. The Consultative Committee set up by Nuffield. This was again chaired by George Taylor, but was more broadly based than Sub-committee A, having representatives from the HMI, the universities, training colleges, the teacher, language associations and Nuffield. At least three people, including Dr. Riddy, the then Staff Inspector for Languages, were members both of this committee and of Sub-committee A. This was in all probability one of the most vital of the committees since it served as a link between the Ministry and Nuffield.

4. An Advisory Committee for Primary French set up by Nuffield, chaired by George Taylor and with a similar kind of representation to that of the Consultative Committee; there was, however, a more pronounced emphasis on language teaching expertise. Its function, which was mainly related to the Nuffield Foreign Languages Teaching Materials (NFLTM) team was, as the title implies, advisory and in no way executive. Its area of concern would have been the broad lines of linguistic and didactic policy of this materials producing group.

5. The NFLTM team (French section) – a salaried group of various specialists (artists, practising teachers and native speakers) headed by an organiser. During the ten years of its existence there were five such organisers, sometimes overlapping, sometimes succeeding one another, as the materials moved from the primary and through the secondary range. The section also had its own advisory panel, mainly consisting of teachers whose role was presumably to advise on the appropriateness and detail of the proposed materials. This twin system of a materials producing unit with its own advisory panel of teacher specialists was duplicated with regard to secondary French, Spanish, Russian, German and the testing materials.

As far as the tasks set out above were concerned, a relatively clear division of labour was possible and even advisable. The first three (the organisation of the schools, teacher training and, to a certain extent, dissemination) required the official status of the Ministry and its representatives. The other items were in the main capable of being tackled by the team set up by Nuffield.

Selection of schools

The first point to be considered was the selection of areas and accordingly the Ministry invited LEAs to propose pilot areas which would meet the following conditions:

1. a given group of primary schools should exclusively feed a restricted number of secondary schools;

2. each pilot area to have an annual age group of about 480 pupils;
3. the schools to provide a cross-section of national educational conditions;
4. local education authorities to be prepared to release teachers for training and themselves to promote internal training.

The response was enthusiastic. Of the 146 LEAs approached, 80 expressed interest and in the event thirteen pilot areas were set up, four in excess of the original number planned. The reasons for this initial extension were to involve the training colleges on a national scale and to cover all possible varieties of educational conditions. At this stage 125 primary schools and 6,000 children were involved.

At the same time authority was given for certain LEAs not included in the pilot scheme to select parallel areas which should be known as associate areas. The number of these was initially modest but when a Ministry-sponsored survey of existing Primary French in 1964 showed that some 2,500 schools were already teaching the subject anyway the number of associate areas was increased to 84 by the autumn of 1967. The associate areas were to be treated exactly like the pilot areas with two qualifications: they bought their own materials; and they would not be subject to the planned evaluation programme. Nevertheless, this meant that the original 6,000 strong age group would rise to 40,000 with a maximum requirement of 1,000 teachers, both figures to grow as more year groups became involved.

Teacher training

The second involvement on the Ministry side was in the training of teachers. The LEAs were asked to provide intensive part-time language courses. These varied in extent but some ran as high as 180 hours, comprising three two-hour sessions per week for 30 weeks. Many were sited in further education establishments and used such audio-visual courses as CREDIFs *Voix et Images* in conjunction with a language laboratory. Attendance at such courses was to be a necessary prelude to a range of secondment courses arranged by the Ministry. These were three in number: a three-month course in Besançon or Paris; a three-month course at an English centre, the main one being Holborn School of Languages; and a three-week course at Vichy.

The last two were to be linked and aimed at giving teachers who had done their secondment in England some taste of life abroad. The Paris course, too, which was an annual affair, was mainly aimed at secondary teachers who would eventually have to deal with the pilot scheme children. It must be noted here that all of these secondment courses were to be extremely successful. In particular, the Besançon course was to send its teachers back with a high degree of fluency and armed with a battery of French songs, games and readers all of which stood them in good stead later.

Before going on the courses the teachers were subjected to mainly oral tests, which aimed at establishing their acuteness of hearing and sound discrimination. All expenses were met and there was little financial burden on the teachers involved, although it is true to say that some LEAs were more generous than others. Difficulties were of course occasioned in the schools themselves since temporary teachers had to be taken on to cover classes and heads were not always ready to cause such upsets to help train teachers who would probably leave them within a year or so. In the long run secondments paid lavish dividends in the case of the mature teacher who was settled in the school, though such teachers were given the opportunity all too rarely. On return from these secondment courses, whose aims were frankly linguistic, the teachers initially also had to attend seminars run by HMIs where the main emphasis was on teaching techniques. It was hoped that at the local level LEAs would do the same kind of thing. To summarise: by means of a closely knit phased programme of training the Ministry, with the support of the local education authorities aimed at building up a competent force of French teachers in the pilot areas. In doing this, and in the way in which they did it, they were saying quite clearly that French teaching was a specialism and that primary French teaching was a specialism within a specialism.

Production of materials

Meanwhile, the Nuffield team was faced with the daunting task of writing and producing a new four-year French course which would cover three years of the primary course and the first year of secondary. They were working very much against the clock, since the team was not in a position to start until the autumn of 1963, and the first materials would have to be tested prior to their introduction into the pilot schools before September 1964. The question must be asked: why was it necessary to produce materials at all since well established courses covering the same age range already existed? There were, for example, the highly successful *Bon Voyage* by Mary Glasgow and CREDIF's impeccable *Bonjour Line*. Indeed, in the initial stages of the project these courses were used both in the pilot areas and in the associate areas.

There was, of course, a question of practicality, for it would have been foolhardy to rely on private publishing firms to maintain a reasonable supply of software which would meet the extraordinary demands about to materialise. Secondly, there was perhaps a feeling, as expressed somewhat guardedly by Spicer in his report to the 1966 Hamburg Conference, that present methods (and one understands by that also materials) were not in keeping with what he felt to be the new approach to language teaching, namely that language comes first and then the formalities of the grammatical rules. It was with this in mind that very early on, together with CREDIF, Nuffield commissioned a Child Language Survey which was to delineate children's actual interests and their style of speech (see Stern 1969 chapter 14, and Nuffield Foreign Language Teaching Materials 1967). The usefulness of this research is exemplified by one of its findings: that 34 centres of interest can be detected in this age group, a most valuable piece of informaton for the writer of a language course. On the linguistic side CREDIF dealt with the French, and Nuffield with the English child's mode of expression. Here, a great deal of useful information emerged in the matter of semantics but when it came to syntax the waters became too deep and the relevance not all that clear.

Although it was a mammoth task, little requires to be said here about the actual production of materials. In general the procedure that was followed was to devise draft materials, to test them out in schools, to redraft them and eventually to have them published by independent publishing organisations. Each set of draft materials usually contained a report form calling for comment and suggestions. In the case of, for example, Stage 1 of the materials which were called *En Avant* the first draft went into 50 schools in January 1964, before the actual project was started. The second draft went into the pilot schools in September 1964 and a third draft went into the associate areas the following year. This particular section was to have a strange history since, although the published version appeared on the market in 1966, almost ten years later a final and very different 'revised Stage 1' was published. The reason was that the final stages of what was to be an eight-stage course were proving to have a whip-lash effect on the earlier stages and even now at the date of writing the publishers are meditating a further compression of the first three stages for the same reason.

Briefly, the Nuffield team had the commitment to produce a four year (four stage) course. This they had done by September 1967. The nomenclature they used was Stages 1A, 1B, 2, 3, 4A and 4B under the general title *En Avant*. At this point the Nuffield commitment was terminated, but the newly formed Schools Council decided to finance the production of another three years teaching materials. This side of the project was ultimately to cost them £892,000. These were to be in two flights – one for the more able pupils and known as *Avant Garde*, while the other, entitled *Dans le Vent*, was designed for potential CSE candidates. When it came, however, to the question of final publication, it was decided to revert to a common core to be known as *A Votre Avis* with ancillary material which could be adjusted to the ability of the pupils.

The involvement of E. J. Arnold as publisher is an interesting one. According to the Nuffield Foundation there was no question of a public tender. Talks were held with various publishers and Arnold was selected as being most capable of doing what was asked. Royalties were retained by the Foundation and the Foundation paid the publication costs and allocated a certain percentage of the profits to the publishers.

It would take more space than we have available to give a fair estimate of the originality of the contribution to language teaching made by the Nuffield/Schools Council materials. They do, however, have the following characteristics:

1. There is a constant stress on the audio-visual element of language teaching, that is to say everything is amply illustrated both by picture and

by film strip, and taped material is always present. They do not, however, constitute an audio-visual course in the sense that every phrase is ineluctably and unambiguously depicted by a picture as was the case with TAVOR. Basically we are always dealing with an illustrated text. The difference is fine, but crucial to the teacher.

2. Conceived as they were for the non-specialist teacher, there is a constant emphasis on teacher direction. In the first three stages such instructions are built in to the course book; thereafter with each stage there is a separate teacher's handbook. Nevertheless, in the later stages there are interesting possibilities for individual work.

3. Throughout there is a conscious effort to deal with the centres of interest of the pupils which is a factor of their age and the stage of the course. This is sometimes at the expense of adjustment of the language to the pupil's existing knowledge thereof. The message often becomes the medium.

4. Greater stress is laid on aural and textual comprehension than on the accuracy and grammatical knowledge required for productive skills. The latter are certainly not neglected but tend to be relegated to the later part of the course.

5. The final stages seem to generate a multiplicity of ancillary material, e.g. integrated readers, situational conversation books and an excellent series of DIY grammar books amusingly contrived to promote individual study of this area.

6. There were also occasional publications of a general nature covering such topics as songs, games and group work with mixed ability classes.

There is little doubt that these materials were monumental and complete. They have always aroused great enthusiasm, particularly among experienced secondary-school language teachers. It is, however, fairly clear that the initial deferment of reading and writing skills and, in the same area, the refusal to insist on even a simplistic acquisition of grammatical knowledge seems to promote confusion and frustration.

Dissemination

Once the scheme was under way, there were two major tasks, namely dissemination and evaluation. The first of these was a joint undertaking of Nuffield and the Ministry.

Both took their job most seriously: there was the periodic publication of a news-sheet, *The Micklegate News* (Micklegate House being the location of the team in York); national free-access courses were organised at the nearby York University, where news was given of developments, chiefly on the examination front; and members of the team gave willingly of their time for lectures in various parts of the country. This contribution was solid and good, in particular in the way in which language experts from all over the country had the frequent chance of meeting each other with consequent attendant benefits.

The Ministry, chiefly through its Inspectorate, undertook a series of national conferences. The first one, held in February 1965 at Harrogate, had as its theme the preparation of in-service courses in teaching methods within the pilot areas. There was a kind of 'crest of the wave' feeling about most contributions, a feeling that this was the way to do things and that what had gone before had been deficient in many ways. Consequential upon this was a failure to invite any contribution which could have been made by the secondary teachers. Their greater involvement could have been crucial but, as it was, primary French was to become a preserve of primary teachers, HMIs and local advisers. It is true that the second conference, held this time at Torquay, was called 'The Implications for the Secondary Schools', but here again the main trend of contributions was to justify the project by pointing out the rather mediocre performance of language teaching and indeed the declining popularity of language compared with other subjects. This was accompanied by a panegyric of what was happening at primary level. Miss N. R. Mulcahy, HMI, for example, said boldly and unequivocally 'the primary schools are succeeding' to which she added emphatically: 'The vast majority of the children love learning French ... their enjoyment is manifest.' (Schools Council 1966, 33–37.) The conference then asked the secondary teachers what they proposed doing when these eleven-year-old linguists arrived on their doorstep. With the questions couched in such a way the answers were perforce somewhat fanciful. Some felt that course work would have to be abandoned and that an amalgam of readers and high level conversation work would take its place. Others felt that at secondary level French would become a tool language thereby expanding the number of information resources available in, say, history or geography. In retrospect the conference was something of a fairy story, completely failing to foresee the traumatic situation which would emerge at transfer to secondary level when pupils who had been excellently taught were side by side with those who had not and, worse still, when a goodly percentage of children were already disillusioned with French at the age of eleven.

Evaluation

Evaluation of national projects had been urged at the 1962 Hamburg Conference and was duly requested by the Consultative Committee in early 1964. The National Foundation for Educational Research was commissioned to carry it out. There were four areas of investigation:

1. the effect of the introduction of French on the level of general achievement;
2. the assessment of the level of achievement in French with special reference to the low ability child;
3. the influence of additional factors on the learning of French;
4. organisational problems in the learning of French.

These were remoulded during the first months of the investigation into five specific questions:

1. Do other aspects of primary education suffer because of the introduction of French?
2. Are there levels of ability below which French should not be taught?
3. Is there any substantial gain in mastery achieved through learning from the age of eight?
4. What methods, attitudes and incentives are most effective in promoting the learning of French?
5. What organisational and teaching problems are posed by the introduction of the subject at primary level?

The investigation was limited to the pupils of 121 primary schools from the thirteen pilot areas and these fed into a largish number of secondary schools (60–80) where the investigation continued. Three year-streams of pupils were concerned. These were the First Cohort (aged 8+ by September 1964 with wider age range in small rural schools); the Second Cohort (aged 8+ by September 1965); and the Third Cohort (aged 8+ September 1968).

In all about 17,000 pupils were involved (5,700, 5,500 and 6,000). Basically the First and Third Cohorts became a kind of control group, the first in particular being used for a certain amount of pre-testing. Only the Second Cohort was subjected to the full enquiry. In this sense one of the limiting factors of the evaluation was the fact that in the final secondary year this vital Second Cohort had dwindled from its orginal number of 5,500 to 1,300 of whom 600 were at grammar school, 360 at comprehensive and the rest at secondary modern schools.

As this was the first known enquiry of its kind, all instruments for evaluation had to be devised and pre-tested. There is an excellent account of these in the final National Foundation for Educational Research Report, *Primary French in the Balance* (Burstall 1974). They were concerned with three aspects: pupils' attitudes to learning; primary teachers' attitudes and pupils' achievements. The actual instruments used in each area were:

1. *Pupils' attitudes.* Three versions to be administered at the end of the second, fifth and eighth year of learning French. These contained questions in English requiring a YES/NO answer and a few open ended ones. Example of the former: 'I'm afraid to speak French in class'; of the latter: 'What do you like most about learning French?' Very rigorous steps were taken to ensure that the questions were right, complementary and suitably couched.

2. *Teachers' attitudes.* One version applied once only after five years of the project, having the same format as that above except that the answers were on a five-point scale: strongly agree/agree/no opinion/disagree/strongly disagree in response to such statements as: 'Teaching French to less able children is a criminal waste of time'.

3. *Pupils' achievement*. Four versions for the end of the first, second, fifth and eighth year of learning French.

    (a) LCA listening comprehension after one year;
    (b) Battery 1 to test speaking, listening and writing after two years;
    (c) Battery 2 as above, plus reading, after five years;
    (d) Battery 3 as above after eight years.

The instruments here devised are something of a milestone in language testing since they aimed at isolating the various skills. Their main features were the use of taped material, visuals and objective testing. They led the way to the style of examining which characterised the so-called 'Nuffield O-level French' first set in 1972 and administered by the Oxford Local Examinations Board; though the Joint Matriculation Board had used some similar methods since 1967. The tests (and attitudes soundings) were also administered at appropriate times to five Control Groups (CG 1–5). For example, the Second Cohort, when it reached the second year of secondary school, was compared with CG1 and CG2 who were both in the same year but had done at least two years less French. There was a further comparison with CG3, who were fourth year grammar school pupils who had done an equivalent amount of French to the pupils in the Second Cohort. The results were not encouraging: for example, CG2 could read and write better and, although in listening and speaking Cohort number 2 by and large always had the edge, yet CG3 pupils were better all round than the grammar school pupils of the Second Cohort. When it came to analysing the results of Battery 3 tests given to the Second Cohort, CG4 and CG5, all of whom were fifth year secondary pupils, there was still no cause for rejoicing.

Table 5.1 compares the average achievement of Cohort 2 with Control Groups 4 and 5, indicating against each skill which group performed better on the Battery 3 test.

Table 5.1 Table of superiority.

	Cohort 2 compared control group 4	*Cohort 2 compared with group 5*
Listening comprehension	Cohort 2 performed better	Cohort 2 performed better
Reading comprehension	Control group 4 performed better	Cohort 2 performed better
Speaking	Both groups equal	Both groups equal
Writing	Control group 4 performed better	Both groups equal

On the basis of this kind of evidence the NFER answered its original five questions somewhat negatively. As far as the rest of the curriculum was concerned, French had caused no harm but neither had it helped. Indeed, at secondary level it had failed to foster interest in the minority languages and this could be construed as a harmful result. The very style of teaching, where the medium is the message, meant that the disadvantaged became even more so. For many children French was a profitless experience. The answer to the question as to whether the project meant an ultimate gain in mastery was 'unequivocally in the negative'. On the questions of method, attitude and incentive there was a feeling that these three were linked, that different levels of ability needed different approaches and that in the final analysis nothing succeeded like success. On the organisational side, the report emphasised the difficulties at primary level which were caused by specialist time-tabling, and at secondary level the impossibility of coping in the same class with pupils of differing ability and varying French experience. The report concluded that a further extension of primary French was not advisable.

The report was a nationwide bombshell. Newspaper headlines made full use of the phrase 'profitless experience'. HMIs were strangely quiet, LEA. language advisers not so. Heads reacted according to the extent to which their own experience tied in with the report's findings. The main vocal opposition came indeed from the advisers, or from certain advisers who pointed out that there was still great enthusiasm for French in many of their primary schools and that, where effective secondary liaison existed, beneficial results were continued to that level. By implication they were arguing that ideal conditions had not existed at that level in the pilot areas. It was pointed out that the 123 primary schools fed into some 60 secondary schools and this gave little prospect of correlation. They refused to accept the idea that five years of French is as good as eight years and, given good teaching and good conditions right along the line, the system must work. To put it bluntly, there was a fairly general refusal to accept the NFER verdict.

Another factor has changed the original picture. This was school re-organisation. Consequent upon the Plowden Report many LEAs had decided to restructure their primary education either on an 8–12 or a 9–13 age basis. The implications for a secondary language department became serious. A three and a half year course from scratch to O-level is unthinkable and very soon this fact alone has led to an intensification of the demand for the new middle schools (ex-primaries) to 'do' French, and ironically enough the demand is in many cases being made from the secondary schools. An example of this process is East Sussex where in 1975 93 per cent of the primary schools had French and where quite recently the education committee passed a resolution in which they said they would like as many primary schools as possible to include it on the timetable. Authorities which have never taken an effective part in the scheme are moving in certain areas on the same lines, and Surrey has similar figures to those of East Sussex. These departures and trends are being currently investigated by a committee under the leadership of P. H. Hoy, a former HMI, together with certain language advisers (Hoy 1977).

In 1973 the Schools Council made a grant of a further £21,500 to finance a two year dissemination project. It was undertaken by the Language Materials Development Unit at York University. The principal area of activity was to disseminate information on the materials and to publicise existing expertise in the handling of them. Courses and conferences were organised, mainly at York, though the team placed themselves at the disposal of LEAs for their own conferences. Lists of teachers with expertise were also drawn up with the help of participating LEAs but in the event they were not widely used. Additionally the team continued work with the publishers in the adaptation of the materials for overseas use and most valuably maintained liaison with the Examining Boards in the matter of constructing alternative O-level syllabuses.

Conclusions

To summarise adequately ten years of such nationwide linguistic effort would call for a volume rather than a paragraph. No one can dispute that because of poor conditions and/or inferior teaching no benefit accrued to a fair number of pupils, but on the other hand there have been many, many instances of continuous and brilliant teaching which proved the job could be done effectively. That this was so had never seriously been in doubt. The issue was rather what would be the effects in the final stages of secondary education, and it was here that some of the major consequences of the pilot scheme are to be found. Some of these may be summarised as follows:

1. Pupils arrived from the primary stage with attitudes to French and France already formed. The better ones had very high expectations precisely because they had been well taught. They constituted a challenge which was not always met.
2. Despite certain deficiencies in primary French outside the pilot scheme most secondary schools extended the study of the language to all abilities.
3. There was increased staff commitment because of this, which in turn made the early introduction of the minority languages difficult.
4. Although O-level figures were to stay constant and A-level figures were to fall, there was massive increase in CSE entries by 1975.
5. A fair degree of co-operation was made necessary between primary and secondary schools.
6. Most importantly, the years 1968–72 saw a great deal of educational ferment in the language departments of secondary schools as they looked at the new approaches and tried to find answers to the problems which had been evoked.

6   Nuffield Secondary Science[1]

Basic information

Sponsor   Nuffield Foundation.

Grant   £164,000.

Location   Mary Ward House (London); from 1968 at the Centre for Science Education, Chelesa College of Science and Technology.

Period of development   1965 to 1970.

Designated pupils   Originally '13–16 average and below average ability', but before the project began this was expanded to '13–16 boys and girls unlikely to take O-level science'. (In effect 70 per cent of the age group).

Organiser   Mrs. Hilda Misselbrook, previously head of science and deputy head of Mayfield School in London.

Project team   Sixteen people, most of them working part-time for the project while continuing their normal work as LEA advisers or college of education lecturers.

Trials   1966 January–March. Feasibility trial of two short sections of material in 16 schools.
1967–68 Development trials in 53 schools.
1968–69 Large scale trials in 212 schools.
1969–70 Large scale trials in 258 schools.
(Fresh texts were prepared for each trial).
By the end of the trial period the project has been tried in virtually every (pre-Redcliffe – Maud) local authority in England and Wales, as well as in N. Ireland and in service schools in Germany. In 1971 Longmans, the publishers, claimed that the project 'had been successfully tried with 10,000 pupils in over 250 schools.'

Materials   In May 1971 Longmans/Penguin published eleven Handbooks for teachers on the basis of the trial material. These are listed in the bibliography.
In addition the project published 34 film loops, 8 film strips/slides and two boxes of illustrations. There are no course books for pupils, but a number of background booklets on particular topics have been published.

The nature of the materials   The materials consist of a wide range of resources through which the project provides a number of alternative routes. In a pre-

publication leaflet the organiser summed up the nature of the materials from the project's point of view. 'The content of the project is based on eight themes. The pupils study material from each one, but flexibility is achieved by the differences in emphasis and depth which teachers give to the themes according to their pupils' needs and interests.
' 'To aid selection, each theme is divided into fields of study and the weightings given to these fields determine whether the theme as a whole is treated as a major or a minor one. Some fields of study might be omitted, thus the material is in no sense a course or a syllabus but rather a quarry from which teachers can select and construct their own coherent schemes.'

Cost　The full set of Teachers' Handbooks currently costs £20.05, but most of the cost of implementation is absorbed by equipment and facilities. As a rough guide, trial schools found that they had to allocate £500 p.a. initially (1970 prices). This may be less if the school is already equipped for Nuffield Combined Science (which is often used as a preliminary to Secondary Science). It may be more if the school is poorly equipped or has no technician.

Evaluation　In practice extensive formative evaluation was carried out by the project team and by HMIs who were observer members of the Consultative Committee. An independent evaluation was funded by the Schools Council in 1969 after considerable discussion. This evaluation was conducted by Miss Dorothy Alexander, Staff Inspector for Science in the IIEA with a grant of £9,000. The evaluation report was published by the Schools Council in 1975.

Origins and background to the project

BEFORE FUNDING

The history that lies behind the setting up of Nuffield Secondary Science is longer and more complex than the two page outline in the *Teachers' Guide* would have us believe. The project itself clearly learnt some lessons from its past, for example 'general science'[2] and the Newsom Report are given only passing reference, yet were significant in creating the context within which the project operated. The project's down-to-earth, non-scholarly style which has been an important ingredient in its success in schools makes it difficult to document influences in detail. What follows is necessarily a cursory outline.

The first point that should be made is that Secondary Science was not simply an afterthought following the success of the Nuffield O-level projects. Through the 1950s the Association for Science Education (as it now is), while campaigning for the setting up of what were to become the Nuffield O-level projects, also took a consistent interest in secondary modern school science. Surveys were made of laboratory provision in modern schools and attempts were made to organise appropriate science curricula.

As Tony Becher later described the situation in early sixties in an interview:

The notion certainly was that maybe after these things [the O-level projects] started, the programme might spread upwards to A-level, downwards to the primary school and sideways towards secondary science. But at that stage it was only an idea that was loosely around. There was no official sanction from the Nuffield Trustees, or from any of the people who were whatever the Schools Council then was.

(SAFARI interview 1973)[3]

The motive was not just for expansion of curriculum reform. 'There was a feeling of the need to try and extend the kind of science teaching developed by Nuffield to the young school leaver. This was felt particularly strongly at the Schools Council and by no-one more than Derek Morell' (Becher, SAFARI interview 1973). The problem was not simply to convince the trustees but: 'to identify the teachers with experience of teaching non O-level kids, who were also going to be articulate enough and knowledgeable enough to work on a project. Inevitably the situation tended to be one where the 'best teachers' were sucked up into the sixth form and GCE grammar school streams' (Becher, SAFARI interview 1973).

The publication of the Newsom Report crystallised the case for setting up a one-year feasibility study. The Nuffield Foundation appointed a retiring HMI, L. G. Smith, and asked him to establish the case for a project and to identify some of the people who might form the nucleus of a project team. The feasibility study, later published as Schools Council Working Paper 1, (1965a) *Science for the Young School Leaver*, was a document with more than one agenda.

> It was certainly intended to be a tactical move in the sense of establishing Secondary Science, and also tactical in the political sense of trying to get increasing commitment from the Schools Council. Strategically, this seemed a difficult area to plunge into, and the notion of getting a feasibility study done seemed an attractive one.
>
> (Becher, SAFARI interview 1973)

The formal story was given in the Nuffield Foundation's 19th *Annual Report* (1963–64):

> Secondary Modern Science Project
> Even more than the A-level projects, this is a field in which there is little background work on which a new curriculum development programme may be based. The science taught in secondary modern schools has often hitherto been a diluted form of grammar school work, and has tended to take little account of the pupils' special needs and interests. Aims, content, and methods of teaching all need re-examination.
> For this research an exploratory period appears to be advisable, before the project proper begins. The Trustees have therefore appointed Mr. L. G. Smith, until recently a member of HM Inspectorate, for a period of nine months, from April to December 1964, to carry out a preliminary investigation to try to establish the general principles and lines of development for the project, and to find experienced practising teachers who might later serve as the main participants in the work.
>
> (73–74)

WORKING PAPER 1: SCIENCE FOR THE YOUNG SCHOOL LEAVER

The working paper is a short document arguing the case for Secondary Science and outlining a structure for the curriculum. It draws heavily on the Newsom Report:

The pupils with whom this paper is concerned are those of average and below average ability between the ages of 13 and 16, i.e. the Newsom pupils. They comprise a broad band of the total spectrum of intelligence within their age groups extending from those at one extreme for whom the simple mechanics of reading and writing present major difficulty to those at the other whose abilities could well lead to success at CSE level. It is sometimes useful to think of the 'average' of this group as a boy or girl who is about a third of the way up the full intelligence range, a pupil whose abilities are often underrated, but one who nevertheless has definite intellectual limitations. The purpose of this paper is to offer a basis for discussion by considering the present teaching of science to many pupils in this range, the aims which it might have and the possible lines along which a Nuffield project might help to achieve them.

Since relatively few Newsom pupils, and especially those of lower ability, have hitherto remained at school after the present statutory age limit, the available experience of teaching them science beyond the age of 15, or of developing courses with this end in view, is meagre, and there is some uncertainty about what might be achieved with them at this stage given good teaching with good equipment under good conditions. There is evidence, however, to encourage the belief that a Nuffield Science project designed specifically to meet the needs of these pupils between the ages of 13 and 16 could not only have valuable and far-reaching effects, but would also be warmly welcomed in many schools. If it is to be broadly applicable, the project would need to take some account of the widely different school situations in which these pupils are taught, and if it is to be widely acceptable it must seek to offer help in such a way that there is ample scope for individuality or initiative in using it. The aim, therefore is not to prescribe a definite course of study but to try to develop a fairly flexible project so that, without losing its essential qualities, it can be adapted within certain limits to meet particular needs.

(Schools Council 1965a)

The paper goes on to quote the Newsom Report generously, using the word Newsom more than twenty-five times in its first twenty paragraphs, either quoting sections of the report directly or using terms like 'Newsom pupils' or 'boys and girls in the Newsom range'. (In contrast the *Teachers' Guide* to Secondary Science makes only one reference to the Newsom Report – in the Introduction – and *never* uses the term 'Newsom child'.)

Working Paper 1 went on to consider the problem of balancing a science curriculum between 'an immediate, intrinsic interest in the work at hand, and the broader interest of relevance to the modern scene so that it is apparent to the pupils that the knowledge which they are gaining has a real and current value to them.' The concept of 'significance', later to be developed in the work of the project was given some prominence.

The strong emphasis L. G. Smith had laid on the Newsom Report was reflected in the Nuffield Foundation *Annual Report* for the following year (1964–65), where the project title was changed from 'Secondary Modern Science Project' to 'Newsom Science Project.'

Newsom Science Project

The needs of non-O-level pupils in secondary schools have recently been singled out for attention in a number of ways, and particularly by the Newsom Report, published in August 1963. Mr. L. G. Smith, a recently retired member of HM Inspectorate, completed his report for the Foundation on the particular problems of teaching science to Newsom children in December 1964, and this has since been published by the Schools Council as *Science for the Young School Leaver*. This paper is also to be taken as a starting point for the work of the Newsom science programme under Mrs. H. Misselbrook, deputy headmistress of the Mayfield Comprehensive School, Putney.

The plan is that a period of up to two years shall be spent on a careful investigation of the problems arising from the great diversity of intellectual ability and interest among the pupils concerned. During this period preliminary materials will also be prepared by a process involving the participation of teachers in British schools. The course materials will be tried out systematically, beginning in September 1967, and it is hoped that the programme will lead to a final and full publication in 1969 or 1970.

The work of the Newsom programme is being guided by a consultative committee whose chairman in Dr. John Topping, Vice-Chancellor designate of Brunel University. Mr. L. G. Smith, formerly one of HM Inspectors, is a consultant to the project. The Department of Education and Science has agreed that HMIs Dr. J. K. Brearley and Mr. T. R. Jenkin should be observers at this committee.

(Nuffield Foundation 1965)

APPOINTING THE ORGANISER

It had been part of L. G. Smith's brief, while writing *Working Paper 1*, to identify people who might later be appointed members of the project team. Hilda Misselbrook was a member of a Schools Council Committee concerned with CSE examining (later published as *Examinations Bulletin 8*), which L. G. Smith chaired, and of which HMIs Brearley and Jenkins were also members.

While at Mayfield school Mrs. Misselbrook had been involved in the transition from a girls' grammar school to one of London's first and largest comprehensive schools. As head of science, and later as deputy head she had naturally been concerned to develop an appropriate science curriculum in an area where there was little in the way of an established tradition. L. G. Smith was clearly impressed by her contributions to the Committee, and she was later asked if she would attend a conference where *Working Paper 1* was discussed. The week following the conference she was surprised to receive a phone call from Mary Ward House. A secretary asked if Mrs. Misselbrook would call in and see John Maddox (then organiser of the Nuffield Science Teaching Project). She imagined the reason for the meeting was that Nuffield were hoping to use Mayfield as a trial school. 'It came absolutely out-of-the-blue when he said, "Would you be interested in organising the project?"'

The 'disguised interview' as a means of selecting project directors was characteristic of curriculum development in the 1960s (see, for example, MacDonald and Walker 1976, 107). As a technique it is open to charges of unfairness, and even of élitism, but it was a method of selection which created minimum disturbance within some of the professional circles where the future project would have to operate. Given the circumstances, we can guess that Mrs. Misselbrook came to the job with expectations rather different to those she might have had if the post had been publicly advertised, and the appointment made after a competitive interview. Curriculum projects necessarily exist in delicate professional, social and even political tissue within which trust, persuasion and personal influence play a highly significant part. The projects exist in situations where consensus is delicately balanced and often needs to be tactfully sustained. The 'disguised interview', at least in the early days of organised curriculum development seems to have provided an appropriate means of selecting and appointing organisers and directors.

Characteristics of the project

CENTRAL ASPIRATIONS

1. Following L. G. Smith's recommendation the project saw itself producing 'a source, not a course'.

> Secondary science does not constitute a course as it stands ... the aim ... has been to produce material which is flexible and capable of adaptation so that teachers can select appropriately and construct courses suitable for their own pupils. Secondary Science might be regarded as quarry from which teachers select suitable material to build coherent courses.
>
> (*Teachers' Guide*, ix)

2. Although the project intended that teachers should construct their own courses, they were also anxious to preserve structure.

> The temptation to use 'good ideas' in isolation should be resisted. Although meant to be used flexibly, the material has been designed to ensure that as far as possible certain major scientific principles are established within a body of fundamental knowledge which has a meaningful pattern. Random selection of 'interesting' material will not achieve this.
>
> (*Teachers' Guide*, 3)

3. Following the *Working Paper*, the project stressed the theme of 'significance'. As used by the project, significance means 'having intrinsic interest' (3) and 'relating what is happening in the laboratory to the real life situation'. (*Teachers' Guide*, 17). 'Any material that failed this test in trials was deleted.' (*Teachers' Guide*, 3). In other words it is the teacher's responsibility to demonstrate significance; it is not necessarily assumed to emerge from anything the pupils seem to enjoy doing. It stems from pupils' needs, as well as from their interests (*Teachers' Guide*, 4).

HOW DID THE PROJECT VIEW THE TEACHERS?

The project argued that science was essentially unified and that science teachers at this level should teach across the full range of science subjects, not confine themselves to specialisms. 'In Secondary Science ... we are concerned with an integrated approach to science ... it is essential for a class to be taught by one teacher.' (*Teachers' Guide*, 80–81). The project saw itself supporting those science teachers who lacked extensive scientific training, who were narrowly specialised, or who lacked experience of non-O-level teaching. In this sense it attempted to make a major contribution towards the development of a science curriculum for the comprehensive school.

HOW DID THE PROJECT VIEW THE PUPILS?

Secondary Science adopted a view of the pupils quite different from the O-level projects, and arguably much closer to the view held by their teachers:

> The pupils with whom we are concerned are not going to be scientists, but they will become the greater part of the adult population.
>
> (*Teachers' Guide*, 15)

> In some cases it may be difficult to get a verbal expression of a generalisation, but if the basic experience is there, it may well be applied in a practical situation later on.
>
> (*Teachers' Guide*, 16)

> Since we are largely concerned with pupils for whom abstract thought is difficult we must not expect them always to be able to suggest hypotheses in the sense of verbal abstractions. They should, however, be able to grasp simple problems, and to devise ways of solving them and of testing their suggestions.
>
> (*Teachers' Guide*, 17)

> Qualities of imagination may not be immediately obvious in our pupils since they may demand abstract thought and an ability to express ideas.
>
> (*Teachers' Guide*, 61)

This kind of view of the pupil has important consequences for specifying teaching methods.

> Pupils who have been used to authoritarian methods of teaching are liable to react rather violently if the change to individual and group work is made too suddenly.
>
> (*Teachers' Guide*, 52)

> These boys and girls are unlikely to look very far ahead in their personal lives, whether at the level of the future job or the long-term consequence of irresponsible conduct. The future is in their opinion a matter of chance or 'fate'. They are not concerned with the results of their own behaviour though usually aware of its immediate consequences.
>
> (*Teachers' Guide*, 50)

> Most adolescents will respond well to a situation in which demands are made on them as sensible and reliable people.
>
> (*Teachers' Guide*, 17)

> Teachers will know that to develop a useful discussion with our pupils can be very difficult.
>
> (*Teachers' Guide*, 17)

THE PROJECT TEAM

Most of the sixteen project team members were part-time and continued in their jobs as college of education lecturers or LEA advisers throughout the project. Mrs. Misselbrook outlined their tasks as follows:

1. Developing a specific part of the trial material. This involved pre-testing experiments, designing prototype equipment, suggesting appropriate visual aids and preparing a text on the pattern agreed by the team as a whole.
2. Visiting trial schools in their own area to discuss the work and advise on problems.
3. Reporting to the organiser on the general and specific difficulties encountered in the schools and the success and failure of each part of the work.
4. Revising trial scripts for which they were responsible in the light of written feedback from the schools and comments from the rest of the team.
5. Working with trials teachers at the briefing conferences and workshops.

(Mrs. Misselbrook, personal communication 1976)

An interesting point to note about the tasks is that visits and observations (under 2 above) related to the project as a whole and not necessarily to the material that the particular team member had contributed.

LOCAL GROUPS

Early in the project two meetings were arranged for all those who had expressed some interest in it. They were held in December 1965 and January 1966. One outcome of these meetings was the establishment of 'study groups'.

The original idea of study groups had come out of a conversation between Mrs. Misselbrook and an HMI. The organiser wanted to extend the team, both in order to get a wide range of content areas included in the project, and to bring in the experience of as many practising teachers as possible. However, at that time there were few practising teachers available who were able to combine the necessary subject expertise and the skills required to write course materials. The idea emerged of establishing local curriculum groups of teachers 'just to see what they could do'.

In the event there was a range of interpretations of the study group idea, from '80 people in a lecture theatre' to smaller working groups. Most were led by college lecturers, and although few did any writing of material, they provided about half the membership of the trial schools, and some remained together throughout the trials period and were still producing worksheets and developing common core CSE Mode 3 exams after the project had ended. In one city the study group notion was taken up by a group already established in response to the Nuffield O-level Biology Project. The group still functions, though now as a biology teachers' centre under the aegis of the Institute of Biology.

Mrs. Misselbrook's original intention of devolving responsibility for developing the content was not fully met, but the study groups became an important feature of Secondary Science, not least because they provided a network for extending the dissemination of discussions about *Working Paper 1*, and for establishing Secondary Science amongst a group of teachers who generally lacked occasions for professional meetings which focussed on the kinds of problems addressed by the project.

TRIALS

In the main trials a large number of schools were needed because the team wanted to test the materials as a whole, and not simply piece by piece. In order to cover each subject area over 200 schools had to be involved. The Schools Council (who circulated the LEAs) also pressed for extensive trials (and in fact suggested 100 schools in the development phase, which the project felt would stretch their contact with the team). The argument they advanced, however, was in terms of future dissemination rather than adequate field testing.

The fact remains that Secondary Science had one of the most extensive field trials on record amongst Nuffield and Schools Council projects, and this was undoubtedly a key factor in its dissemination. It was virtually 'disseminated as it was developed'.

Feedback on the materials from trial schools had previously been a rather hit and miss affair. Secondary Science considered taking a lead from Nuffield Physics and sending schools two copies of each set of materials so that they could return one with comments pencilled in. On the advice of L. G. Smith they decided instead to send out questionnaires which asked more specifically about problems encountered with each bit of the materials. The bulging filing cabinets that remain attest to the success of this method; not only did teachers complete the questionnaires, they often went on to add detailed comments and accounts; a flow of information that appears to have increased year by year.

Materials writers took this feedback into account when rewriting each section. They also had reports from their fellow team members, and sometimes from the HMIs who were observer members of the Consultative Committee. In addition each theme was given a group appraisal (during 1968–69) by members of the team plus one outside consultant who had detailed knowledge of the fields of study involved.

EQUIPMENT AND MATERIALS

For those unfamiliar with science it is important to emphasise the enormous amount of work that went into selecting, designing and testing equipment and trying out experiments.

In retrospect it is amazing that the project succeeded in meeting its deadlines in getting materials out to schools, though it has to be admitted that errors did creep in. One of the early trial school teachers recalls:

> The apparatus list included 200 grams of ferro cube, which no-one had heard of. We ordered 100 volumetric flasks to be told it was a 'bit of a mistake' which meant I had to 'phone the suppliers and say 'could you take them back, Nuffield have made a bit of a mess . . . ' One school bought a 'fridge and then found all they really needed was ice, which they could get from the kitchens . . .
>
> (SAFARI interview 1973)

ORGANISATIONAL STYLE OF THE PROJECT

As we have seen, the project covered a wide range of subject areas, involved a large number of teachers and schools in the trial of materials, and had to co-ordinate the work of a large, geographically scattered team. As a result the organisational style that emerged was distinctive and perhaps less like that of the O-level projects than is often realised. Secondary Science was one of the first British curriculum projects to move away from what is conventionally called a 'centre-periphery' design towards an organisational style with 'multiple dispersed centres'.

Mrs. Misselbrook was a key figure in setting the style and tone of the project. A tireless worker and traveller, she expected all who worked with her to be as committed as she was. It is interesting to note that it took someone with a strong leadership *style* to attempt to disassemble the notion of a strong central team, for Mrs. Misselbrook tried at all points to increase teacher participation in the development of materials and to localise the process of curriculum reform. At meetings she almost always identified herself as a teacher and succeeded in making the project seem like a project by teachers for teachers. There can have been few other curriculum projects that have involved so many practitioners in the development phase; a sign perhaps that its views of the curriculum, the schools and the pupils were realistic rather than idealistic.

THE CONSULTATIVE COMMITTEE

The Consultative Committee met under the chairmanship of Dr. J. Topping, then Vice-Chancellor of Brunel University (who incidentally chaired Project Technology's Consultative Committee for much of the same time). It consisted of L. G. Smith (who had been the principal author of *Working Paper 1*, and who took an active part in the project attending all team meetings in the first two years, and commenting on each draft of the materials), representatives of colleges and university departments of education, and LEAs, science advisers, with HMIs Brearley and Jenkins attending as observers. The Committee met regularly, usually twice a year and was broadly supportive of the organiser. In some cases members of the Committee worked to secure help outside the regular meetings. For example, one recurrent problem was that non-specialised science courses were often not considered adequate qualification for entry to ONC courses. This was an issue taken up by several committee members.

EVALUATION

The Schools Council funded its evaluation of Secondary Science at a time when there was a general interest in building evaluation into projects. It took considerable discussion to match the Council's desires with the project's intentions, and by that time it was really too late to conduct an evaluation that would be truly 'formative'. But as we have already indicated the project was organised in a way that incorporated a considerable amount of evaluation by the teachers. team members and by HMI.

The problem faced by the official evaluator was clearly a demanding one, for working part-time and beginning late in the project it was clear that she had to respond to the situation that existed. As she later wrote in a Schools Council report:

> The situation was somewhat daunting in February 1969, when the evaluator was faced with:
>
> 1. What could easily be a useless exercise because of its timing.
> 2. A project which was producing a very large amount of material from which teachers could select, which meant that everybody was likely to be choosing something a little different.
> 3. A project which aimed at providing useful material for some 75 per cent of the pupil population aged 13–16.
>
> (Alexander 1973, 177–83)

But by the end of March Miss Alexander had decided on the direction the evaluation should take. In a report to the Schools Council she wrote:

> It would seem to me that the main points to concentrate on are: first, the question of significance, and secondly the aspect of activity and element of investigation in the pupils' work, coupled with repetition and variety for consolidation. These are the items which seem to be most frequently referred to, both in the written materials, in the Schools Council publication [*Working Paper 1*] and in the advice given by the team generally when discussing the project at their meetings and with the teachers.
>
> (Alexander. 1973, 179)

The concept of 'significance' proved 'difficult to pin down in any aspect which is capable of simple measurement'. It seemed to the evaluator to have both short-term and long-term connotations, and by concentrating on the latter, she was able to mobilise the idea of attempting to measure pupils' interest in science to obtain at least sidelong glance at the way the project team's intentions were being born out in practice.

Using an attitude measure previously developed by the NFER (*Pupil Opinion Poll: Science No. 104*) classes in fifty of the trial schools were sampled along with a control group of classes from paired schools. The test was administered in September 1969 when the experimental group first entered the trials, and again in June 1970. The results clearly had to be treated with caution since the experimental group entered the trials at a late stage (perhaps, though, making them more representative of post-development schools). The timing of the testing periods raise further questions (would pupils respond differently, in June and September whatever the course taken?). Perhaps most important, the test was not tailor-made and appears to have been standardised on a rather different group of children. Nevertheless, despite the many qualifications surrounding the interpretations that were made of the results, these did reveal that: 'Both control and trial schools showed a deterioration in attitude towards the social implications of science but the deterioration in the attitude of the trial schools was significantly greater than the change in attitude of the control schools' (Alexander 1974).

It is important to realise that this result does not necessarily imply failure on the part of the project. Any curriculum which effectively brings consideration of contemporary issues in science and technology into the classroom, may well result in disillusion amongst pupils. Better science teaching may not necessarily lead to greater optimism about the potential of modern science in relation to current social issues.

The second element of the evaluation consisted of an exploratory observational exercise carried out in ten schools. This was based on the assumption that the observers were people 'whose normal job included certain times when they went into the classes and observed them at work, but who were not necessarily trained for any sophisticated use of this kind of technique.' The schedule that was devised was made as simple as possible, though turned out to be difficult to standardise. The aim was to focus on one issue . . . to find out the quality of pupil participation'.

Overall, the evaluator summed up her conclusions as follows:

> The positive factors emerging from this investigation indicate that, after one year of use, the teachers' interest in the Secondary Science materials has been maintained; the pupils' attitudes towards their teachers has improved, and the teachers' style of teaching has been modified. However, teachers normally react more quickly to changes of content than they do to changes of approach and one year is probably too short a time in which to effect major changes in the attitudes of either pupils or teachers.
>
> (Alexander 1974, 37)

Legacies

The project has generally received widespread support from teachers and other concerned audiences. What kinds of points do its advocates emphasize, and what criticisms are made by adversaries? The dialogue that follows is fictitious, but the statements that are made are taken from interviews and conversations SAFARI has had with various people concerned in different ways with science teaching.

Adversary: From the start Secondary Science was a compromise. In accepting a view of the pupils that emphasised their lack of ability and intellect it merely reinforced what most teachers believed already and confirmed them in authoritarian methods.

Advocate: I don't believe the project 'accepted' this view of the pupil as unable in the way you suggest. I think they were astute enough to recognise that this was the view most teachers held and that unless they recognised it the project wasn't going to get very far. What the team did, I think, was to recognise the way most teachers felt and then proceed as far as they could in changing their views. After all the *Teachers' Guide* is full of suggestions about 'discussion', about getting the pupils to do experimental work themselves, about 'significance'. You can't fairly call it authoritarian.

Adversary: I accept that in the mid 1960s teachers may well have had these kinds of views but I think things have changed. Many teachers now look on Secondary Science with some embarassment because it takes a 'Newsom view' of the pupil. What the project should have done is to take the accepted view of the pupil, examine it closely and challenge it. This is what the Nuffield O-level projects did. They said, 'The way we look at the pupils is wrong. They are capable of far more than we usually expect of them. Let's see what will happen if we change the way we teach.'

Advocate: And how many schools now do Nuffield O-level chemistry in that spirit? Kings College? Westminster? Christ's Hospital? The ones who were doing it anyway? The point about Secondary Science was that it was a massive exercise, not just a curriculum experiment. It came on the heels of comprehensive reorganisation, of the spread of CSE examining and the raising of the school leaving age, and it was an important curriculum ingredient in all these wide-scale policy changes. It's not too much to say that in some places it made such changes possible and reasonably successful when they might have been much worse.

Adversary: But the cost of becoming part of the system is that you end up supporting its basic values and beliefs. In some of the new comprehensives (which often aren't comprehensive at all) Secondary Science is almost the only curriculum on offer in science. The result is that a lot of pupils are cut off from doing A-levels in science simply because the gap between Secondary Science and A-level is so great. It's a case of streaming school by school instead of class by class.

Advocate: I don't think the project would accept that the gap between Secondary Science and A-level is so great, and perhaps the problems are really more general problems about sustaining a sixth form with small numbers. I still feel that the greatest strength of the project lies in the fact that its central educational values are very close to those of most teachers, and that it leads them just about as far along the progressive path as it is possible to go. If the project had gone any farther it would have lost the support of the teachers.

Adversary: I think you have hit on my central criticism of the project. It is a project for teachers, not for pupils. It's not close to the values of the pupils, and all the talk of 'significance' shows it as a very teacher-centred concern.

Advocate: But surely the only way to improve things for pupils is via the teachers?

Adversary: Well, I still feel that if a more challenging view of the pupil was placed at the centre of the project the effect, in the long run, would have been to do more for the pupils.

Advocate: You clearly have a rather critical view of the teachers which the project doesn't seem to share ...

Adversary: There's not one note of criticism against teachers in the whole project, but surely the only reason for having a curriculum project is to *change* teaching. I really don't see how you can run a curriculum project without a very clear view of what you don't like about current practice put right at the centre of the project. They even fudge the issue of subject integration.

Advocate: I think you have to appreciate the situation at the time the project was operating. Until very recently science was only taught in grammar and public schools, and when it was taught in secondary modern schools it was often as 'rural studies'. There was no real tradition of science teaching for comprehensives except that of O-level and A-level, which just seemed unrealistic for at least 2/3 of the pupils. So you had ex-grammar school physics teachers with no idea of how to teach most of the pupils they now faced, and non-graduate secondary modern teachers who knew the pupils but often didn't know the science. It's hard to imagine looking back, but there really was no tradition of mass science teaching in the early 1960s. And Secondary Science has played an enormously significant role in creating one. You only have to look at the sales figures, or walk in to any comprehensive school science lab.

Adversary: I accept that, but it's the very ease of uptake that worries me. I feel that any project which has been taken up so quickly and easily on such a large scale just can't be good. I feel the project missed a critical opportunity to really establish curriculum *change*, rather than curriculum *spread*. If they had been more bold, more analytical about what they were doing, then they would have produced something more challenging. I can see that this would have put widespread dissemination at risk, but I feel curriculum development should take that kind of risk. The kinds of changes you talk about would have been filled by other agencies anyway: textbook writers, colleges of education, LEA advisers and so on. The 'new tradition' you make such a lot of has really been formed by a new generation of science teachers entering the profession from places like Chelsea anyway. I still feel that, although the project did a good, workmanlike job, and worked hard, they failed imaginatively. We can only guess at what might have been.

Advocate: Most likely miserable failure!

Adversary: Well, actually I think failure might have been quite useful. You can learn a lot from mistakes.

Advocate: I admire the intellectual elegance of your criticism, but I think that quality is just what is wrong with it. Curriculum development isn't an academic exercise, but much more a shop floor, nuts and bolts activity. The strength of the project is perhaps that they never engaged publicly in long-drawn-out debates like those you would want to have seen. They just got on with producing the materials and getting them out into schools. The ultimate test is that those materials are still being used, increasingly so. But I'll bet that if they'd had the debates they would have been forgotten by now by all but a handful of people.

HILDA MISSELBROOK

Nuffield Secondary Science: A Response

Before tackling some of the statements in the chapter and the 'dialogue' it is worth commenting that some of the misunderstandings about the project may have arisen because of the economies made in in-service work two or three years after the project was published.

It was never expected that the guides alone would fully equip the majority of science teachers to teach Nuffield Secondary Science. In science, where a large number of teachers feel happier 'doing experiments', less tangible but very important ideas can easily get lost in the pressing need to come to terms with the 'nuts and bolts of the shop floor'.

Out of their context, the quotations on page 9 in the chapter give a misleading impression. A project with an optimistic approach appears pessimistic and negative. Take, for example, the fourth quotation. In the *Teachers' Guide*, this statement is followed by 'There is no doubt, however, that in practical situations they can often be resourceful and ingenious and show an insight which they might find difficult to express verbally'. Again, the sixth quotation is taken from a paragraph dealing specifically with difficult classes *only*.

The important ideas – *significance*, *flexibility* and *selection* – get scant attention in the article. To refer to significance as a 'theme' is unfortunate in the context of Nuffield Secondary Science! The statement that 'It is the teacher's responsibility to demonstrate significance; it is not necessarily assumed to emerge from anything the pupils seem to enjoy' is a distorted condensation of all the many aspects of significance discussed in the *Teachers' Guide*.

The adversary asking for curriculum 'change' rather than 'spread' forgets that in 1965, Science for All was only twenty years old. *Working Paper 1* shows that in the early 1960s not many curricula in the full sense of the word were in existence. At this time the only sensible method of development was to work empirically and to involve the teachers as fully as possible from the start.

The criticism that our approach emphasises the pupils' lack of ability is the hardest to understand since, throughout, teachers were urged to be alert to evidence of the potential of the individual. Awareness of a pupil's difficulties does not imply an acceptance of limitations; it is the first step towards overcoming them. We expected teachers to make demands on their pupils – to stretch them – just as the project made demands on the teachers. It may not be a coincidence that many of the teachers involved in the development trials have since taken further degrees in education.

The project has undoubtedly contributed to the greater interest and involvement shown by science teachers in curriculum development at local and national level. The debates, discussions, analysis and curriculum changes demanded by the adversary are now happening in the schools.

Notes

1. I am grateful to Barry MacDonald and other colleagues on the SAFARI Project who provided the background research from which this chapter was written. I would also like to thank Hilda Misselbrook, Tony Becher and all the teachers, advisers and others who have shared their experience of Secondary Science with us.

2. 'General science' has a long history going back to the origins of the professional associations at the turn of the century. It has always had a minority following, especially among senior members of the profession, though by the early sixties was generally regarded unfavourably and associated with content-laden, low level science taught by rote. To some extent the best of the tradition was kept alive through the late 1950s by HMIs who ran courses (primarily for secondary modern school science teachers) initially at St Lukes College, Exeter, and later throughout the country. When the Nuffield Foundation began to look for people to prepare a feasibility study for a project in secondary modern school science it was natural for them to turn to HMI. As one science HMI later used to joke, 'Secondary Science is really an extended-Exeter!'

3. *SAFARI* (Success and Failure and Recent Innovation) was an evaluative research project funded by the Ford Foundation (1973–6). Directed by Barry MacDonald, SAFARI considered four completed curriculum projects (Nuffield Secondary Science, Project Technology, Geography for the Young School Leaver and the Humanities Curriculum Project) and attempted to track their imprint on the education system. Much of the work of SAFARI is reported in *Changing the Curriculum* by Barry MacDonald and Rob Walker (Open Books 1976).

7 Science 5–13

Basic information

Sponsor Schools Council

Grant £137,200 (+£18,000 from Nuffield Foundation, £10,340 from Scottish Education Department +£2,000 from Plastics Institute)

Location School of Education, University of Bristol, 1967–74

Project team

Len Ennever	Project Director
Albert James	Deputy Project Director
Wynne Harlen	Evaluator
Roy Richards	
Sheila Parker	
Don Radford	
Mary Horn	

Materials Teachers' guides, published by Macdonald Educational, are listed in the Bibliography

Introduction

What follows is the story of a project in action through the eyes of three members of its central team. When there is a difference in emphasis or interpretation I have done my best to represent it. The views expressed have been selected from tape-recorded conversations with Wynne Harlen (project evaluator) and Sheila Parker (a team member), and the project director, Len Ennever's, taped reply to some questions I sent him through the post. The material was gathered during the summer of 1976. My selections from it are inevitably guided by my own views about what is significant for understanding the process of curriculum development. The story presented here is far from clear and complete in places, but I hope it will stimulate the reader to further inquiry. With this in view I have cited at the end some further sources of information about the project.

Basic ideas

Before the story of the project can begin I must briefly try to summarise its basic ideas as they are described in *With Objectives in Mind*, a project publication aimed at helping teachers to understand these ideas. The passages attributed to Len Ennever are either actual quotations from this book or comments made by him after reading a draft of this chapter.

ASSUMPTIONS

1. In general, children work best when trying to find answers to problems that they have themselves chosen to investigate.
2. These problems are best drawn from their own environment and tackled largely by practical investigation.
3. Teachers should be responsible for thinking out and putting into practice the work of their own classes.
4. In order to do so they should be able to find help where they need it.

PROBLEMS

Within this framework the project team urged that they sought answers to the following problems:

1. What kind of science is right for children?
2. What do we want them to achieve through learning about science?
3. How can we best help them achieve it?

SOME ANSWERS

What kind of science?

Ennever: Exploration of the environment is certainly involved – the exam-ination of what is there.... There may be experimenting, there may be measuring, but much of the work will be finding out.

They will organise their experience into some pattern personal to themselves ... most of our children will be happier talking about the speed of cars, falling stones and moving planets than about velocity and acceleration which are abstractions drawn from experience of moving objects.

To a discerning teacher those who have such powers (of abstraction) and those who have not, reveal themselves through the kind of problem that they choose to tackle, and the kind of answer they propound.

The project team defined development in terms of Piaget's pre-operational, concrete operational, and formal operational stages. They warned teachers to be careful: that our own ideas about science and our own ideas of what they might achieve through it do not dull our perception of the individual natures of these children and what they need to develop their different potentials.

What do we want children to achieve?

The team believed that science could contribute to educational ends which transcend subject boundaries, e.g. 'self-realisation', 'broadening experience', 'educating the whole child'. Scientific learning may not always contribute to such aims, because these general ends give no indication of the particular contribution science activities can make to them. The team concluded that they give no help in planning day-to-day work in science.

Ennever: ... We must add to them others that are sufficiently specific for the purpose. This was a task that occupied us for some time.

We discussed with panels of teachers in different parts of the country what might be their aims and objectives for children when working with them in the field of science. In the light of these discussions we shaped aims and objectives for children learning science that were acceptable to us and, broadly, to the teachers with whom we had talked. At their suggestion we wrote them down in a form that we thought useful in schools, well aware that this pattern of guidelines was only one of many that could be equally satisfactory and useful.

They started on this task by defining an *overall aim* of '*Developing an enquiring mind and a scientific approach to problems*'. The overall aim was then broken down into eight *broad aims*:

1. Interpreting findings critically.
2. Developing interests, attitudes, and aesthetic awareness.
3. Observing, exploring, and ordering observations.
4. Developing basic concepts and logical thinking.
5. Posing questions and devising experiments or investigations to answer them.
6. Acquiring knowledge and learning skills.
7. Communicating.
8. Appreciating patterns and relationships.

The final stage of the specification process was to break each of these broad aims into the specific 'behavioural objectives' appropriate for children at different developmental stages. The complete list of objectives is published in *With Objectives in Mind*, and at the end of the other units.

How can we best help children achieve the objectives?

Ennever: They [objectives] do not indicate to teachers anything about the materials or apparatus their children should use or about the experiments or activities they should undertake. Whether or not children achieve certain objectives in a situation in which these objectives potentially could be achieved depends on the way the situation is managed.

According to the team, teachers can best help pupils by selecting activities which *match* the levels of development individuals are at. Two kinds of knowledge are required for *matching*. First, knowledge of the level of development pupils are at and secondly, knowledge of activities which are appropriate at the different levels.

TEACHER SUPPORT

The team believed that they could help teachers help pupils to 'develop an inquiring mind and a scientific approach to problems' firstly through analysing their overall aim into specific behavioural objectives, and secondly the production of units which suggest learning activities through which these objectives can be achieved at the appropriate levels of development.

How objectives can help teachers

The team believed that 'our broad aims apply to all children but they have little practical application unless they are further broken down in ways which take into account the age of the children and, most importantly, their stage of mental development'. They also argued, again on grounds of practicality, that specific objectives should be expressed as desired and observed changes in pupil behaviour (behavioural objectives).

Ennever: Having an aim cannot lead to satisfaction unless it is possible to recognise its achievement. So aims are most effective when they are expressed in terms of expected changes in children, and changes which can be observed.

The function of the team's statements of objectives appears to be four-fold:

Ennever: 1. ... being conscious of them helps the teacher to take advantage of the potential elements of science which are in any of their activities.
2. Working with objectives takes some of the insecurity out of discovery situations.
3. ... Teachers who consider these objectives in relation to individual children ... will find out what ideas the children already have so as to frame objectives for them accordingly and they will therefore know how firm a foundation, if any, they have upon which to build.
4. To help teachers assess whether activities have been matched or mismatched.

SUGGESTIONS FOR LEARNING ACTIVITIES

The team have produced detailed suggestions for activities through which their objectives might be achieved in the form of published handbooks for teachers arranged in a series of sets. Details of these are given at the end of this chapter.

Each unit in the first four sets was written in skeleton form after work on the theme in a few volunteer schools. The units were then commented on by all team members and by some teachers, were expanded into a trial edition, sometimes of 4,000 copies, and were used for trials and evaluation, first in 12 pilot areas, later in 27. After being evaluated the trial units were rewritten for publication.

The team argued that from their experiences at the trial stage a good unit must satisfy the following criteria:

1. *Attractiveness* to children and teachers.
2. The content must possess *relevance* for children inasmuch as it engages their attention and provides opportunities for inquiry.
3. It can be *implemented* in schools.
4. It is *open* to further development by the teacher.
5. It must *demonstrably further the teacher's objectives* for the children.
6. It must *give the teacher the help he needs*, both long term – citing realisable objectives, and short term – with methods and apparatus.

Ennever: These units do not in any way constitute a course or even part of a course. They are illustrations of ways in which a teacher might go about helping children to achieve objectives she has in mind for them.

... the evaluation of the pilot trials was aimed at revealing the extent to which the trial unit helped teachers to consider profitably the objectives for children learning science and to implement them. There is positive evidence that the units are of value in doing this.

There were no books for children, since by their terms of reference the team were bidden to produce books for teachers. One of the project's tenets was that teachers could best help children to learn science by selecting experiences and activities appropriate to their abilities, and engaging the attention, of individual children.

There has been strong and continuous pressure at home and abroad for the project to produce materials for children. A proposal to do this, and to establish a national dissemination centre has been accepted by the Schools Council.

The project in action

THE ORIGINS OF THE PROJECT

Wynne Harlen (Project Evaluator):   The project began in September 1967, about 18 months after discussions had begun between the Schools Council and the Nuffield Foundation about the possibility of setting up a jointly sponsored project in primary science. It was originally conceived as a continuation of the Nuffield Junior Science Project (January 1964–August 1966), with the Nuffield Foundation contributing a fixed sum, but the continuing responsibility for support resting with the Council. Shortly after the start of the Science 5–13

Project the Scottish Education Department was welcomed as a third sponsor, contributing 10 per cent of the Schools Council grant in return for the participation of Scottish schools.

Len Ennever (Project Director):   It was thought that the Nuffield O-level projects would be more firmly established if there was a foundation of science in primary schools on which to build. So the Nuffield Junior Science Project was set up in 1963. I was at that time an HMI concerned with the Nuffield programmes and also with the general area of science in primary schools. I was asked to make liaison between the Nuffield Primary Science Project and the Ministry as it was then. The Nuffield Foundation provided funds for the curriculum development but said that not one penny was to be used for teacher training. However, the Schools Council, which was founded in 1964 – a year later than the Nuffield Junior Science Project – said that they would provide courses for the teachers from the twelve Nuffield pilot areas if the local education authorities would pay the teachers' costs, give money for trials expenses, provide apparatus and provide a centre for each area where teachers could meet and discuss. That was the start of the train of Teachers' Centres set up around the country.

Wynne Harlen: While sharing many of the educational convictions of the Nuffield Junior Science Project, the new team naturally wanted to form its own ideas about how it would try to help teachers, rather than continue the production of the kinds of materials developed by the earlier team ... Soon, the new project developed its own line of approach to the solution of the problems it confronted, and it was appropriate that it should drop its initial name 'Junior Science Project', which linked it rather too firmly with the Nuffield Junior Science Project. The title 'Science 5–13' was chosen at the first meeting of the project Consultative Committee. (Harlen 1975).

Len Ennever: The Nuffield team were repeatedly asked by the chairman of their consultative committee – Professor Kerr – to say what their objectives were. They were reluctant to do this because they said that the objectives were inherent in the work. After the team's secondment period of three years was up in 1966, the project was declared closed. I was then asked if I would resign from the Ministry having reached the minimum retirement age and run a new project covering the same age range as the Nuffield one and taking into account amongst other things the areas of difficulty they had revealed. I was appointed in April 1967.

STAFF APPOINTMENTS

Wynne Harlen: I remember reading in the project archives [after her appointment as project evaluator] correspondence between the Nuffield Foundation and the Schools Council about the need for further work – even before the Nuffield project ended – and my impression was that there was a preference for starting with a completely new team. The Nuffield team were idealistic, they didn't receive our ideas about objectives very favourably at first. It seemed to them to be likely to prevent or destroy the lively open-ended work which they were promoting. We wanted this open-ended work too, but felt teachers needed a lot more help; more structure of ideas. I think the value of this has now been appreciated by the Nuffield team as well as by others.

Len Ennever: My experience with the Nuffield projects had convinced me that project staffs would be far more effective if they could be housed together in the same building and could work in more or less daily contact but with some measure of independence. The University of Bristol provided a house and, though advertising for staff and providing an appointments committee, gave me practically complete freedom of choice in selecting staff members. In general the University could not have been more helpful to the project.

Wynne Harlen: I was appointed by Len. We got to know each other because I was working in Bristol the year before the project started and he was already there. We met very formally [at a staff meeting in Bristol]. I showed him what I was doing on the Oxford Primary Science Evaluation, and everything went from there.

Len Ennever: Before starting work, the general lines of the project were settled by preliminary discussion between the Schools Council staff, the staff HM Inspector for Science, and myself . . . The Schools Council had insisted that one member of the team should be an evaluator; the first ever. We were lucky enough to find Wynne Harlen on the staff of the School of Education and ready for a change. She was appointed and was not to produce units of work as the other members of the team were, but was to be accorded a considerable measure of independence in how she approached her work. Yet she was to work with the team in order to understand what their intentions and aims were. This turned out to be a very happy arrangement which, having worked in such a way as an HMI for 18 years, I found it very easy to foster and maintain.

Wynne Harlen: I had been working on the Oxford Primary Science Project which didn't spell out its aims at all. I came to it in its fourth year trying to ask questions about what they thought they were doing and meeting a great deal of resistance. I told Len about this . . . Len didn't give definite guidelines but he must have had something like this role for me in mind.

Len Ennever: The terms of reference for the project, which were modified after discussion with the Schools Council, and stated by them, were not definite as to the necessity for the project to state its aims explicitly, but every body concerned with the design of it was convinced that it was necessary to do so.

Wynne Harlen: Len knew everyone [team members] before. Sheila Parker he knew of I think, Don Radford he knew from being an inspector . . . Albert James and Len had met on courses; he came on the scene later. There was only

Sheila, Don, and I for the first year ... so that was the initial core. Yes it was very much by recommendation ... I had to have an interview actually. So I suppose he had to go through the procedure.

CONSULTATION PROCEDURES

Len Ennever: The Consultative Committee had on it Professors William Taylor, Kevin Keohane, Geoffrey Matthews, and Peter Kelly; also some teachers, and members of related projects; there were 25 or so members in all. They met regularly, once or twice a term, and their influence was entirely beneficial. They were critical in a friendly way of what we did but they, by their terms of reference, imposed no restraints on the way we carried it out. We listened to each other and the dialogue that took place was wholly helpful.

The other committee was the area representatives committee, consisting of LEA advisers and others, drawn in the first place from those who were helping to conduct the evaluation procedure, originally to discuss evaluation procedure and iron out difficulties. This was very much down to earth; much more coal-face work was done by the members and it proved extremely valuable. It was through this committee that we operated a system of help to uncommitted areas. When requests for lectures or help on courses and so on came in we would write to members of the area representatives committee who would find someone to make the necessary response. It was through influences such as these that the work of the project spread beyond the pilot areas; some of the new areas became sufficiently well organised to send members to the area representatives committee.   Later regional Science 5–13 groups were organised to provide mutual help for regional groups of LEAs. There are eight of these and they cover most of England. Scotland, which is very active, bases its work on colleges of education. North Wales looks to Liverpool for help. South Wales runs its own courses for teachers, but has not formed a group. Many countries abroad run courses and ask for help from the project team. As the project drew to its close [it ceased to be funded in September 1975] the consultative committee and the area representatives committee met jointly and from them emerged the 'after-care committee' which still exists. It meets regularly but less frequently than the original committees, and is largely self-supporting. Of late, the financial climate has taken a turn for the better.

THE AIMS OF THE PROJECT TEAM

Stenhouse draws a distinction between the aims set by a project for its teachers and its aims as a team, e.g. research, reform, development. I probed the latter with members of the project team.

Len Ennever: They were embodied in our terms of reference and were shaped in team discussions about teaching aims. These regular and formal as well as irregular and informal discussions gave us clearer ideas as to the project's own aims. Among these an important one was 'to help teachers identify their own aims and objectives, relevant to their own circumstances'. Of necessity this was a long term project aim. High priority was given to personal contact between members of the project team and teachers who were making trials of project materials. Contributory to this was the desirability of setting up working groups of teachers to give each other mutual help in implementing aims. We did this at first in the pilot areas we had chosen, and then in wider and more loosely joined areas.

Wynne Harlen: We never really spelled out the aims of the project team as distinct from the teachers. They were not explicitly talked about at all. Looking back on it, what is one to say? My role in it was always someone who was to put a structure on what teachers were doing and might already be doing.

Len always described us as 'pulling out science from what was already done' rather than pushing a new kind of subject to go into the curriculum. I think he had a pretty good idea of what he was doing although he never made it explicit. I'm not sure that was shared by everyone.

Sheila Parker (team member):   Our self-image as a team was perhaps to do with helping teachers to be professional by looking through what they were doing to try and have some rationale for why they did things. Did children make progress and all that sort of thing? structuring it a little bit. That wouldn't necessarily be the views of every single person in the team; we started with four people, then it became five, then six, and finally $6\frac{1}{2}$.

DEFINING TEACHING AIMS

Len Ennever: Teaching aims were discussed in a preliminary way by the team but it was realised early on that teachers' views should be sought. So discussion groups were set up in different areas and the business of objectives for children learning science were hammered out. At the teachers' request these were printed; their basis is discussed in *With Objectives in Mind* and they are printed in every unit.

Wynne Harlen: I had just been writing science items for the Bristol Achievement Tests. For that I had to think out for myself what you would want children to achieve at different stages. And it wasn't too difficult then to say 'Well, look I can produce a document – a grid of things that I think we should be working towards with children. Let's discuss it.' I did this. It isn't anything like what came out in the end because I remember it had five stages and a different number of headings. But it was a matrix: stages of development with objectives linked into the stages.

That's where it all started. Len went to America for a month and he left us with the problem of putting this into shape and talking to teachers about it.

We had meetings with teachers in the teachers' centre in Bristol, and I did some near my home. Gradually my document was torn about and changed, but the idea of objectives was accepted by Len very early on. I always give him credit for this. He seemed to see where an idea was going even when the person who had the idea couldn't. He was the one to pick out the good ideas and to encourage people to develop them.

It was with Sheila and Don that I had to thrash out what this idea of objectives meant.

Sheila Parker: Curriculum evaluation is a sign of the times ... We faced the problem of 'what kind of structure can we offer to teachers', knowing that some of the criticisms of the preceding project were about the lack of structure, and we played around with content and method ... and arrived at objectives at a stage when Wynne was very anxious that they should be there. That's the origin of 'objectives'. Some statements about childrens' behaviour were implicit in the developers' minds and Wynne really crystallised them in terms of statements that could be used in the evaluation. I am not saying that the project team arrived at objectives, that's not true. We arrived collectively through the evaluator ... but the individuals in the development team certainly had different views about the function of these objectives ... One objection was that 'they destroy everything we are trying to do in the classroom', that 'one was making precise what was not precise', that 'where you were making statements about objectives you were fitting on a veneer of structure which was inappropriate in the classroom situation.'

THE DEVELOPMENT OF MATERIALS

Q.:   The project's units were written for teachers, not for pupils. Why?

Len Ennever: The project produced a considerable body of materials willingly, by intention, and these were materials for teachers, which is what our terms of reference demanded.

Wynne Harlen: The project wanted children to propose their own inquiries and tackle their own problems, and we felt that this was impossible if you presented ready-made problems to children.

Q.:   How did the team set about developing the units?

Len Ennever: During the trials of our units in the 12 pilot areas in England, and the several added to them in Scotland, members of the project team. each assigned to two or three areas, discovered for themselves what HMIs had known for years; namely, that for most teachers the printed word was not sufficient and that personal contact with originators of ideas and materials was essential. The need was partly to have someone's hand to hold, and someone with whom to discuss problems. As a result project members profitably spent a high proportion of their time in pilot areas and among other things helped the promotion of teachers' groups and their work. During these visits team members made detailed reports on the work seen, the comments made, and the judgements of those who commented. Thus a bank of informed criticism was built up on the draft editions of the units that were put out to trial. These comments and their graded values were of tremendous use when rewriting the trial units for final publication. Close personal contact helped us decide which teachers' comments carried most weight. During the whole of its period the project held regular meetings of team members to discuss materials and the reception of them by teachers. Responses to the demands made by teachers were constructed and thus the project became one of organic design in which the original aims and intentions were modified by the experience we gathered.

Wynne Harlen: I suppose our main arguments in the team were about the kind of unit we should be producing ... what sort of help should we be giving. We tried a lot of times to look to see what topics ought to be covered and whether we were covering them. And this always ended in failure. We never managed to agree on the main topics. I suppose we were looking for a core and never agreed about it ...

Len Ennever: Others studied the same problem and we did not agree about their solutions either. There is no single solution.

Wynne Harlen: The topics were very much related to those that wrote them ... the way they were developed reflects this. Sheila definitely worked from groups of teachers. I went to lots of her meetings. She would throw in ideas and she would somehow manage to enthuse them and they would come back with loads of work that she could then put into the unit. Another member wasn't like that at all. He would write the unit probably using books ... and then the teachers were allowed to try it and he would modify it a little bit. But he didn't actually draw on their resources for ideas for the first draft.

Q.: How did the project's units differ from the teachers' guides produced by the Nuffield Junior Science project?

Wynne Harlen: First of all the statement of objectives was intended to give a lot of support in terms of what you should be aiming for in suggested activities and what the children should be getting out of them.

Secondly, in giving the background information that we did for each topic. We changed this a bit. In the beginning all the units were going to have a book for teachers and a background book. As time went on that background tended to be absorbed into the book for teachers, but it is still there.

Thirdly, I think giving much more specific help with activities, giving many more examples of the way things had been done and organising these under headings. Although it isn't a programme, of course, there is far more chance of a teacher picking up 'coloured things' and being able to do a term's work on that and feel very secure with it, than there is in picking up a Nuffield teachers' guide.

Q.:   How did the publishers influence the production of the materials?

Wynne Harlen: The publisher came in very late. No, I don't think they influenced ... I'm trying to think ... because they did in fact produce trial units for our first trials. They kept us waiting for ages for them and in the end we went back to doing them ourselves for later trials. So they were on the scene earlier than I thought. They must have been on the scene by the end of 1968 actually.

Sheila Parker: They irritated initially because of the constraints they put on us with changes of editors.

Len Ennever: The method of publication was the standard Schools Council method; namely, of invitation to many publishers, discussion with them and with the team, and finally acceptance of one form of publishers by both the Schools Council and the team itself.

The publishers were very slow to produce trial editions and held up the work for many months. In the end we produced them ourselves and had them replicated by the university. Later, however, when the several changes that had taken place in the publishers' firm had sorted themselves out, we settled down to a friendly relationship. A good designer was engaged and gradually the form of the publications emerged and received a very warm response from the teachers. We know now that the appearance of the books and the good quality of their design is an important factor in their acceptance by teachers ... half our sales, which are considerable, are exported.

THE EVALUATION OF THE PROJECT

Q.:   Was it an independent evaluation?
Wynne Harlen: No, I never thought of it as independent. It was intended to be supportive and therefore there was a very close interchange between me and members of the project.
Sheila Parker: Well I don't think it was independent ... it was part and parcel of project development.
Q.:   What were the aims, methods and outcomes of the evaluation?
Wynne Harlen: It was aimed mainly at revising materials. But I remember meetings where we discussed the results of trials, but because they are never cut and dried there were members of the team who wouldn't take the indications. You couldn't prove that it was better to rewrite it in another way and so if you couldn't prove it you may as well leave it. That was the line that was taken by some but not all. Sheila, for example, rewrote her earlier unit completely but I'm not sure the evaluation had a major role here because she had seen the main issues for herself.

Sheila Parker: Yes, but it was nice to know that all of this 'great thing' was saying what you yourself subjectively thought ... Initially the evaluation was very much concerned with the respectability of evaluation and a concentration on measurable results ... in terms of the classic model of evaluation ... But Wynne changed her mind. As I remember it, the change was part expediency, the cost of this great superstructure. But it was also taking into account the teachers' comments about the difficulties they had with this procedure. It wasn't just expediency but the realisation that the task wasn't merely saying to teachers that if they used this particular material the children would get such and such, but that one wanted to encourage teachers to talk about outcomes.

Wynne Harlen: The evaluation was a team thing really. We didn't feel we got much out of the test results ... Oh, it was a terrible business and also when it was reported to teachers I felt that we'd put far too much credence on the sorts of figures we got. They couldn't take them as mere indicators to put with a whole lot of other evidence ... They were really reading too much into them.

The approach eventually adopted was to collect information about the way the units were being used by observation in the trials classrooms, and to combine this with comments from teachers gathered by questionnaire and direct discussion. In this way particular criticisms or suggestions could be interpreted in the light of the teaching methods and working context of the teachers making them.

Wynne Harlen: I was struck by the emphasis teachers put on a need for help with organisation and some of the things which you would regard as their normal teaching style. They felt uncertain about these things. A lot of the subsequent rewriting of units tended to help with these problems.

Sheila Parker: In our particular team Wynne was the kind of person who, although she was helping and *with* the team, one felt she was objective enough to pull you up by your boot-straps.

Wynne Harlen: It maybe that we did have more reflective discussions because there was an evaluation. It might have been very easy to have got along without them otherwise, because the team were busy producing activities and so on.

DISSEMINATION

Q.:   Was there a plan?

Len Ennever: Right from the start dissemination (publicity it was called then) became a built-in quality in the project. It happened this way. It was clear to us that the ideas we had to offer to teachers were deep-rooted as far as their effect on the understanding of children's education was concerned and as far as classroom practice was involved. It appeared that these ideas would be slow to gain acceptance. Therefore it seemed necessary to us that an early start be made on helping teachers and others to become familiar with them. Thus when we produced trial editions of our units as far back as 1969, instead of producing sufficient just for the trials we would produce 4,000 or so of each unit. These materials we gave to the pilot areas for work that they were doing for us, but we let it be known that schools, LEAs or colleges could purchase the trial materials and comment on them if they wanted to. Thus the view we took was the opposite of some; namely, instead of playing the cards close to our chest, we said 'These trial editions represent our thinking at the present stage and we hope you'll help us modify and improve them'. Well, the sale of these trial editions was quite considerable and represented an important source of income to the project; indeed, it was largely because of this income that we were able to support so many activities, courses, and visits etc. We ran many residential courses for teachers that we could not have done without this financial help.

As dissemination was seen at the Schools Council, and elsewhere, to become more and more important in the design of projects, a number of studies were conducted and plans for dissemination were made. In our case we extended and varied them so as to further our long-term objective of leaving behind us, when the project finished, local groups examining their own objectives and implementing them in their own circumstances with mutual help. Mostly the activities that we undertook were based on the pilot areas, or the associated areas that had grown up to join them. A map of centres of dissemination of one sort or another showed that practically the whole country was covered.

Sheila Parker: There was no grand strategy for dissemination to my knowledge. You can identify after the event what you want to see in it as it was.

Wynne Harlen: We talked about courses, and held many of them, local and national.

Sheila Parker: ... The concept of dissemination was new at the time ... you've got to remember that Len was a very experienced HMI who used the old boy network to a large extent.

Wynne Harlen: And he knew that if he invited certain people to meetings, courses, or conferences, that things would get going. And he knew where to hold these to get them going and it was using all that sort of thing ... maybe there was a sort of strategy in his mind but it wasn't ever put down on paper ... We would hold x number of conferences and courses during the lifetime of the project; eight or ten, or something like that for about 100 people each time in selected centres you see ... colleges of education, mainly colleges of education ...

Q.:   Who was on Len's informal network?

Sheila Parker: His ASE [Association for Science Education] network was very important, besides that of the HMIs.

Wynne Harlen: And all his contacts with other project people and their contacts whom they knew would help, such as people, who had been on various consultative committees of Nuffield projects. Len was on most of the important consultative committees.

Sheila Parker: And he had made lots of contacts with senior LEA advisers.

Wynne Harlen: He would say 'it's time we did something for college people. Let's have a conference for them'. To some extent that was timed when we had material that was suitable for college people. Before that we concentrated mainly on showing draft materials to trial schools and later it widened as publisher's drafts became available.

Sheila Parker: All sorts of things in that respect were very useful – such as Len's decision to make trial materials readily available and setting up some machinery where people could write in and buy it 'warts and all', as he put it. In the long term this proved to be very, very effective.

Q.:   How adequate was the network for dissemination purposes?

Wynne Harlen: I don't know, because it so much depended on people staying put ... doing certain jobs. A lot of them moved away as a result of local authority reorganisation.

Q.:   How successful was the dissemination in getting implementation at the classroom level?

Sheila Parker: Patchy. It's a very interesting example of the kind of curriculum development which inevitably must have some influence on others, particularly something like the Schools Council's History, Geography and Social Studies Project at Liverpool. At that level I think it's had some kind of influence. With respect to the extent to which it has been taken up in schools I think the result has been disappointing overall. There are areas where you can say 'yes, there's another 5–13 happening there' but many of these are in areas where conditions were right before the project came along. I suppose Liverpool would be an exception. There was a particular set of circumstances. They battled against difficulties. I don't know Liverpool directly because it wasn't one of my areas ... but as I understand it there is virtually no science going on in primary science other than 5–13. Whether that science is 'pure' 5–13 is another issue, but nevertheless there is a real impetus there for developing science in the primary school. But as for the country as a whole, and locally where the project was housed, it is not too encouraging, though understandable.

I'm sure one significant issue in dissemination is personal contact. There is sometimes too much change in terms of the support system for teachers within LEAs ... I suppose what I am really saying is that it is not just personal contact but that there are no real area networks existing independently of the project itself. There's one developing now in Avon. It's perhaps a bit glorified to call it a network but there is a sudden surge of 'grassroots' interest in 5–13. I can't speak for the authorities, but I think they are interested in the number of teachers who now want courses about Science 5–13; which is ten years after the project. It is interesting that the stimulus for this was an LEA in-service day in Avon. There was an exhibition of work by some good 'Science 5–13' teachers which was very influential indeed; it appears that teachers have now started the dissemination ball rolling.

Len Ennever: Other areas as active as Avon are Kent, Surrey, South East London, West Yorkshire, South Wales, Nottingham, North Western Counties and parts of Scotland.

Wynne Harlen: You don't see the kind of use of Science 5–13 that we really want. No, leave out Science 5–13, because we do not see much primary science going on at all. And it's still an embarrassment if someone comes up and says 'Can we go to see a school where there is good primary science?' You just can't, unless I send them to Liverpool or somewhere like that. Some people would say that pupil material would be the answer. We have this aftercare committee, and there is still a great division in that. I would hold out against pupil material because I would frankly say that I would rather not have science in the primary school that is going to be the normal kind of stuff that you get from the usual kind of work-card.

Len Ennever: Our objectives of necessity applied to a great deal of what went on in school other than teaching in a classroom and teaching in a particular subject area. And one of the things we saw was that when this was understood and acted upon, particularly by heads and staffs together, the project, its activities and thinking as it were sank into the sands of the school – it became absorbed. There were some schools that arranged the whole of their curriculum on Science 5–13; they used it as the starting point for most things; infant schools in particular. It would be a little difficult after one or two years of such working to say which schools were doing Science 5–13 and which were not. As we saw it, when schools are using Science 5–13 it is very often difficult to know the extent to which they are doing so; good practices spread.

REACTIONS TO THE PROJECT

Len Ennever: By and large the project was very warmly received by teachers and local authorities, and still is at home, and particularly abroad. Such criticism as there was can be seen from Wynne Harlen's *Science 5–13: A Formative Evaluation*. There were one or two bits of criticism from research workers which we thought were unjustified; namely, on the uptake of the project. Mostly it was concerned with the period even before the project had produced any published material, and we thought these criticisms were of no great value either to the general public or to ourselves. It wasn't necessary for the project to react to these kinds of criticisms; but very careful note was taken of the comments and criticisms that were gathered during the trials, and during the working of the project in its courses and day-to-day associations with teachers and others. They were discussed by members of the team in meetings, and in all cases a considered response was made to them.

Sheila Parker: Initially the project was under quite a lot of criticism, and in some cases hostility [from Ex-Nuffield Junior Science supporters], largely through misunderstandings of what the project was about and particularly about the interpretation of the objectives. There was in some people's minds the feeling that we were an alternative; very, very different from the original Nuffield science, which is nonsense . . .

Wynne Harlen: They felt we were putting a structure on to it, and that we were going to begin to prescribe what primary activities should be done. The only other bit of hostility I remember was from Scotland in relation to our 11–13 Stage 3 material. They didn't like that because 'it didn't have the structure' and we had quite a difficult meeting. . . . They wanted a structure of subject matter. Some of the *Times Educational Supplement* reviews were pretty nasty. We didn't like them.

   I don't remember 'pupil materials' being a great issue initially. Maybe we just prevented discussion of it. Because we said teachers have to make the decisions, we didn't raise it then, we put it out of court as a topic. But since then there's been a lot of talk about it.

Len Ennever: There is a collection of press cuttings in the project archives. I don't think they amount to anything of great help. Probably one of the most useful things would be to go through the diaries of the teachers which were written during the period of evaluation. These we found most valuable. We read them again and again and they helped us a great deal in coming to conclusions as to the levels at which we should write our materials.

Sheila Parker: One strength of the project lies in its attempt to bring structure into what was rather a nebulous area. Perhaps its greatest strength was its power to bring teachers together to think about a problem in curriculum terms. Its weakness lay in its tendency to rely on too much assumed intercommunication between people. Certainly its statements of objectives are off-putting in the extreme to many teachers who meet the published materials 'cold' and solely through the written word.

LEN ENNE·VER

Science 5–13: A Response

When we began running residential courses for teachers in our trial areas, we started each programme with a thorough-going treatment by lecture and discussion of objectives. A glaze came over the course-members' eyes which was not dispelled until we had started them on some relevant practical work. We got the message; so we changed our tactics and involved them right from the start in interesting practical work related to what might go on in their own classrooms; then we discussed with them what they thought they had got out of it, and what children might achieve if engaged in work of a similar kind.

This was much more profitable; it put objectives in perspective, and they saw them not as a miscellany of discrete ends to be achieved, but collectively as a guide to open-ended work with their children. Ultimately, the statement of objectives made by the project was seen not as a unique solution to a problem – there could be many different statements, all viable – but as a framework to support their own pattern of thinking shaped by their own circumstances and suited to their own children. The individual aims and objectives derived their power from being built into a structure – the better designed, the more powerful – rather as Wittgenstein's hempen rope made of short fibres, weak in themselves, could be built into a hawser strong enough to moor a ship to the quay.

Our aims became, not to tell teachers what to do, but to motivate them to think about solutions to their own problems related to their own circumstances and posed by their own children. The progress towards that end was inevitably patchy and slow; the encouraging thing is that it continues at home and abroad, and shows signs of gaining momentum.

Understandably, sometimes and in some places we were misrepresented and misunderstood. At times some teachers looked to us to tell them what to do: we helped them to take their first steps, and tried to provide help to support them as they went on. Their best help came locally because it was related to their own conditions and available on their own doorsteps; more than that, it could be mutual. In fact it took many forms: local authority courses – science advisers were invaluable and most helpful to teachers and to us – teachers' centre courses and ad hoc groups to study specific problems and sometimes even to write about them. Abroad, in those cultures where educational organisation is centrally derived and the ground for us is rather stony, some teachers gained new insights from open-ended investigations. True, they are not ready for attitudes that challenge authority of book or person – that is, not ready for whole-hearted acceptance of those attitudes – but some of them use our materials, and in doing so think for themselves.

A new project will start shortly, staffed by some members of the original Science 5–13 team, aimed at disseminating knowledge of Science 5–13 materials and thinking, and at designing materials for pupils to use. It should join on very well because the original project proved to be open-ended itself, and left behind enough residual organisation to be of some value. But the image that remains to us, who fashioned it, is one of new work and hard thinking carried out with dedication and loyalty and above all, with immense enjoyment.

8 Project Technology[1]

Basic information

Sponsor Schools Council

Grant £270,000

Location Loughborough College of Education

Director Geoffrey B. Harrison

Period of development 1966 (pilot year)
1967–70 (main project)
1970–72 (extension)

Designated pupils The project itself uses phrases like: 'all children'; 'as many children as possible, of all ages and abilities'. The Schools Council usually refers to 'pupils in the age range of 11 to 18'.

Concerns 1. To see that all children become aware of the technological forces which are working on them, and which they have at their disposal, and that they are aware of their ability and responsibility to control these forces.

2. To see that as many children as possible, of all ages and abilities, have the opportunity to become involved in the technological design process.

3. To help all children push forward the frontiers of their own technological resources in terms of theoretical knowledge and practical skills.

Curriculum area The project tried to resist classification within a subject area and talked about making an impact on the 'total curriculum'. Schools council promotional literature usually groups the project under 'science'.

Teaching materials (Fuller details are given in the bibliography.)

1. Project Technology Handbooks. A series of handbooks for teachers designed to 'fill gaps in the teacher's knowledge and experience, help him or her initiate technological activities and give guidance on the availability, use and construction of apparatus'. Sample titles include: *Simple Bridge Structures*, *The Ship and her Environment*, *Engine Test Beds*, *Design with Plastics*, *Simple Fluid Flow*, *Industrial Archaeology for Schools*. The series is published by Heinemann Educational Books.

2. Review material. Case studies and accounts of ideas in practice: three volumes published by English Universities Press – *Applications of Science*, *Science Fairs* and *School Technology in Action*.

3. Technology briefs. Word-card style presentation of ideas for projects aimed at 'inspiring' pupils and 'involving them personally and directly in the technological design process'. Published by Heinemann Educational Books.

4. Course materials. Complete courses in basic electronics and control technology and course units in photocell applications and *Fibres in A-level chemistry*.

5. SATIS – an abstracting service for teachers.

6. *Bulletin* (re-named *School Technology* in 1971): a quarterly journal.

Examinations The project was involved in setting up and supporting an A-level course in Engineering Science, and a GCE O-level/CSE mode 3 in Control Technology.

Surplus buying agency The project established this agency (with nine sub-depots around the country) to buy government and industrial surplus materials, equipment and components in bulk and sell them to schools.

Regional centres Some thirty regional groups were established in which schools, higher education institutions and industrial concerns together provided a source of support for the development of technology within the school curriculum. Some of these centres have become continuing institutions, usually with local authority finance.

Schools In 1971 the Schools Council claimed that the project was disseminating its *Bulletin* to over a thousand schools, each linked to a regional group. (*Working Paper 38*, 7).

Institutionalisation At the close of the project Trent Polytechnic appointed the project director as director of a new institution, the National Centre for School Technology. This unit provides a continuing home for the work of the project and runs courses for teachers. (At the time of writing (October 1977) the DES has announced a 'teachers in industry scheme.' Financed by the DES and LEAs and organised by the Institution of Mechanical and Electrical Engineers, the scheme includes two one-week courses at NCST.)

Evaluation The Schools Council gave a grant of £17,263 to Keele University to conduct an independent evaluation of the project. The evaluator was David Tawney and the period of the evaluation from 1969–71.

Outline history of the project

The prehistory of the project, that is the period up to the point of funding, is most simply told through the story of one man, Edward Semper. Semper has recently retired, but he was the headmaster of a technical grammar school in Doncaster. He had gone to the school in 1952, having previously taught maths and physics in a Bradford grammar school, and mechanical engineering and mathematics at Bradford Technical College. He had also completed a master's degree thesis on the curriculum of the technical high school. He believed strongly that the technical school held the potential for an alternative curriculum to that of the grammar school. A curriculum that would be equal to the grammar school in demanding intellectual and academic standards, but which was 'attuned to the needs of the modern age rather than to the needs of the past'. Arriving in Doncaster and finding a school which had once been a junior technical school, but which had since become a more conventional grammar school, Semper submitted proposals to the governors to reorientate the curriculum, and joined the Association of Heads of Secondary Technical Schools (AHSTS). This was a small body (some three hundred or so), but in the period that led up to the Crowther Report, it proved to be an important one since one of its members (Dr. Frazer of Gateway School, Leicester) was an influential member of the Crowther Committee.

The educational philosophy of the Association is represented in the Crowther Report's notion of 'An alternative road'. The 'Alternative road' was conceived as a curriculum equal to the classical scholastic curriculum of the grammar schools, but based on the assumption that 'some boys learn best by deducing from applications rather than reasoning from principles'. The 1944 Education Act had implicitly embodied the same notion in establishing a tripartite system of grammar, technical and modern secondary schools, but the Association was concerned that in many local authorities pupils had no access to technical schools. Throughout the nineteen fifties they saw the promise of the 'alternative road' shrinking in the face of what was in fact becoming nationally a predominantly bipartite system.

Following a meeting between Council members of the AHSTS and the Committee of Principals of Colleges of Advanced Technology, an approach was made to Boris Ford, (Professor of Education at Sheffield University)[2] to find ways of formulating a programme of curriculum development and research. Ford mentioned that a post of lecturer was vacant at the time and suggested that Semper should occupy it for one term to work up a detailed proposal.

Happily Semper secured secondment for one term from his LEA to take up the post (from October 1962 to February 1963). Once there he formed an ad hoc Development Committee under the chairmanship of Boris Ford which included academics, industrialists and HMIs. The minutes of its early meetings reveal that its discussions centred around the theme of initiating a 'possible enquiry . . . into the factors affecting the intellectual curiosity of adolescents and the use of personal investigation as a means of learning.' Key features of the discussion were, a concern with 'creative problem solving' (as opposed to the learning of 'theory' and 'abstract ideas'), and with the nature of 'inventive thinking' as opposed to rote learning.

It is important to stress that the emerging proposal was not just for the establishment of a new subject in the curriculum, or simply for the updating of existing subjects. The proposal concerned the development of an alternative curriculum, and alternative theories of learning. The people who proposed them seemed to think of themselves primarily as 'educators' rather than as engineers or subject specialists. Although this broad educational theme was later to be overlaid by other concerns, it is a stance that the project has consistently retained, despite some of the misunderstandings and misgivings it has created in others.

Having produced an outline proposal Semper set about the task of trying to raise funds. There were few precedents and few guidelines at this time, which was before the establishment of the Schools Council. The obvious place to turn was the Nuffield Foundation, but they were fully engaged with the early Nuffield science projects, and did not yet contemplate funding beyond them.

So Semper began trying to raise money from industry; the AHSTS had already contacted the Committee of Principals of Colleges of Advanced Technology, the Education Committee of the Federation of British Industry (now the CBI) and the British Employers' Federation. Semper continued these contacts and addressed conferences in Leeds, Cardiff, London, Oxford, Sheffield, Liverpool, Newcastle, Burton and elsewhere. Semper's persistence began to produce results.

In January 1963 (25 January) the *Times Educational Supplement* carried a long article on 'The Broader Road'. In April 1964 Shell sponsored a teachers' course on 'Technology and the Sixth Form Boy' and Semper's address was widely publicised. The same month the AHSTS held a conference in Sheffield devoted to 'Curriculum Research in Applied Science and Technology' (to which Prince Philip sent a goodwill telegram). On the fund-raising front, D. R. O. Thomas of the British Steel Corporation, as a representative of the FBI, held a series of fund-raising dinner parties for his fellow industrialists. Promises of funding were forthcoming but were conditional on matched funding from a government or educational source. However, Semper found it increasingly difficult to get any response from such institutions.[3] In 1964, as Harold Wilson rode to power on a campaign highly charged with the rhetoric of a coming 'white hot age of technology', Semper seized the opportunity to write directly to the new Prime Minister offering his Committee's project as a contribution to this tide of history.

Two other contributions need to be noted in the run up to the establishment of Project Technology. One was the publication, in 1965, of a report by G. T. Page called *Engineering Among the Schools*. Page was information officer for the Institution of Mechanical Engineers, and for some years the Institution had shown concern about the quality of recruitment to its profession. (Other engineering bodies shared this concern, as did some University departments.) The initiation of the report was stimulated by a research study by Hutchings (Hutchings and Heyworth 1963) which showed that more-able sixth formers were opting away from engineering and applied science. This study was given considerable publicity in both the professional and the popular press. (This was, we must remember, a point in history where the intense 'space race' between the USA and the USSR demonstrated the decline of Britain as a world technological leader.)

Page's report took the interesting form of a survey of 'good practice' in the school level teaching of applied science and engineering. (Incidentally Terry Page was not an engineer, but an arts graduate.) By looking to 'good practice', and describing it in some detail, the report both created a sense of optimism about curriculum possibilities, and indicated practical measures that might be taken. In this way it provided an interesting counterpoint to Hutching's more orthodox research study.

Writing at almost the same time as Terry Page, D. I. R. Porter, a staff inspector in HMI, was commissioned by the Schools Council to write what was to become Curriculum Bulletin 2 *A School Approach to Technology*. Donald Porter had a strong interest in craft and his report argued the case for correcting the balance between academic and practical elements in the secondary school curriculum. Those readers who came to his report concerned about recruitment of a technically qualified workforce were led into the broader debate about the whole curriculum initiated in this context by the Association of Heads of Technical Schools.

Meanwhile Edward Semper's approach to the Prime Minister had brought results. The DES, and subsequently the newly formed Schools Council, took up the matter. Early in 1965 Semper and Dr. Edwards (chairman of the ad hoc committee[4]) were invited to meet Derek Morrell and Robert Morris, joint secretaries of the newly-formed Schools Council, and to discuss his proposal with them.[5] The outcome of this meeting left Semper with a choice. If he and his committee wanted to remain independent, and to use the industrial money that already had been promised, then they could expect a grant of about £10,000 from the Schools Council. If, on the other hand, the committee was willing to hand over the proposal to the Schools Council, they would develop it as a full project and fund it to the extent of at least £100,000. It must have been a difficult decision for Semper, for it was inevitable that he had grown to identify with the project, but when the consulted his committee (by post), they seemed agreed that the most expedient thing was to hand it over. After all, many of them must have felt that Semper would be the Schools Council's natural choice as a project director.

In May 1965 the Schools Council held a meeting at Belgrave Square. Nominally the aim of the meeting was to discuss current developments in the field of school technology. Unknown to most of the invitees, a strong hidden agenda was that this was a chance for the Council to assess the potential of possible project directors. Amongst those who attended were Semper, Somerhoff (from Sevenoaks School), Aitchison (craft adviser for Nottingham), Donald Porter (HMI), John Maddox (Co-ordinator of the Nuffield Science Teaching Project), Terry Page (from the Institute of Mechanical Engineers), and the newly-appointed head of the Department of Design at Loughborough College of Education, Geoffrey Harrison.

Geoffrey Harrison had the unusual distinction of having trained and practised as a civil engineer before entering a teaching career. He had subsequently taught at Dartmouth College[6] and at Dauntsey's School. It was the work he had done at Dauntsey's that had caught the attention of Don Porter while he was researching for his report, for Harrison had established an engineering department in the school, with a strong emphasis on individual project work. At the Belgrave Square meeting he impressed the Schools Council staff, who found him a man of ideas, interested in social policy, and not just in making sixth form science teaching more technologically orientated. They also felt he had the necessary multiple skills of the project director – the skills of the salesman, the diplomat and the negotiator.

From the point at which the Schools Council took over the funding, Harrison became the key figure in relation to the history of the project. Yet up to this point he was an outsider to most of the events described here. Semper remained involved in Project Technology,[7] indeed his school created the CSE control technology course, but it was only some years later that Geoffrey Harrison learnt the full background to the project he came to direct.

Continuing legacies

I have described the prehistory of Project Technology in some detail, though set against the actual pattern of events this account is highly compressed and so inevitably distorted. It seemed necessary to give this account in order to try and explain how it was that a proposal that arose from a group of headmasters, concerned to provide an alternative to what they saw as an outdated curriculum, became a development project in 'technology'. I also wanted to try and explain how it came about that a proposal originating with a body committed to an alternative to the scholastic tradition in state education, should produce a project that came to be directed by a man who was strongly identified with the public schools. I would not want to claim to have solved these puzzles, but I hope that the information that I have provided provides a context within which these appear interesting questions to ask.

There are other reasons for wanting to include this account of the background to the project, for the influences and events that created the context within which Project Technology was formed did not simply dissolve once the project was underway. Because the project was to adopt a wide ranging and all inclusive strategy, these influences remained to reappear in other forms and other guises. Many of the actions taken by the project were to be in collaboration with some other, more permanent institution. For example, the A-level in Engineering Science[8] was sponsored jointly with an Examining Board (the JMB); the local and regional technology centres were set up in conjunction with the local education authorities; SATIS, the abstracting service was set up with Esso Petroleum. Ideas also often had multiple roots, and were to reappear in other forms. For example, the theme of 'creative problem solving' that Edward Semper stressed in the early meeting of his development committee after reading Getzels and Jackson's influential book (1962), was not simply replaced by Project Technology's more operational conception of the technological design process in project work, but tended to resurface in different forms. Edward de Bono spoke at several Project Technology conferences on lateral thinking, and in 1974 the Regional Centre for School Technology at Sheffield Polytechnic appointed a research worker to look again at the area of creative problem solving. To give another example, the recurring interest of central government in the supply of scientific and technically trained man-power was undoubtedly one of the factors behind the decision to fund the project. Over the years this concern has changed its focus from recruitment to the professions, to the production of a technologically aware citizenry, to a concern about the image of industry in the eyes of school leavers.

The creative problem-solving tradition, stemming back at least to Crowther, the involvement of headteachers, the cultivation of links with the professional associations, leading academics and industrialists, the 'capturing' of the experience of a small number of schools with an existing technology currriculum: it was the fitting together of these separate but overlapping interest groups that made Project Technology viable, but, once incorporated, each interest group became, in a sense, a lobby within the project's audience. Even before the project began it already had traditions and expectations written in to an invisible charter. For a project that Becher (1971) was later to see as typifying Havelock's 'social network' model of dissemination, it is interesting to see how many networks were in fact forged before the development phase of the project began. (For further analysis of the project as a typification of Havelock's model see MacDonald and Walker, 1976.)

A final reason for wanting to stress the early history of the project is to point to the influence of cultural tides and fashions. The involvement of Harold Wilson and the Duke of Edinburgh in the story, and the ability of the project to mobilise the support of people like Basil de Ferranti, Frederick Dainton, author of 'the Dainton Report' (HMSO 1968) and the Vice-Chancellor of Warwick University, reflect a long-standing, general concern about this area of the curriculum. One of the questions that remains is what effects have changes in fashion – from Harold Wilson's 'white hot age of technology', to the conservation and ecology movements, and on to the current concerns with high unemployment and economic stringency – had on the project? Are they simply a background against which the project operates, or do they have a deeper significance? After all, a project which claims that it is crucial to change the intellectual and educational climate which fixes our view of the applied sciences is likely itself to become caught up in wider (if diffuse) shifts in the tides of cultural concern.

Enter Prince Philip, Duke of Edinburgh

Establishing the project at Loughborough turned out, from the Schools Council point of view, to be a complicated and tedious process. It was the first time that the Council had funded a project through a local education authority, and Harrison was anxious to clarify all ambiguities about control of the project at an early stage. The situation was complicated by the fact that he had only just been appointed to the College and was involved in developing a new B.Ed. course, doubling the size of his department, and arguing the case for a new £200,000 building with the DES. Although for the main development phase of the project he was seconded full-time, it was clear from the outset that he would be unable to devote all his time and attention to the project.

Nor was the task clearly defined. Almost by definition the project lacked a clearly identifiable audience of teachers. Craft teachers might have constituted such an audience, but their emphasis on precision and finish might have clashed with the project's emphasis on problem solving and engineering approximation, and the clash was almost a moral one. Nevertheless, Donald Porter was anxious to pursue this route, feeling that the engineering approach offered a way forward for craft teachers. In the event the relationship between craft teachers and the project remained hesitant, perhaps because the project was wary of the low status that craft teachers tend to carry, and felt that a strong association might hamper them in the pursuit of their aim to raise the status of applied studies within the total curriculum.

Science teachers presented another possible target audience, but not only were science teachers largely preoccupied with Nuffield science at this time, they also had ideas of their own about applied science in the school curriculum. In 1968 the Duke of Edinburgh agreed to become Patron of the Association for Science Education and at an ASE Meeting, he addressed the Association on the subject of applied science teaching. The speech had a considerable impact, on the public as well as on the professionals. Prince Philip suggested that perhaps, instead of teaching Boyle's law in the usual way, it might be an idea to begin with the bicycle, and to develop the theory from that. Following the speech he set up an Action Committee with the intention of encouraging support for applied science teaching in schools from industrialists and scientists. The Action Committee was established in ignorance of Semper's committee and the Schools Council's involvement, and the existence of it presented something of an embarrassment to the Schools Council and Project Technology. In those days the network of people at the centre was a close one, and after hasty negotiations the Action Committee was reconstituted as the Schools Science and Technology Committee (SSTC), including both Harrison and Semper amongst its members, and with John Banks, then a programme officer at the Schools Council, as its secretary.

Although the SSTC had no funds to distribute, it was a powerful committee in terms of membership, including Nobel prize winners and captains of industry like Basil de Ferranti. Nor was it simply a show-piece committee. It met regularly, once a month, over a period of three years.

From Project Technology's point of view, the successes of the SSTC included establishing the National Centre for School Technology at Trent Polytechnic (with Harrison as director), and setting up the Standing Conference on Schools Science and Technology. These national bodies supported the development of a number of local and regional centres for which the Southampton Centre was an (independently founded) prototype. Less obviously, the SSTC acted as a buffer between Project Technology and the ASE. The ASE had been instrumental in setting up the Nuffield science projects, and in a sense felt that any extensions they might want to make in the direction of applied science had been taken from under their feet by the establishment of Project Technology. The relationship was to remain an uneasy one, and one not helped by Harrison's apparently imperialist stance in developing the project. Inevitably some sections of the ASE felt threatened by the project's free-wheeling creativity in establishing committees, institutions and networks.[9] Earlier in this account I stressed the continuing traditions that surrounded the project. There is though another aspect of the story, for as well as continuity there are marked discontinuities. In this case these seem to centre around the Schools Council's reluctance to develop close contacts with the subject associations, particularly with the ASE, and the AHSTS. Perhaps it was the job of the consultative committee to create these contacts, but they seem to have failed to pursue this role actively. Certainly the AHSTS ad hoc committee expected to be more closely consulted.

Committees, networks and institutions

The School Science and Technology Committee was to give way to another, expanded committee, the Standing Conference on School Science and Technology (SCSST), but at this point it is better to leave written description of these different committees and turn instead to a diagram reproduced in one of the School Technology Forum publications.

This diagram gives some indication of the institutional complexity that surrounded and involved Project Technology. The project's willingness to accept and entertain this complexity led to a diffuseness in its image and activities that some members of the Schools Council found difficult to understand. The current image of curriculum development was of a group of people primarily engaged in the production of materials, with schools firmly in a consumer role. It was fashionable in some quarters to look to the educational context surrounding the project-school relationship as one which created constraints on innovation, but this was not expected to divert projects from what was seen as their primary function. Harrison conceded the point to some extent. In official presentations he always took care to feature the materials production activities of the project: for example, in the paper 'Objectives and activities' given to the Scarborough Conference in 1969 the heading 'Teaching material' accounts for three of the eight typescript pages. And the claim was justifiable; the project did produce quite an extensive range of materials which were distributed widely. In 1971 in Schools Council *Working Paper 38*, the project claimed to have 'more than a thousand schools, each linked with one of the regional groups' receiving *School Technology* and other project materials. Where the

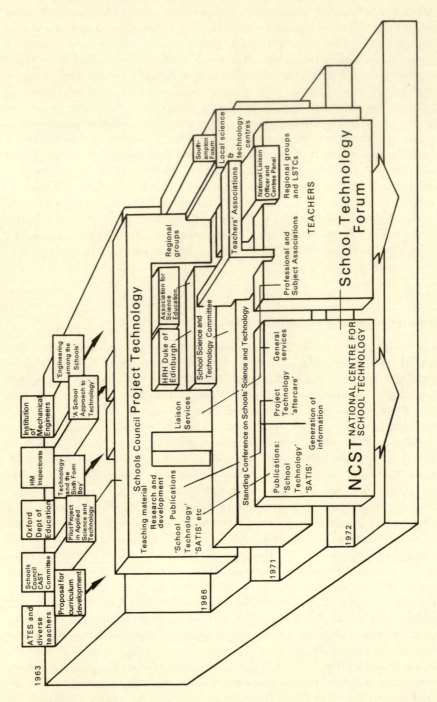

Figure 8.1 Emergence of school technology

project diverged from the pattern set by other projects was less in the production of materials than in the cultivation of a network of trial schools within which the use of the materials was carefully monitored and checked.

Many people expected more from the Council's most expensive project. They found the materials peripheral (for example the extensive sections on industrial archaeology), or just puzzling. Harrison, for example, insisted on including the *Journal* format as a 'teaching material'. All these things made sense given the strategy adopted by the project, and especially given its prime commitment to the creation of support structures for technology teaching in school. But it was just this strategy that people found hard to accept, and the fact that the project always seemed to be supporting others rather than promoting their own materials and hard-selling their own message disconcerted many, especially those at some distance from the project team.

Paradoxically, when the project succeeded in its own terms, that success was often invisible. For example, when it succeeded in establishing networks and institutions it often found itself unable, and unwilling, to claim or control them. Geoffrey Harrison commented in an interview:

> The whole point of the regional centres is that they must come as local initiatives. Therefore the setting up of those centres is something you have to forget as having to do with a national initiative from Project Technology. It has taken a great deal of our time to talk to local committees about what is required in the form of local support, but that's not part of the public success of Project Technology.
>
> (SAFARI interview 1974)

The philosophy of support eloquently articulated by Harrison was widely interpreted by others as a lack of direction and control from the centre. Many of those involved in the Project, both in schools and in the Schools Council, were unable to escape the assumptions of the R, D and D model.[10] They listened to the rhetoric of the social interaction model but still expected the materials to arrive. In the end, many became confused, disappointed and cynical. '£270,000 and nothing to show for it' became a common judgement on the project.

SAFARI asked one headmaster, a man who did not seem a natural cynic, what his experience of the project had been. He explained that his school (a secondary modern) had been involved in a cooperative venture with two neighbouring schools, a boys' grammar school and a public school. Working under the direction of the conservation officer of the local canal (a retired naval officer), the boys had designed and built a craft for clearing water weed. The public school had made the weed cutting gear, the grammar school had designed the boat, and his school had built it. When the time came to launch the boat his boys could not be there. We asked him what had happened. 'The boat?' he said. 'It sank. Just like Project Technology.'

While disappointment was a common reaction at the periphery (though it was certainly not universal), the response from the centre was much stronger. Project Technology touched some tender political sensitivities at the Schools

Council. When Geoffrey Harrison dispersed his autonomy through the support network, he in effect crossed territorial boundaries. At one point early in the project, the team wanted to set up a particular regional group in a rural county. Harrison was aware that this could be a risky operation and was anxious to identify someone who would be 'sympathetic, had the right attitudes and the right enthusiasm'. Receiving little response from the LEAs and the technical colleges, he discovered that someone known to the team from the pilot study had recently been appointed principal of a suitably located city college. The approach to this man, asking if he would take the initiative in the area, was followed by a letter to Harrison from the chairman of the Schools Council Programme Committee demanding to know why the project hadn't approached a particular county technical college, which the writer knew well and deemed more appropriate. Harrison quoted the letter as ending with these words: 'It is time that those at the periphery of the Schools Council understood what is required of them from the centre.'

The Schools Council may grant projects autonomy even when the projects don't perceive it as such. Shipman, for example, suggests that the Keele Integrated Studies Project interpreted the Council's grant of autonomy as lack of interest and enthusiasm (Shipman 1974). Projects cannot be fully autonomous, however, since they inevitably act as agencies of the Schools Council and so reflect its delicately poised situation between local and central government agencies and the teacher unions. When the actions of projects seem to question the basis of Council structure, direction and policy, then corrective action tends to follow swiftly: hence the apparent over-reaction to Harrison's regional initiative.

Curriculum development projects often talk in terms of the 'barriers' that exist between curriculum innovations and classrooms. Project Technology saw itself working to reconstruct and reorganise the barriers in ways that would foster classroom developments, rather than acting as if the barriers were not there. The aim was to create 'a service to meet the needs of teachers and schools and not an agency to tell them how to do their job' (*Working Paper 38* 1971).

Evaluation

The independent evaluation carried out at Keele University found it hard to come to grips with the strategy adopted by the project. This situation was not helped by the fact that the principal investigator (David Tawney) continued in his full-time job as a lecturer in the education department while his head of department retained formal responsibility for the grant. Inevitably, given the state of evaluation at the time, the study concentrated on those things that were amenable to orthodox study. In the event the evaluation collected data on the readership of the *Bulletin*, produced feedback on materials, and ran tests which attempted to investigate the effectiveness of some of the more coherent courses, such as Control Technology. While the project pursued its prime aim of creating support structures, the evaluation team found themselves in the somewhat frustrating role of being the only contact many schools had with the project team.

A final thought

It is interesting to note that Project Technology was the first large-scale curriculum development project to break out of the orthodox mode of concentrating on materials production and school trials. The reasons why a project in the field of engineering, partly staffed by engineers, broke away from a model known as the 'engineering model' remain puzzling and obscure.

Project work – an illustration

In Schools Council Working Paper 18 *Technology and the schools* (1968) Geoffrey Harrison gave an account of the feasibility shape of Project Technology and included a list of possible areas for project work.

UNCLASSIFIED LIST OF PROJECTS

This list is not intended to be comprehensive. Moreover some of the projects have been undertaken several times under different conditions and with different age and ability levels.

Hovercraft – design and construction of fan, ductwork etc., stability and directional control.

Linear motor – design and construction, useful application.

Vacuum forming – design and construction of machine, properties and characteristics of various forming materials.

Moire fringe applications – measurement, analysis of numerical machine control, interference patterns, e.g. links with finger-printing.

Rocketry – design and construction of firing mechanisms, using solid fuels, experimental data obtained during captive firing.

Pulse-jet engines – design, construction and instrumentation to measure characteristics.

Engine test rigs – instrumentation of various engines, 2-stroke, 4-stroke, design and construction of simple dynamometers, indicators, b.h.p., i.h.p. and thermal h.p. tests, efficiencies.

Stress analysis – strain viewing using polarised light, use of strain gauges.

Structures – design, construction and testing of simple structures using balsa wood and similar materials, bridge construction, etc.

Electronic timer – alternative methods, e.g. photo cells and scaler.

Sound transmission – by modulated light beam – design and construction of transmitter and receiver.

Linear air track – use of for investigational purposes – design, construction of tracks of varying types, investigations in dynamics using track.

Electronic programmed control of working models – design and construction of control devices, preparation of programme.

Radio control – design and construction of transmitter and receiver, the servo-mechanisms on the device.

Wind tunnel – construction and investigations – design and construction of the tunnel and fan, smoke production unit, measuring equipment, airflow around various objects – aerofoil sections, buildings, etc.

Lasers – design, construction and operation.

Electronic equipment – construction of power packs, signal generators, oscilloscope etc.

Metallurgical investigations – crystal structure, microscopic inspection, equilibrium diagrams, effects of controlled heat treatment.

Go-karts – design and construction of steering geometry, suspension, gearing, braking.

Chromatography – dyestuffs, analysis of metals.

Simulated automatic machine control – drilling operation etc.

Applications of photo-cells – light seeking devices, industrial process control applications.

Ultrasonic devices – design and construction of ultrasonic control mechanism.

Graphical representation of mechanical movement – use of mechanisms, linkages, cams etc., e.g. graphical representation of a car journey.

Material testing – design and construction of testing devices, tensile, comprehensive, fatigue, wear and impact tests.

Equipment for disabled people – design and construction of devices to assist cripples to mount steps, etc.

Hydraulics applications – flow tanks, impact of jet, wave mechanisms.

Mechanical handling – construction of test rigs, automatic devices.

Photography – enlarging, film-making, aerial photography using balloons, high speed and time lapse photography.

Harmonographs – design and construction of apparatus, analysis of results.

Scale and experimental model engineering –manufacturing techniques, original design, links with electronics.

Electronic organs –electronic and mechanical aspects of design and construction of circuits tuning.

Mechanical calculating devices – integrators and computers.

Radio telescopes – design of aerial and operating mechanism, receivers, amplifier.

Astronomical telescopes – optics, operating mechanism.

Land yachts – design and construction involving investigations into sail design, stability, steering geometry, suspension, braking.

Weather station equipment – design and construction, remote reading of wind speed/direction, rainfall etc.

Logic circuits – relay operated, transistor operated logic, puzzle circuit design based on Boolean algebra, computer circuitry.

Moisture-testing equipment – development for moulding sand and other materials.

Binary adder and subtractor – construction of transistorised binary counter, alternative methods of input, e.g., telephone dial pulses or signal generator, applications as a precision timer.

Hydroplanes – design and construction. Analysis of factors influencing stability and speed.

Greenhouse control – automatic or programmed.

Kymograph – design and construction of apparatus to study muscle action, variable speed drive, linkages etc.

Cricket bowling/fielding machine.

Score board – remote control, for use on sports day or cricket matches.

Harmonic analysis – device for·drawing two sine curves and their resultant curves on blackboards.

Cupola – for melting cast iron scrap.

Board duster – to facilitate easy and quick erasing.

Test tube cleaner.

Automatic book-binder.

A plastic injection moulding machine.

Tensile testing machine – suitable for use on a school laboratory bench.

Plane table – incorporating swivel and tilting table and telescopic legs.

Cine tilter – for horizontal and vertical tilting.

Tractor – a lightweight riding tractor for use around the school.

3-wheel and 2-seater car – design and construction complete with body.

Automatic timetable device.

Mechanical clock – large two-face clock for mounting on roof.

Punched card system – for issuing and returning library books.

Electronic modulator – for use in school music department.

Lawn mower – for elderly physically handicapped person.

Automatic winding machine – for school turret clock.

Milk bottle dispenser.

Flight controls simulator.

Self steering mechanism – for a yacht.

Wave tank – as an aid in the teaching of geography.

Theodolite – for use in geography department.

A light-beam communicator.

Automatic sunshine duration recorder.

Enamelling kiln – electrically heated.

Solid fuel rocket engine – design and construction.

A free-pendulum clock – pneumatically controlled.

Electronic music-composing machine.

Colorimeter – for investigation of the rate of enzymatic reactions.

Electronic thermometer – for use on animals.

Underwater microphone unit – for the collection and recording of sounds made by fish.

Thermostatically controlled incubator – for locust and stick insect eggs.

Respirometer – to investigate the effect of temperature upon the gaseous exchange of germinating wheat grains.

Thermal and acoustic properties of building materials. – Construction of *test rigs* and arrangement of data.

Investigational approach to the design and construction of musical instruments.

Determination of acceleration due to gravity – alternative methods – accuracy.

Determination of the speed of sound – alternative methods.

Determination of the speed of light – alternative methods.

Transmission of diagrams/photographs by wire, use of photo transistors etc. – alternative methods.

Efficiency of ships' propellers – design of test equipment, problems of 'cavitation' etc.

Small-scale climatic conditions control – effects on animal/plant life.

Design, construction and use of equipment to measure human reaction times under varying conditions – statistical data obtained.

Man-made fibres – method of production, testing etc.

The design implications of time and motion study in the kitchen.

Investigations into traffic control – speeds, tidal flow etc.

Transistor logic control of traffic lights.

Investigation into *ship stability*.

Investigation into *resistance to motion of ships' hulls etc.*

Investigation of *acoustic reverberation lines of school class rooms.*

Harmonic analysis of musical instrument tones.

Stability of axially-loaded columns and struts.

Investigation of the *factors determining the deflection and distortion of simply supported and cantilevered beams.*

Use of Schlieren systems to investigate change of *refractive index of a gas.*

Properties of shells for roof construction.

The strength of concrete mixes.

Yacht research involving hull shapes and wind effects.

Investigation of the *magnetic field in a d.c. machine* under varying conditions of load.

Research into *current carrying properties of semi-conductors.*

Investigation into *phase shift of electric current in transformers.*

Young's modulus – to design and construct an apparatus for the illustration of the elastic properties of wires.

A 'sensitive' planishing/work-hardening machine with interchangeable hammers and anvils.

A device to sort foil milk bottle tops from straws and to wash the tops.

Sensitive methods of electro-chemical analysis.

A machine for winding resistors.

Table 8.1 Prepared by Geoffrey Harrison for an international conference in 1973, illustrates how he approached the problem of conceptualising 'design' as a means of teaching and learning

	Purposes	*Methods*	*Examples*
1. 'Pure' creativity	(a) To develop capacity for divergent thinking.	Paper exercises: group work or individual; sketching and evolution of ideas graphically.	How to drop an egg safely from ten feet on to concrete.
	(b) To give opportunity for unfettered thinking about solutions to 'original' problems.	No syllabus 'knowledge' needed.	How to cut finger nails on the right hand.
	(c) To learn, progressively, the *operation* of the design sequence of problem identification and analysis, synthesis of multiple hypothetical solutions, optimisation etc.		How to bridge a gap given limited resources. Developing a 'movement' toy for 6-year old child.
2. Reinforcement of learning	To reinforce or directly provide the means of acquiring specific 'concepts' and 'knowledge'.	Simple design briefs designed to make pupils explore specific problem fields.	The nature of stability in a mechanical system, e.g., a rocket, a boat, an aeroplane. Rigidity of 2D and 3D frameworks. Electrical switching and logic circuitry.

Table 8.1 (continued)

	Purposes	Methods	Examples
			Plastic and electric structures. Energy conversion model vehicles, catapults.
3. Technical design	Developing specific capability in detailed technical design and reinforcing knowledge taught by other means.	Either paper or real exercises. Short design briefs with narrow specifications.	Amplifier, gearbox. Transformer, structural element. Composite members.
4. Integrated design	To complement the usual study of narrow fields of knowledge by developing an integrated view of useful knowledge.	More open design brief requiring a solution consisting of several different design problems contributing to the whole. Preferably a fully realised design but in the interests of economy and money, it could use modules and re-usable framework components.	A controlled device, e.g. garage door opening to a signal, a sorting device, a controlled model vehicle. All requiring electrical, electronic, mechanical, structural and systems engineering.
5. Creative design	Experience of the *total* design process from identification of the problem to the final realisation of the optimum solution. Including all economic, social, material, technical, aesthetic factors and restraints. The perception of the total inter-relationships.	Student choice of project according to their personal interests, with teacher's approval to ensure relevance to course.	Device controllable by a disabled person, e.g. page turner, coffee maker, wheel chair, typewriter, kiln controller, controlled electrical model car etc.

Table 8.1 (continued)

	Purposes	Methods	Examples
	The development of resourcefulness, initiative, confidence etc.		
6. Investigational	To develop a scientific problem solving approach to an investigational requirement.	Either (a) closely controlled assignments or (b) more open-ended investigations.	(a) Effect of heat treatment on physical properties. (b) Thermal insulation effect of double glazing.

Source: Pemberton and Eggleston 1973.

ROBERT MORRIS

Project Technology: Response I

I suspect that before Edward Semper arrived in Curzon Street to meet me and Derek Morrell, as joint heads (then) of the Curriculum Study Group (the Schools Council not yet having come into existence), his concern for 'an alternative curriculum, and alternative theories of learning' (page 117, lines 37–8) must have sobered down. For, as I remember, his proposal to the DES for an 'educational research' grant, was to enable Doncaster Secondary Technical School, in association with a handful of other *local* schools, to develop a more creative curriculum *in the workshop*.

However, Semper's ideas for creative, rather than imitative, handicraft made sense to me, so I consulted Don Porter, who led us (Derek and we) to the Institute of Mechanical Engineers and to their Consultant, G. T. Page, who at that very time was engaged in the study which led to *Engineering among the Schools*. Page had already by him a substantial list of schools (including Sevenoaks and Dauntseys) which were *already* trying 'the project approach' to handicraft, as advocated by HMI Don Porter and his colleagues.

So, what seemed at first to be an idea 'worth trying' proved, in the event, to be an idea 'being tried'.

Consequently, we had the idea of trying to harness the 'trying' schools to a National Project Technology in preference to Semper's local effort. However, we were under a moral obligation to Semper. He had put in a bid for DES funds and his application had to be accepted or rejected. So we decided to invite him back to Curzon Street and put to him the situation as we saw it. To his credit – and his own sense of vision – Semper at once saw the advantages in making an attempt to launch a national project, and, after consulting his association, agreed to support our alternative proposal.

The story then shifts back to the Institute of Mechanical Engineers and their agreement to sponsor a one-day conference to discuss how, in a project, schools might be linked together in such a way as to inform and reinforce each other. It was out of this large gathering of teachers that the basic ideas for the structure of Project Technology took root.

When, soon afterwards, the Schools Council was formed and project money became available, we had to find a project Director. Our method of choosing one in those days was to assemble the likely lads and for them all to talk! It may not have been a very good method, but it was open and above board. It was not as sneaky as the loaded phrase 'a strong hidden agenda' (page 119, lines 31–2) would suggest.

As for the suggestion (page 119, lines 27–8) that Semper's association would have expected the Council to appoint Semper as Director, I must confess that no one in those days ever contemplated headmasters as being director-fodder, or even expected them to be interested in anything other than trying to make something happen. Certainly, to my knowledge, Semper never gave the slightest hint of wishing to be more involved than he came to be, namely one of the most valued members of the Consultative Committee for the Project.

Finally, why did it seem to fail? Or, why did it not spectacularly succeed? My answer to that is a simple-minded one.

1.   Its philosophy

The one 'method' was to be a project approach in which the initiatives were to come *from the pupils*. Such a method precludes the development of teaching material other than that of the 'for example' kind. Prescriptive material would be at variance with the objectives.

2.   Its clientèle

Handicraft teachers are not as a rule sufficiently well steeped in science to apply scientific principles to the solution of a technological problem.

Conversely science teachers are not as a rule practical enough to adapt to the creative needs of a workshop.

Neither group is accustomed to 'project' work.

GEOFFREY HARRISON

Project Technology: Response II

There were very many teachers, already practitioners of the engineering project approach, who helped to stimulate Project Technology into existence. Rob Walker's chapter credits too few such people and reference should be made to *Engineering Among the Schools* for further information.

Success and failure of a project can only be gauged over an appropriate period of time. It was obvious at the start of Project Technology that a period of many years would be needed for the significant change in attitude which was sought. The Schools Council never accepted this but expected instant success and take up. It is interesting that the sales of teaching materials were greater in 1977 than in 1976. The Council never gave support to the idea that a dissemination *system* would be required and the development of the regional organisations (SATROs), the Standing Conference on Schools' Science and Technology and the School Technology Forum, all necessary for the dissemination of Project Technology, were not seen as fit activities in which the project team should engage. This did not stop the team putting considerable effort into all three developments!

I find Walker's final paragraph fascinating. It was precisely *because* the team comprised engineers that the system of curriculum development which was designed did not conform to the conventional but falsely named, 'engineering model'. The genuine engineering approach, which is well spelled out in the project's own materials, required a very careful analysis not only of the problems identified, but also of the constraints against which any solution would need to battle. The project identified and recognised these constraints and prepared materials and activities accordingly.

Notes

1. The material presented here derives from the Ford Foundation's SAFARI Project, a study of the mid-term effects of curriculum development projects based at CARE 1973–6. Much of the fieldwork and its interpretation is due to the efforts of Barry

MacDonald and Lawrence Stenhouse. We are of course also indebted to all those who shared their experience of Project Technology with the SAFARI team, particularly Geoffrey Harrison, Edward Semper OBE and John Banks.

2. Prof. Dent (Ford's predecessor at the Sheffield Institute) had established a study group of technical school heads which met at regular intervals. As this group included the president of AHSTS it seemed natural for them to turn to Boris Ford for advice.

3. A programme outline was submitted to the DES, the Institution of Mechanical Engineers, The Royal Society and the Nuffield Foundation.

4. And vice-chancellor of Bradford University.

5. In the event Dr. Edwards was involved in a car accident on his way to the meeting, and was unable to attend.

6. Robert Morris, Joint Secretary of the Schools Council at the time, had also taught at Dartmouth College.

7. Notably as chairman of the S. Yorks regional group.

8. A-level engineering science developed from a joint initiative by Semper and Professor Harry Edels. Deryk Kelly, a member of Semper's staff joined the JMB working Party and later became science coordinator for Project Technology.

9. Geoffrey Harrison comments: 'I like the sound of ... "Harrison's apparently imperialist stance ..."! But it was entirely democratic. The trouble being, as in most democracies that it is difficult to actually get the "demo" to be "cratic"! The ASE was consulted time and time again and always refused to have anything to do with the project, officially anyway. There were always many active members of ASE also who became very involved.'

10. The Research, Development and Diffusion Model was described by Havelock (1971) as one of the main forms for generating and implementing innovation in a large-scale system. The focus is on the activity phases of a developer responding to perceived needs in the system. The phrase has been widely used to describe much of the curriculum development activity of central agencies like the Schools Council.

ALASDAIR ASTON

9 The Humanities Curriculum Project[1]

Basic information

Sponsors Schools Council and Nuffield Foundation.

Grant £234,328 (£174,328 from the Schools Council and £60,000 from the Nuffield Foundation. Of this, £68,000 went to evaluation).

Location Philippa Fawcett College of Education, ILEA, then from 1970 at the University of East Anglia.

Period of development 1967–72.

Designated pupils 14–16 average and below average who did not experience special reading difficulties.

Organiser Lawrence Stenhouse, previously principal lecturer in education at Jordanhill College of Education, Glasgow.

Project team Project director, with initially four and later six team members, plus a schools officer, film research officer (based in the British Film Institute) and research librarian. In addition, from 1968 an evaluation officer, later with three assistants.

Trials Conducted in academic years 1968–70 in 32 schools from 29 (pre-Radcliffe–Maud) local authorities in England and Wales, plus 4 approved schools.

Materials From 1970 onwards Heinemann Educational Books published eight packs of thematic materials for pupils, each pack including general teacher's handbooks to the project and teacher's handbooks specific to the packs. The packs are:

1. *War and Society*
2. *Education*
3. *Relations between the Sexes*
4. *The Family*
5. *Poverty*
6. *People and Work*
7. *Living in Cities*
8. *Law and Order*

In addition materials were prepared on *Race* but these were not published. Each pack of materials contains a resource bank of texts, pictures and sound tapes sufficient to service a group of twenty pupils. The project also published many documents on project design, teacher preparation, dissemination and evaluation. Videotapes were also made available.

Cost   Each pack of materials costs £48 to purchase. It is important to budget for fairly frequent film-hire and for pupils to travel on out-of-school enquiries. It has been suggested that the provision of student groups of not more than 20 is a precondition for success and this may be regarded as a budgeting item.

Evaluation   Funded by the Schools Council; was conducted from 1968–72, directed by Barry MacDonald and published from 1975 onwards.

Humanities curriculum project

The Humanities Curriculum Project, sponsored by the Schools Council and the Nuffield Foundation, was set up in September 1967 to extend the range of choice open to teachers working in the humanities with adolescents of average and below average ability by offering them teaching materials and research support. The aims of humanities teaching had been outlined in 1965 in Schools Council Working Paper 2 *Raising the School Leaving Age* and the project's director, Lawrence Stenhouse, has referred to this as the point of departure for the project:

> The problem is to give every man some access to a complex cultural inheritance, some hold on his personal life and on his relationships with the various communities to which he belongs, some extension of his understanding of, and sensitivity towards, other human beings. The aim is to forward understanding, discrimination and judgment in the human field – it will involve reliable factual knowledge, where this is appropriate, direct experience, imaginative experience, some appreciation of the dilemmas of the human condition, of the rough-hewn nature of many of our institutions, and some rational thought about them.
>
> (Schools Council 1965, para. 60)

The Working Paper continued by hinting at two difficulties in implementing such a programme:

> All of this may seem to some teachers like a programme for people who have both mental ability and maturity beyond the reach of most who will leave at the age of sixteen. The Council, however, thinks it is important not to assume that this is so, but rather to probe by experiment in the classroom how far ordinary pupils can be taken.
>
> (Schools Council 1965, para. 61)

And later:

> But adult procedures in the classroom ... will not be successful if a different kind of relationship between teacher and pupil obtains in the corridor or in extra curricular activity. If the teacher emphasises, in the classroom, his common humanity with his pupils, and his common uncertainty in the face of many problems, the pupils will not take kindly to being demoted to the status of children in other relationships within the same institution. Indeed, they may write off the classroom relationship as a 'soft-sell'.
>
> (Para. 97)

These remarks were important determinants of the project and may be regarded as part of its 'prehistory'. By emphasising the common humanity of teacher and pupil, and by inviting teachers to treat the school leaver as a young adult, they challenged the assumption of the Newsom Report (CACE 1963) that the leaver was a special case. Other important preconditions of the project are to be found in the writings (particularly his *Culture and Education*, 1967) of Lawrence Stenhouse. A propensity for academic rigour and an affinity with the Scottish encyclopedic tradition almost anticipate one of his later remarks to the effect that experience with the project tends to suggest that we have seriously underestimated large numbers of our adolescents.

When the project director was appointed to the project, he told his sponsors in the Schools Council and the Nuffield Foundation that he expected the right to fail, implying by this the right to experiment boldly. Although they were taken aback somewhat, they certainly accorded the project a great deal of freedom. The project itself preferred curriculum work that was speculative rather than evangelical, and cumulative rather than *ad hoc*. On the other hand, public opinion throughout would seem to have exerted continual pressure in the direction of advocacy of the project's position. The team wished to derive hypotheses from case-study in an effort to build theory. The notion of action research was under frequent threat from outside. Eventually, however, with quite vigorous independence the procedure adopted was presented in the following terms:

1. Select a cogent general educational policy statement in the curricular field in question.
2. By relating its logical implications to the realities of the classroom, produce the outline of a teaching strategy consistent with the aim which is feasible in practice.
3. Attempt to develop the strategy, testing its logical consistency in discussion and its feasibility in experimental schools.
4. Make case studies of experimental schools to generate hypotheses regarding the problems and effects to be expected in implementing the curriculum in a wider range of schools.
5. Use this case study experience to design dissemination procedures which will attempt to meet the anticipated problems.
6. Monitor the effects in dissemination both by case study and by measurement.

In so far as the project had a general (as opposed to a teaching) aim, it was the embodiment of this view of curriculum research founded on substantive premises in the curricular field (see below). Interestingly enough, although this aim concerns itself with research and experiment, it has implications for reform and development.

The project team also attempted to formulate a statement of teaching aims which would summarise the insights of the team into the logic of the teaching. The formulation changed and developed. And the central team itself did not have a blanket consensus. The aim finally adopted for the *The Humanities Project: an Introduction* (1970) was: 'to develop an understanding of social situations and human acts and of the controversial value issues which they raise.' It was intended that this should imply an application of the perspectives of social science, history, the arts and religious thinking to the understanding of human issues. Such understanding should take account of the need to attempt objectivity on the one hand and to tap imaginative sympathy on the other. And it was believed that the crucial problem in handling human issues was controversiality.

The Project also stated five major premises:

1. that controversial issues should be handled in the classroom with adolescents;
2. that the teacher should accept the need to submit his teaching in controversial areas to the criterion of neutrality at this stage of education, i.e., that he should regard it as part of his responsibility not to promote his own view;
3. that the mode of inquiry in controversial areas should have discussion rather than instruction, as its core;
4. that the discussion should protect divergence of view among participants, rather than attempt to achieve consensus;
5. that the teacher as chairman of the discussion should have responsibility for quality and standards in learning.

(*The Humanities Project: An Introduction*, 1970, 1)

The overall task of the project was to discover a teaching strategy which would implement these premises in the classroom, to report this strategy and to support teachers who wished to develop it with training and, if necessary, with materials.

The experimental framework or design adopted by the project necessitated the involvement of teachers as experimental colleagues from whom the central team would be able to learn. The 32 experimental schools participating in 1968–69 and 1969–70 were seen as development schools rather than as trial schools, since, at that stage, the project's concern was with producing a prototype rather than with generalising or with statistical sampling.

In 1968 there were induction conferences for the experimental schools who were introduced to the project's aim and premises, informed of possible problems and chaired in discussions by central team members who had carefully considered the role of teacher as chairman. The central team thought that the inquiry into human issues would involve research on the part of pupils, written work, visits, improvised drama, art work, and so on. The inquiry would deal with controversial issues, would be undertaken by young adults approaching independence, would involve teacher neutrality and would necessitate the provision of materials. The experimental schools were asked to test and develop hypotheses about teaching method and to test, and perhaps to add to, the materials offered by the central team.

Experimental materials were provided by the project for the schools in 1968–70. Basing their approach on the notion of areas of inquiry (see Schools Council Working Paper 11 *Society and the young school leaver*), the project team had assembled packs of material on eight main themes – education, war and society, relationships between the sexes, the family, people and work, living in cities, poverty and law and order. These themes contained issues which would divide society, especially a pluralistic society, and were thus controversial. The themes were also adult in content and, in some respects, interrelating. From very large initial collections the editor of each pack pared down the collections in the light of the experimental schools' suggestions to about 250 items – printed, pictorial, and audio-taped. In each collection there was also a list of recommended films. These basic resource collections were eventually published by Heinemann Educational Books from 1970 onwards. The materials collected on a ninth theme, race relations, were not published at that time but formed the basis for a further continuing project. Each pack contains 20 copies of each item of so-called paper evidence, plus two teacher's kits containing a general handbook to the project, a handbook specific to the theme, a sound tape and a single copy of the students' printed items.

The most widely available piece of teacher's material produced by the project is, of course, *The Humanities Project: An Introduction*. In addition to exploring the project's aim and five major premises, it offers advice gleaned from the experimental schools on the materials, the nature of group discussion and the climate of groups. Furthermore, it identifies the responsibilities of the chairman by suggesting that he ought to:

1. set a context favourable to discussion;
2. encourage group identity and group loyalty;
3. foster in the group a commitment to the inquiry;
4. ensure a clear articulation of the subject under discussion;
5. keep under scrutiny the relevance of the contributions to the discussion;
6. protect divergence of view;
7. introduce appropriate evidence;
8. maintain continuity between discussions;
9. see that the rules of discussion which have been accepted are observed;
10. mediate critical standards which support work of quality in the group;
11. ensure that an inquiry is rounded off in a way which organises the understanding gained.

(20)

The handbook provides advice on how to get discussion going and also suggests reasons for which a chairman would introduce new materials or people:

1. to enable the discussion to progress along lines being developed by the group or to provide a new stimulus when discussion flags or goes round in circles;
2. to represent a view which the group has not considered or to document a minority viewpoint not adequately represented in the group;
3. to challenge consensus or complacency;
4. to sharpen the definition of a view by asking its proponents to face critical evidence;
5. to offer concepts which would clearly be helpful to the group.

(23)

Furthermore, the handbook lists the main types of useful contribution made by chairmen to the discussions:

1. asking questions or posing problems in relation to resources;
2. clarifying or asking a member to clarify what has been said as a basis for discussion;
3. summarising the main trends in the discussion;
4. keeping the discussion relevant and progressive;
5. helping the group to use and build on each other's ideas;
6. helping the group to raise and define issues for discussion and to decide on priorities;
7. by questioning, providing intellectual stimulus and encouraging self-criticism.

(25)

One very important result of the experience of the development schools is the 'Self-Training Procedure for Teachers' included in the handbook, with an important checklist of points to bear in mind when playing back and analysing tapes of discussions. The handbook also contains notes on activities other than discussion, assessment, notes for planners and annotated transcripts of audio-taped classroom discussions in extract.

The publishers of the materials, Heinemann Educational Books, seem to have worked in fair harmony with the central project team and were not, by testimony of the director, over-prescriptive about design. During the dissemination phase, however, many teachers were critical of the quality of the print in the students' materials and of the publishers' policy not to market individual items to replace losses.

Naturally enough, a project that was acutely aware of its procedures published many of its own documents informally and formally. Some of them are reports on individual experience, others are advice and recommendations to organisers, others again are the results of evaluation. An extended list is to be found at the end of this account, together with a bibliography of other writings about the project.

The evaluation unit of the Humanities Project differed distinctly in role from those of many other projects. In the first place, the evaluation of teaching materials was in this project taken to be part of the task of the development team. Secondly, the project offered the evaluator no behavioural objectives. It was expected that the greater part of the evaluator's work would be in case-studying schools and, indeed, the title under which Barry MacDonald was appointed was Schools' Study Officer. In a 'non-objectives' approach there was no ready-made niche for the evaluator and this posed problems to the unit. After several shifts of emphasis the evaluation team eventually defined its task thus:

1. To ascertain the effects of the project, document the circumstances in which they occur, and present this information in a form which will help educational decision-makers to evaluate the likely consequences of adopting the programme.
2. To describe the present situation and operations of the schools we study so that decision-makers can understand more fully what it is they are trying to change.
3. To describe the work of the project team in terms which will help the sponsors and planners of such ventures to weigh the value of this form of investment, and to

determine more precisely the framework of support, guidance and control which are appropriate.

4. To make a contribution to evaluation theory by articulating our problems clearly, recording our experience and, perhaps most importantly, by publishing our errors.

5. To contribute to the understanding of the problems of curriculum innovation generally.

(Stenhouse 1973, 165–66)

Barry MacDonald himself has said that 'when curriculum development is becoming increasingly the concern of a number of new and relatively in-experienced agencies, there is a need for those involved in the field to contribute what they can towards an understanding of the problems of change' (Stenhouse 1973, 166).

One of the problems for the evaluation team in this project was that identifying the task took such a long time that delivery of findings tended to be slow. It is arguable that earlier publication of some of the work could have had an important effect on some high-level decisions.

The Humanities Curriculum Project had a consultative committee that was both influential and bold in its decisions: it tended to ensure that discussion was thorough and subsequent support strong. Its members included representatives from the local education authority administration, the Schools Council, the University of London, HMI, the teaching profession and the central project team.

Dissemination had not been built into the project's experimental design but had begun to be considered by January 1969. In order to avoid anything as haphazard as 'diffusion' the team decided to organise dissemination through a network of understanding people who would act as points of reference in their areas of the country. Initial communication via open days was followed by training via central courses and later by support via local associations of teachers. The responsible task of leaving something by way of after-care placed immensely heavy staffing burdens on the central team who yet recognised the importance of what they were doing. Some eventual conclusions drawn from the experience of dissemination, as expressed by Jean Rudduck, who was responsible for organising this aspect of the project, are that 'innovation is difficult to accomplish, that there can be no effective curriculum development without teacher development and that dissemination, if it is to breed a continuing experimental attitude, must depend on education rather than on training' (Rudduck 1973).

The project caused considerable hostility. Critics in the main attacked the notion of neutrality often without understanding the reasons for its introduc-tion: i.e. the emphasis on student learning, the nature of divergent society, the dangers of indoctrination and of polarised discussion. Particularly affronted were inspirational teachers with wisdom to transmit and those generally opposed to change of any kind, especially in the traditional roles of student and teacher. Others, not understanding the project's definition of evidence as proof of the existence of a point of view, accused the collections of materials of many shortcomings, some of which had to do with 'truth'. It was also claimed that the materials were too difficult from the point of view of reading level.

To these few and the many other criticisms the project's main reaction was that of fostering public debate so that at least the issues could be better understood after full discussion, for example in the press. In the main, teachers and press have given credit to the team for this openness that insists that it is the project's job mainly to ensure that a fully informed discussion takes place. Pupils, be it noted, have for the most part approved of the project, albeit for widely differing reasons.

It is difficult to assess the present situation of the project. It may be that it is in the process of disappearing as such, but that it has given impetus in many areas to an investigation into learning theory and to teacher awareness. That may have been its main effect.

LAWRENCE STENHOUSE

The Humanities Curriculum Project: A Response

A brief account inevitably tidies, making the process of curriculum research and development sound less excitingly speculative, more efficient, than it is. The logical structure of the project unfolded, often in response to contingencies of action or challenges to theory.

The major achievement of the project was the exploration of the role of neutral chairman which embodies important strategies appropriate to all discovery and inquiry teaching. In this role the teacher maintains his position in authority but moderates his claim to being *an* authority by insisting that students do not rely on him as an arbiter of truth. This expresses a concern that schools should be about knowledge as understanding, not merely inert facts, and that pupils should not be asked to acquire competences without enhancing their powers. I believe that interest in this aspect of the project's work is at present increasing, and that it will endure.

The principle of neutral teaching is apparently subject to misunderstanding. The most common misunderstandings are these:

1. People tend to think that the teacher is being asked to represent himself to pupils as a neutral person whereas he is assuming the role of a neutral chairman because he is a committed person who wishes to make room for others to develop their commitment;
2. It is apparently assumed that the project made the elementary error of believing that a chairman could be perfectly neutral, whereas, of course, there are no perfect performances and neutral chairmanship represents a set of criteria for the judgement of teaching;
3. Teachers often neglect to explain and negotiate their role as neutral chairman with the students, whereas it is clear that they too should be in possession of the criteria.

The aspect of the project which most worries me now is the problem of reading levels. The project was attempting to produce the conditions which would induce students to struggle with reading matter of serious content – it was, as Aston hints, a throwback to the tradition of the nineteenth-century encyclopaedic reader and a protest against the devaluing of content in pursuit of motivation. We have evidence that teachers persistent in the face of initial discouragement can shift from the pattern 'we read, we understand, we discuss', to the alternative 'we read, we do not understand, that's why we discuss'; and that when they do so, the project yields marked improvement in reading performance. But it is difficult to persist in the face of discouragement. It would be ironic if the back-to-basics movement led to HCP! For back-to-basics is most often a call for a return to competence *without autonomy*.

I still believe that any pupil who cannot read the kinds of evidence provided in HCP by the time he leaves school is disadvantaged.

Note

1. A general introduction to this project in action appears on pages 7–12 of Schools' Council Working Paper 56, *Curriculum Innovation in Practice*.

10 Design and Craft Project

Basic information

Sponsor Schools Council.

Grant £73,710.

Location Leicester University; then Keele University.

Period of development
April 1967 – Start of feasibility study
April 1968 – Start of research
April 1971 – Start of two-year extension
A total of six years, 1967–73.

Director S. J. Eggleston, Professor of Education, Keele University; previously Senior Lecturer, Leicester University.

Project team Senior Research Fellows – A. R. Pemberton, D. Taberner
Field Officer (from 1971) – Louis Brough
Writer/Editor (from 1971) – Russell J. Hall

Trials In five areas (Cheshire, Hertfordshire, Leeds, Leicestershire and Wiltshire). Other areas added later, including Northern Ireland and BFES Germany.

Materials Published by Edward Arnold Ltd. from 1974. Further details are given in the bibliography.
Materials and Design: a fresh approach
Design for Today and filmstrips
Looking at Design and filmstrips
You are a Designer
Connections and Constructions
Education through Design and Craft
Design and Karting
Creative use of Concrete
Designing with Plastics
Design with a Purpose – a film available from National Audio-Visual Aids Library.
Education through the Use of Materials – Schools Council Working Paper 26, Evans/ Methuen Educational, 1969. The report of the feasibility study.

Preface

John Eggleston, Director of the Design and Craft Project, provides us with an immediate clue to the rationale behind the project in the title of his article, 'Focus on creativity – new perspectives on design education' (Eggleston, 1973a). He offers the reader reasons for the change from traditionally held views on this part of the curriculum. He believes the two critical factors are the movement away from the acquisition of knowledge towards open-ended discovery approaches and the new realisation that our environment, public and private, is a matter in which the host of individual decisions is the key determinant. Eggleston illustrates the latter point by indicating how ordinary men and women affect the environment by deciding how they shall lay out their gardens, decorate their houses, construct their sheds, park their caravans and use their money and leisure time.

The notion that industry requires workers with set skills is now outdated by the new technologies and the movement away from primary industries towards service industries. This provides a whole new range of tasks involving decision-making and other responsibilities, which make a particular set of hand skills inappropriate.

Alongside decision-making at work comes an increased opportunity for decision-making in leisure and at home, and thus we require an education that is related to the environmental context of a technological society and one which assists the individual to associate positively and actively to it.

This use of the word *design* in school reflects the wider social implications of much of the work, just as it seems to be an educational hope for social change. Bernard Aylward suggests that design is a form of control which can only be exercised by participation in the process (Aylward 1973).

Introduction

The Research and Development Project in Handicraft (to give it its original title) grew out of a series of meetings by craft teachers set up to discuss the contribution of workshop subjects to the education of young people growing up in the twentieth century. The rapidly changing social and industrial scene was beginning to make teachers of workshop subjects question the validity of their subject which, in many ways, looked backward rather than forward. The influence of William Morris, which was reflected in the Arts and Crafts Movement and had an approach and moral philosophy of the medieval craftsman, was still apparent in many schools, as was the residual effect of the Bauhaus Movement. In addition, recent developments in the field of applied science and technology, and the sponsorship of Project Technology by the Schools Council, emphasised the need for parallel innovation in the less technological area of craft studies, often referred to as design.

Such was the situation when the School Council decided to accept the proposals which were to form the basis of the feasibility study. The one year feasibility study which began in April 1967 terminated in a report (Schools Council 1969) which not only identified the contribution craft teachers were making, but whose title added a new cliché to educational verbiage – 'education through the use of materials'.

The feasibility study was concerned with: 'an examination of an approach to education in which pupils, using tools and materials, are enabled to explore the adult world (Schools Council 1969, 5); and whose roots lay 'in the desire of handicraft teachers to develop courses that will meet the changing needs of young people, particularly those who will be spending an extra year in full time education after the raising of the school leaving age' (School Council 1969, 7).

The report articulates the educational reasoning behind various types of craft activity and describes some of the more popular areas of work. It makes a considerable contribution towards helping teachers to relate theory to practice by providing a rationale and a list of educational objectives in an area of the curriculum with a dearth of educational literature.

The central task of investigating the feasibility of promoting research in workshop crafts, that could offer useful guide lines to teachers in the task of extending and reshaping their curricula to meet the challenge of the raising of the leaving age, was broken down into three main areas:

1. to identify and classify the educational objectives of handicraft teaching;
2. to survey the range of handicraft activities currently being undertaken in secondary schools in order to identify the most promising methods of attaining the educational objectives;
3. to examine possible methods of validating the effectiveness of the new and existing handicraft curriculum in attaining its educational objectives.

(Schools Council 1969, 8)

The strategy adopted hinged on the formation of five groups of teachers who would work with the project team during the feasibility phase. The groups represented different kinds of local education area and centred on Cheshire, Hertfordshire, the City of Leeds, Leicestershire and Wiltshire. The team relied very heavily on the good offices of advisers, HMIs and education officers for details of interesting, novel or successful work and for access to schools, although contributions were invited from other teachers. The areas of activity selected for possible development were chosen because, 'they seek to attain a wide range of educational objectives and offer scope for further development'. They were:

1. design – a problem solving experience focussing on such factors as function, materials, cost and aesthetic judgement. Other problems might be based on discrimination exercises;
2. design for living – based on the variety of factors which affect the quality of life in the home;
3. preparation for occupational role – for those motivated by their interest in particular occupational roles;

4. Community Service Projects – to promote unity between school and society at large;
5. school service projects – related to the immediate school environment;
6. recreational equipment projects – recognising the importance of education for leisure;
7. foundation courses – the essential prelude to many other activities.

(Schools Council 1969, 13)

The teachers' groups operating in the feasibility study began to recognise that the validation of their subject depended, to a large extent, on their ability to define the objectives they sought. Some of the objectives they proposed had been traditionally recognised, if only intuitively, whilst others were new to the changing situation. The dynamic nature of the process of change was acknowledged and the objectives thus sought were grouped into traditional, contemporary and anticipatory sections. For example, more traditional objectives concerned with the acquisition of motor skills and the appreciation of fine craftmanship, with their attendant satisfactions for children, were contrasted with others more appropriate to many of the alternative attractions of contemporary society. We see an attempt made to establish a link between the needs of the individual and the nature of a rapidly changing society.

Teachers' groups stressed the high priority which objectives concerned with the development of character, social awareness, creativity, logical thinking and aesthetic judgement should have. Workshop teachers, like others, believe they have something special to contribute in these fields. The complete classification of their curriculum objectives is as follows.

Classification of curriculum objectives (not in order of priority)

1. MOTIVATION TO ACHIEVE OBJECTIVES
   (a) Intrinsic, e.g. harnessing of natural curiosity; desire for achievement; creative drive.
   (b) Extrinsic, e.g. desire to please – or not to displease – parents, staff, pupils; long-term goals (necessary qualification, skill in order to make something).

2. PERSONALITY TRAITS AND ATTITUDES

E.g. span of concentration; ability to organize work; ability to study independently to a given date for completion; ability to postpone immediate satisfaction for future goal; inquiring mind; questioning attitude to given opinion/statement; moral values; tolerance and understanding of differences; expectance and adaptability to change; ability to work as member of a team; recognition of needs of others.

3. CREATIVE DEVELOPMENT

E.g. personal expression through manipulation of materials; ability to make judgements about design; ability to make and test original hypotheses; creative personal relationships; original and interpretative work through the use of tools and materials.

4. SKILL

(a) Communication (two-way) e.g. verbal/numerical; spoken/heard; printed-/written, visual image.
(b) Motor e.g. direct manipulation (without tools) of materials such as clay; manipulation of materials through use of hand tools (tools for which all power is provided by the operator); manipulation of materials through powered hand tools (tools driven by energy from a source external to operator but which are guided by the operator); manipulation of materials by machine tools.

5. LOGICAL PROCESSES/STRATEGIES

E.g. deductive/inductive processes; problem-solving techniques – involving a definite answer – involving a judgement.

6. KNOWLEDGE

(a) Information e.g. facts and linked series of facts.
(b) Principles and concepts
(N.B. Knowledge here implies understanding, not verbal knowledge of definitions).
E.g. understanding of principles and concepts related to technology and materials; understanding of the relevance of technological change in present-day society; understanding of the relevance of aesthetic judgement in present-day society.

Within this framework there will obviously be variations in emphasis according to age and ability. Nevertheless all the objectives outlined above should receive adequate consideration in the handicraft curriculum at some point during the child's school career.

During the discussions it became obvious that many craft teachers believed that the contribution which design and craft activities made to the wider areas of education was latent rather than manifest and, as such, defied the immediate process of evaluation. Teachers' reactions varied because some had urged a more systematic approach to assessment, no doubt as some confirmation of their beliefs, and as a basis for the future justification of their work. The problem of evaluation posed particular difficulties because of the nature of many of the objectives and the nature of the work. The time-span involved, the complexity of the pupil response in terms of the cognitive, the affective and the psycho-motor, and the dearth of easily used evaluatory instruments made many teachers unsure of their ground and others sceptical of an objective approach.

The project team

That the project should develop in the School of Education at Leicester University was due to a number of reasons, not least the 'foolhardy enthusiasm' of its Director, John Eggleston, a former craft teacher (Eggleston 1974). The Leicester Education Authority had encouraged much local curriculum development in craft and design activities and there were a number of enthusiasts ready to support further innovation. Professors Bantock and Tibble, of Leicester University, knowing something of the field, gave sympathetic support to the proposals and helped the movement to take shape.

Professor Bantock attended the first meeting of the project at the Schools Council and from then on became Chairman of the Advisory Committee which guided the project. In some ways the unlikely marriage between the project and Professor Bantock was to prove to be one of the strengths of the organisation: his close involvement throughout the life of the project and his connections with the university sector played an important part within the legitimisation process.

The acceptance of the project by teachers depended to a certain extent on their acknowledgement that whilst the team knew something of their particular subject field, at the same time it had the 'respectability', in academic terms, of the university. Thus John Eggleston's own background as a craft teacher turned university lecturer was an important factor in linking the two. The choice of two research fellows from the subject field, A. R. Pemberton and D. Taberner, provided an interesting triumvirate who were to guide the project to its completion. Within the division of labour it fell to the research fellows to interpret, analyse, record and assist the development of many design activities leaving the director to emphasise his own educational beliefs (sociologically flavoured) through to final statement.

Although Eggleston believed that the ideas on the project should come from the teachers, and in this he differs from some project leaders, he nevertheless emphasised those aspects of design courses which contributed to his ideological view of the relationship between education and society. It is interesting to try to imagine what emphasis, for example, a psychologist in similar circumstances would have placed on the acquisition of manual skills and the physiological benefits thus derived. The strategy adopted included discussions, recording and analysing the ideas of teachers in the belief that successful practitioners were the key to further developments. The request that the teachers groups should include a percentage of 'non-committed' teachers brought forth some interesting comments both inside and outside the meetings.

Eggleston was concerned about the individuals' participation within the decision-making of society and he believed that through the involvement of ordinary people, they could be educated for survival in a rapidly changing technological society. He had a desire to increase the status of craft and design subjects so that they expressed an acceptable non-verbal sensitivity at least equal to that achieved in the more traditional 'intellectual' areas. The

Crowther principle of the 'alternative route' (Ministry of Education 1959) became important as the team sought to provide experience with materials as a basic (and necessary) ingredient in the education of all pupils.

One interesting difference in this project concerns the status of the director, who was never formally appointed to a paid position. His was an honorary appointment based on an agreement with the University that he would devote what time he had, after his lecturing duties, to the direction of the project. Such a situation poses some interesting questions about accountability and freedom. For example, being without contract might imply unlimited freedom, but in practice, the need to succeed was even greater and perhaps this restricted the amount of 'kite-flying' which one might have expected.

The appointment of the director to a chair of education at Keele University gave the project a new start within the programme of work being conducted in preparation for the raising of the school leaving age. The title of 'Handicraft' became inadequate to describe the multiplicity of activities involved and mounting pressure from teachers resulted in a change to the Research and Development Project in Design and Craft Education.

The team were supported by a number of local authority co-ordinators who established day-to-day communications between the team and the schools, both during the trials and at the dissemination stages. The Advisory Committee (Schools Council 1975, Appendix 1) became the policy-making body, although in effect the team had to take a strong individual line to achieve the many publication and other deadlines.

On reflection, the team proved to be too small and insufficient for the ambitious programme undertaken and they required much more specialised assistance and advice at national level. Shortage of servicing personnel, expert advice and backing from the Schools Council meant that the team was overstretched on many occasions, resulting in insufficient time being available for observation of the effects of their efforts. After a relatively quiet start the movement quickly gathered momentum and with the best intentions the team lost some contact with schools, activities and co-ordinators.

The team worked particularly hard, and successfully, on the diffusion programme, training LEA representatives to carry on with the follow-up work. This stage of the project was recognised by teachers as providing an effective in-service support although not all authorities were able to second sufficient people to make the desired impact.

This discussion has tried to concentrate the attention of the reader on to the team because, in practice, they play a major part in the acceptability of the research and development project in the eyes of teachers. In this particular subject area, which has traditionally suffered from being regarded as 'vo-cational' and 'practical' – at one time even being referred to as 'the badge of pauperism' (Board of Education 1913) – the team had a considerable task to perform. To compromise the beliefs of craftsmen and educators, to introduce an integrated programme with its inevitable political difficulties in schools, to achieve the amount of published material thought necessary and to cope with the many practical difficulties with such a small team is an indication of the magnitude of the project and the importance of the mark that they have made.

Design and craft project

When the project proper became part of the programme of work in preparation for the raising of the school leaving age, the focus was to be on the work of average and below average pupils. This initial objective was extended to cover the whole ability range because of the need to upgrade, rather than downgrade the notion of designing in the eyes of many educationists and to accommodate Eggleston's personal views of social equality.

The heart of the project's work was to be the development of problem-solving approaches, suitable for use in the secondary schools. In his article 'Focus on Creativity' Eggleston speaks of providing 'opportunities for greater decision-making in leisure and the home' (Eggleston 1973). Alan Pemberton, Senior Research Fellow, emphasises the intellectual nature of the process when he argues that participation at this active level requires more than emotional response; it needs: 'a skill to identify and understand problems, to sift information and present reasoned argument' (Pemberton 1973).

This involvement in problem solving whether it be in the home, at work, in the community or at leisure was the factor which has clearly influenced the organisation and scope of the project and its published material. Problem-solving in this context is commented on by Pemberton: 'in some situations they [the pupils] will act as designer or producer; in others as consumer or user. In all they will require the ability to obtain and analyse information and make assessments' (Pemberton 1973).

The introduction of design process as a structure to aid the solving of problems is central to the developmental work. Studies have shown the relevance of problem-solving and self-expressive approaches (by students and teachers) to a broad band of curricular activity. The design process is a valuable tool which provides a framework for action within which the various aspects of a problem can be considered in a logical sequence. Within the tools and materials field designing offers many opportunities for solving problems and to this end five areas were selected for special treatment. They offered opportunities for students to participate actively, through their own decisions and practical activities 'to the development of their own social, industrial and material environment' (Schools Council 1969), not only in school but outside in the wider community. The areas selected were:

1. *Materials and design* – in which pupils gain experience of the basic design process. In addition to the skills and techniques normally associated with practical work, the pupil is offered opportunities for discovery, expression and problem solving.

2. *Materials and Domestic Life* – concerned with the use, maintenance and development of the home as it affects the individual's quality of life.
3. *Materials and Community Development* – concerned with the specific needs of others.
4. *Materials and Leisure* – concerned with the stimulation of activities that will contribute to the profitable use of leisure.
5. *Materials and work* – attempts to introduce pupils to the world of work.

Much of the project was concerned with analysing, recording and developing case studies and the published materials provide evidence of strategies adopted in different areas of successful practice. The multi-disciplinary approach to problems has been encouraged as one of the important areas for development. Together with a desirable integration of disciplines, there is also the belief that such problem situations can be offered to suit the variety of interests of pupils. The approach can be applied to the basic design activities, just as it can be used in the solution to complex problems in which material, ergonomic, social and other factors interact. Thus individual learning programmes can be tailored to suit the 'age, ability and aptitude' of the pupil.

In line with current anxiety about the contribution education can make to our economic wealth and in recognition of the motivational significance of such studies, the project attempts to introduce the manufacturing process into the context of general education. Pemberton comments: 'Clearly work simulation is a vehicle of general education and cannot be considered as vocational or pre-apprenticeship training. However, a useful bonus may be in outcomes that enable students to assess their likely career prospects.' (Pemberton 1973).

Clearly, links with further education, activities based on leisure pursuits, community projects and work simulation can provide pupils with easily recognisable short-term objectives with their attendant interests and motivations. The relevance of such activities to all pupils is clear, though the distribution of them to certain groups of under-achievers in schools tends, unfortunately, to underline the vocational aspects. The project has endeavoured to promote 'expressionistic' activities and those in which aesthetic judgements need to be made and Eggleston quotes the host of opportunities which exist for their development. (Eggleston 1971).

Differences of opinion have arisen in those areas in which the visual element is important, and art teachers especially have been highly critical of the end-products. A difficulty does arise here because it is so easy to equate the end-product with a similar artifact which may be bought in the shops and the reasons for its design and making are often ignored. Nevertheless, this problem of balancing expression and productional skills is a real one and one which will tax educators for a long time yet. The benefits of the 'journey' need be assessed alongside the other achievements and it is too easy to fall into the trap of assessing only the end-product. It would be dangerous also to ignore the short-term pupil objectives in the teachers' quest for higher order aims.

The great variety of possible design problems poses considerable organi-

sational and administrative difficulty for many teachers who often find themselves in unfamiliar surroundings. The assurance of Bruner is not always
sufficient to support the hard pressed teacher: 'When the teacher becomes a
learner then his teaching takes on a new quality.' (Bruner 1963).

Providing the teachers' managerial skills are cultivated the dynamic nature
of the process can be exciting and rewarding – but in reality not all see it this
way.

The publishing stage was of obvious importance, but it posed many problems
for the team. Having produced draft material, they despatched this to the
Schools Council for them to find a suitable publisher and, presumably, to agree
a contract acceptable to them. When the publisher had been chosen, the team
were left to finalise the details of the packages and materials without the
professional advice they required in terms of graphical and presentational skills.
The understandable urgency on the part of the publisher to meet the constraints of the market to a large extent presented the team with a *fait accompli*
and consequently materials not entirely to their liking.

In retrospect the Schools Council might have produced a number of other
central services which could have given real support to the team in their
negotiation with outside agencies like LEAs, trial schools and others at the
dissemination stage. Important time savings and increased efficiency might
have been achieved, thus leaving the director and his colleagues more time for
other (perhaps more suitable) tasks.

The initial idea of communicating results of discussions and case studies was
good but the manner of the presentation, especially for a design project, was less
than ideal. It is probably true in education, as elsewhere, that if the quality of
the material has a hint of amateurism about, it it may deliver its own 'kiss of
death'.

That a project endeavouring to support the development of non-verbal
sensitivity should have generated a large number of words is indicative of the
difficulty in the dissemination of ideas. Eggleston nevertheless can be assured
that the arguments and case studies will remain for teachers to study even
though the real message for all is in participation.

Final comment

The project's emphasis on problems of an inter-disciplinary nature, though
based on school workshops for the most part, presented schools with a number of
difficulties. Inevitable 'political' differences arose when departmental co-
operation was proposed resulting in some 'go it alone' tactics. This tended to
take away the integrated nature of the learning and programmes became
dependent on a single teacher from one subject area.

In some situations the lack of organisational skill resulted in stereotyped work
and the real benefits of 'individualised learning' became lost. Often the
simplicity (or assumed simplicity) of an end product would lead teachers into

instant designing situations and thus the solutions became copies of other, and often inadequate, answers to the problem. Highlighting successful practice can be a double-edged sword, though providing the teacher regards it as an example of an interesting, perhaps unique, approach, there is much to be learned. Unfortunately the products of many schools became so alike that the situation was reminiscent of the days of the Millbank Scheme (Dodd 1974). This criticism applies especially to the 'design and make' section where a 'Keele style' became very evident. The chess sets, condiment sets and collages vied with the hovercraft to become the updated version of the infamous toothbrush rack. In some early programmes of work the key words of expression, freedom and exploration led many into difficulty and some courses foundered because of lack of direction and purpose. The situation was reminiscent of that referred to in a report published in 1922. 'Even if a lad is satisfied with his efforts, that is no gauge of the educational value of such efforts, for the crudest possible work – work absolutely devoid of beauty and a mass of technical solecism – frequently satisfies the youthful "designer"' (National Scheme for Handwork Committee 1922).

Following these early mistakes, observation indicates a tighter control and a more highly structured approach, with perhaps more attention paid to problems with a greater functional element. This slight shift of emphasis has resulted in work of a higher technical standard though there is still evidence of supposedly expressive work of a shoddy nature. Criticism is also levelled at craft teachers because of the standard of design achieved as they endeavour to strike a balance between expression and skill.

The confusion which surrounds 'means' and 'ends' indicates some of the difficulties of evaluation. One of the important activities of the project was to establish a CSE examination to illustrate the compatability of designing and assessment and Denis Taberner, Senior Research Fellow, moved to the North West Secondary Schools' Examination Board to continue work in this field. Such research as the assessment of special studies, multi-certification and group certification is likely to prove invaluable in determining the essential features of the learning and the role of the teacher within it.

It is generally easier to support the status quo and the introduction of designing has required different kinds of organisational skill. Some teachers have been stimulated by materials produced but others have been swamped by it. Dr. Briault, Education Officer of the Inner London Education Authority, spoke recently of the threat to innovation being the extreme conservatism of teachers and this seems to be the case in many school workshops. Nevertheless, there is evidence to indicate a trend towards much more individualised learning and the provision of opportunities for pupil participation.

The real effects may still be to come in the slow change of teacher attitude towards innovation and particularly to activities in this field. The introduction of the design process as a methodology for tackling problems of an open-ended nature may also bring increased educational rewards. Some of the possible gains have been nullified by practical constraints to do with economic factors, teacher shortage and college re-organisation.

Amongst the findings of the project is the confirmation that practical subjects have a relevance to the education of all pupils:

> One of the most striking impressions of our feasibility study has been the potential contribution of the workshops to the education of the most able pupils as well as the education of the average pupils. It is inevitable, therefore, that the study will make a contribution to the education of pupils of all abilities throughout the secondary age range.   (Schools Council 1969, 21)

The theoretical underpinning which the published material offers craft teachers may be seen to have been of vital importance in their increased professionalism. The evidence of integrated schemes and successful co-operation is not likely to lead to wholesale inter-disciplinary work across the curriculum. A likely outcome may be the increased realisation of the possibilities which exist for integrated schemes and the desirability of links with agencies outside the subject boundaries. The impact has clearly been felt and, as a result, many more teachers are questioning the nature of their approach, particularly in those areas which extend outside the bounds of the school. Community service is not new but it may be said that the Design and Craft Project gave considerable impetus to its development. The logical form of the design process has meant that teachers can now offer an approach which can be applied to many different kinds of problems and thus they are not confined to the well trodden path of many traditional woodwork and metalwork activities.

Taken in tandem with Project Technology, this project has supplied another part of the development of 'working with materials' thus ensuring a much more rounded approach to learning with tools and materials. The clear message is that designing is not the emotional response to a problem but is a logical planning approach in which intellectual ability is a vital factor. If that message has been received with any degree of clarity then the £70,000 has been well spent.

Shortly after the conclusion of the project the DES funded a research project based on the Royal College of Art to investigate 'Design in General Education'. This is one of the more tangible effects of the Keele exercise but there are others which, in the end, may prove to be of the greater value. 'Trail blazing' is perhaps too strong a phrase for an exercise involving a research and development project but it may be said to be 'path finding' of a high order in a particularly difficult area.

JOHN EGGLESTON

Design and Craft Project: A Response

Tom Dodd's account of our objectives is accurate, his description of our difficulties sensitive, and his view of our achievements is just. Innovative work in design and craft is fraught with difficulties, particularly in a project such as ours, where both making initiatives and their realisation is undertaken by individual teachers with diverse ideologies and backgrounds. Some teachers responded enthusiastically but simply created a new orthodoxy to replace the old. Others worked with a disconcerting crudity. The structure and internal politics of some schools led to major impediments. We deliberately sought to retain such teachers and schools rather than to abandon them, taking the view that a project that only works in optimum conditions is unlikely to be relevant to the conditions of the majority of schools and teachers. We are convinced that this decision, though contrary to some of the advice we were given, was the right one. The patient work of teachers, advisers, heads and the members of the project team during and since the project have overcome many of the problems dramatically; barren areas have blossomed.

And it is important to emphasise that the problems affected only a small minority of schools; the imaginative, creative work that has developed in very many schools is, as Dodd emphasises, a better guide to the achievements of the project. I have reviewed these results in a recent book where I have considered the whole developing field of design education (Eggleston 1976).

Even during the life of the project, it was realised that the real results would be long term rather than short, and that a continuing dialogue by teachers would be essential. So a magazine, *Studies in Design Education and Craft*, was set up, independent of project funds. Now well established as an independent publication, each issue contains accounts by teachers of their innovations and developments in design education as well as discussion of objectives, evaluation and much else. The quality of the contents is perhaps the best indication of what is now being achieved in the schools.

Design education now has its own identity, an impressive degree of recognition from other subject specialists, its own professional organisation, its own journals and books and is achieving in many schools a range and quality of work that strikingly transcends that of the previous decade. Above all it has its own momentum. Perhaps the best evaluation of the Keele Project is to recognise the extent of the contribution that it has made to this transformation.

11 Geography for the Young School Leaver

Basic information

Sponsor   Schools Council.

Grant   £127,300. This includes all additional funds made available to the project up to the time of writing and £600 from Northern Ireland for the period 1976–79 for support and dissemination.

Location   Avery Hill College of Education, 1970–76.

Designated pupils   14–16 average and below average ability pupils (originally).

Period of funding   Development phase 1970–74. For dissemination and support from 1974 to 1976 and on a reduced level 1976–79.

Project team   1970–74 Rex Beddis and Tom Dalton – co-directors (each $\frac{1}{2}$ time). 1974–79 Pamela Bowen and Trevor Higginbottom research officers. Trevor Higginbottom was funded for a further two years full-time to act as national co-ordinator for the project. He is now an adviser with the Sheffield Metropolitan District Education Authority and continues to act as national co-ordinator.

   Co-ordinators to support the schools in their locality were appointed during the project trials. 12 regional co-ordinators were appointed at the dissemination stage in 1974 and they continue to operate. LEAs were invited to appoint local co-ordinators. Regional co-ordinators receive expenses and honoraria for their services.

Trials   Pre-trials work was carried out in a small number of schools in the south east London area. Testing of the first pack of materials began in 1971 in 23 schools clustered in five areas of England and Wales. 22 'associate' schools were also involved.

Materials   Three published themes: *Man, Land and Leisure; Cities and People; People, Place and Work.*

   Each published theme contains a teachers' guide; 30 copies of numerous resource sheets for pupils; other audio-visual material. Published by Thomas Nelson & Sons Ltd. from 1974.

   Teachers Talking: a magazine about GYSL. The first two issues were produced by the project. Since 1976 it has been published biannually by Nelson, still edited by the project team and containing mostly articles by teachers on the use and development of GYSL.

Introduction

Geography for the Young School Leaver Project has arguably achieved a success unrivalled by any other Schools Council project, and that at a time of financial stringency, when the education system has supposedly wearied of innovation and when the Schools Council sorely needs to display its merit marks. The project has attained a considerable penetration of the market, the classroom resources and teachers' guides have been favourably reviewed by teachers, educationists and geographers and almost every local education authority has established a GYSL teachers' group, appointed a co-ordinator and in most cases provided financial assistance. This 'success' resulted from an ambitious interpretation of the brief which was 'to examine successful work being undertaken with pupils in the 14–16 age range; to define the contribution that geography might make to these pupils, particularly those of below average ability, whether taught as a separate subject or as part of an interdisciplinary course; and to investigate the ideas that might be understood, the skills that might be developed and the values and attitudes that might be considered'.

Origins and early plans

In this decade two other projects in geography have been funded by the Schools Council; Geography 14–18 and Geography 16–19. They are both exclusively for secondary pupils and one is for the more able pupils of the same age range as GYSL. Developments in the subject at university and research levels, particularly in human and applied geography, can be seen as creating an advantageous climate for proposals for the reform of school geography.

The project team referred in meetings to the publications of Chorley and Haggett (1965) and to the Madingley lectures[1] which endeavoured to communicate the innovations in geography to teachers. There was also the American High School Geography project to look to as an example of the sponsorship of 'new geography' at school level. Chorley and Haggett wrote, 'The thread linking research, university teaching and school teaching, a thread already pulled taut, should not be allowed to part' (1965). To this warning GYSL responded by representing at school level the areas of concern, the concepts, the techniques of model building and quantification, etc. which would reflect the advances made in geography in the preceding two decades.

This being the intellectual rationale behind the three upper secondary geography projects, it might also be worth considering pressure from organised geographers. The Geographical Association and the Royal Geographical Society help to confer identity on teachers of geography and the latter organisation, particularly in the 1950s, was vociferously defending the subject against encroachments by social studies and environmental studies (Williams 1976). At one GYSL conference in 1975, the comment was made that 'Geography has never been in a stronger position, no question of it fading away ... Environmental studies and humanities will not shake geography'. The team, however, did not expressly support a single subject approach.

Geography for the Young School Leaver was one of the last of the RSLA projects but its only concession to the Newsom thinking of the 1960s was in its resources and suggested classroom procedures which were selected with the average and less able in mind. In view of the changes in thinking in the early 1970s the team considered it would be 'terribly out of step' to propose a curriculum for the average and less able with the implication that a different fare was appropriate for the more able. A common course was advocated, despite the existence of another geography project aimed at the more able:

> common schools imply equal opportunity and equal access to knowledge. While technique and methodology may vary with different ability groups, it should be possible to identify aims and content applicable to the whole age range. (Introduction to *Teachers' Guide*).

The team members themselves at dissemination meetings would apologise for the 'mid-sixties RSLA title' and the publisher's advertising booklets would bear the titles and logos of the three themes on the cover rather than the project name. The team emphasised that it was not 'geography for yobos' and even attempted through the Schools Council to change the title in 1976 to escape the restrictions it implied and also to make it more feasible as a submission for an alternative O-level course.

The Schools Council's growing concern with dissemination is also an important background feature. The Schools Council Working Party on dissemination and in-service training belatedly rejected the prosaic notion of diffusion which characterised much earlier research development and diffusion work and recommended a greater attention to positive promotion and after-care. Thinking about dissemination occurred early in the project's development (though the word was 'diffusion' in pre-1973 documents) and undoubtedly this, the perceived merit of the team's productivity and the funder's concern with dissemination had something to do with the granting of no less than four extensions of varying generosity, partially or wholly for dissemination.

Thus developments in academic geography, geographers' organisations, comprehensivisation and RSLA (and the changing emphases in policy and debate within these), together with Schools Council's deeper contemplation of strategies of curriculum development (possibly prompted by a consideration for its own survival) had implications for the destiny of the project. Taken together with the widely attested dissatisfaction of geography teachers with conventional geography courses, there were favourable signs beneath which the project worked.

The development work of the project

The production of classroom materials was from the outset accepted as a prime task of the project; a need for materials especially for the least able was made plain by early committee meetings, by a brief survey and by early piloting experiences in five local schools. The 'situational analysis' survey also confirmed that interdisciplinary courses for the less able were widespread, a fact which they recognised in their *Teachers' Guides* with suggestions for interdisciplinary work.

The three themes to be developed – leisure, urbanisation and work – were confirmed very early after a consideration of many other possibilities. A consideration of objectives in geography teaching in general and with regard to the three themes in particular was pursued throughout the project and the objectives model of curriculum development was to be one hallmark of the project's 'philosophy'. Problems of later 'diffusion' also occupied the team from the beginning. It was with these in mind that the 23 main trial schools were in five clusters in England and Wales so that teachers from different schools could meet and discuss the project and serve as nuclei for later 'diffusion'. Each school was visited where possible at least once a term, usually by two project team members, who would also meet termly for one whole day with the trial teachers in one region. A co-ordinator, usually an adviser or college lecturer, was appointed for each cluster to offer more locally based expert support to the teachers. This experience at the trial stage led to 'collaboration' being another hallmark of the project.

A further 22 schools were involved as associate schools in testing the project material. These received much less support from the project. The idea was that this increased number would widen the spectrum of participating schools and enable a better grasp of likely problems at the dissemination stage. The associate schools also did not have the benefits of a co-ordinator and inter-school collaboration, and this provided interesting comparative information.

The team sees the production of materials as just one facet of the policy for dissemination and implementation, and they reject any charge that GYSL is simply about materials. The three-fold strategy consists of:

1. The publication of resources and guides which are to serve as a short-term support for teachers, but more importantly as 'a catalyst in the continuing debate concerning the contribution of geography to the curriculum'.
2. The setting up of the local curriculum groups which will prepare local resources, alternative case studies and further curriculum units, serve as a forum for discussion and exchange of ideas and 'act as an advisory team to assist other teachers in the local authority willing to develop the project's style of work'.
3. Collaboration with external examination boards so that teachers wishing to incorporate the project's work into an examination course may more easily do so.

Thus the changes the project hopes to provoke in the teaching of geography (and not just to the specified age/ability group) are to be seen in relation to the institutional arrangements it hopes to establish for the reception and development of the project in local authorities and schools.

The choice of themes was influenced by four main principles:

1. The work should be concerned with all aspects of pupil development — understanding ideas, acquiring facts, developing skills, engaging attitudes, etc.
2. The themes should be of interest and relevance to the pupils now, but should also be of more than transitory significance.
3. There should be a structure of ideas which focus attention on the concepts of the discipline. These ideas may be initiated by a consideration of the local environment and community. By linkage and analogy these could be extended to more distant parts of Britain and the world.
4. The methods used should encourage full pupil involvement and participation.

Within the themes, the 'new geography', especially social geography, is very much to the fore, involving analysis of spatial patterns and decision-making in the environment. Through case studies the aim is to show that conservation, immigration, location of factories or shops conform to certain patterns. Pupils are intended to grasp the universality of these patterns, in contrast to traditional geography which remained very much in the descriptive mode, dealing with unique instances. The process of spatial development is studied by reference to social factors and decision-making; geographical determinism plays a far smaller part in the consideration of such issues as play space, high rise flats, holidays and journeys to work.

There is an emphasis on precision, not just through quantification and the use of graphs and statistics, but also in the definition of concepts, and there are also elements of prediction on the basis of knowledge built up of the variety of factors and the models which may be developed.

The moral issues which arise in considering such issues are regarded as indispensable to the subject area. The project strongly advocates work in the sphere of values and attitudes, but not as a means to inculcate middle-class standards; conflict in land use, the differing qualities of housing areas and pollution are issues inextricably bound up with moral judgement. As one team member put it: 'The hope is that judgements will be made, as far as possible, on the basis of evidence and that pupils will realise that differences of opinion and attitude will exist and demand some form of choice, give and take and compromise.'

In dealing with the topics and issues, particularly where value questions are raised, and to do justice to the principle of relevance, the value of drawing on other disciplines and subject specialists is recognised, and the project team have been in no way averse to the use of the project within an interdisciplinary context.

In terms of styles of learning, the project encourages a move away from the 'didactic' method to one which 'involves' pupils more; individual and group work, discussion, field work, role play, games and simulations are examples of the 'activity' methods that are suggested in some detail for pupils. The emphasis is on guided discovery approaches with great variety, well structured by the teacher. The team stress that these activities should 'enable the pupil, whatever his ability or level of motivation, to test evidence, to interpret, to use his own judgement ...' There is a requirement here, it would seem, for different attitudes on the parts of both teacher and pupils, and consequent changes in teacher-pupil relationships.

In both suggesting styles of learning and in the development of resources, a major consideration has been the problem for the teacher of the ability and attitude of the less able adolescent. Whilst choice of teaching techniques and resources is made with regard to the achievement of specified learning objectives, the aim is also that they should be interesting and engage the pupils; the resources are bright and colourful with modern layout to make an impact on pupils and thereby help to overcome the problems of low motivation in so many of these pupils. The resources, the team emphasises consistently, are exemplars, serving to show how the geography curriculum might be developed. The bounteous supply of resource sheets together with other audio-visual material is intended to be used flexibly, adapted and supplemented and eventually replaced as curriculum development within the schools and local groups moves on.

The illustrative content, the case studies and the resources are examples and the first task upon which most local groups have been engaged is the production of parallel studies of a local national park, urban area, etc. This local material still exemplifies the key ideas in the project but being closer to the experiences of the children and offering possibilities of field visits, it introduces a more marked reality and relevance which will serve to motivate pupils.

The resources in the published packs and many parallel resource units developed subsequently by teachers, are seen as a medium of stimuli and data, a basis for developing the techniques, understanding the concepts and addressing the complexities of the issues. This contrasts with the view of conventional text book resources which have tended towards descriptive information to be learnt.

Assessment, according to the team's view, is to function not merely to grade pupils but also to evaluate the success of the teaching provided. Tests are to be of comprehension and application, not mainly of recall as most school geography testing has been.

If the foregoing can be seen as the 'cart' of GYSL then the horse is the curriculum development model which provides the power and rationale for the whole vehicle. Drawing on Bloom and Krathwohl (1956 and 1964), Taba (1962) and Kerr (1968), the team employed what would be called a 'rational curriculum development model'.

This model, also intended as a basis for teachers continuing the development work of the project, starts with objectives which are derived from a consideration of

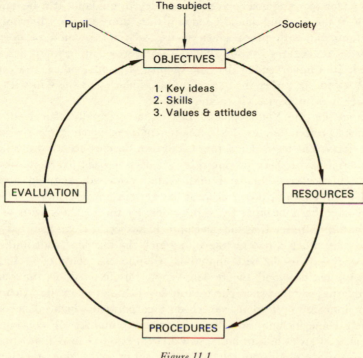

Figure 11.1

1. the pupil – and what topics are of immediacy and relevance to him;
2. the subject – the conceptual revolution in geography, its techniques, and the developments in human and applied areas;
3. society – issues of the time, the forces at work and the changes taking place.

The objectives are framed in terms of discovering important ideas, mastering relevant skills and developing attitudes.

Having established the 'why' of teaching through specifying objectives, the task of resource development follows. The areas of study and the style of presentation are chosen with the aim to engage pupils and exemplify the key ideas. The design of procedures, how best to use the resources is the next step. Variety is the keynote, and pupil-centred approaches predominate. Assessment is the final step and in the cycle of curriculum development gauging pupils' levels of attainment is secondary to evaluating the teacher's success. The objectives specify key ideas and skills, and evaluation, by whatever means – formal tests, question and answer episodes, analysis of pupil work – is intended to produce information about how appropriate the lessons or units of instruction are and how effectively they have been taught. By this measure of the extent to which learning goals have been achieved, guidance can be gained as to how (or if) the teaching should be modified in future practice. By comparing *teacher* attainment with pre-specified goals, need for revision of objectives, resources, or procedures (or for that matter assessment techniques) can be considered. It is not intended that the quality of pupils' values and attitudes should be tested but rather their selection of evidence and the skill with which they master it to support a viewpoint.

Geography for the Young School Leaver, as originally conceived, was a development project, but as this development took place it clearly inclined towards reform. The team claims that GYSL is a 'teacher-based' project. Much of the material having been produced by teachers, it was tried in classrooms in the trial schools across England and Wales, criticised, adapted and even subjected to an editorial board of local teachers in South London. The team claims to have been inspired by and guided by the teachers with which it worked, but one can see that the development project it clearly started out as, developed very much a reform stance in which the teachers' contribution was almost exclusively to do with materials. Despite the continuous and close contact with teachers and the responsiveness this fostered, in the relatively unfettered situations that such curriculum development teams find themselves, significant innovatory elements have been incorporated which go beyond the basic brief. These include radically new content, emphasis on concepts, core curriculum, new styles of learning, a new style of resource provision, a new role for assessment, emphasis on relevance, topicality and value questions, the interdisciplinary potential, the objectives based curriculum development model. Though logically cohering in the development phase of the project, the question is whether this unity comes through to teachers, whether it is *in total* acceptable and feasible for teachers and whether they might not select from it those aspects which best suit their needs – in particular the attractive, motivating resources.

The curriculum development model, the kernel of the project's development 'philosophy', receives great emphasis in dissemination meetings as the team wishes to avoid the situation where teachers' views of the project are dominated by resources. The team expresses the wish that there were some self-destruct mechanisms in the resources so that they would act only briefly as a support for innovating teachers, introducing them to a style of curriculum development, and would motivate local groups to sustain the development of the geography curriculum through collaborative effort. The team even distances itself from its material products by referring to them as 'the Nelson version'.

Dissemination

Diffusion/dissemination had occupied the thoughts of the project team from its earliest days. A large number of meetings were addressed in 1972 and in the 1973–74 academic year dissemination was in full swing. The team has seen its task as 'changing a system' and recognised that curriculum development in their terms is a long process with many constraints. With this in mind, the project addressed the system at a number of levels. Through the Schools Council curriculum officer for the project, a discussion paper was sent to every LEA in England and Wales outlining the role that they might play in the implementation of the project in their area – the appointment of a co-ordinator, possibly with some free time from lecturing/teaching duties, and support for teachers wishing to adopt the project. Three conferences for LEA representatives were held early in 1973 to explain the project and delineate the strategies LEAs might use to support teachers wishing to become involved with GYSL. Thus a solid approach was made to the management levels within LEAs before teachers were exposed to the project. Before the main phase of the project finished in August 1974, eleven regional three to five day conferences for teachers were held, to which representatives from all CSE boards were invited. The *Man, Land and Leisure* resources were available by May 1974, *Cities and People* by October and *People, Places and Work* by May 1975, so that teachers contemplating embarking on a two-year course for their average and below average pupils in September 1974 would be able to base it on GYSL. Few projects were fortunate enough to have such a short time period between the termination of their main dissemination efforts and the point of implementation.

The regional courses were intensive and had the varied format of lectures by team members, trial-school teachers, college lecturers and examiners, discussion groups and workshop sessions.

The lectures, though stressing the academic content of the project and the 'philosophy', evinced significantly a 'project-for-the-people' character with references to '4D on a Friday afternoon' and the 'wet wellies on a Monday morning' realities of innovation at the 'chalk face' of curriculum development. The enthusiasm of most teachers at the conferences was considerable and, as usual, a representative from the publishers was present to deal with queries on the commercial side.

As a project with a long-term developmental view of curriculum change, with involvement on the part of large numbers of teachers teaching and learning through the published materials as the springboard to continuing development, the evangelistic campaign with an emphasis on sales is inescapable. So too is a certain ambivalence in the project message so that its appeal should be to *every* geography teacher; despite an extensive array of innovatory facets, the message is softened at points by references to how the emphasis in geography should be 'slightly different', that for the teacher who is a little worried about the swing away from what he knows 'here, there's an opportunity for some good solid regional geography'. Thus at times the radical nature of the project was underplayed to make it easier for teachers to engage in it. Teachers representing the project at dissemination conferences also provided, and were asked for, information about its success with the less able and less motivated pupils and such information was very positive in its support. There was, at times, from such teachers an importance attached to the published resources which did not correspond to the team's position: 'we [teachers] must guard these [resources] with our lives'.

Further dissemination and support

From September 1974 further funding was received for one year, and later for a second year to enable a member of the project team to continue as national co-ordinator of the project. This is a role Trevor Higginbottom continues to play on a limited part-time basis for the period 1976–79, yet further funds having been successfully requested from the Schools Council.

Further dissemination and consolidation conferences were held, though on a more local basis, in 1974–76 and the local groups were set up in greater numbers. The local, regional and national network of co-ordinators was established with termly meetings of local co-ordinators within their regions, and separately of regional co-ordinators, permitting considerable exchange of examination syllabuses, test items, resources and experiences.

In the conferences during this period, when many schools and local groups were already actively working with the project, points of emphasis by the project change. With common examinations at 16+ being widely debated and feasibility studies in some areas under way, the 'common core' potential of the project was greatly emphasised. In addressing one meeting the national co-ordinator said that the only word he would agree with in the project's title was 'for'. Not only was this a claim for the project's applicability to a wider age and ability group – 'The project could be used as a basis for remedial or Oxbridge pupils' – but to a wider curriculum area also. One project team member claims there are no skills which are specifically geographical and further that the project, and geography in general, should aim to 'give insights' and 'youngsters should be concerned with political decision making in the local area', which is opening the way still further for an integrated approach to the humanities curriculum.

As Stenhouse puts it, the products of a curriculum development project are 'educational proposals' (Stenhouse 1975). Certainly to make it a classroom reality GYSL was more widely communicated over a longer period with greater energy than other projects have found it possible to do. The strength and extent of the co-ordination network has no doubt contributed much both to spreading the word and to supporting and urging forward those already involved. The deliberations at the regional co-ordinators' meetings offer interesting insights into the strategies thought necessary by the project to effect change and the nature of the system within which they see themselves working. Dissemination for GYSL became not simply a matter of uniformly extending a message far and wide, but developed to a stage where problems in particular areas could be analysed and solutions discussed. Approaches to decision-makers were deliberated, documents which might generate support at this level were specified, the careful wording of examination syllabus submissions was emphasised – 'These are political documents', and throughout 'wheeling and dealing' terminology enters.

'Curriculum development' avowed one of the team 'is about personalities', and with no ready-made system through which a national project can be converted into wholesale school practice, informal, particularised, sometimes ulterior strategems are required. The support of decision-makers, LEA advisers and examination board personnel particularly, was sought throughout. Teachers were encouraged to keep their authority informed, send documents which might further the cause of collaboration. At one local meeting the teachers were urged: 'If we are to sell the idea of local curriculum development, let's start with the head'. As implementation was taking place in schools and teachers were seen to be dealing with the nuts and bolts of local resource provision, consideration was given to 'the next stage' and how local groups could be moved into a wider and more fundamental development of the project.

Such a co-ordination system is a support for teachers at both the intra- and inter-schools levels and a driving force to maintain the project as a dynamic developing entity. Though the original materials of the project will not self-destruct, the hope is that they will be rendered obsolescent through local developments shared throughout the country.

The response to Geography for the Young School Leaver

The customers, teachers and pupils, have praised the project (Hebdon *et al.* 1977). Though the novelty of the project has raised eyebrows and been rejected by some, the quality of the resources, the relevance of the subject matter and the stimulating nature of the classroom activities are particularly esteemed, despite the lengthy preparation time needed. Customer satisfaction is one measure of success, though one by which not all curriculum development projects would care to be judged. From its beginnings as a development project emerging as reform, it can now be viewed as a stimulus project, and the team certainly see that in the long term its major achievement may well be the setting up of the collaborative network.

With its main audience of teachers and administrators, GYSL has forgone the benefit (some might say, avoided the irrelevance) of debate with academics. Geographers have in general endorsed the project as sound geography, though it is suggested that the project has settled for a list of second order concepts. Others have suggested that a consensus view of society is represented by the project (MacDonald and Walker 1976). If the project aims to engage pupils in discussion of burning issues of our world and sees the school not just as responding to change but as a potential agent of change, then this implicit model of society deserves attention. Other claims against the project are that it is insufficiently child-centred, has not clearly thought out a pedagogy to handle the values and attitudes aspects, has used an inappropriate development model i.e. an 'objectives model', while curriculum development purists denigrate the provision of materials. The team's response typically has been that of modesty; the published products of GYSL are but starters through which much has been suggested but little prescribed. The local groups are to continue to work, fill the gaps, correct the errors, etc. and so criticism of the project to some extent is premature. The project team can argue with some justification that the central project has been translated into over 100 local development projects. The flexibility of Mode II and Mode III CSE examinations and now the availability of an O-level based on the project present considerable opportunities for development and, with the support of geographers in higher education, the potential for local groups grasping these opportunities would seem good. Resources, test items, syllabus examples produced by local groups are being 'banked' for circulation to and use by other teachers; and new curriculum units are being developed, particularly on the Third World and physical geography, with the new GYSL O-level course in mind.

The logic of the project's curriculum development model, the cycle of objectives, resources, procedures and assessment, is compelling, but one can question the extent to which this is more of a rationalisation than a rationale for both project team and the teachers. Although modification may go on in local groups through the inclusion of additional concepts and new issues, supplementary materials and procedures, assessment as a measure of course effectiveness has never been strong in our schools. Arguably, assessment at the trials stage was of 'utility' at classroom level with the average and below average – a question of whether pupils' interests were engaged rather than whether learning (conceptual development) took place. If evaluation for teachers rests principally on 'how well it goes down with 4Z' (MacDonald and Walker 1976), the project will in the end be sold short. Even applied to the whole ability range it could remain a tool of divisiveness, judged as *socially* acceptable for the less able and *educationally* successful for the more able. A premature speculation perhaps, in view of the fact that co-ordinators – local, regional and national – are expected to constantly raise broad educational issues related to project use and not just see that the group busies itself with test items and resource provision.

The position now (September 1977) is that local GYSL groups are at work in 102 of the 104 local education authorities of England and Wales, and more than 2,000 schools are said to be working with the project. There are also groups in Scotland and Northern Ireland. The project's extension to the higher ability pupils is being consolidated with 19 schools involved in the pilot O-level examination and approximately 100 schools are expected to present pupils for the first main examination in 1978. By managing the examination system in this way the common course principle of the project is supported. Interestingly, the project team claims to have been 'dragged' into the examination field by teachers.

The mass acceptability that the project has won may imply that it is not challenging, not radical and no great advance (though mass acceptability of projects is one criterion by which the Schools Council will undoubtedly be judged). The team will claim that curriculum change is a long process, that GYSL has scarcely begun and that through the recently instituted curriculum groups, linked and co-ordinated, the potential of the project will out – in due course. Charity James has urged that curriculum development should aim to make it possible for the less able to learn the same sorts of things as the more able (James 1968); the team has tried to do just that, but 'the control and occupying of time of increasing numbers of children who would rather not be in school at all' (Young 1972) could be a partial fate of GYSL. But what curriculum development project can do more?

TREVOR HIGGINBOTTOM

Geography for the Young School Leaver: A Response

The author's generous comments relating to Geography for the Young School Leaver suggest that he may have succumbed to what he refers to as the project's 'evangelistic campaign'. However, he still needs convincing on a number of issues:-

1. The project does attempt 'to appeal to *every* geography teacher'. National curriculum development is not simply about working with teachers who are already heavily committed to innovation. The charge of 'ambivalence in [the presentation of] the project message', in order to ensure a large take-up, is perhaps a little unkind. Certainly any team member involved in dissemination work with teachers must judge his audience and respond accordingly, even to the extent of emphasising some aspects of the project's philosophy rather more strongly than others. Once teachers are involved, however, it is hoped that all the many facets of GYSL can be explored. This should certainly be possible if they are members of an active LEA curriculum group.

2. The suggestion that the project has 'forgone the benefit of debate with academics' is erroneous. The team has in fact maintained a continuous dialogue with many colleagues working at the frontiers of geographical and educational research. However, it has always been felt that the major emphasis should be on work with teachers, who are seen as the key figures in the curriculum development process. This issue highlights a dilemma faced by central project teams: the need to meet what sometimes appear to be the conflicting demands of two different audiences, drawn from the 'academic' and 'practical teaching' worlds of curriculum development. For example, in the late 1970's the majority of the 'academic' world appears to be seriously questioning the value of the 'objectives model' and yet many members of the 'practical teaching' world, influenced no doubt by the DES Green Paper, exhibit a seemingly insatiable appetite for this mode of curriculum planning.

3. Curriculum purists may 'denigrate the provision of materials' but these

certainly appear to be welcomed by many teachers. It is totally unrealistic to suggest that colleagues working at the 'chalk face' of curriculum development should produce all their own materials, particularly in view of the fact that classroom pressures appear to have increased in this decade. GYSL has always taken a compromise stance on this issue, with the publication of exemplar teaching materials and the provision of many opportunities for teachers to develop further curriculum units. This policy is well illustrated in the project's GCE Ordinary Level scheme.

4. The 'common course principle of the project' is now being applied in many schools, with the adoption of common CSE and GCE syllabuses. Examination performances suggest that 'educational success' can be achieved with a very wide ability range. This does, however, raise another key issue: should GYSL ever have become involved with external examinations? Here at least one team member does have to admit to a degree of ambivalence. Certainly those external examination schemes which incorporate group syllabuses have helped the project to create long-term collaborative frameworks. When continuous assessment has been involved the teacher has often been provided with feedback which has become 'a measure of course effectiveness'. Much of the project's philosophy has been incorporated into examination syllabuses, including 'child centred approaches' relating to coursework. But are other important aspects of GYSL, such as value and attitude clarification, unexaminable and therefore often not included in teaching programmes? And what happens when the central team loses control of an external examination scheme?

5. Whether or not GYSL is 'challenging, radical and a great advance' obviously depends, in the final analysis, upon teacher interpretation in the classroom context. The project's view is that teachers are more likely to implement the total philosophy if they are working within a framework which involves collaboration between those at all levels in the educational system.

It must be admitted that GYSL leaves many questions unanswered, particularly in relation to the affective area of the curriculum. But the relatively small team has inevitably had to work within a limited programme and has certainly experienced a number of major constraints. For example: in some cases lack of effective support at the LEA level (even now almost half the authorities have no geography adviser); shortage of teacher time for local curriculum development activities; lack of interest in some teacher training establishments; unfavourable climates for curriculum change within some schools; the attitudes of a number of CSE geography panels.

One of the most important outcomes of GYSL as far as the central team is concerned is the realisation that there is a need to give almost as much consideration to the management of innovation as to the nature of the innovation itself.

Note

1. Courses for teachers of pre-university geography held at Madingley Hall near Cambridge, under the aegis of Cambridge University's Extra-Mural Board.

12 History 13–16

Basic information

Sponsor   Schools Council.

Grant   £126,600.

Location   School of Education, 31 Lyddon Terrace, The University of Leeds, LEEDS LS2 9JT.

Duration   1972–77 (Phase 1, which is the focus of this chapter) 1978–81 (Phase 2).

Designated pupils   *What is History?* is intended for the full range of ability in the third year. Schools have used it with other year groups. The 14–16 course is intended for potential CSE/GCE O-level candidates. It has been used with children in the bottom 40 per cent ability range. Teacher feedback to the evaluator suggests that the aims and objectives of both courses are attainable with children of all ability levels, though in some cases this will inevitably lead to an adaptation of the project materials.

Project organiser   The project was directed by David Sylvester from its establishment in 1972 through to 1975. Sylvester then left to become an HMI and was succeeded by one of the team members, Anthony Boddington.

Team members   David Sylvester (Director 1972–75)
Tony Boddington (Director 1975–77)
Gwenifer Griffiths (1975–76)
William Harrison (1972–75)
John Mann (1974–75)
Aileen Plummer (1972–77)
Denis Shemilt (Evaluator 1974–77, Director 1978–81)
Peter Wenham (1972–74)

Materials   Published by Holmes McDougall. Further details are given in the bibliography. They include *A New Look at History* (a handbook setting out the project's ideas), *What is History?* (a multi-media third year course), *Modern World Studies* and *Enquiry in Depth*.

Evaluation   Funded by Schools Council, it began in 1974 and is being carried out by Denis Shemilt at Leeds University. The full report, due to be completed in the summer of 1978, will be filed at the Schools Council. A writing conference will produce a distillation of the full report for use by teachers and people involved with in-service work in particular. The project team has also produced a manual which explains the workings of the project in detail, gives examples of practice and of development work which has used the project as a starting point.

Origins of the project

In the late 1960s the established place of history in the curriculum was being challenged by a variety of reformist movements. In 1968 the Historical Association's journal. *History*, carried an article by Mary Price on 'History in Danger' which analysed the problems being encountered by the subject and defined a number of curative strategies. The article summarised teachers' fears of the 'real danger of history disappearing from the timetable as a subject in its own right'. These teachers saw history 'surviving only as an ingredient of social studies, or civics, or combined courses of one kind or another' (Price 1968).

In the period since 1968 a number of innovations related to history teaching can be discerned which follow suggestions made in the article. The suggestion that history syllabuses should be reformed has been partly taken up although there is still evidence of Lamont's complaint that 'History does not repeat itself; examination papers in history do' (Lamont 1971, 192). A new range of history syllabuses has been devised, concentrating particularly on types of 'world history'. Further, the suggestion that history teachers should be provided with a forum for new ideas and information has been adopted with the launching of the Historical Association's new journal *Teaching History* in May 1969.

With respect to a curriculum project for history, Mary Price considered that the Schools Council was uninterested, and herself felt that 'salvation for history did not lie that way'. The judgement about the Schools Council proved incorrect, for in the ensuing years opinion at the Council, focussed on discussions within the History sub-committee, moved in favour of a curriculum project. A number of 'experts' outside the Council, such as Peter Carpenter at Cambridge, were consulted and proposals were encouraged. In response to this lead a number of proposals were submitted including one from David Sylvester, then teaching at the school of Education of Leeds University. The Leeds proposal was subsequently accepted and in 1972 the project began its work.

Sylvester's proposal suggested that 'many teachers would find helpful a project which would provide stimulus, support and materials to help them revitalise their own practice in general, and more particularly help them to encourage more pupil participation in their study of history' (History 13–16, n.d., 2).

Setting up the project

In making the appointments for the project David Sylvester laid great stress on the need for teaching experience. This priority was reflected in the announcement in the project newsletter of the appointment of the three research officers, 'all of whom come straight from teaching in schools'. (Project Newsletter April 1973). Initially, Aileen Plummer, Bill Harrison and Peter Wenham were appointed. Later Tony Boddington joined and Denis Shemilt, one of Sylvester's colleagues at Leeds, became the project's evaluator. The staff was completed by the appointment of a full-time secretary and a part-time clerical assistant.

The leadership of David Sylvester was very important in the formative period of the project when aims and objectives were defined and materials prepared. Sylvester's experience in school was mainly within the private sector and after three years he left to become a member of the Inspectorate. He was replaced by a team member, Tony Boddington, who in contrast had been head of history in a state school – a comprehensive in Hull. Besides the ongoing activities, Boddington was left with primary responsibility for dissemination and publication of materials.

Initial activities

The first brief the project defined was 'to review current practice in the teaching and examining of history'. This brief was pursued energetically in the first term (from September 1972) and was interpreted as 'a selective programme of research into the current state of theory and practice in the teaching of history' (Project Newsletter April 1973). The selective programme took the form of:

1. *Visits to* various schools, teachers' centres and colleges of education; BBC Schools Broadcasting Department; ILEA World History Project; Vindolands Archaeological Centre; Granada Television education officer.
2. *Questionnaires to* wardens of teachers' centres; secretaries of local associations of history teachers; history teachers in schools; pupils of history in schools.
3. *Meetings with* some local associations of history teachers; HMIs; Schools Council projects – Geography for the Young School Leaver; History, Geography, Social Science 8–13; and Cambridge School Classics Project; observers at meetings of two 16+ feasibility study panels in history – NUJMB/WMEB and Oxford/SREB; evaluators' panel at Schools Council; Schools Council Field Officers; some lectures in university departments of education and colleges of education.

Review of history teaching

For the detailed review of practice in Schools, Sylvester reported that 'LEAs were invited to send us the names of schools where interesting history teaching was taking place' (Sylvester 1973, 443). In spite of this initial bias in favour of 'interesting', normally interpreted as 'better' practice, the results of the review seem to have been clear. Commenting on the teaching of history 'over the past twenty years or so', the project stated: 'In this period, history teachers have not, in general, consciously aimed to improve their pupils' thinking abilities, but have concentrated rather on making history interesting and on transmitting a body of factual knowledge about the past' (History 13–16 n.d., 5).

The dominant pedagogy of history teachers was reflected in their syllabus designs. The project gave a content summary of a 'typical history syllabus 11–16':

Age 11–12 Ancient World History to Norman Conquest
      12–13 British, European and World History 1066–1485
      13–14 British, European and World History 1485–17th,
          and 19th centuries
      14–16 *Either*   Modern British History 1815 ⎫ to the
          or   Modern British and European History 1789 ⎬ present
          or   British Social and Economic History 1700 ⎪ day
          or   Modern World History 1870 ⎭

The project commented that 'It is a logical pattern if it is accepted that it is based on a view of history as a subject with a chronological structure' (History 13–16 n.d., 26). The project was unwilling to accept such a structure, arguing that 'adherence to this structure has been the cause of many of the past ills of history teaching in schools and more than this, that in giving only a linear view of history it gave a limited one' (Sylvester 1973, 145). Therefore history teachers should place less emphasis on chronology. Once this is questioned, the way is open for alternative patterns of syllabus making (History 13–16 n.d., 26).

New definitions

Following the review of practice, the project attempted some new definitions of school history. These definitions moved from considerations of how to define a new history syllabus through to the implications of such considerations for classroom practice.

In questioning the use of chronological structure as the basis of history and in seeking to define an 'alternative pattern', the project reported, with laudable honesty, some of the difficulties. Firstly,

> though it tried, the project could find no adequate conceptual structure to history which would either meet with general consensus, or form a basis for the teaching of the subject. Concepts there are, such as change, continuity, revolution and reaction, challenge and response. Other more specific concepts may be particularised, such as trade, war, family and government.
> [Conclusively the project adds] The list could easily run into thousands, and consequently . . . could not do for history what Jerome Bruner originally suggested was possible for all subjects, and base the teaching on its conceptual structure.
> [Secondly, the project] failed to isolate an adequate methodological structure for history. That historians look at evidence and then write a story of some past human experience is a general description of the historian's method which would receive fairly universal acquiescence, but it does not provide an adequate framework for the teaching of history in schools.

[Thirdly, the project considered structuring a syllabus on a taxonomy of educational objectives but again concluded that] though this has relevance for the teaching of history, it is inappropriate as a basis for syllabus framework.

(Sylvester 1973, 145)

To summarise, history is a subject which has an immense variety of content but which lacks any structure which can dictate how this content should be studied.'

(History 13–16 n.d., 17)

Because of these difficulties the project decided to devise a syllabus which was 'based on the uses of the past for adolescents'. There were to be four sections in the syllabus, each of which was in the opinion of the project, of specific use to adolescents:

1. Studies in modern world history because 'it helps to explain their present'.
2. Depth study of some past period because 'it helps them to understand people of a different time and place'.
3. A study in development of a topic because 'it provides material for the understanding of human development and change in time and also of the complexity of causation in human affairs'.
4. History around us because 'it contributes to leisure interests'.

(History 13–16 n.d., 18)

Defining a pedagogy

The definition of the project's history syllabus was therefore based as much on an understanding of adolescents' needs as on an understanding of history. Such a position has certain pedagogic implications which the project consistently pursued:

It has been contended in this paper that history is not a body of knowledge structured on either chronology or any other conceptual framework. Such a negative position is not however helpful when it comes to thinking about the appropriate teaching methods to be employed. If history is not a coherent body of knowledge what is it? The suggestion here is that it might be more meaningful to see history as a heap of materials which survives from the past and which historians can use as evidence about the past ... History in this sense involves a perpetual act of resurrection in which pupils and teachers reconstruct the past and so make it become real and 'present' to them ... It implies active enquiry of pupils into the various kinds of primary and secondary sources which make up the raw materials of history.

(History 13–16 n.d., 37–38)

The stress on adolescents' needs and 'active' pupils had been present in the first proposal to the Schools Council: 'Many teachers would find helpful a project which provides stimulus, support and materials to help them revitalise their own practice in general and more particularly help them to encourage more pupil participation in their study of history' (History 13–16 n.d., 2).

The teaching methods advocated were summarised in the New View booklet:

The general conclusion which emerges ... is that since the outcomes hoped for are attitudes and abilities rather than memorization of facts, classroom methods should be favoured which create an active learning situation for the pupil rather than those which cast the teacher in the role of a transmitter of information.

(History 13–16 n.d., 5)

Developing strategies

Following the review of practice and the ensuing re-definitions of school history, the project's strategy, outlined by Sylvester, was two-pronged:

1. to produce exemplary materials for teacher and pupil use in a newly conceived history syllabus;
2. to co-operate with examination boards in developing a varied approach to the examining of history at GCE O-and CSE levels.

The project's strategy can be readily scrutinised because of the commendably public approach adopted: besides wide coverage through visits the project produced a regular newsletter which described the evolving strategy in detail. In April 1973 the newsletter reported: 'The process of finding trial schools is now under way. It is hoped that there will be about 20 to 25 trial schools of varying kinds grouped in clusters in different parts of the country.'

Co-operation with trial schools broadly followed this sequence: firstly, in the school year 1973–74 the project and associated trial school staff sought to develop and try out materials related to the project's new definitions of school history. On average, this work, which mainly involved the 13–14 age group lasted for about half of each of the three school terms. Secondly, in the school years 1974–76, trial schools were expected to teach the prepared syllabus to O- and CSE level.

The detailed support of trial schools varied from school to school, but generally took three forms:

1. Materials were produced and supplied (free of charge) to support teaching of the new syllabus topics.
2. Project staff visited trial schools to advise on teaching and course-work assessment procedures.
3. The project initiated (in my experience with considerable success) regular group meetings among trial school teachers in the various local 'cluster' areas which emerged. The meetings were held in trial schools or in local teachers' centres and involved teachers being freed by their local authority from teaching duties for half a day or a day.

Provision of teaching materials

Of the three kinds of support the first strategy – provision of materials – was undoubtedly seen by teachers as the most important. At the annual conferences held by the project at Leeds, the team seemed to follow this perceived priority. Most of the 'briefings' by project staff focussed on explanation and discussion of 'the materials'.

In talking to teachers participating in the conference, the preference for support in the form of materials was constantly reiterated. A teacher in a secondary modern school about to turn comprehensive said: 'What I've come for is to get some survival kits for next year ... If you've got something to hand out you can survive, if you haven't, you're in the firing line ... Above all, it saves me the time and bother of preparing worksheets.' (Interview at Briefing Conference, Leeds University, Summer 1974).

Most, if not all, of the booklets were in fact written by the project staff at the headquarters in Leeds University. The booklets, which were well presented and produced, were available in advance of the annual conference in 1974. Detailed discussions with Holmes McDougall took place some time after this date, so that it would seem that the publishers were offered a more or less complete package of materials to consider.

Comments on the teaching materials

Alongside the more or less unanimous teacher support for the materials strategy at the annual conferences, a number of teachers expressed their concern at the language employed in the booklets. A girl teacher in an urban comprehensive summarised this position:

> I don't think they know much about the kind of kids we are working with ... The kids are full of imagination and life, but big words and long sentences can throw them ... They get bored and that's the end ... My feeling is that in some of the booklets the language that they use would stretch the average sixth-form candidate.
> (Interview at Briefing Conference as above)

The pupils themselves expressed other reservations. Most common of all was a reaction against the 'tyranny of the booklets' replacing the more familiar tyranny of the teacher dictating notes at the front of the class:

Teacher: What do you think of the booklets?
Student: It's like reading a fairy tale, isn't it?
Teacher: What do you mean?
Student: Well, as I read the booklet on the Red Army I didn't realise they were communists and I found myself thinking. 'Oh, they're good guys'. But then I thought 'But they're communists – I don't think much of communists ... They are sort of inevitable winners ....' I found myself wanting to know about the losers, what sort of people were they? ... was their defeat sort of certain? Why did they lose and not the communists? You could come to your own decision then ... and not be brainwashed by the book. (Fourth-year pupil at Stantonbury School, Buckinghamshire).

Developing an examination syllabus

The project saw the need to define a syllabus for examination because:

> teaching and examining are different ends of the same continuous process ... The examination is central to our work. Teachers must necessarily, for their students' sake, make the examination their priority and a history project designated 13–16 cannot shirk this issue if it is to be realistic in its approach and to have effective results to its work.
> (Sylvester 1973, 143)

The negotiations with examination boards did not develop smoothly. In 1974 Sylvester was in touch with boards as the annual conference actually took place, trying finally to confirm on the telephone that they would accept the project's syllabus.

A complicated examination format was finally accepted for GCE O-level/ CSE to be jointly operated by the Southern Universities Joint Board and the Southern Regional Examination Board. There are two examination papers: Paper 1 counts for 40 per cent of the total marks and tests the students' understanding of Modern World History, the study in depth and the study in development; Paper 2 counts for 20 per cent of total marks and aims to test the exercise of historical skills through 'questions based on unseen evidence'. Coursework assessment covering a wide variety of student work accounts for the other 40 per cent of the marks.

Evaluation

The evaluation of the project was undertaken by Denis Shemilt from the early stages through to the preparation of a report in March 1977. A number of interim reports were given to the annual conferences in the form of lectures by Schemilt.

The focus of Shemilt's evaluation was on the *pupils* taking the new courses. At one point in the final report Shemilt notes: 'The locus of trials and of evaluation has been a group of children not a group of teachers' (Shemilt 1977).

Shemilt compares the project to the trials and application of 'a new surgical technique'.

Following this analogy Shemilt concludes:

> On the History 13–16 trials, no one died, though many suffered; none endured the extremities of madness, yet some despaired; most displayed a level of historical understanding significantly in advance of their peers in control schools, but then they *did* have the advantages of Hawthorne effect, experimental effect, and all the covert behavioural influences following in the wake of curriculum development trials.

With respect to the new definitions of pedagogy so consistently articulated and advocated by the project, Shemilt states that: 'Very little can be said about the impact of teacher philosophy and pedagogic style even though, *a priori*, it seems certain that these factors are of the utmost importance.'

Nonetheless, some indirect insight can be elicited for 'trial teachers encountered many problems with the project', although he warns that most 'were of an individual nature and could not be used to reliably forewarn the teacher new to History 13–16'. Certain of the problems then listed, however, seem potentially generalisable rather than idiosyncratic. For instance:

> One of the more frequent pitfalls stemmed from the plethora of supplied materials. History 13–16 aimed to emphasize 'concepts and skills' rather than a 'body of

content', but *in practice* it demanded detailed mastery of several discrete content areas far in excess of normal O-level and CSE requirements.

[He adds a familiar theme] Admittedly, in its provision of such superabundant materials the project aimed to ensure a teacher's freedom of action, to supply him with alternative means of teaching the concepts and skills at issue, but many teachers felt obliged to cover the 'topics' in the detail suggested by these materials.

(Shemilt 1977)

Conclusion

History 13–16 has a very impressive record: large numbers of guides and materials have been produced and meetings and conferences held. The thorny problems of examination and pedagogic style have been consistently confronted. Significant numbers of schools are now teaching the new history syllabus. In a real sense the project has done all that could have been expected of it.

The major weakness of the project is one common to most curriculum reform movements and projects, namely, the strategies for achieving basic change in classroom pedagogy. Such change has proved enormously difficult to encourage because of the range of constraints which persuade teachers to transmit factual knowledge to more or less passive students. 'Active learning situations', where the teacher ceases being merely a transmitter of facts, are certainly far more elusive than the implementing strategies drawn up by the project ever hint at.

The project hardly offers a coherent scheme at this level; more a mixture of *laissez-faire* and hope. The former is illustrated by comments about how to deal with third-form history: 'It is a problem which most teachers must work out for themselves, in the light of the differing circumstances in which they are placed.' (History 13–16 n.d., 29).

Hope is evident in a range of statements. The strategy for getting teachers to use more evidence was described in this way: 'The project hopes to give teachers a rationale for making evidence central to history teaching and also give to them, by the production of materials, some of the tools for the job.' Sylvester 1973, 144).

Fundamentally the project's hopes seem to have been for a change in pedagogy through *exhortation*. This is well illustrated by the attempts to get teachers to use discussion methods: 'Teachers will need to be willing to discuss with pupils their own reasons for teaching history and for seeing it as useful educative for adolescents.' (History 13–16 n.d., 25).

In seeking to change classroom pedagogy a curriculum project is approaching one of the vested traditions within teaching and one supported by a huge range of rational and irrational arguments. Traditional teaching patterns have not and will not be changed by exhortation or by *new* materials that can be readily put to use in teaching with the *old* method.

DAVID SYLVESTER

History 13–16: A Response

The evidence provided by the evaluation and by observation in classrooms would suggest that, contrary to the reviewer's conclusion, some changes have been made in traditional teaching methods by the project. There have, however, been no mass conversions or wholesale changes, and whether methods other than exhortation and new materials, as implied but not disclosed by the reviewer, would achieve more, needs putting to the test. It is relevant to state here that the project did consider producing detailed programmes of pupil work which teachers would operate, but decided against this, preferring to assume that teachers were professional people, willing to think about their job and able to devise their own programmes to suit their pupils in their particular situations. This assumption may have been over-optimistic, but if it was also misguided then it may be doubted whether any methods will produce worthwhile pedagogical changes. Exhortation, and the discussion it implies, still seems to be the most appropriate method if the aim is the education rather than the indoctrination of teachers and pupils, and particularly if the subject is history where complete objectivity is unattainable and opinion and interpretation is its life-blood. So the hope remains that if more in-service time can be found for exhortation and using the materials, pedagogical changes will slowly follow.

The centrality of assessment and examinations in the project's work has been noted. It was always foreseen that once the project had ended the examination boards would have a central role to play as guardians of the project's ideas. It is important, therefore, that the future activities of the boards are studied for, if the examinations depart from the project's ideas and if, in particular, the history method element is decreased (the existing 20 per cent of the marks given to this seemed to some to be too small at the outset) then the project's ability to change teaching method will seriously diminish.

Further study is also needed to assess whether the project's emphasis on fieldwork and the study of the visual historical environment continues as a basic part of the school history teaching. Another area which needs consideration is the extent to which teachers develop new approaches to evidence work and new materials for different studies in development, for depth studies in other historical periods and for further contemporary political problems.

Finally the studies begun in the evaluation need to be extended. More work is needed on pupil acquisition of the various historical concepts outlined by the project, such as evidence, development, change and causation. The project began with the hypothesis that school pupils can do real history and not be mere recipients of historical information. Testing that hypothesis needs to be carried further.

13 Sixth Form Mathematics Curriculum Project

Basic information

Origins   The project was set up in January 1969 on the initiative of Professor Jack Wrigley of the University of Reading and the Mathematics Committee of the Schools Council. The relative decline in the numbers of sixth formers studying mathematics as well as science had become a matter of concern. At a conference held in 1966 at the University of Reading, it was noted that new mathematics programmes in sixth forms seemed to reveal a disturbing lack of consensus. The new project was set up with the intention of investigating sixth form mathematics generally and, if feasible, courses would be devised to make mathematics intrinsically more attractive to sixth formers. Thus, it was hoped, more of them might be encouraged to continue their studies beyond O-level. The Dainton Committee, set up in February 1965 and reporting in January 1968, independently recommended that it should be the normal practice for pupils to study mathematics until they left school. (para. 179) and this offered further encouragement to the project.

Location   The School of Education, University of Reading.

Sponsor   Schools Council.

Grant   £129,860.

Director   C. P. Ormell (1969–78).

Project team
   J. B. Morgan: Editorial Adviser (1970–76)
   F. L. Knowles: Research Associate (1971–74)
   D. D. Malvern: Research Associate (1971–73)
   C. Bentley: Evaluator (1969–76, part time)
   Mrs. B. E. Sewell: Research Assistant (1973–76 part time)
   W. Flemming: Research Associate (1975–76 part time). Co-ordinator (1976–78 part time)

Preliminary survey   A preliminary survey, as yet unpublished, indicated three factors which were militating against the successful teaching of mathematics to non-specialists in the sixth form:

1. Perhaps as a result of their earlier experiences of the subject, many sixth-formers were relatively weakly motivated towards the learning of mathematics.
2. Teachers had often already tried most of the teaching devices and approaches to the curriculum they knew during the O-level courses and seemed to have no

further means at their disposal for arousing or re-awakening interest in mathematics.

3. Mathematics was a subject which seemed to lack relevance and thus meaning for the student.

The project materials as they were developed had therefore to take account of these factors which had become known early in the life of the project.

Production of materials In an initial pilot phase (1969–70), three packages of 'relevance oriented materials' were produced. A proving trial of the first package, *Indices*, was carried out in nine schools and was followed by trials of all three packages in 30 schools. The significant development from this period was the emergence of a style of presentation which came to be called *semi-programming*. This permits an element of self-instruction without debarring the use of the texts for reference back to earlier work.

During the main production phase (1971–74), revised versions of the three initial packages and thirteen others were produced and tested in some 107 schools. Each school tested one or, occasionally, two packages. Five schools introduced the complete two-year course beginning in 1972 and nine other schools started one-year courses in 1973. All these schools entered candidates for the AO examination in 1974.

During the period from 1974 to 1976, final revised versions of the materials were prepared by assembling various draft booklets into larger books to form one student discussion book, five starter books (intended to bring pupils beginning from different attainment levels to a common position) and three main course or continuation books. Five of these final versions were published in readiness for the session 1976–77 and the remaining three books appeared during the spring of 1978. A Teachers' Guide was published in July 1978.

Since 1969, the project has produced a large number of booklets and articles. These have included newsletters, various explanatory accounts of the philosophy underlying the work of the project, the rationale of the course, the method of assessment and the use of the materials in classroom practice.

Assessment The examination at AO level has been available to schools since 1975. It is conducted by the University of London School Examinations Board which acts as co-ordinator for the various examining bodies.

Published materials These are published under the general title *Mathematics Applicable* by Heinemann Educational Books. They include a pupils' discussion unit, starter units, continuation units and a teacher's guide. Further details are given in the bibliography.

The mathematical aims of the project

Mathematicians who today are interested in the application of mathematics to important and everyday problems have come to interpret their method of working in a particular way. They consider that the salient features of some situations can be incorporated in a suitable series of mathematical statements called a *model*. The mathematical relationships embedded in the model can be exposed through manipulation of the model by mathematical means and the implications of the model as initially conceived can be shown up. If certain changes are made in the original situation and hence in the mathematical statements of the model, the consequences of these changes can be seen. All this is accomplished without the need to construct actual physical models: for instance, the whole of the public transport system of a city can be planned without a bus having to leave the garage, or a bridge can be designed in various alternative forms to cater for different demands without a single load of concrete being mixed. The reliability of the results obtained in this kind of exploration of possibilities is dependent on the amount of significant detail incorporated into the model in the first place, upon the accuracy of the deductions made and upon the care taken in the interpretation of the results, always bearing in mind that there may well be elements in the problem which are not quantifiable or otherwise expressible in mathematical terms. Mistakes can be expensive when bridges fall down or a fault in a transport system causes a rush-hour traffic jam!

Seen in this way, applied mathematics is not a branch of mathematics or physics but is a discipline in its own right. In constructing a model in the first place, data has to be obtained from sources outside mathematics and indeed the mathematical model may be constructed by someone who calls himself by a name other than *mathematician*, say a physicist or an engineer. In any event, the construction of models of this kind requires skill and practice; it also requires imagination. While such categories are but a very rough and ready guide to ways of thinking, it is often said, with some justification, that mathematicians are convergent thinkers. Here, in model-making, is a much more creative activity which clearly calls for some divergent thinking. While a full analysis of the thinking lies outside the requirements of present considerations, as does the nature of the model when once it is constructed, one aspect is particularly worth mentioning here. At some stage during its construction the model is essentially a descriptive one and for many purposes this is all that is needed. On the other hand there are occasions when a model is required to be rather more flexible so as to be able to provide information about what would happen if certain important features were altered within a given range of permitted changes. This is a projective characteristic of mathematical models: essentially models are more general than the actualities they initially represented. For instance Kepler's laws describe planetary motion (though they do more than just this) and they depend on an inverse square law associated with central forces. What would the laws describe if the force were changed to obey say, an inverse cube relation?

This, then, is perhaps the commonest way in which mathematics is put to practical use. It would seem obvious therefore that this fact with suitable examples should form part of the standard mathematics curriculum in schools. That it does not would appear to be a condemnation of the limitations which are conventionally placed upon what is taught and, further, an introduction of an element of model building into pedagogy might very well open up new ways of viewing at least some aspects of the existing curriculum. Since it is possible that many people demand of essentially difficult subjects that there should be some practical pay-off in terms of the applicability of knowledge, it is also possible that the incorporation of modelling might occasion greater respect for and interest in the subject as a whole. This is not, of course, to deny that children can and should, as far as is possible, be brought to the appreciation of mathematics for its own sake as a human achievement not only in the organizing of sense impressions but in abstracting from them.

It was considerations of this kind which were in the minds of the director and his colleagues when the project began in 1969. A start was made with adapting the idea of modelling to the work of the non-specialist sixth-former with whom the problem of teaching mathematics was an acute one. At the start, there were three important questions needing answers. Can modelling be taught to pupils at this stage of education and, if so, to what extent? Does it motivate their learning? In what respects is it useful to try to teach it?

Philosophy

At this point it is worth mentioning that the director felt that there was philosophical support for the general view that it is the applicability of mathematics which is crucial both as concerning the nature of the subject and its pedagogy. Force was added to his argument by the empiricism expressed by C. S. Pierce from about 1878 when he began to construct the philosophical system which he first called *pragmatism* and later *pragmaticism* (Pierce 1878). Pierce begins from the point of view of the experimental scientist. 'Every statement you make to him [the experimentalist] he will either understand as meaning that if a prescription for an experiment ever can be given and ever is carried out in act, an experience of a given description will result, or else he will see no sense at all in what you say (Hartshorne and Weiss 1932–35).'

By this and other similar statements he implied that all our conceptions, however abstract, derive their meaning from things in terms of what the things will do or can be used for, of how we may act upon or with them. It is easy to see how this view might react with the idea of modelling, changing it from *a* discipline to *the* discipline of importance. Remarks made by Kline, von Neumann (Ormell 1971) and even Wittgenstein (Ormell 1972) ('Don't ask for the meaning, ask for the use.') can also be adduced to support the modelling view. Interestingly, none of this would have surprised the Leibnizians of the eighteenth century: Lambert makes a remark with special reference to algebra and his theory of magnitudes in which he actually uses the phrases later used by the director in reference to the whole of mathematics '. . . this science only determines which combined possibilities out of all the possible combinations derive from . . . the theory of magnitudes . . . and how they permit translations from one to the other' (Lambert 1764).

While anyone embarking on a new development in education must adopt a more or less consistent philosophy, it is perhaps unusual for the director of a mathematics project to exteriorise a philosophical position at the outset. Although the intellectual background does give some strength to this project, it is not on these views that the course must be judged. The value of the course lies in whether or not it succeeds in teaching elementary modelling and in motivating learning.

The course and the texts

The course may be run without using the published material but teachers are advised to refer to the books for guidance as to what is required and what work should be done. All the books are written for non-specialist sixth formers who are likely to have main subject interests over a wide range including 'biology, economics, geography, social studies, architecture, humanities etc.' (undated project notes) and an element of self-instruction is envisaged if the texts are used. The books are related as in the following diagram:

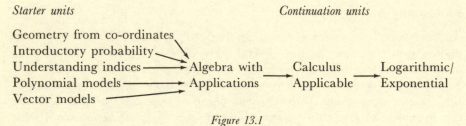

Figure 13.1

with the discussion unit *Mathematics Changes Gear* as an introduction to the whole course.

From the very wide range of possible topics, there has clearly to be some selection and the course has been arranged to give its main thrust towards the use of logarithmic and exponential functions. This is chosen as the principal target because of its particularly wide range of applicability as, for example, in physics where 'almost every phenomenon studied ... seems to involve models containing exponential terms' (SFMCP n.d., a). The fact that the course is not intended to supplant main subjects in the sixth form but is to remain a minority time study emphasises the need for selection: the course demands either four 40 minute periods per week for one year or three for two years. Of this at least a quarter is used for taught lessons in which the teacher is to present mathematics 'as a possibility pre-viewing discipline' and he is to handle 'the description and explanation of real-life situations as well as the mathematics' (SFMCP n.d.). Furthermore, a teacher is likely to cover ground more slowly than he would expect.

Clearly, since the teaching of modelling is not at present a normal part of the mathematics teacher's brief, some guidance is needed about what kinds of activities need special emphasis and these include reading about problems in common language, visualization and spatial imagination, the interpretation of and the sketching of graphs and the simplification of diagrams; all are additional to the more obvious need to be able to make a formal representation of a problem in mathematical terms (SFMCP 1976a).

'The ultimate aim ... is to initiate the pupil into the art of mathematical modelling in respect of actual situations, real or imagined' (Flemming 1977) and this cannot be fully realised by working from text-books. The partly predigested exercises of the texts provide a gentle initiation and training and the learner then moves on to short essay exercises based on simple open-ended instructions such as 'Invent a situation involving a linear model and introduce an element of probability into it' or 'Discuss an indicial [*sic*] modelling situation of your choice.' (Five examples of such essays actually produced by pupils on the course are provided to assist participating teachers.) Sometimes it is possible for groups of pupils to work together on larger-scale studies and one such possibility is the *Local Feasibility Study* which is 'aimed at throwing light on the implications of interesting proposals relating to a particular school or area'. (SFMCP 1972). The use of *quasi-facts* is recommended as a basis for working since the collection of proper data would be too time consuming. Topics suggested as suitable include the proposal to install a moving pavement up the hill into school, the building of a ski-slope or the raising of a tall TV aerial where reception is poor and detailed advice is given on how to follow through whatever topic is chosen (*loc cit*). After preparation of this kind, the pupil is able to proceed to coursework essays of his own and one such essay formed part of the examination requirement until 1978.

The examination

Participants in the project may not wish to take a public examination but, since they are sixth-form pupils, a very large proportion of them will be entered. It is expected that entrants will already have either a pass in mathematics at O-level or a very good CSE result of at least Grade 2 before entry to this AO-level examination. Until 1978, the examination consisted of four elements: a coursework essay and three examination papers. Since the design of the examination was far from traditional, a detailed description of it is called for.

The coursework essay was of up to 200 mathematical or verbal sentences (including any program statements) which might be the best of a number of such pieces of work written by the candidate. Submitted in May, it was first marked by the teacher under very detailed guidance from the project team and was then moderated by the Examinations Board. This essay might have been about the setting up of an accurate mathematical model of some situation of significane outside mathematics or it might have been a discussion of the implications of a proposal or hypothesis using simple models whose empirical validity is taken for granted. Examples mentioned in the project literature include studying the patterns of wear on a corridor floor and the siting of road signs on a footpath (SFMCP 1973). The coursework essay attracts 20 per cent of the final marks.

Examination papers 1 and 2 were each one hour in length and were taken on the same day, while paper 3 was of two hours duration. The first paper aimed at testing a candidate's 'grasp of mathematical concepts, standard methods and techniques'_ and it consists of two questions set on topics from the *Starter Units*, three on standard methods and one requiring 'some preliminary thought concerning methods'. (SFMCP 1976b). Paper 2 tested the translation 'from a less formal level' of information and back again, asking four questions of each type. Each of papers 1 and 2 carries 20 per cent of marks. Paper 3 was a sustained discussion of a projective application based on twenty questions. In this paper, hints, checkups and notes were provided but the use of a hint was penalised by a loss of marks. *Hints* were given under seals which, once removed, could not be replaced. *Check-ups* were provided to avoid a self-doubting candidate's taking up a hint after he had acted correctly without it. *Notes* were for the general clarification of the problem. Paper 3 carried the remaining 40 per cent of marks. Paper 3, clearly seen by the weight placed upon it as a major element in the assessment, was considered to test 'a mixture of visualisation, abstraction, interpretation and purposive mathematical manipulation' (SFMCP 1976b).

So as to streamline administration and reduce costs somewhat, from the 1979 examination the first two papers are combined to form a single Paper 1 and the old third paper becomes Paper 2. On this second paper fewer hints are given and they are on a separate card. From the same date the coursework requirement ceases, since the need to produce an essay of a suitable standard has proved to be rather a burden for teacher and pupil alike. Removing the requirement allows more time to be devoted to the course (SFMCP 1978).

The original and somewhat elaborate examination pattern represented a wholly new departure in a public examination at this or any other level. It offers an approach to testing the creative aspects of a subject often thought of as a routine one together with the techniques needed to develop them.

Evaluation

It has not been usual in mathematics projects in the United Kingdom to make provision at the outset for systematic evaluation of the work being undertaken. (Only one other secondary mathematics project did so in the 1960s.) The project team did from the inception include an evaluator whose work has proceeded concurrently with the development of the materials. Not only has the team wished to improve the texts as the result of trials and to evaluate the examination at the pilot stage so as to set a suitable standard, but there has been an attempt to determine what are attitudes of both teachers and pupils to the individual parts of the materials. This has led to substantial and detailed reports (Bentley 1971; Bentley and Malvern 1972; Bentley and Malvern 1975) some of which are not yet published. Generally, the results recorded in the reports indicate favourable responses from pupils and very favourable ones from their teachers. Throughout, pupils' attitudes have been measured on Lickert-type tests (Lickert 1932) with either five or six intervals, though unfortunately full details of the methods used are not given in the printed reports. The analysis of the results is presented in the form of frequency diagrams of the responses to some of the questions put together with rectangular distributions for comparison. An idea of the magnitude of the early investigations is given by the fact that the 1971 report refers to the pupils of seven schools and colleges, six in southern England and one near Madras. Similar methods of analysis have been used for the examination evaluations (SFMCP n.d.) with the addition of the provision of percentage performances on the individual examination questions. Particularly interesting are graphs of the numbers of hints used: a careful comparison of this data with the actual examination papers would have been very enlightening but is not given in the report.

The evaluation of a project presents great difficulties for the experimenter. It is not possible to teach the same group twice over by different procedures in order to find out which method is best, and obtaining matched groups is of doubtful reliability since it is not evident what are the criteria on which the groups should be equal. In any case, large sample controls are in practice very difficult to maintain: a control group was used in 1964–65 in the Shropshire Mathematics Experiment when there was a straight comparison of the performance of the experimental group and that of the control on skills which both would achieve in the normal course of events, but almost 40 per cent of the control group failed to complete all the tests. In the *Mathematics Applicable* course the important aspect to be evaluated would not have been common to the experimental and control groups. What could have been common was manipulative ability in various areas of mathematics but no natural control group for this existed and it would not have been reasonable to try to create one. As the 1972 report wryly puts it: 'Control groups have not been used as this was considered impracticable. Not only would it have involved producing new 'dry-as-dust' material with identical mathematical content to that of the packages, but a hundred or more additional unenthusiastic schools would have had to be found to test it' (Bentley and Malvern 1972). And that does not mention the necessary validation of the new material!

If the best-buy approach, then, is not possible, the alternative, and this is the one chosen, is to determine whether the new product, *Mathematics Applicable*, lives up to the manufacturers' specifications. Now it is a curious phenomenon that when projects are evaluated, they are always shown to be successful and this is not due to cheating in the results. There could be at least four reasons for it. First, it is a characteristic of non-comparative testing that it is dependent upon value judgements. Second, there is the effect of the enthusiasm of involved teachers for something new which breaks away from what has tended to become routine and the consequent enthusiasm generated by them in their pupils. Third, the scale of an experiment is always relatively small. As with the scaling up of a laboratory process to factory production, new problems are encountered when a more general implementation is attempted since minor effects unnoticed in the small scale are magnified and detailed control is in any case more difficult. This problem suggests evolution by small steps rather than revolution by large ones. Fourth, there is the fact that new projects are only taken up by enthusiasts in the first place. The only way that this inevitable bias can be corrected is by carrying out tests when the work is itself becoming more commonplace and routine and by investigating results when the work is taught by teachers who are not volunteers. Furthermore, projects in general tend to collect results only from the fairly successful schools: data about failures is rarely accessible to them and is often sensitive material anyway. An interesting field of investigation for all concerned with curriculum development is the examination of reasons why teachers have rejected an approach from the outset or why they have given up after, perhaps, an enthusiastic start. It would of course be equally interesting to know about teachers who have made a reluctant start, perhaps after coercion, but who have continued with increasing enthusiasm.

In the evaluation of the project, the team has, then, made an effort to monitor the degree of success their materials have had in producing the desired results. They have been able to investigate some aspects of the project and they conclude that, by and large, the material is interesting to many pupils and teachers, that it is not too hard, and that the course reaches its goals of teaching some aspects of modelling. They have not yet been able to discover whether in the long run pupils are any better off for having learned these elementary ideas of modelling. Indeed, it is hard to see how this could be discovered: to ascertain whether any educational venture succeeds in fulfilling non-behavioural objectives is incredibly difficult.

The reports conclude with a number of free comments made by pupils. It is a pity that there has not been time or manpower to follow up at least some of the most tantalising ones.

> '. . . I find verbal teaching easier than reading'
> '. . . [the package] was a good attempt.'
> '. . . My enjoyment of it [mathematics] lies in solving questions. Knowing why makes little differences.'   (Bentley and Malvern 1972)

> 'If you knew your formulas you couldn't go wrong – the exam was clear and easy – but I didn't know my formulas.'
> '. . . the exam relied on application of principles rather than rote learning of formulas and details.'   (Bentley and Malvern 1975)

Clearly, the comments printed in the report are a selection only. It is interesting to note the general air of favourable comment which could be due to a desire to please but may well reflect genuinely favourable feelings. The latter would be consistent with the other results obtained.

The future

Any mathematics project must see itself as contributing to the overall development of mathematical education. No project can expect to hold in the palm of its hand the solutions to all the fundamental problems of teaching mathematics: the project under discussion has set out to introduce systematic instruction in a mathematical discipline hitherto, to a great extent, ignored at the elementary level and, in doing so, to provide motivation for at least one group of pupils. This much has been accomplished, but it would be a pity if the project ended without first producing for publication full reports of its work, especially the details of its evaluations of which there are nine draft reports, the most useful mathematical parts of its newsletters and the many examples of elementary model-building which have been devised. There is also a quantity of material concerned with the teaching of mathematics to biologists, some further feasibility studies, work on the design and assessment of coursework and much detailed work on examination design. None of this has yet been published. After all, this material has taken the time and effort of a number of contributors: it is not easy to produce and should on no account be lost.

Furthermore, the stated objectives (Lockard 1972) in the first place included a review of the value of the various parts of the sixth-form mathematics and the relationship of mathematics with physics and other subjects. Matters such as these are of crucial importance in the proper development of future sixth-form courses and especially so if proposals for new examinations now being discussed are adopted. The publication of all the findings of the project on these matters would be most useful and particularly so if they gave rise to practical recommendations.

The attempt to modify the curriculum and its pedagogy by devising a project generates the problem of what is to happen to the ideas after the end of the period of formal development. On the one hand, there is the risk that good ideas will disappear altogether and, on the other, the danger that continuing on a formal, even if voluntary, basis will result only in the formation of a closed group of initiates. In neither case is there much influence to be felt. For the present project some policy needs to be adopted and if the work is to continue to develop, a much wider appeal must be made. Whatever the administrative arrangements, there must be provision to help teachers to become properly familiar with the ideas of modelling and ways in which this can be taught at an elementary level.

Lastly, in the longer term, it is desirable to conflate the experimentally supported views of the team about motivation with work currently being done in studying cognition since it is exceedingly dangerous to tinker with the content of mathematics courses or with their organization without taking into full account what is known about the learning process. This would clearly involve further experimental work and, indeed, perhaps another project.

CHRISTOPHER ORMELL

Sixth Form Mathematics Project:
A Response

I read Raymond Heritage's chapter on the Sixth Form Mathematics Project (Mathematics Applicable) with interest. It is always nice to know how the work one has done or with which one has been closely associated appears from a different point of view. In this case there is the additional pleasure in finding that Mr. Heritage is broadly appreciative of the result, and, in particular, of the philosophy underlying the enterprise. He has clearly carefully read and assimilated the themes of most of the draft material the project has produced since 1969, in addition to the published material. So in general terms we agree: on the underlying assessment of needs, on the importance of modelling, and on the technical implementation of a modelling-based course for non-specialists in the $16+ - 18+$ age range. Where we differ is on points of detail only; on some aspects of the epistemology of mathematics; and on the exact role of the study of 'cognition' in designing new curriculum materials. I shall say a few words on each of these points, if only to help to sharpen the issues involved, and to leave the reader in a better position to form his or her own opinion.

Heritage speaks of 'application of mathematics' and of the use of mathematical models to describe 'situations'. He then introduces the idea of 'changes' in the situations concerned, and emphasises the value of the models in drawing out the implications of these changes. He goes on to say that the modelling idea is so important that 'applied mathematics' is no longer a 'branch of mathematics' but 'a discipline in its own right'. It is good to see that he gives such a strong account of the value of modelling, but one wonders whether the terminology in which he discusses this has quite caught up with the content of the message. The new way of conceiving mathematics certainly renders the old term 'applied mathematics' rather an awkward one. Generally speaking 'applied mathematics' refers to certain parts of dynamics and statistics which have been developed for handling very specific problems arising in these areas. The new modelling approach, however, enormously widens the range of mathematics which might be needed in handling a model representing a proposal or an hypothesis. For example, the full gamut of elementary algebra, calculus and geometry is needed again and again, and it has certainly not been customary in the past to describe this broad range of mathematics as 'applied mathematics'.

It is this kind of consideration which has led to the recent widespread use of the term 'applicable mathematics' to cover the fairly extensive area of mathematics needed in constructing and operating models. In our work we have extended this development somewhat by applying the term 'model' to simpler and more 'projective' examples than hitherto. At the same time we have sought out ways of involving virtually the whole of what is often called 'the core' of elementary mathematics in handling models. In this way the extension of the idea of mathematical modelling gradually reaches the point where the whole of elementary mathematics is involved. Instead of the term 'applicable mathematics' picking out a *sub*-set of elementary mathematics which is potentially applicable to real problems, therefore, the whole of elementary mathematics is seen to be applicable to real problems. Thus the term 'applicable mathematics' loses much of its point, and we come to see that elementary mathematics as a whole has become applicable: hence 'mathematics applicable'.

By the same token one starts to wonder whether the term 'application' of mathematics does not already contain a built-in premiss about the prior existence of (elementary) mathematics-for-its-own-sake. We argue that it does. Once elementary mathematics as a whole has been seen to be applicable, the term 'application', too, ceases to be quite as appropriate to the situation as it was previously. In other words the capacity for mathematics to be used as a source of building bricks for modelling, and as an operating system for manipulating models systematically blurs the old distinction between 'mathematics' on the one hand and 'its application' on the other.

We agree with Heritage that the study of what he calls 'cognition' is extremely important. We believe that the work being carried out at present will confirm our view that existing syllabuses in mathematics are seriously over-crowded. A smaller body of topics studied in greater applicative depth would in our view greatly improve the quality of the 'cognition' being achieved by the average child. Heritage rather implies that the existing syllabuses are doing a good job, so that even to 'tinker' with them might be to cause significant harm. We do not take this view at all. We feel that the average quality of the 'cognition' being achieved is rather poor, that 'tinkering' is unlikely to produce a discernable difference, and that nothing less than a full-scale return to low density syllabuses is likely to improve the situation. Some would prefer to drill the topics of these low density syllabuses in the attempt to improve the quality of the cognition. We have tried to show another way; one which is capable of appealing to the youngster's imagination, sense of relevance and concern for the real world.

14 Scottish Integrated Science

Basic information

Sponsor   The Secretary of State for Scotland (N.B. This was not a funded project but a scheme developed by a working party set up to review one aspect of secondary education in Scotland.)

Grant   None. Expenses of the working party and administration were borne by the Scottish Education Department and Local Education Authorities but no public statement of finances was made.

Location   None. The working party, all of whom had other full-time jobs, came together as and where they could to discuss the substance of the scheme.

Director   None. (The Chairman of the working party set up by the Secretary of State for Scotland was A. J. Mee, HMI.)

Period of development   1964 to 1969.

Designated pupils   From 1964 to 1966 the concern was with pupils in the first and second years of secondary school who would *not* be following courses leading to the Scottish Certificate of Secondary Education. In 1966 the remit of the working party was changed to one relating to a common course for *all* pupils in the first two years of secondary school. (In Scotland the age of transfer to secondary school is 12+ years.)

Concerns   'The broad aims of science education should be that pupils acquire

1. some knowledge of the empirical world about them
2. a little of the vocabulary and grammar of science
3. an ability to observe objectively
4. an ability to solve problems and think scientifically
5. an awareness of the culture which is science.'

Teaching materials   There was no 'package' of teaching materials as such. The working party provided a syllabus, objectives and some guidance for teachers in their general report (*Curriculum Paper 7* Scottish Education Department, 1969); they also prepared a set of worksheets that teachers could use if they wished (Heinemann Educational Books, 1969 and 1974), but these were provided as an aid rather than a definition of the course. Since that time other worksheets and textbooks have been developed as suitable for the scheme (Scottish Central Committee on Science 1977a, b, c and d; Scottish Education Department undated; Buckie *et al*. 1978; Mee *et al*. 1971).

Examinations   Although there is no public examination in Scotland that is based on this course, it was explicitly designed as an alternative to the first two years of the four year courses in biology, chemistry and physics for the Scottish Certificate of Education.

Schools   In 1971 a census (Brown, 1975) showed that this scheme had been adopted by more than 80 per cent of all the secondary schools in Scotland.

Institutionalisation   The pattern of continuous curriculum development in Scotland has ensured that this scheme is always under the scrutiny of the Scottish Central Committee on Science; development and evaluation work is administered by the Dundee Centre of the Scottish Curriculum Development Service.

Evaluation   Evaluation of this scheme has been somewhat fragmentary. This chapter and Jeffrey (1977) each provide an account of the various studies that are relevant.

Introduction

Has this been a successful curriculum development? In the case of Scottish Integrated Science one is tempted to answer: 'Yes, very much so; 80 per cent of all secondary schools in Scotland have adopted it and a further 14 per cent are following the content it prescribes.' These figures, established in 1971 (Brown 1975) and confirmed in 1975 (Brown, McIntyre, Drever and Davies 1976), suggest that teachers and administrators have, to a large extent, accepted the innovation and attempted to implement it. However, such information is of little use unless supplemented by answers to other questions such as:

What has led to this high level of adoption?
What was the nature of the innovation?
Do teachers understand what was intended by the developers and have they found it possible to implement what was intended?
Is the innovation leading to the intended pupil learning?

In attempting to explore such questions I will, firstly, outline the way in which the course was developed; secondly, describe the four major innovations with which the developers appeared to be concerned together with teachers' reactions to and understanding of these innovations; and, finally, briefly comment on various studies evaluating different aspects of the course.

Development of Scottish Integrated Science

This course was not the outcome of a curriculum *project*; it developed as part of the continuous process of gradual curriculum reform favoured by a Scottish educational system that is much more centralised than that of England and Wales. One of the reasons for the widespread adoption of the integrated scheme was undoubtedly the extent to which it was in line with various national policies.

In 1964 the Secretary of State for Scotland set up a Working Party to review the secondary school science curriculum for those pupils who would *not* be following courses leading to the Scottish Certificate of Education. This reflected the then current policies of the Scottish Education Department (SED) and the LEAs that were directed towards providing new and enlightened programmes for such pupils (the 'alternative' separate science syllabuses had been designed for the more academic pupils in the early sixties). However, a shift in political emphasis to the importance of common courses for mixed ability groups in comprehensive schools had occurred by 1966, and the Working Party's remit was changed to one which was interpreted as requiring the preparation and evaluation of:

1. A common course in science for *all* pupils in the first two years of secondary school (S.1 and S.2)[1]
2. A course for non-academic pupils in years 3 and 4 (S.3 and S.4).

The following discussion relates only to the first of these.

The new task seems to have been accepted without demur, which is not surprising since eight of the 16 members of the Working Party were from the policy making bodies (SED and LEAs). Furthermore, we might expect that the eight teacher members (from schools and colleges of education), realising that a common course for mixed ability groups within comprehensive schools was to be the pattern for the early years of secondary education, would have been quite willing to turn their hands to developing a course designed to ease some of the problems that such reorganization would inevitably present.

The distribution of power among, and freedom of, members of this central authority/teacher alliance is not clear. Both chairman and secretary of the Working Party were HMIs, which reflects the ultimate control retained by the SED over what should or should not be (a) considered, and (b) written down as a result of those considerations. Nisbet in describing curriculum development in Scotland at that time comments: '. . . the process of change is seldom adequately documented so that it is difficult for those outside the system to know precisely what has happened' (Nisbet 1970). However, in a later paper he goes on to point out the advantage of a system whereby

> . . . the proposals which emerge are more likely to be in line with national policy. They will generally be practicable; they arise from consensus of informed opinion within the system; they are seen as carrying the approval of authority; and . . . there is a greater chance that they will influence policy.   (Nisbet 1975)

The perennial political pressure on science teachers is the public examination system, administered in Scotland by a single board. In 1965 the SED transferred control and responsibility for the examinations to an autonomous Scottish Certificate of Education Examination Board (SCEEB), but there remained close contact among HMIs, Working Party members, SCEEB science subject panels and Examination Board officials. This informal contact facilitated the agreement whereby the proposed course for S.1 and S.2 would be equivalent to the first two years of the four year O-grade courses in biology, chemistry and physics. If this agreement had not been achieved it seems very unlikely that teachers would have been prepared to put their academic pupils 'at risk' by following what would have been seen as a 'non-certificate' scheme.

In 1969 the Working Party published its report *Curriculum Paper 7* (SED 1969b), incorporating the syllabus for the new course. Legally, the SED has no direct responsibility for the school curriculum (SED 1969a), LEAs and schools being free to accept advice or not as they choose. In practice, a document like *Curriculum Paper 7* that:

1. the SED sends free of charge to all schools as an official communication;
2. takes for granted the implementation of policies such as comprehensive education and mixed ability classes;
3. presents a course designed by teachers, LEA advisers and HMIs specifically for such implementation;
4. provides assurances that public examinations will be tailored to fit the new programme;
5. is reflected in the in-service courses (over which the SED exerts considerable control);

is ignored at peril by the teachers!

The development of this course reflects some of the features of the relatively small Scottish educational system (less than 500 secondary schools with fewer than half a million pupils). It is not difficult for those who develop, disseminate or evaluate curricula, control examinations, organise in-service work and advise or train teachers to consult each other. These influential individuals meet frequently and can facilitate speedy, realistic curriculum reform within the existing framework – a system that Nisbet (1975) describes as tending 'towards the paternalistic and not designed to develop criticism or imaginative original ideas'. This suggests that reforms may be quickly achieved but are unlikely to be radical.

Innovatory aspects of the course

It appears that the Working Party were concerned with innovations in four broad areas of Scottish science education. Firstly, this was to be a common course aimed at a new group of 'target' pupils – mixed ability classes in comprehensive schools. Secondly, the way in which the knowledge was organised was to be changed: science was to be presented in an *integrated* form. Thirdly, appropriate teaching methods ('stage-managed heurism') were recommended. Fourthly, the course was to be structured in relation to pupils' achievement of specified objectives.

A common course designed for mixed ability groups

Previously, courses tended to be designed either for the 'junior secondary' (non-certificate) or for the 'senior secondary' (academic) school or stream. In this case, the intention was that the science course be 'essentially part of general education' (SED 1969b, 11) and should 'suit the needs of a common course to be taught to unselected classes' (9) making 'provision ... for different rates of working and for different depths of understanding' (23).

Curriculum Paper 7 did not attempt to *justify* a common course for mixed ability groups, it was *assumed* as part of the framework within which the curriculum was to be developed. Teachers have expressed vociferous opposition to this policy, but the only relevant documented study (based on interviews with science staffs of 50 schools: Brown *et al.* 1976) found that 15 per cent more arguments were presented 'for' the common course than 'against' it. These researchers found also that while teachers frequently emphasised the necessity of individualising tasks for pupils in mixed ability groups, the available resources were considered inadequate for this purpose.

The Working Party shared the view that individualisation was desirable, prepared a set of worksheets (Scottish Secondary Science Working Party 1969, 1974) and claimed that:

> Where possible, the frames into which each worksheet is subdivided are in a hierarchical order of depth of understanding ... the concept with which the sheet deals can be elicited from results of work done in the earlier frames so the less able pupils can grasp the essential point of the teaching without proceeding to the end of the sheet. To keep the very able pupils at full stretch however some additional exercises have been included'
> (SED 1969b, 23)

The publisher appeared to exert little influence on the writing of the sheets and was eager to co-operate in the production of material stamped with official approval.

The dissatisfaction of some teachers with these worksheets led to development of other sheets or teachers' guides by individual schools or LEAs and, through representations from one of the teachers' unions to the Consultative Committee on the Curriculum,[2] to the establishment of a *new* Working Party with the tasks of reformulating groups of objectives for each section of the course and of producing worksheets, all of which were to take account of different levels of pupils' abilities.

The recent publications of the new Working Party (Scottish Central Committee on Science 1977a, 1977b, 1977c, 1977d) have clarified a number of aspects of mixed ability science teaching that had been neglected. For example, *Curriculum Paper 7* suggested that some of its specified objectives might be too difficult for some pupils, but it offered no help on how to decide which objectives were relevant for which pupils. We are now provided with specifications of sets of objectives seen as appropriate for three groups of pupils (the less able, the average and more able, and the most able), and these groups are described in terms of relatively permanent characteristics that the pupils within them might be expected to display (e.g. 'slow rate of cognitive development', 'a feeling of personal adequacy', 'highly intelligent'). In addition, a series of core worksheets has been developed of which rather fewer than a quarter have extension sheets. These extensions, labelled 'a' 'b' and 'c', comprise materials selected as being at levels consistent with the states of intellectual development (i.e. levels of concrete/abstract thinking) of the three ability groups, and illustrations of characteristics of concrete and abstract thinking are provided to help teachers to assess the stages of development of their pupils and to allocate them to the appropriate extension sheets.

However, there is very little guidance offered to teachers on appropriate procedures and suitable teaching strategies to use in classes with pupils of a wide range of abilities where different pupils are undertaking different tasks. Teachers are urged not to categorize pupils into permanent ability groups that are always allocated 'a' or 'b' or 'c' extensions but rather to continually reassess the pupils' performance and to match pupil to extension accordingly. But no guidelines on how this is to be done are provided; the exhortation to the teachers is 'be flexible'.

The considerable organisational demands on the teacher in a classroom where different pupils are doing different things towards different objectives are recognised. Effective management of this new context is seen as dependent upon the 'organisational skills of teachers'. Unfortunately few of us have developed skills that will enable us to see immediately how we can deal at one time with a number of groups doing different work (e.g. with the introduction of what each different group is to do; with the division of teacher's attention among different groups or extensions; with the discussion of results and conclusions appropriate to each different group; with the stigma that may attach to the 'less able' extensions; with the problems of having to split 'friendship' groups that are not of homogeneous ability; and so on). It seems likely that statements such as 'it is the responsibility of the individual teacher to use his or her professional judgement and skill' and 'it is the teacher's duty to ensure that the class remains as one social unit' will have to be supplemented if teachers are to implement the intentions of the differentiated programme.

Integration

Curriculum Paper 7's recommendation was that an integrated course for S.1 and S.2 was appropriate since 'science must somewhere be seen as a whole' (SED 1969b, 18), it should be taught by one teacher rather than three and in a form so that the 'unity of science should be made clear' (18). This implied that the content of the course was to be selected and organised on a different basis from either that of the earlier non-certificate general science, or that of the certificate biology, chemistry and physics. However, there were two important constraints influencing the choice of content. These were that it should

1. demand a minimum of new equipment for the schools;
2. be acceptable as a base for later certificate work in the separate science syllabuses.   (Jeffrey 1977)

During the sixties the schools had acquired considerable new stocks of apparatus to accommodate the 'alternative' separate subject courses for academic pupils. The obvious procedure was for the Working Party to choose content that would make the best use of this equipment, and the most appropriate content for this purpose was that of the separate science syllabuses. Furthermore, such content would be appropriate also as an alternative course to the separate syllabuses (since it would be identical!) for certificate work. As a result, the content prescribed for the integrated course corresponded very closely to the separate science courses. In the case of chemistry and physics the wording was identical. 'That biology is not also identical is only because of the form in which the biology syllabus was published by the Examination Board' (SED 1969b, 19).

What then did the Working Party mean by *integrated* science?

Statements such as '... the approach to science ... teaches some fundamental concepts' (25), '... energy and the structure of matter are fundamental to the rest of the course' (21), and 'Pupils should acquire ... awareness of the inter-relationships of the different disciplines of science' (16), might imply that science was seen as a single conceptual framework with 'energy' and 'the structure of matter' as two components of that framework. Such a framework would be expected to influence the organisation of the material and the order in which the various contents were covered. However, no specification was provided of any of the other components nor of any inter-relationships among them. Furthermore, though the content was divided into 15 sections, no particular ordering of them was recommended (apart from the early treatment of energy and structure of matter), and 'many of the sections stand alone, little, if in any way, dependent on what has gone before' (21). Those sections that could not be labelled biology or chemistry or physics consisted of either material previously duplicated in the separate science (e.g. Section 4 'Evidence for the fine division of matter' was covered in both chemistry and physics), or related material from two or more separate sciences that is now more conveniently juxtaposed (e.g. Section 13, 'Support and Movement' draws on 'Force' and 'Work and Energy' from physics, and 'Support in Animals' and 'Muscles' from biology).

It appears, then, that the curriculum *as a whole* was not designed in relation to some unified conceptual structure of science.

There is some indication that 'integration' was interpreted in the sense of some sort of unified process of scientific enquiry:

> ... there is a much reduced emphasis on the retention of the factual content of the syllabus. Instead an attempt has been made to expose pupils to many other aspects of the work of the scientist; the apparatus at his disposal, the experimental methods he uses, the different processes of thought by which he arrives at his conclusions.
>
> (SED 1969b, 10)

This statement is not reflected in the syllabus. Apart from Section 1 'Introducing Science', the vast majority of recommended topics are focussed on collecting *substantive information* and not on the practical and theoretical *procedures* of science. That is not to say that pupils will not learn something about those procedures as they carry out experiments and watch the demonstrations that lead to substantive results (it would be surprising if they did not), but it does demonstrate that the course does not reflect the emphasis on procedures and methodology that is claimed by the rhetoric of *Curriculum Paper 7*.

It may be the case that the Working Party viewed 'integration' in terms of 'science as an integral part of everyday life'. They saw the course as providing explanations of 'ourselves and the natural phenomena with which we are surrounded' (SED 1969b, 11), demonstrating the influence of science on 'our morals, our ethics, and our whole cultural environment' (13) and illustrating 'the contribution of science to the economic and social life of the community' (16). There are many social and technological problems that knowledge from a single subject area is inadequate to solve, and some integrated courses are built around such problems. That is not the case for this course, and since it relates so closely to the alternative separate science courses it is difficult to see how it can be more socially relevant or useful than they are.

Brown *et al.* (1976) found that the meanings ascribed to 'integration' by the teachers were both varied and vague beyond agreeing that it entailed each class being taught all its science by one teacher. Arguments 'for' and 'against' integrated science were evenly matched. The teachers perceived advantages (greater feeling of security for the pupils arriving from primary school, less boredom for the teachers than continuous repetition of single subject lessons, better chance for teachers to know and assess their pupils, closer teacher–pupil relationships, easier to patch over shortages of teachers in particular areas of science) and disadvantages (teaching unfamiliar subjects, inadequate foundation for academic pupils, problems of equipment supply and distribution). However, the teachers' concerns were in different areas from those of *Curriculum Paper 7*. The only common ground was the agreement that the one-teacher arrangement led to better teacher–pupil relationships. The teachers stressed their inadequate training for teaching a course, large sections of which came from specialist areas other than their own – a problem anticipated but given little attention by *Curriculum Paper 7*. The *particular* problems of the individual school influenced the teachers' views of the course. Schools with staff imbalances among subject areas favoured integration, while schools with widely dispersed science accommodation favoured separate subjects, but the Working Party provided no developed discussion of these factors. Both Paper and teachers argued in terms of political constraints, but there was evidence of conflict between the Paper's assumption of the appropriateness of the course as a preparation for O-grade[3] and the teachers' different views. Arguments about the suitability of the course for producing an informed lay population in addition to trained scientists, and as reflecting the true nature of science, were given considerable attention by the Paper, but they were largely ignored by the teachers.

It appears then that 'integration' in this context referred only to a new arrangement – one teacher teaching all the science to one class – and that the 'demonstration of the unity of science' claims for the course were somewhat pretentious.

STAGE-MANAGED HEURISM

The importance of selecting the 'right methods for presenting science to these young people' is stressed by *Curriculum Paper 7* (SED 1969b, 22). 'Stage-managed heurism' is recommended and appears to be synonomous with the more widely used 'guided-discovery'. The method is presented as some sort of compromise between discovery learning and programmed learning. It is suggested (22) 'that science is a subject which is admirably suited to discovery methods, indeed the very process of discovering appears to us to be as important as the knowledge discovered'. On one hand, such methods were seen as giving the pupil 'classroom situations which allow him to discover things for himself . . . exercise selection of approach and method and he should never be in possession of the final and correct answer before he begins his investigation'. But, on the other hand, we are warned that pupils 'have neither the skill nor the experience to work on their own without support'. Just what level of support was being recommended is not clear. Despite their admiration for discovery methods the Working Party imply a very high level of control by the teacher:

> The introduction to the work on the worksheets, the discussion afterwards, all of the demonstration work and the actual teaching which will establish the concepts under investigation, are still completely in the teacher's hands. In other words the teacher still has complete control over the end products of the various activities.
>
> (SED 1969b, 24)

Furthermore, they suggest (24) that the most appropriate support might be found to be programmed learning material (the antithesis of discovery learning).

Brown *et al.* asked teachers what they understood by, and practiced as guidance (or support). They conclude:

> The teachers gave very little support to the Paper's suggestions (a) that pupils themselves should exercise control over their experimental approaches and methods, and (b) that guidance on how to solve problems should be kept to a minimum. They placed great emphasis on pupils being in possession of *correct* answers and not going away with inaccurate information, and there was little evidence of willingness to follow the directive of the Paper to expect and accept negative as well as positive results. (Brown *et al.* 1976, 49)

As a method, the teachers treated guided-discovery with hostility, presenting nearly eight times as many arguments 'against' as 'for'. They saw it as inappropriate for the abilities of their pupils and for science, as inadequate for the demands made by the syllabus and later certificate work, and as impracticable within the time allocated to science and in relation to their own perceived lack of training in such methods. However, the responses implied the rather limited interpretation of guided-discovery methods as 'pupils deciding and doing *everything* for themselves without assistance'. It seems likely that the curriculum writers had a wider range of interpretations in mind. Brown and McIntyre (1977) report that an attitude questionnaire, reflecting this range and administered to a group of teachers comparable with the earlier sample, revealed mildly favourable attitudes towards these more broadly-based conceptions of guided-discovery. The authors argue that this is an example of inadequate conceptual clarity from curriculum planners which invariably leads to teachers having little idea of what was intended and either ignoring the innovation or misunderstanding it and reacting with disfavour.

TEACHING TOWARDS SPECIFIED OBJECTIVES

Curriculum Paper 7's method of approach (SED 1969b, 9) was one by which 'First and foremost aims and objectives have been formulated'. Earlier Scottish science courses had identified broad aims, but this was the first time that explicit specification of general objectives for the course ('knowledge and understanding', 'attitudes' and 'practical skills') and specific objectives for each section of work, had been provided.

The Working Party suggested that activities in the classroom could, and should, be planned in relation to achievement of the specific objectives which would then lead to attainment of the smaller number of general objectives (16). Moreover, the objectives were seen as the underpinning for the testing of pupils, the first stated function of which was seen as 'To assess if the curriculum is achieving its objectives' (25).

However, no information was given on how the recommended classroom activities, specific objectives and general objectives were related to each other, and in most cases the specific objectives were not stated with sufficient precision for their attainment by pupils to be tested.

Despite the first sentence of this section, Jeffrey (1977), a member of the Working Party, reports that the general objectives were developed *after* the content and broad aims. We are given no details about how the content (largely determined by the alternative science courses) was seen as likely to lead to attainment of the chosen aims and objectives. This lack of explicit linkage may partly account for the very small number of schools that Brown *et al.* (1976) found to be consciously planning classroom activities in terms of achievement of the specified objectives. The teachers' concerns seemed to be with getting across the *content* of the syllabus, and constructing tests in relation to that content, rather than pupils' attainment of the objectives.

There are a number of features of the recent work of the *new* Working Party (Scottish Central Committee on Science 1977c, 1977d) that may lead to more concern for objectives in teachers' thinking about their teaching. Firstly, the linkages from the general aims of science teaching, to the objectives for the course, to section objectives, to individual lesson objectives are examined and illustrated. Secondly, some effort has been made to clarify the meanings of the course objectives seen as appropriate for achievement by pupils of each of the three ability groups. Thirdly, a recommendation (with exemplification) is made that assessment should be criterion-referenced where the criteria are determined by the stated objectives and expected outcomes. It may be the case that these features provide the clarification of meaning and procedural referents that appear to be necessary prerequisites of any effective curricular innovation (see, for example: Brown and McIntyre 1977; Doyle and Ponder 1977).

Evaluation of the course

Evaluation of this scheme has been somewhat piecemeal; the various stages have been summarised by Jeffrey (1977). Prior to publication of *Curriculum Paper 7*, the Working Party appear to have used oral accounts from teachers in pilot schools and HMIs for feedback on which to base the changes in the early materials. No details of their procedures are given.

They showed early concern for the development of test material for assessing pupils, and provided modest financial support to two research students for this purpose. These tests were administered to pupils of various levels of ability in both streamed and mixed ability classes (King 1972, provides a description of the development, administration and results of half of these tests). Some fairly sweeping conclusions were drawn from these studies by the Scottish Education Department: that these tests were valid measures on which to evaluate the curriculum, that all pupils were learning adequately from the curriculum, and that streaming had little effect on the learning of the more able but a considerable and lowering effect on the least able. The content validity of the tests was assumed to be established by means of a screening process in which individuals examined the items and judged them as relevant or not to the objectives of the curriculum. Unfortunately, this procedure does not ensure that the items reflect the curriculum 'as it is taught'. A study in Sweden (Dahllöf 1971, 54–58) found low correlations between the distribution of mathematics test items and the time devoted to the teaching related to those items (five out of the six examples gave correlation coefficients that were less than 0.35). It was concluded that the tests were generally unsatisfactory instruments for evaluating that teaching. If the content validity of the Scottish tests has not been established, then any pronouncement about what has or has not been learnt by pupils from the course must be treated with caution. Even if the tests are valid, it is impossible to judge how useful such work is as curriculum evaluation unless we have documented details of how the conclusions were reached.

A substantial grant was provided for evaluation of a very limited aspect of this curriculum – the attitude objectives (Brown 1974, 1976, 1977). This study examined the arguments for inclusion of the objectives, their meanings and purposes, the factors influencing achievement of the objectives, the attitudes of pupils following separate subject courses as compared with those following the integrated course, and the changes in pupils' attitudes over the two-year course.

A number of studies have provided information about the extent to which this curriculum has achieved what was intended, although their primary research questions have related to other matters. Project PHI (Roebuck, Bloomer and Hamilton 1974) was concerned with assessing the value of introducing audio-visual equipment and self-instructional procedures to remote secondary schools in the Highlands and Islands. The work was carried out within the framework of the Integrated Science course, but the findings focussed mainly on the solution of educational problems in isolated areas rather than on the science curriculum.

Hamilton (1973, 1975) studied the innovation of the scheme in two schools and its relationship to Bernstein's (1971) educational paradigms (integrated and collection type). As well as looking at the course as an exemplar of a theoretical model he reports a number of interesting findings, such as the use teachers made of the section tests for discriminating among pupils rather than for the diagnostic purposes intended by *Curriculum Paper 7*.

At Stirling University a study is in progress of teachers' classroom strategies and tactics in relation to the four innovations of the course, and the relationships of such strategies and tactics to pupils' attainment of the specified objectives. Nevertheless, the fundamental questions being asked in this study are general ('What factors influence the success of innovations?') rather than specific to this curriculum.

An evaluation of the new materials (Scottish Central Committee on Science 1977a, 1977b, 1977c and 1977d) has been carried out. The main aims of this programme were: to assess the achievement of the objectives by pupils in 30 schools using criterion-referenced tests; to collate detailed comments from teachers on the content, presentation and suitability of the course materials; and to investigate general features of the course such as the success of group teaching and the organisation of the course in the classroom. The findings and conclusions of this study have not yet been published.

Concluding remarks

The widespread adoption of the Integrated Science course in Scottish schools, the influence it has exerted on curricula in the Caribbean, Asia and Africa (as witnessed by UNESCO publications) and the context it has provided for a number of general studies of the innovatory process are compelling measures of its success. However, a close look at the extent and nature of the pedagogical changes that have been introduced reveals them to be very modest. The progressive styled innovatory narrative of *Curriculum Paper 7* is not matched in the detailed structure of the 'new' course.

It was, perhaps, unfair to expect the Working Party to develop adequately the sorts of complex ideas that they were dealing with in the time available to them. This points to a serious disadvantage of this type of curriculum development system; Working Parties composed of busy people with other full-time jobs, under pressure to get information for teachers into print quickly, and who have little time or opportunity for reading specialised literature, are unlikely to appreciate the pitfalls and requirements of effective curriculum development. This can lead (as demonstrated by the four innovations discussed here) to the superficial presentation of new ideas for which the relevant concepts are inadequately described, and to failure to provide a coherent programme of evaluation.

The great advantages of the system 'are the close contact between the curriculum developers and those expected to implement change, the continuity and opportunity for gradual change maintained over many years, the relative ease with which working parties can be set up in response to problems encountered with the curriculum in the classroom, and the way in which national educational policies and innovations can be mutually supportive.

Notes

1. The age of transfer to secondary school in Scotland is at 12+ years.
2. The Consultative Committee on the Curriculum (CCC) maintains a general oversight over the school curriculum and advises the Secretary of State for Scotland on curriculum matters.
3. 'O' grade – national examination taken by pupils at same age as those sitting GCE Ordinary Level in England and Wales.

DAVID JENKINS

15 Man: A Course of Study[1]

Basic information

Sponsor The National Science Foundation (USA).

Grant Development $4,800,000.
Dissemination and implementation $2,160,000.

Locations Educational Development Center, Cambridge, Massachusetts.
Publishers and organisers of world dissemination: Curriculum Development Associates,
1211 Connecticut Avenue, NW. Suite 414, Washington DC.
   British training and dissemination organisers: MACOS Secretary, CARE,
University of East Anglia, Norwich.

Period of development 1963–68.

Designated pupils 10–11 year olds, but the course has been used with pupils aged
up to 16, and some of the materials with students and adults.

Organiser and team A large team during the development phase, latterly with
Peter Dow as director.

Consultants Jerome S. Bruner, Professor of Psychology, Center for Cognitive
Studies, Harvard University; Irven DeVore, Professor of Anthropology, Harvard University; Asen Balikei, Professor of Anthropology, University of Montreal.

Materials Films, booklets, teachers' guides and other materials. For full details see
bibliography.

Evaluation by Janet P. Hanley, Dean K. Whitla, Eunice W. Moo and Arlene S.
Walter, published under the title *Curiosity, Competence and Comunity*. Two-volume edition now out of print, single volume (condensed) included with the teachers'
materials.

Man: A Course of Study is an American curriculum, one of the major products of
the reform movement in the 1960s. Its claim to be included in a book concerned
with curriculum development in action in the United Kingdom is that it has
been disseminated on an international scale. Experience of it in Britain has been
to a large extent mediated through the appointment of an 'official' dissemi-

nation agency, the Centre for Applied Research in Education at the University of East Anglia. When it arrived at our shores, one could have been forgiven for supposing MACOS to be the packaged curriculum *par excellence*, if not actually teacher-proof at least endowed with daunting authority. The relevance of 'dissemination' to 'development in action' is complex and ambivalent, particularly as the style of dissemination has proved controversial. It has not primarily been concerned with preserving messages intact between the original producers of the programme and its future consumers, but with introducing what some have seen as a distorting lens. It is arguable in principle that adaptation of an educational programme to meet the conditions of a culture (and schools sub-culture) other than the one for which it was primarily designed, is itself a form of curriculum development.

Man: A Course of Study was originally developed in the United States by Education Development Centre Inc. (EDC), under grants from the National Science Foundation. The implicit view of curriculum development was authoritarian, valuing expertise. One of the strong thrusts behind the curriculum reform movement in the States was the perceived need to update the knowledge component in schooling. The reformers sought to close the so-called 'knowledge gap' by involving the ablest scholars from the various fields; such scholars were seen as gatekeepers, offering access to the growing edge of academic disciplines. MACOS became the outstanding example of high level sponsorship and the use of subject experts alongside teachers in curriculum design and development. Consulting scholars in EDC were Jerome Bruner, then Director of the Centre for Cognitive Studies at Harvard University; Irven DeVore, Professor of Anthropology at Harvard; and Asen Balikci, Professor of Anthropology at the University of Montreal.

Although the way in which the projected 'course of study' stabilised into a published programme is not closely examined in public accounts, professional gossip suggests that some of the predictable polite tensions that are normal and unremarkable in large scale curriculum projects reappeared here. High level funding has a magnet effect, encouraging prestigious support, but risking the possibility that those seeking involvement might 'bend' the brief in the direction of their particular interest and enthusiasms. (This is also true of a dissemination agency). Equally the realities of sponsorship and funding encourage that brand of 'funding talk' that allows enterprises to be 'fronted' by reassuring national figures whose accounts may not tally with those rowing in the middle of the boat. But Bruner himself is inclined in retrospect to discount the 'top-down' flavour of the *Man: a Course of Study* curriculum development. Admittedly teachers were 'flattered' by the emergence of support and interest from the prestigious universities, but the collaboration was real. The professors not only recognised the difficulties and dignity of the teaching profession, but themselves tried out the material with teachers and children in two summer schools. Nevertheless there is an implicit residual problem relating to the perceived authority of the programme itself, one that we shall return to in discussing dissemination. This notion of the 'authority of the programme' was seemingly endorsed when, at the insistence of the National Science Foundation, Curriculum Development Associates (the American dissemination agency) made teacher training a formal prerequisite to the purchase of the materials. This application of the principle of apostolic succession to the teaching of MACOS, nominally at least, was repeated in the United Kingdom. Not untypically there have been tensions and rivalry between EDC, the developers, and CDA, the disseminators.

It may be useful to describe *Man: A Course of Study* briefly in terms of its underlying conception, course structure and curriculum materials. The original blueprint is found in Jerome Bruner's *Toward a Theory of Instruction* (1966). It is remarkable, in retrospect, how widely-based an exploration Bruner envisaged, certainly one transcending any subject-based approach to curriculum, and organised around great questions, theories, and substantive issues. Bruner described the *content* of the course as 'man: his nature as a species, the forces that shaped and continue to shape his humanity'. The broad lines of approach to man's humanness were predetermined as the 'five great humanizing forces' that shaped man's destiny: tool making, language, social organisation, the management of man's prolonged childhood, and man's urge to explain his world.'

More remarkably, the five 'humanizing forces', redefined as 'subjects', had been subsumed under three large, and largely speculative, questions. It was intended that these questions should reverberate through the course:

What is human about human beings?

How did they get that way?

How can they be made more so?

'We seek', wrote Bruner, 'exercises and materials through which our pupils can learn wherein man is distinctive in his adaptation to the world, and wherein there is discernible continuity between him and his animal forebears.'

When the first commercial edition of *Man: A Course of Study* appeared in 1970, it was possible to compare the product with the original inspiration. The first point to notice is that the material is rich, multi-media, extremely sophisticated, attractively presented and expensive. The five humanizing forces had survived intact, although explicit concern with human language had diminished (or alternatively had become diffused and implicit, buried into the foundations of the comparative cultural studies). More than one would have supposed from a reading of the blueprint in *Toward a Theory of Instruction*, the material had become biassed towards film. The man-animal comparisons focussed sharply on a small less-than-self-evident selection: salmon, herring gulls and baboons. The exploration of the human condition arrowed-in on a single typical incarnation, the near-extinct culture of the Netsilik Eskimo, whose life style was to be followed and explored in depth throughout the cycle of the seasons.

But the underlying conceptual structure of the course had also become a surface feature of MACOS, explicitly embedded in the curriculum materials, particularly the cartoon-format 'concept booklets'. These pressed some of the main ideas of the course, seeking to promote understanding through explicated example. Titles included *Life Cycle, Animal Adaptation, Innate and Learned Behaviour* and *Natural Selection*. These booklets could easily be seen as authoritative, instructional ('based on Harry Recher's research into herons and puffer fish') rather than material for enquiry or discovery. The *Teachers' Guides*, too, were written prescriptively.

It would be wrong, however, to hoist Bruner with his own petard and castigate him as *only begetter* of a course of study that ignores his own important distinction between 'teaching to spectators' and 'teaching to participants'. The balance between instruction and discovery/enquiry is carefully maintained. Indeed the formal aims of *Man: A Course of Study* make it clear that the course is intended to engage the curiosity of the student. Its explanations and concepts have the status of 'working models'. The aims in part refer to process, in part to extremely broad cognitive and evaluative maps that in a sense offer the learner little more than orientation:

1. to give our pupils respect for, and confidence in, the powers of their own mind;
2. to extend that respect and confidence in their power to think about the human condition, man's plight and his social life;
3. to provide a set of workable models that make it simpler to analyse the nature of the social world in which we live and the condition in which man finds himself;
4. impart a sense of respect for the capacities and humanity of man as a species;
5. to leave the student with a sense of the unfinished business of man's evolution.

Given the much-expressed view that there is a persistent antinomy in *Man: A Course of Study* between the 'cognitive map embedded in the materials' and its commitment to enquiry-based learning, it is interesting to see how these original aims, as expressed by Bruner, are reworded in the evaluation report *Curiosity, Competence, Community*, (Hanley *et al.* 1969) and labelled 'Brunerian'. The report suggests that the programme aims at 'enlarging human capacities rather than refining narrow skills', and is 'structured around a "community of learning" rather than around hierarchial or status-defined roles such as "student", "teacher", or "authority".' This, we are told, exemplifies a Brunerian approach to curriculum, operating under three assumptions:

1. That learning is in good measure a social process by which children and teachers can articulate and share ideas with one another.
2. That competence over a body of knowledge will lead to increasing self-confidence and comprehension of one's operating assumptions about life.
3. That the world can be observed, conjectured about, and to some degree ordered and understood using the tools of the behavioural sciences, and that an individual life can be viewed as part of the larger flow of human existence.

(Hanley *et al.* 1969)

Nevertheless CDA's introductory brochure to *Man: a Course of Study* describes the material 'created from ethnographic film studies and field research' as representing 'the most recent *findings* of the behavioural sciences' (my emphasis). The course is said to begin with a unit on the life cycle of the salmon partly so that the unit might 'introduce the vocabulary and intellectual framework for the studies that follow'.

One of the reasons for taking an interest in the internal ambiguities of *Man: a Course of Study* is that the adaptation of it characterised by the Centre for Applied Research in Education at the University of East Anglia is premised on a line of argument developed by Lawrence Stenhouse. In my view this line adds up to reinventing the promise of the programme. Like much of Stenhouse's work, which is highly idiosyncratic as well as imaginative, its ambition is to turn a personal preference (decently veiled) into a public tradition. But readers may prefer first to get some purchase on the internal tensions between the epistemology of MACOS which might be labelled classic, and its pedagogy, which is romantic. The authors of *Curiosity, Competence, Community* produced a summarising four-dimensional analysis, which considered *Man: a Course of Study* in relation to its conceptual themes, its data sources, its classroom techniques and its learning methods (Table 15.1). There is some evidence of mismatch across the columns.

One aspect of *Man: a Course of Study* that links it with Stenhouse's Humanities Curriculum Project is its repudiation of a 'behavioural objectives' approach to curriculum design. This means simply that it discouraged the view that success is to be measured by conventional testing for evidence of student learning, and

Table 15.1 The conceptual and pedagogical goals of *Man: A Course of Study*.

Conceptual themes	Data sources	Classroom techniques	Learning methods
Life cycle (including reproduction)	1 *Primary Sources* Student experiences	*Examples* Individual and group research, e.g.	Inquiry, investigation (problem-defining, hypothesizing,
Adaptation	Behaviour of family		experimentation,
Learning	Behaviour of young children in school	direct observation or reading of texts	observation,
Aggression	Behaviour of animals	Large and small group discussion	interviewing, literature searching, summarizing and reporting)
Organization of groups (including group relationships, the family and community, division of labour)	2 *Secondary Sources* Films and slides of animals and Eskimos Recording of animal sounds	Games Role Play Large and small group projects such as art and construction projects	Sharing and evaluating of interpretation Accumulating and retaining information
Technology	Recordings of Eskimo myths, legends and	Writing of songs and poems	Exchange of opinion, defense of opinion
Communication and language	poetry Anthropological field		Exploration of individual feelings
World View	notes		Exposure to diverse aesthetic styles
Values	Written data on humans, other animals and environments		

Source: Hanley *et al*. 1969.

achieved its wish by refusing to specify the goals of the programme in testable terms. This stance is not just of technical interest; it forced the evaluation team to examine the programme *in action* and develop an educational critique. Janet Hanley and her co-authors of the evaluation report *Curiosity, Competence, Community* (1969) write:

> During the process of evaluating *Man: a Course of Study*, we frequently encountered from educators and researchers questions as to behavioural goals. The course has not been framed within the confines of a behavioural psychology, nor have its developers thought specifically in behaviourist terms as they prepared and tested it. Rather the course was developed within a humanist framework by way of its emphasis upon the anthropological, biological and ethnographic. Its organising question 'What makes man human?' has always been asked in the broadest possible sense, and its framers, from Bruner on, have emphasised the resonance of the question within the material.

Evaluation tended to confirm what one might readily have guessed, that teachers were facing up to the challenge of *Man: a Course of Study*, but that many of the issues raised were professionally demanding, and required further thought. In particular an educational critique of *Man: a Course of Study* was being articulated with increasing persuasiveness by Richard Jones. At its crudest Jones' critique, published in *Fantasy and Feeling in Education* (1968), suggested that the formidable *intellectual* challenge of the programme was obscuring the need for any defensible exploration of man's *humanness* to find a way of handling emotions in the setting of the classroom. Evidence from clinical observation of single classrooms revealed teachers treating, say, senilicide (in times of hardship the Netsilik eskimo may abandon his grandmother on an ice flow) as if it were emotionally neutral. In a tape-recorded post-lesson discussion a psychologist remarked 'What emotional skills would they have learned this morning if they followed our example? Here's a story about a useless old lady who's expected to commit suicide. Get it? Now let's see how they build an igloo.' But institutions will, if possible, assimilate rather than reject their critics, and Jones' strictures simply ended up as seminar material for teacher training sessions run by the dissemination agencies.

Another problem that emerged from the evaluation report, *Curiosity, Competence, Community* was ethnocentrism. The course, it was suggested, might be generating side-effects, inculcating attitudes opposite to those it was designed to instil. Far from sensing a 'common humanity', some children were finding the eskimo culture alien, even bizarre. Empathy is clearly more readily forthcoming when the human quality responded to is technological inventiveness (e.g. constructing a sledge) rather than an emotional expression in an unfamiliar idiom (e.g. the eskimo myths, which some children ridiculed).

Perhaps more disturbingly, the evaluation report dichotomised the teachers it observed into two broad kinds, 'idea-centred' and 'student-centred'. The student-centred stereotype appears warm and mothering ('an archetypal elementary school teacher'). She is strong on collaborative social learning in the *Man: a Course of Study* classroom, but is herself hazy intellectually on the concepts of the course. That is, she seeks to teach what she does not properly understand herself. But 'idea-centred' and 'student-centred' reflects in a much more general sense the internal ambiguities of the course, which at times suggests a kind of curriculum optical illusion, perceived differently by different people.

Opposition to the programme, however, came less from its friendly neighbourhood evaluation than from that truss of ideological self-righteousness, the American 'Bible Belt'. Fairly typical was the controversy that arose surrounding the introduction to MACOS into Arizona schools. The following extract is from a circular sent to parents by an anti-MACOS action group in the Madison district:

> Kill useless old grandma, eat the wife's flesh and save the bones. Murder baby girls, exchange wives, learn to think like a baboon, and study animal mating. Simulated hunts and role playing are included which condition children to accept a primitive culture as normal ... We are told this is a pilot or experiment ... Why experiment with a course that is *not* state approved? Would you allow a brain surgeon to experiment on your child?
>
> A steady diet of blood letting and promiscuity is presented through games, records, nightmarish films, booklets and pictures ... The children are also taught that we humans are related to the chimpanzee. The immature impressionable child is thereby induced to believe that man is only an advanced animal.

The political pressure brought to bear against *Man: a Course of Study* was surprising vehement, involving several congressmen. Odd that a programme so *demonstrably* American in preserving the twin myths of the frontier and the perfectability of man, should attract hostility for running counter to fundamentalist myths of the origin of the human species.

When we turn to *Man: a Course of Study* in Britain, we immediately encounter rich paradoxes. It all began with a piece of pure opportunism. The Humanities Curriculum Project team were in America for an HCP workshop sponsored by the Ford Foundation in Ohio State University. The style of workshop session evolved by Stenhouse and his team was to approach the HCP in terms reverberating its own pedagogy; that is, to treat *the curriculum innovation itself* as a 'controversial issue'. In effect, this meant that training sessions were conducted by 'neutral chairmen'. One of the participants at the workshop who found the open stance attractive was Frances Link, leading lady of Curriculum Development Associates. Mrs. Link was about to leave for Miami to conduct a *Man: a Course of Study* workshop, and it was agreed that John Elliott should accompany her. Stenhouse guessed rightly that at the back of her mind was the possibility of setting up in the United Kingdom a centre of dissemination of the programme and the training of teachers.

Elliott was at that time distilling the central ideas of the Ford Teaching Project. He directed this action-based research into enquiry and discovery-based teaching at the conclusion of his HCP contract, subsequently taking it with him to the Cambridge Institute of Education. Elliott's reaction to *Man: a Course of Study* was critical. He considered its claims to be open-ended bogus, pointing to the conceptual map 'embedded in the materials' and to the 'double-think' involved in giving man a value definition but still calling the programme an open-ended enquiry. Elliot's reservations about *Man: a Course of Study* probably contributed to Lawrence Stenhouse's decision, when offered the British agency, to place it with Jean Rudduck 'as disseminator' rather than with John Elliott 'as trainer'. He was perhaps also afraid that it would be simply annexed into the Ford Teaching Project.

At that time Lawrence Stenhouse 'needed *Man: a Course of Study* very badly.' It appeared unlikely, at least in the immediate future, that he would attract further curriculum development funding from the Schools Council. There arose what Stenhouse describes as 'an extraordinary situation': 'We knew nothing about the curriculum or very little. We had not taught it; we had not seen it in schools; we had had nothing to do with its development. Initially we were learning about the curriculum ourselves ... trying to explore it with other people.' The underlying paradox stood out as nicely ironical: how might this style of dissemination be squared with the moral imperatives associated with obligatory training?

Stenhouse's way out of the partly-acknowledged intellectual dilemma was characteristically subtle. Might not *Man: a Course of Study*, like HCP, be disseminated by training teachers in a way that echoed the perceived pedagogy of the course? This mimesis of the pedagogy by the training style was quite explicit: 'The principle of the conferences became to treat *Man: a Course of Study* as an object of discovery and enquiry, and try to teach it by discovery and enquiry methods'. Thus the dissemination of MACOS was brought under tribute to one of Stenhouse's recurring research interests, the exploration of authority relationships in relation to academic knowledge. The dissemination model chosen by the Centre for Applied Research in Education is one that emphasises the responsibility of the teacher, rather than the authority of the programme. The object of the exercise is three-fold:

1. To make *Man: a Course of Study* more accessible as a potential choice for teachers in primary, lower secondary or middle school.
2. To report on the experiences of teachers using the materials, while recognising their right to determine what is right in their own situation.
3. To maintain a dialogue concerning what problems and possibilities are perceived in the school.

The idea of the 'dialogue' is a central one. Stenhouse characterises the differences between CARE and Curriculum Development Associates as follows: 'They are interested in disseminating a curriculum; we are interested in disseminating a dialogue. We are not basically and primarily interested in disseminating the curriculum. I think that's true' (Interview with Stenhouse).

This may be in tune with the sub-culture of British curriculum development, which tends not to proceed by way of authoritative recommendation. Nevertheless the stance involves 'taking a view' of *Man: a Course of Study*, which was accepted on the understanding that a certain amount of reinterpretation and renewal would take place. Both the discovery tradition and the instruction tradition are seen by Stenhouse as involving inherent contradictions. As he says 'whereas in the instructional tradition the teacher is caught relentlessly in pretending to know more than he knows, in the discovery tradition he is caught relentlessly in pretending he knows less than he knows'. In contrast CDA's Frances Link begins from an emotional commitment to the programme. The authority she finds most difficulty in getting rid of is emotional authority. Stenhouse admits to finding more difficulty in getting rid of intellectual authority. When alternative ways of advancing *Man: a Course of Study* were canvassed in Britain (in Bulmershe and Madeley Colleges of Education), Stenhouse did not hesitate in using his authority 'to prevent the style being captured'.

When a group of teachers met at the 1975 Standing Conference on Curriculum Studies 'to report on the experience of teachers using the *Man: a Course of Study* materials', it was felt that the packaged curriculum materials, particularly the films, were a relatively fixed element, while the pedagogy might be interpreted selectively. Actual use of the material varied widely, which was perhaps a tribute to the non-recommendatory stance of the dissemination. On the other hand because it is possible to infer from a dissemination 'based on the pedagogy of the course' how the disseminators would themselves approach it in classrooms, teachers felt able to define their own practice in terms of the 'implicit orthodoxies' underpinning the UK dissemination programme. This orthodoxy was perceived as preoccupied with the nature of evidence (cf. the Humanities Curriculum Project) and anti-instructional to the extent of silencing out the sound track on the more informative films, to reinforce their witness as surrogate raw data.

One must expect a training organisation to have its own cultural milieu, and that of the Centre for Applied Research in Education has developed historically around the kind of problems posed by the remit of the Humanities Curriculum Project. Nevertheless the MACOS curriculum has been made accessible, and teachers validated it in their own attempts at modification and adaptation. Quite a number of Yuri Gellers of British education were able to give examples of MACOS spoon-bending. These included:

1. An attempt to keep the material support while 'rejecting' or 'rejigging' the theory. One school overlaid MACOS with an explicitly Christian gloss that would have gone down well in Arizona.
2. Adding to or extending the material. One school grafted on the Tristan da Cunha section of the Keele Integrated Studies *Living Together* pack.
3. Finessing the strategy associated with the media element. Several schools followed the British dissemination agency's idea of silencing out sound track rather than following EDC's *Note for Teachers*; (Lawrence Stenhouse dissents from this interpretation of events, but I remain unpersuaded.)
4. Emphasis-shifting towards comforting ideologies (e.g. the primary school ethos as extended into the middle school).

5. Pursuing private agendas. Ms Cutler, a liberated and vocal secondary school teacher, proved to the satisfaction of many that the MACOS interpretation of the social organisation of baboons is 'sexist'.

6. Updating the knowledge component. This ironically is where the original development team came in. But several teachers had seen, immediately prior to the conference, a television film about a learning chimp Washoe, who had mastered the quasi-linguistic syntax of his computerised prison-laboratory. It was asserted that MACOS had, overnight as it were, become dated in its 'findings' on man-animal distinctions. One beneficial spin off was that this insight allowed individual teachers to escape the authority of the programme.   (see Jenings 1967b)

Overall it might be said that the significance of *Man: a Course of Study* in Britain has been its use as a vehicle for the further professional education of teachers. But whether the now-you-see-it-now-you-don't 'reinterpretation' of MACOS for the cultural conditions of British education quite counts as 'curriculum development in action' is an issue best left to the reader.

JEROME BRUNER

Man: A Course of Study: Response I

I have the general feeling about Mr. Jenkins of an almost complete pre-occupation with the politics and ideology of education as an institution. He is very sophisticated at it as well. And he operates on the assumption that those who are involved in anything having to do with education are just as sophisticated as he is. Historically speaking, that is a big mistake. Because in point of fact when we were all at work on *Man: a Course of Study* we had in mind principally the issue of reducing the authoritarianism of teaching by making the materials such that they would challenge learners, pupils and teachers alike, and make them something closer to brothers in inquiry.

Now, as you know from the heights of the latter 1970s, that is a very naive idea! Yet that in fact is what we were trying to do.

I would also add that we chose our material in such a way that not only intellectual but valuational issues would have to be approached afresh and without received authority. I still differ with Richard Jones on the issue of whether one can or should produce emotional unmasking in class if one is not prepared to take responsibility in a quasi-therapeutic way for those unmasked – be they teachers or pupils.

I cannot say much about the promotion and dissemination of the course after 1970–71. Frances Link and her group worked mightily and undoubtedly introduced many changes. Nor can I say much about what Lawrence Sten-house and Jean Rudduck had in mind when they took over dissemination of the course in Britain. They undoubtedly introduced changes too. But the course was ultimately designed with change in mind. I always had the feeling that the main thing that was worthy about the course was that it could be used as well for teacher training, and that used in that way it would produce quite upredictable results in what teachers would do with the course afterwards. I gather from everything I have been told that this is indeed the case.

The heavy burden of film in the course was one of the inevitabilities of the local Cambridge scene. Zacharias had a big film studio going and it was also the case that the Canadian Film Board and DeVore had most of their materials on the Netsilik and on baboons in the form of film record. But film has a way of pre-empting reality by too much emphasis on how things *look* and how they *appear* to work. It always risks becoming a substitute for imagination. I certainly reduced the emphasis on film as much as I could and I also worked very hard to use film as a stimulus rather than as a given. I don't think that we fully succeeded by any means in bringing film into balance.

I think it is fair to say that I exerted all the power I could in the direction of keeping the balance that finally emerged in the course between initial aspiration and materials used for achieving that aspiration. Undoubtedly, the aspiration in the form of the questions that I had used initially have put a predisposing structure into the materials. That structure is undoubtedly Brunerian! But let me only urge that it is intended as the goad to a dialogue rather than an imprisoning matrix from which the student's mind cannot escape. Politically, I suppose that would be considered naive. Ah well.

JEAN RUDDUCK

Man: A Course of Study: Response II

Man: A Course of Study and David Jenkins's chapter of *Man: a Course of Study* are alike in some respects. In each there is excitement, glamour and challenge. They are both, in their ways, as beguiling as the Lotus Isle, and visitors – users of the course and readers of the chapter – need to have their wits about them. Neither course nor article presents the whole truth, and the rhetoric can easily dull one's responses and persuade one that it's all there and it's all right.

Jenkins certainly raises important questions about knowledge and control in relation to the dissemination of curriculum development. MACOS presents a thesis about the nature of learning; Jenkins presents a thesis about the influence of authority. On the whole what he says about the dissemination of the course in the UK is sound and well-supported with evidence, but the weakness of the thesis is that it is restricted to general principles and is not tested against the details of current practice. Jenkins seems most interested in the 'grand originals': Bruner, Link and Stenhouse, but the programme of dissemination in this country is planned by a group of teachers from schools and colleges who give up a lot of spare time to thinking out how to improve the quality – and quantity – of support for teachers interested or involved in MACOS. They are not managed by Stenhouse through some miracle of remote control. What one misses in Jenkins' account is the sense that some of the ordinary everyday aspects of teaching and training MACOS are worth writing about.

Here and there in the chapter are points where an alternative view might reasonably be set alongside Jenkins' own.

First, the handling of emotion in the classroom or the ethnocentrism of pupil and teacher response: these are problems that are widespread in our schools. MACOS does not create these; it merely focuses them and helps teachers to pay attention to them.

Second, it seems right, within the framework of enquiry teaching, that the instructional resources should be built into the materials rather than into the teacher's role. In this way, the teacher is free to make a critical response alongside the pupils. Both teacher and pupils take their place within the community of learners.

Third, Jenkins' preoccupation with the soundtrack of the animal films – which have taken on an absurdly Machiavellian power. Of course teachers might experiment with the impact of film run without soundtrack for an initial viewing, but we would not recommend the exclusive use of the picture alone for if teachers shut off the sound they are shutting off the instruction and they may then be forced back into the 'teacher' role of the instructional classroom. Soundtrack as well as visual image provides material for critical enquiry.

Note

1. This account is based in part on taped interviews with Lawrence Stenhouse and Jerome Bruner, and an informal conversation with Frances Link. It is not my supposition that these people would wish to add to their kindness by endorsing the account as written, for which I must take individual responsibility.

ELIZABETH ADAMS

16 Ford Teaching Project

Basic information

Sponsor Ford Foundation.

Grant £25,795.

Location Centre for Applied Research in Education, University of East Anglia and subsequently Cambridge Institute of Education, Shaftesbury Road, Cambridge.

Director John Elliott.

Period of development Main Project 1972–74, Extension 1974–75.

Designated population Qualified teachers.

Concerns The analysis and improvement of the logic and practice of teaching through inquiry and discovery.

Curriculum area Across the curriculum in primary and secondary schools.

Action research Conducted in classrooms in about a dozen schools primary and secondary.

Materials produced Working papers: these are listed in the bibliography. Film: 'Fish in a Tank'.

Evaluation Begun in 1976 on a small grant to John Elliott from the Ford Foundation. Informal follow-up by self-selected group of teachers prepared to pursue action research in their classrooms.

Background

As Wrigley has pointed out 'to evaluate, assess or examine important activities is not easy'. (Wrigley 1976). Teaching is such an activity and the Ford Teaching Project was set up to come to grips with some of its more recalcitrant features. Detailed records of all aspects of the project were kept throughout its two year period of funding, 1973–75. Since 1976 further support from the Ford Foundation has ensured the non-commercial control of materials and has made some provision for continuing discussion of the issues thrown up by the project. In 1976 its headquarters moved with its director from the Centre for Applied Research in Education at the University of East Anglia to the Cambridge Institute of Education. The project was based in East Anglia because it derived from the Humanities Curriculum Project which, from 1970–72, was located at East Anglia for the last two years of its funding by the Schools Council. The teaching problems which the Ford Project set out to study had been pinpointed by the Humanities Curriculum Project. After five years in the Humanities team, John Elliott became director of the Ford Teaching Project.

The only other research officer in the Ford Teaching Project had very different but equally relevant experience. Clem Adelman came to East Anglia from the University of London Chelsea Centre for Science Education where he had developed new audio-visual techniques for observing and recording in classrooms. Tina Reay was the third member of the team, with responsibilities for the transcription of the tapes. The names of these officers and of all the teachers, advisers and other educators who became involved in the project are given in its publications concerning in-service education, of which a select list may be found at the end of this paper.

In the Humanities Project a number of competent and sympathetic teachers experienced unexpected difficulty when trying to work with adolescent pupils on inquiry/discovery lines. Although they had worked to understand the project and believed that their principles and practices were in accord with it, some of these teachers were defeated by the demands it made on them. Not only was goodwill not enough: acceptance and internalisation of ideas too were seen to be insufficient. The Ford Project was set up to identify the nature of the problems encountered in classrooms where teachers were initially in favour of teaching and learning by inquiry/discovery methods; and to develop some means of helping such teachers to bridge the gap between their aspirations and their performance.

In the event, what transpired was less a bridging of the gap than a marriage of research and practice in a creative union. Such a bringing together of two partners was envisaged by John Nisbet in a plea for just such action research as the Ford Project achieved. (Nisbet 1974). As Nisbet said 'In the long run, the real influence of educational research is through its effect on the attitudes of those who teach'. No other research or curriculum project to date can produce more convincing evidence than the Ford Project of such influence on teachers.

The first practical task for the project team was to identify the teachers in whose classrooms the research could be conducted. This proved to be a greater problem than had been expected. Knowing as they did that there were many teachers with some awareness of their comparative lack of success in inquiry/ discovery teaching, the project team failed to anticipate the difficulties of making contact with such teachers. They had to ask local education authorities in the vicinity of Norwich for the names of teachers likely to be interested in and suitable for the project. When a number of suggestions was received they assumed, mistakenly, that each of the selected teachers was ready to reflect on his own classroom performance and to have it subjected to scrutiny. It was not until later that members of the team realised that some of these teachers had lacked any initial preparedness. They had simply been asked by their education officers to participate in the project.

In the rush to collect a group of teachers for the research, the team somewhat underestimated the importance of the school as a unit. Two or three local inspectors agreed to be associated with the project and to facilitate meetings of teachers and the use of accommodation in schools and teachers' centres; but the support of the head of the school was not fully achieved in the case of every school 'supplying' a teacher to the project.

The project was launched at Easter, 1973 at a first conference attended by a group of forty or fifty teachers from a dozen or more primary and secondary schools. In the words of the team's account of this conference (Ford Teaching Project 1973), these teachers 'met to forge the basis of an action research programme into the problems of implementing inquiry/discovery approaches in classrooms'. Their threefold task was defined in the following terms:

1. To specify the aims and principles governing inquiry/discovery based teaching;
2. To identify, diagnose, and document a range of teaching problems which are raised by attempts to realise these aims and principles in practice;
3. To attempt to establish practical guides to teaching by discovery or inquiry methods.   (Ford Teaching Project 1973)

The rest of this document makes clear that the research team began as they had promised: by interacting with the teachers, by showing a readiness to learn with and from them and by putting responsibility on them to make case studies in their own classrooms.

The importance of this approach to action research can hardly be over-emphasised. Tizard claims that: psychologists are now more likely than they were to try to solve their problems through experiment and the study of practice ... In other words, if we want to improve skills or competencies we have to study how to do so directly (Tizard 1976). And later in the same address he pleads with psychologists to decide to tackle *significant* problems that are within their field of competence – and keep working on them. The Ford team did just that: and their own mode of action research provides a model of the inquiry/discovery teaching which they set out to investigate.

In the summer following the Easter conference several papers were written by members of the team to describe the principles guiding the project and the processes of action research by which the work was already being carried into classrooms. While consideration of these early papers reveals how clearly this project was envisaged, comparison with documents published only a year later gives some indication of the development of the members of the team as well as of the teachers and advisers with whom they worked.

A paper on the methodology of teacher development (Elliott 1973a) discussed how a research team was to get teachers to reflect on their own practice and adopt a research role. It identified difficulties of self-monitoring in the classroom as the central problem being probed by the project. It listed five examples of the obstacles which teachers at the Easter conference had reported meeting when trying to innovate. It indicated also the tendency shown by those teachers to find explanations external to the classroom situation rather than in any feature of their own performance.

Written after one term of working in schools, the paper made clear that little progress in the project seemed possible without intensive and heavy intervention by the team. The latter part of the paper distinguishes between 'soft' and 'hard' forms of intervention, both of which were directed towards giving the teacher evidence that he might not be doing what he thought he was doing in his own classroom. In the 'soft' approach, use was made of an observer sitting in the classroom, taking field notes, talking to pupils and subsequently asking the teacher the kinds of questions that gave him cause to reflect. It also provided for the group of Ford teachers from any one school to meet those from other schools in the project every term. The 'hard' approach was appropriate for those teachers with enough security to face reality after not too prolonged a run-in. It involved the use of an observer, 'the stranger in the classroom', who would work with pupils as well as with the teacher on the problems and misunderstandings of any teaching/learning situation. The attempt was not to undermine what the teacher was doing but to make him more aware of his impact by providing access to pupils' accounts of their classroom experience. The paper concluded:

> We feel that after a term's hard work we are moving towards a situation in which about half the teachers involved are beginning to embark on systematic self-monitoring ... How far the development towards the teacher doing his own action research will go it is too early to say. Already we have observed reactions from head teachers and power figures in schools towards what is emerging. Perhaps the test of an institution's capacity for innovation is in the long run the capacity of its guardians to tolerate and support the self-monitoring of its members, and the outside intervention which is necessary to establish this.   (Elliott 1973a)

Another significant paper produced during the same period came to grips with the conception of action research as it impinges on the teacher and the researcher respectively (Elliott and Adelman 1973b). The Ford Project was rooted in the idea that the teacher's power to act autonomously was a necessary condition for teaching to take place. The researchers therefore set out to enhance the teacher's awareness – his practical, his situational and his self-awareness – by putting him in the position of being able to monitor the consequences of his classroom actions. According to the team such monitoring depended on the teacher finding out systematically from the pupils how they saw what he was doing.

In concluding this paper, the team made clear a distinction between what action research meant for the teachers concerned and the full implications of the research which the team itself had undertaken. The project was testing certain theories about theories: the two hypotheses being restated as follows:

1. That it is possible for a group of teachers working in a variety of contexts to identify problems and effective strategies for resolving them which are highly generalisable.
2. That action-research methods which promote self-awareness by monitoring pupils' accounts of teaching are the best means of helping teachers to fruitfully diagnose their most persistent and generalisable inquiry/discovery problems.

(Elliott and Adelman 1973b)

The explication of the project is completed in the ensuing paragraphs:

Whereas our teachers are doing action-research into inquiry discovery teaching, we are doing action-research into effective ways of supporting action-research of this kind. Our research on the central team must be seen in relation to the aims of the project and not the teachers involved in it. This important distinction is often blurred.

The hypotheses the project itself is testing are ... about the possibility of getting teachers to produce worthwhile generalisations across their own experience and the possibility of getting them to explain their most persistent problems in terms of their own unconscious influences on their situation. In other words they are second-order theories about the possibility of a first-order theory of inquiry/discovery teaching and are tested by the success of our teachers to produce the latter. Our action research is therefore logically dependent on that of our teachers.

(Elliott and Adelman 1973b)

In November 1973 such action research by teachers was aided by the publication by the Ford team of Document J: *Understanding Life in the Inquiry/Discovery Classroom: some questions for reflection.* This short paper also served to give interested outsiders some sense of the work in hand. It might be thought that, had it been available early in 1973 there would have been fewer difficulties in locating teachers suitable to take part in the project. However, like the rest of the pile of papers and booklets about the Ford research, this document was an outcome of the interaction between the teachers and the research team. It could not have been written before the need for it was thrown up. It is an example of the mass of written and visual working materials produced at every stage of the project as a means of making and consolidating, advances in the research process itself.

Mainly by means of groups of questions, Document J invites reflection on the ways in which, by their own actions, teachers positively nurture or inadvertently prevent independent reasoning on the part of their pupils. Does the teacher, for instance, prevent pupils from initiating problems for inquiry? Does he invite their agreement to certain views with rhetorical questions such as 'Do we all agree'? What is he trying to do about such constraints as the requirements of public examinations? What strategies is he adopting, and with what evidence of success, for increasing his pupils' powers of developing their ideas into coherent and testable hypotheses?

Before the end of the project it was possible to produce a handbook (Ford

Teaching Project) to help teachers to identify the constraints that they themselves imposed on the development of independent reasoning among pupils: possible also to share these findings with members of a seminar on curriculum development in teacher education at a conference of the Council for Research into Teacher Education (Elliott 1975a).

Throughout the early stages of the project teachers encountered difficulties in talking to each other and to the research team about inquiry/discovery methods because there was disagreement as to the meaning of these particular words and of other phrases commonly used to speak of classroom styles. Effective communication was hampered and the possibilities for self-monitoring were reduced until meanings were sorted into understandable categories. Members of the team worked on the distinctions made by teachers until they had worked out a schema of contrasted terms (Adelman and Elliott 1973). The description of the terms was improved subsequently, but the essential three-fold classification was established early in the autumn of 1973.

The terms most often bandied about among the teachers included: formal, informal, structured, unstructured, framework, teacher-directed, self-directed (child), guided, open-ended, dependent (child), independent (child), subject-centred and child-centred. Despite the plethora of terms, the team found that teachers could agree fairly well on certain dimensions of meaning. The three main aspects which they agreed on were: formal–informal; structured–unstructured; directed–guided–open-ended.

The formal–informal dimension was used to pick out the degree of intellectual dependence or independence of pupils on teachers. The structured – unstructured dimension related to the degree of subject-centredness as compared with child-centredness of the teacher's aims; in other words, the dimension of the product of learning as compared with the process. The other three terms, that is, directed–guided–open-ended, were points along a single dimension concerned with the amount of directiveness in the methods used by the teacher and the degree of control he exercised over how the pupil learned. The document cited above is interesting because it shows the process by which theory was developed empirically out of communication between teachers and the research team. The schema itself was important as it served to attach particular meanings to certain words used to describe classroom situations: without it, the project would have floundered in a morass of undefined terminology. By the end of the project, the schema had been thoroughly worked over and later papers gave diagrams and explicit notes of interpretation. In one of these the three sets of categories are summarised as follows:

1. Situational Categories: informal–formal.
2. Primary Aim Categories: unstructured–structured.
3. Method Categories: open-ended–guided–directed. (Elliott 1975b).

In this account Elliott proceeded to combine categories to produce a comprehensive typology making it possible, in logic if not in practice, to identify ten types of teaching. In another paper read to a research convention in America (Elliott 1976) he made an analysis of the theories with regard to five major categories which teachers were being asked to use in their attempts to identify their own mode or practice. For example: theory 1 was in the following terms:

Informal–Structured–Guided

A teacher can pursue preconceived knowledge outcomes by guiding students towards them without imposing constraints on their ability to direct their own learning (Elliott 1976).

About this item, Elliott says:

> If a teacher became aware that he was adopting a structured–guided approach he would know that theory 1 was tending to guide his practice. He could then test the extent to which it was being realised by assessing whether his approach actually protected and fostered self-directed learning. If it didn't then he was in a position where he needed to generate new theory.

He later commented that the team found that a large number of teachers thought they were able to protect self-directed learning and pursue pre-conceived knowledge outcomes at the same time if they adopted responsive (guided) rather than directive modes of teaching. They found, however, on reflection, that the structured guided approach did not work. They discovered that such approaches left pupils in a state of intellectual dependence although the teacher had not intended this. Such teachers learned to recognise that they were using a formal, not an informal, approach; they learned further, that to fulfil what they thought they were doing, they needed to switch to a more informal and unstructured approach.

If one were to use the language of the schema to describe the work of the project team with the group of teachers, one might summarise it as an informal teaching and testing situation in which those being taught were not rendered intellectually dependent upon the research team. Secondly, it was an un-structured programme in the sense that the outcomes were not fully anticipated by the team but were influenced by the teachers: and, moreover, that further, unknown outcomes have continued to emerge since the completion of the two year project. Finally it could be described as a guided project, sensitive to the needs shown by the individual teachers as each became involved in the problem of trying to analyse his own work in his own classroom.

The schema was not the only outcome of the early work of teachers and research team. What they agreed in discussion was that in pursuing inquiry/discovery methods both primary and secondary teachers were protecting and fostering self-directed learning. The project thus became committed to helping teachers to sort out the values and principles implicit in their ideas of self-directed learning. One approach to such clarification was by considering the learner's position: was he free to bring out his ideas and to have them looked at in the classroom; and was he free from external constraints on his self-direction and reasoning?

The lists of criteria for helping teachers to deal with these questions were among the most practical of the materials evolved during the project. A document (Elliott and Adelman 1973a) on general methodology produced during the second term provided these criteria within a context of what various teachers had said in earlier discussions. The same document carried useful summaries of the stages in classroom innovation and of the sequence by which teachers waiting to foster independent reasoning could watch their own safe development from formal–structured–directed (or guided) towards informal–unstructured–open-ended patterns. At the time the team were writing these papers – and a number of other articles either for project members or for wider consumption, as detailed in the bibliography – Ford teachers were engaged in their own classrooms in every stage of trying to implement a stable pattern of inquiry/discovery teaching, some for the first time, others after earlier failures or set-backs. The explicit recognition in these documents of the contribution to the progress of the project by particular teachers must have helped to sustain those most seriously involved in an exhausting task: a task, moreover, likely to erode the spirit of the dedicated teacher having to face for the first time in his career certain realities about his classroom performance.

When a teacher's professional self-esteem is built on confidence that he is a successful practitioner of inquiry/discovery methods, it is not funny for him to have to admit that by his own mode of questioning or by his persistent failure to understand, even to countenance, his pupils' questions, he is standing in the way of their developing their powers of independent reasoning. Such new awareness can have a traumatic effect on any teacher – but yet, as a member of the Ford Project he had to continue to cope with his everyday life and his school duties.

For its part the team found that probably more than half the teachers attached to the project had little sense of the gaps existing between their aspirations concerning inquiry/discovery teaching and their own performance, and these teachers had no initial readiness to adopt a reflective stance concerning these matters. Later, after the conclusion of the project, Elliott said that he then considered that at the beginning of the project only one of the forty teachers was self-monitoring to any significant extent; that another dozen probably had some genuine sense of their teaching being problematic; and that the remaining two thirds were neither ready nor able to adopt an objective stance to their practice.

Committed to working with this particular group of teachers and under pressure to achieve progress and produce findings within the limited time of the project's funding, the team was driven to working out procedures whereby a teacher with much less initial preparedness than the research team had reckoned on could be brought to examine what actually occurred in his classroom between himself and his pupils. Triangulation and feed back were the procedures developed to meet this need.

According to Adelman (1976) the strategy of triangulation was introduced at the beginning of the project in March 1973. Throughout the next four terms triangulation was the chief instrument whereby some teachers, apparently quite lacking in initial preparedness, were enabled to recognise the gap between aspiration and performance, if not in their own, at least in colleagues' classrooms. Other teachers, having a degree of initial awareness that some of the recalcitrant difficulties of inquiry/discovery teaching might be brought within their control, were enabled to extend the possibility of success in their own classrooms.

In the ordinary classroom it is scarcely possible for the teacher and his pupils unaided to provide honest accounts of what each thinks is happening; still less for them to agree about the point at which breakdown occurs between what the teacher intended and what transpired. Intervention by a research person sets up a form of triangulation which developed during the project into a series of procedures including the use of film, tape-slide, video-tape, tape recording and notes. First, agreement had to be reached regarding the ethics of the situation so that confidentiality was maintained and honest observations encouraged. Next, the teacher would explain to a team member what he aimed to do in some particular lesson that was to be observed. During the lesson the teacher's words were taped as were those of any of the pupils who came within range of the recorder.

The observer/interviewer attended the lesson without taking part or obtruding his presence. The pupils came to appreciate his role as he occupied himself making notes, tapes and pictures. Afterwards he asked some of the pupils as well as the teacher for their accounts of the lesson, usually interviewing the teacher first.

In the second stage the pupils were interviewed, the team member being in the position of already knowing the teacher's point of view. With the pupils' permission the record of their accounts and of their discussion with the interviewer were played back to the teacher. At that point (stage three) the teacher could see the need to explain the differences between his story and what the pupils said about his lesson. As the interviewer had been present during the lesson, his personal knowledge was always available in the background of these discussions.

The use made of all these accounts and the degree to which these interviews and discussions led the teacher towards enhanced self-awareness depended upon the sensitivity and skill of the observer/interviewer from the research team, upon the security of the individual teacher and upon the qualities shown by the pupils. All members of every triangulation group were, in the early days, feeling their way in a new situation calling for a standard of honesty of expression for which their professional lives had ill prepared them. Adelman speaks of the stalemate with regard to honest accounts. Only when that stalemate was broken could teachers begin to get feedback on their own initiative from pupils or be in a position to begin research into their own teaching without the need for an observer's intervention.

At stage four, transcripts of the lesson and of all the accounts and interviews were put side by side so that the different pictures of each particular incident in the classroom could be compared. By collecting together such a triangulation study the team sought to give the teacher valid material on which to base improved classroom teaching. They used them also as a source of improved theories about teaching and learning.

Some of the triangulations carried out very early in the life of the project show the growing pains of the procedure. One example is the account of a lesson given in a primary school in March 1973 and made available as a classroom document in the autumn of the same year (Adelman 1973). It was published later under the title: *The Tins* as part of Unit 1 (see bibliography). Among much other documentation a secondary school biology lesson given in June 1973 was similarly made available a few months later (Elliott 1973b) and was subsequently published, in this case with contributions from the teacher concerned, as part of Unit 2 under the title *Three Points of View in the classroom*.

These publications serve to illustrate the volume and nature of the records called for by the triangulation method as practised in the Ford Project. It is probably fair to say that in the whole history of educational research in this country no comparable collection of first hand materials relating to the interface of teacher and pupil has ever been made, let alone worked over systematically. Every one in the project had to make records: pupils as well as teachers; teachers as well as the research team. For most teachers the very idea of playing back a record of their classroom performance was a novel and suspect undertaking. Moreover, the making of audio-visual records of class-rooms was outside their personal experience and was inevitably intrusive on their normal privacy. However, the project called for the simple yet effective audio-visual methods of recording which Adelman introduced and which were backed up by increasingly sensitive interviewing techniques developed in the process of action research itself.

Reference has been made to the published Units which became available at Easter 1974 during the first nationally advertised conference held to disseminate knowledge about the project and to get reactions from people with no previous experience of it. The conference gave project teachers and inspectors as well as the actual research team opportunities for clarifying their theories through describing their practices. Those attending the conference learned something about an unusual action research programme. They may or may not have recognised its seminal importance. In any case, such a conference can serve a useful purpose as a selector of those teachers, lecturers and inspectors who might be prepared subsequently to undergo the discipline of the triangulation and feedback procedure themselves in the classroom.

However, given some potentially receptive teachers prepared for study and commitment to action research in their classrooms, where is their support to come from? Who is to provide the intervention without which project teachers had been unable to receive the feedback which only their pupils could give? Where are the observer/interviewers to come from?

Possibly some school governors could learn and practise the observer/interviewer's role. Perhaps some persons now occupying positions as teachers, lecturers, inspectors or researchers could find ways of developing their professional functions so that they could become acceptable to other teachers, lecturers and inspectors as the stranger in their classrooms. At the time of writing the original project team has dispersed to other duties and no training programme has been funded. Despite their other commitments, however, the Ford research team and a number of the teachers and inspectors most heavily involved in the project have kept in touch with each other. In 1976 they set up a Classroom Action Research Network to enable like minded educators everywhere to inform each other directly of their classroom investigations into their own work as teachers. From the membership of the Network a teachers' committee or council has been established to validate and legitimate all further work emanating from the Ford Project.

In retrospect it can be seen that with the aid of some audio-visual equipment and the intervention of a skilled outside observer/interviewer, teachers from a wide range of primary and secondary classrooms can accept the discipline of the triangulation and feedback procedure to the point where, within a few terms, they are able consciously to modify their teaching and to reduce the disparity between what they intended doing and what happened in their lessons. In his summary of the work of the project Elliott said that the main premise on which the project was founded was 'the more able a teacher is at self-monitoring his classroom practice the more likely he is to bring about fundamental changes in it' (Elliott 1975b). In the same paragraph he pointed out that the main problem was to get teachers to self-monitor their practice.

This reflection underlines the crucial importance of the observer's role. A teacher traditionally expects a visitor – whether from the head's room, the authority's office or some college or research unit – to assess, evaluate or form judgements, and to get them wrong; to advise actions, suggest panaceas or recommend curriculum packages, which are unsuitable. Commonly, the teacher assumes that the outsider will seek to patronise or manipulate him. He may be prepared to credit the head, the inspector or the research worker with high and honourable intent regarding his career as a teacher, but he is not likely to be ready to give any of them his unreserved trust. (After a bit of project experience, of course, the teacher may glimpse a comparison between his reception of his well-intentioned visitors and his pupils' attitude to his own efforts at developing independent reasoning, or whatever he thought he was doing.)

The importance of the project does not lie in the pros and cons of inquiry/

discovery teaching. What emerged as the main finding might seem to be a self evident truth: that only the teacher himself can change what he does in the classroom and that his success will depend upon close interaction with his pupils. Corporate excellence in the classroom depends upon genuine communications not simply down the line but up, down and sideways.

One outcome of the project could be that some teachers develop new ways of helping pupils, in their turn, to gain insight into their own purposes and to acquire disciplined habits of recording their own progress and attainments.

Apart from the classroom situation itself, the project could have repercussions on pre- and in-service teacher education. A period of investment in training teachers, in up-dating them, in preparing them for promotion and in providing them with higher educational qualifications, has been followed by drastic reductions on all these fronts. What was missing during the boom years was any systematic attempt to measure the value of studies and courses to teachers as teachers; or to enable the teachers to realise their revised intentions or new found enthusiasms once they had returned to the unsupported isolation of the classroom.

With the cuts in educational expenditure has come a new stridency about accountability. The question being asked is: what is the public getting for its money? It is a fair question and has never been given a proper answer.

This new drive on accountability leads straight back to the Ford Project. Teachers can be made accountable for what happens in school when they have acquired competence in relating what they intended to do with what they actually did and with what the pupils perceived and learned. Assessment by other agents must be based on the teacher's account otherwise it is invalid. But teachers should note that the account is overdue.

JOHN ELLIOTT

The Ford Teaching Project:
A Response

In describing the difficulty we had in selecting potentially reflective teachers Elizabeth Adams states that 'the team realised teachers had lacked any initial preparedness – but had been asked by their education officers to participate in the project'. As I understood it, the problem was not so much one of preparation – I was constantly in and out of schools discussing the implications of commitment to the project – but of getting teachers who were genuinely motivated towards self-reflection. The way a central project has to negotiate access to teachers imposes constraints on locating such teachers. First, one has to negotiate support with the officers of the LEAs who then nominate certain schools. The heads of these schools, having been singled out by their LEA, find it difficult to refuse an invitation to participate. They subsequently 'consult' selected members of staff who also find it difficult to refuse, because as one teacher put it 'the head after all writes your references'. The procedure of negotiating down through 'the hierarchy' is not ideal for recruiting teachers who feel a genuine need to examine their practice more closely. The result was that about a third of the 40 teachers recruited were involved at a very minimal level. Some eventually found reasons for dropping out, but they were few. The majority in this group remained attached without commitment to the project's tasks. One reason some teachers gave for this 'attachment without commitment' was that in applying for promotion they could cite 'involvement' in the project.

Elizabeth can be forgiven for neglecting to mention the fact that teachers were grouped in terms of school-based inter-disciplinary teams, under specially appointed co-ordinators, and conveying the impression that they operated as isolated individuals in schools. Many school teams collapsed as units of co-operative endeavour. This was partly due to the perceived threat of making one's classroom accessible to colleagues. But it was also due to the lack of institutional provision which would permit teachers to meet and observe each other in school time. I attempted to negotiate such provision with head teachers in intitial discussions, but was largely unsuccessful. Only in our middle schools, where traditions of team teaching and team meetings had been established, did 'the teams' survive (and indeed they thrived in these schools). Individuals tended to operate in isolation from their colleagues and preferred to open their practice to either 'outsiders' from the research team, or teachers from other schools. In my view such preferences have important implications for school-based in-service education – a teacher doesn't necessarily learn best from his fellow members of staff.

At one point in her chapter Elizabeth states that the teachers found 'that the structured – guided approach did not work'. The majority of our teachers initially adopted a *short-term* 'structured-guided' approach i.e. they intended that pupils would learn certain things over a relatively short period of time while at the same time wanting them to arrive at their conclusions independently from their authority position. As they began to self-monitor their teaching approaches more systematically they came to realise that these two intentions were rarely both realised. Some experienced what Robert Dearden has called 'the discovery teacher's dilemma'; namely, pupils who reason independently to the 'wrong' conclusions. (Dearden *et al.* 1972). Given the short time span the teachers set for coming to the 'right' conclusions they discovered their tendency to put pupils back 'on track' by providing more and more hints and clues as to what the 'right' answer was. Other teachers became aware of the dominance of 'the guessing game' in their classrooms.

This usually began with the teacher asking a question to which the pupils responded with silence, knowing that if they refused to respond the teacher would gradually provide them with more and more hints and clues until they could simply guess the answer. Again, given the short amount of time teachers allowed for pupils to draw 'right' conclusions, they found themselves 'as time pressed on' colluding in the 'guessing game' the pupils wanted.

We had one teacher who adopted a long-term structure-approach, and he discovered that within this approach he was able to reconcile the pursuit of preconceived learning outcomes with protecting and fostering independent reasoning. However, in making the transition from a short-term to a long-term structured approach we felt some teachers would only cut out the guessing game by adopting an unstructured approach – in which they did not have any preconceived learning outcomes in mind for an interim period.

Elizabeth reports that 'the team was driven' to using triangulation procedures with teachers who had 'much less initial preparedness'. In this context I feel it is important to clarify this idea of 'initial preparedness'. Some teachers were not particularly self-monitoring, to start with, solely because their working conditions in schools did not provide any support for such an activity. In different institutional conditions they would have been able to self-monitor their practice with relative ease. Other teachers simply lacked much capacity for reflection as persons. The triangulation procedures were used with the former group. It would have been dangerous to adopt it with the latter group. Here 'softer' approaches were required.

Elizabeth rightly indicates the crucial role of an 'outsider' in stimulating self-reflection. Such a person can not only compensate for deficiences in the support system within schools, but I am now convinced that the majority of teachers need someone disengaged from 'the action' to 'mirror' their actions. Self-monitoring does not negate, indeed it seems to require, monitoring from 'outside'. The reason for this I think lies in the fact that teachers' actions in classrooms, although once conscious and deliberate, tend to be habitual, routines, and unconscious. In order to become aware of them they need 'the mirrors'.

17 Reflections

These closing reflections are my own attempt to put together what I have learned by reading the papers in this book and to interpret it to myself. The theoretical bias I bring to this task can be well enough judged from my *Introduction to Curriculum Research and Development*. (Stenhouse 1975). My bias in the value area of politics is best summarised by saying that I am less concerned to plan a reform of society than to make its intellectual and cultural resources so widely accessible that as nearly as possible all its members rather than an establishment of privilege – to which I belong – can participate in the shaping of the future. Perhaps the reader should also know that I am inclined to think that the nineteenth-century eclectic reader, the development of a system of teacher education not based on apprenticeship and the curriculum development movement are the most successful attempts to improve teaching which have been mounted in England.

The improvement of teaching is not the linear process of the pursuit of obvious goals. It is about the growth of understanding and skill of teachers which constitute their resource in meeting new situations which make old aspirations inappropriate or unattainable. Just as painters respond to their time and to the development of their art, so teachers must respond to the changing social situation, to developments in knowledge, and to advances in pedagogy; and as the history of art discloses in 'schools of painting' patterns of response, often coherent only in retrospect, so the history of teaching produces schools of thought and practice, or movements. These run down as changing circumstances throw up new challenges, and – just as importantly – as the teacher as artist embodies into his art all that a particular style of response can teach him. Progress in human affairs is not like progress in physical sciences: as we begin to see the lines on which to design a strategy for solving the puzzle, the puzzle itself is changed. Progress comes as we deploy in the face of the new puzzle, what we learned from our intelligent failure to solve the old. Success is a fiction: the distinction is between intelligent and contained treatment of the problems of action and the disasters of incompetence. It is important to learn from history.

Historically, the movement or school of thought which immediately preceded and overlapped with the curriculum movement in England may be broadly characterised as 'progressivism'. The origins of this movement go back a long way and it has many strands, so that any short characterisation of it is bound to distort. I shall emphasise two aspects: 'child-centredness' and 'the school as a community'. In the complex setting of progressivism these themes among others came to be dominant particularly in teacher education, initial and in-service, and in public debate.

The context of this dominance was the pattern of problems and opportunities in state education which emerged at the close of the Second World War in the wake of the 1944 Education Act. This placed secondary education for all at the top of the educational agenda. In spite of the emergence of the 'central school' in some LEAs in the thirities, the system before the 1944 Act was firmly based upon an all-age elementary school attended by pupils between the ages of five and 14, but creamed from 11 onwards by selective access to grammar schools for the few.

The aspiration towards secondary education for all in effect created piece-meal and over a number of years two new schools: the primary school – a genuine first school in contrast to the elementary school; and the secondary modern school – a non-academic school to be staffed and equipped to what were thought of as secondary standards. The first gave a focus of identity and a possibility of power to those who saw their field as 'the education of young children'. Much more radically the second called for a secondary – not merely elementary – education which was not to be justified in terms of ambition and social mobility: an education for life which provided more than basic skills.

In both circumstances progressivism seemed to have a great deal to offer.

Child-centredness in the first school at its best asked teachers to recognize the central importance of child study and the close study of children learning and reminded them that both forms of study were accessible to them at first hand in their own classrooms. The idea of school as community suggested an analogy with the family as a means of humanizing the adult-child relationship and also of creating in schools the community of children which existed in the larger families of grandmother's time.

In the secondary modern school the school-as-community theme was do-minant. Education for citizenship was the theme, but it was not teaching *about* the society of Britain, but rather participation in a community in which citizenship was caught, not taught. This community of the school was seen as humane and, in an A. S. Neill sense, rationally justifiable. Child-centredness was represented as the study less of child-development than of the common, and the differentiating interests of the pre-adolescent and the adolescent, interest being seen as a criterion for the selection of curriculum content.

The Plowden Report and the Newsom Report may perhaps be taken as representations of how these progressive strands looked on the threshold of reaction against them, by which time they had been adopted by the establishment and, some of the adherents of progressivism would claim, weakened in the process.

It is difficult to estimate how fully progressivism penetrated the system, though it seems fairly widely accepted that it influenced directly a minority rather than a majority of schools and in perhaps fewer than 10 per cent of the schools of the country was it implemented in a form that would be defended by its publicly known adherents. It seems to have been powerful in teacher education, but students who absorbed it during initial training soon had it knocked out of them by experienced colleagues who practised the formal teaching inherited from the elementary schools and grammar schools. However, though the system as a whole never went progressive, progressive thinking underlay some of its best practice – and was adopted as a means of justifying some of its slackest and least acceptable.

A new wave of problems was thrown at the teaching profession in the shape of comprehensive education and the raising of the school leaving age to sixteen. I propose to argue that it was this that shaped the curriculum movement as it found expression in the Schools Council.

The early history of that movement began in the United States, and certain aspects of *Man: a Course of Study* exemplify its characteristics. It was an attack on progressivism in its American form (where it was less expressive of child-centredness than of community, life-adjustment and vocationalism) in the name of academic standards. The call was for a return to knowledge as content but up-to-date knowledge; and 'up-to-date' implied knowledge as it is understood in the research communities of the universities. Thus the move away from a community-centred approach to a content-centred approach was expressed through the alliance of scholars and school teachers in curriculum development.

It was this up-dating and improvement of content which appealed to the Association for Science Education and led them to appeal to the Nuffield Foundation for support. In the Foundation Farrer-Brown and Becher shaped the model of funding and project structure and determined that the Foundation rather than the ASE should initiate, support and control the pattern of development. On the whole, control was modulated to protection since the policy of 'finding the right person and giving him his head' focussed control as control of appointment.

Characteristic of the English situation was a much more equal relationship between scholars and school teachers. Where the American formulations speak of scientists and teachers of science in schools, the British tend to speak of scientists in schools and universities. And the background of the teachers endorsed this. The projects were O (and later A-level), and hence aimed at the elite: the project staff were weighted towards public and direct grant schools.

Another important theme of the early Nuffield projects was the emphasis on heurism in teaching methods which went back to Armstrong, and was linked to the problem of the use of laboratories. The changes visualised in the content of science were seen to imply changes in teaching method.

SMP, too, was based on an alliance between mathematicians in schools and mathematicians in universities which aimed at a revision of mathematics teaching which captured the excitement of modern developments in mathematics. In this case, the development continued to remain in the control of the group which took the original initiative towards reform and who succeeded in raising money and institutionalising themselves as an independent entity.

An interesting contrast can be drawn here with NATE, which neither expressed itself in the manner of ASE by moving the establishment to systematic development, nor undertook curriculum work independently in a manner which could have established the financial strength of SMP.

Both the early Nuffield projects and SMP were in the first instance directed towards the grammar schools. The problem they faced was how to ensure that the academic elite in the British schools was equipped for the competitive world of the post-colonial era.

The curriculum movement most closely associated with the Schools Council was an adaptation of the instruments forged by the Nuffield Foundation to meet the new problems: comprehensive education, the raising of the school leaving age, and later the rise of the middle school. Its architect was Derek Morrell, a career civil servant, who together with an HMI, John Witherington, produced its most significant document, Schools Council Working Paper 2 'The Raising of the School Leaving Age.' The builders were R. A. Becher of the Nuffield Foundation, who persuaded his trustees to support Hilda Misselbrook's Secondary Science project, and G. K. Caston and Joslyn Owen of the Schools Council. Becher negotiated the Nuffield support which allowed Caston and Owen to get the Humanities Curriculum Project off the ground, and that was symbolic of the handing of the Nuffield tradition to the School Council as a resource with which to meet RSLA.

What of the problems which comprehensive education and RSLA threw up? The raising of the school leaving age to 16 denied the shelter from ambition and opportunity which the secondary modern school had partly enjoyed because it held every pupil in school long enough to be granted or denied a General Certificate of Education. The comprehensive school embodied in a single and usually large institution both winners and losers in that race. And whereas the division of grammar and secondary modern, by virtue of the differential opportunity associated with social class, kept the social classes apart, in many circumstances the comprehensive school mixed them under conditions in which working-class pupils were in a majority.

In these circumstances, the consensual model of the school as a community was called into question, as were both the faith in rational society and the implicit paternalism which underlay that model. The authority which had been deployed by teachers to create institutional shelter for child-centredness in a censored enviroment was desperately threatened as the comprehensive school revealed its power insistently to reflect the problems of the society in which it was set.

It was at this point that curriculum research and development was adopted by the state system through the agency of the Schools Council, and applied to the problems of the comprehensive school. No longer was it a matter of updating the curriculum for the academic: it was an attempt to meet the problems of extending a genuine secondary education to people who were not of that elite.

There remained a residual discourse of the kind used by platform speakers who have little to say, but say it confidently and well. Much talk still of adjusting to the rapid changes in knowledge with a modulation of that theme into rapid changes in society – as if education had not been able to ignore these in the past. Lip service, too, to the interests of the pupils, though a readiness to look elsewhere than their expression on Saturday afternoon and Saturday evening to diagnose them. Much talk of the Newsom *child* (!) and the residual memories of the practical cast of mind which used to justify the tripartite system.

Some of this talk went on in Schools Council committees and in the Inspectorate and the Advisory services. But it is the great achievement of the early Schools Council projects for the secondary age range that they avoided it. Their search was for an expression of knowledge which could be justified as worthwhile to the secondary school child without being merely a mirror of his interests. The theme of interest was transposed into that of relevance. Child-centred approaches became discovery – and inquiry-based learning.

Nuffield Secondary Science, the Humanities Curriculum Project, Project Technology and the Design and Craft Project are first generation examples of this movement. Typically, they were not subject-based, but I want to claim that they were not about the integration of subjects as this is often understood.

There is a doctrine of integration which pursues the possibility of teaching a group of subjects through a curriculum which interweaves them. It may be characterised as an interdisciplinary teaching of disciplines. Each of the subjects is recognised as an entity which contributes to the study in terms of its own logic. This approach to integration is that investigated by the Keele Project in the integration of the humanities. The subjects most commonly taught in integrated patterns are English, geography, history, religious studies and social studies. The most extensive application of the approach in the secondary school is in the lower forms, particularly where there is an element of mixed ability teaching. *Man: a Course of Study* has been successfully used as a basis for integration, though teachers need to build round it to cover the full humanities subject range.

The projects aiming at the fourth and fifth years of the secondary school did not pursue integration in this sense. Secondary Science asserted the unity of science rather than interdisciplinarity and tried to provide a disciplined alternative to the post-war 'general science'. The Humanities Curriculum Project, declaring that is was seeking 'a vernacular equivalent of the classics,' sought a disciplined form for general studies conceived as an induction to adult education (though it conceded that this would make a good core for those who wanted to integrate). Project Technology supported the development of problem-oriented applications. Nearest perhaps to integrating disciplines, it is better thought of as claiming technology as a discipline in its own right: creative in the face of practical problems as pure research is creative in the face of theoretical problems. And Design and Craft sought to make good a similar assertion about creative responses disciplined by design criteria in settings where the craftsman's skills – rather than those of the scientist and mathematician – were the key.

One of the most interesting problems in the history of the curriculum movement is the widespread failure on the part of the educational establishment to perceive what these projects were about. So fixed in many people's minds were the doctrines against which the projects were reacting (and these doctrines were often in the remits) that, in spite of the projects' repetitious insistence on their stance, they were translated into 'progressive' solutions to the problems of the day.

Thus, for example, each project might be seen in terms of relevance, if relevance meant relation of the school to the real world. But so powerful was the progressive climate that relevance in this sense was rapidly translated into relevance to the interests of the pupils. I well remember a headmaster denying that *Relations between the Sexes* was relevant to his 14 and 15-year-old pupils on the grounds that they were not interested in sex, and my rejection of his criterion by the assertion that because the theme was relevant, it was his job to get them interested!

These projects, then, and the subject projects such as Geography for the Young School Leaver and History 13 to 16, which were their immediate lineal descendents, were content-centred rather than child-centred, and this can be taken to be one of the contributions of the curriculum movement. It is easy, of course, to overemphasise polarities such as 'child-centred) and 'content-centred', particularly when each affects only a minority of schools as compared with those where the mainstream of 'teacher-centred' approaches exists. The labels need to be carefully defined, and that is not a task I can undertake here. What is at the heart of the curriculum movement is an emphasis on knowledge as the basis of schooling. Knowledge exists as the inherited resource of society: the problem is to give people access to it. Epistemology and the sociology of knowledge lie at the heart of the curriculum movement.

Two recurrent consequences of this emphasis crop up in the curriculum movement: a stress on powers, rather than mere competences; and a stress on discovery and inquiry rather than instruction as a basis of learning.

Knowledge, as it is used here, does not mean mere information, but logics and skills so interwoven as to strengthen the capacity to think and to act effectively. Knowledge is inseparable from the development of the powers of the individual. Exercises and information can produce the competence needed by a warehouseman or bank teller without increasing the autonomy of the person. An education of privilege in the traditional grammar schools and the universities always did something to develop the capacity and confidence of the individual as an autonomous citizen, albeit imperfectly enough at times. In this tradition the curriculum movement emphasized skills in the context of knowledge. For example, *Man: a Course of Study* and the Humanities Curriculum Project could both be viewed as reading 'schemes'; but the first contains graded *scientific* reading materials which contrast strongly with the lack of knowledge content in the more vacuous reading schemes common in primary schools, while the Humanities Project was actually influenced by the nineteenth century eclectic reader, though it attempted to structure the diverse sources by treating them as evidence for a discussion of controversial issues. Both aim to teach skills in the context of developing autonomy.

The emphasis on knowledge also led to discovery- and inquiry-based methods. An older tradition of education looks to the teacher as the source of information and the man of knowledge; but this position appears untenable when the status and nature of knowledge is reviewed. Knowledge is developing too fast and is too diverse for a teacher to claim mastery of it. Moreover, it is knowledge precisely because it is accessible through reasoning and judgement and not merely on the authority of persons. This is not to say that authorities are not to be accepted, but it does mean that they should be accepted critically and with some reservation or conditionality. Thus, the case is made for a form of teaching in which the evidence both of direct experience and of persons as potential experts is questioned and explored by teacher and class together. The teacher urges the pupil to learn in the way the teacher learns rather than to know what the teacher knows. This is the basis of discovery- and inquiry-based teaching.

Now, in fact, discovery- and inquiry-based teaching is so different from instructional teaching in logic and in its implications for the teacher's strategies for controlling his classroom – and discipline based on the teacher's security as a procedural authority is a necessary element in all schooling – that it is not easily implemented by teachers who, in spite of lip-service to discovery and inquiry, are almost all trained only in instructional methods.

This problem of shift of method and logic has been the crux of the curriculum movement. Teachers have generally expected that curriculum research and development will make life easier; but because curriculum research and development has been concerned with improving the quality of classroom knowledge by changing teaching strategies, the initial effect has been to make severe demands upon the teacher. As Barry MacDonald put it, the teacher who wishes to improve his teaching by changing his teaching style and logic initially faces the 'burden of incompetence' (1973). He turns his back on the skills he has developed in order to develop new skills. Though he is experienced, he makes a novice of himself. It is surprising to me and, I think, a tribute to the profession that the minority of teachers who have had the tenacious professionalism to take on this task is as large as it is.

John Elliott's Ford T (Teaching) Project, which developed from the experience of the curriculum movement faced this problem of teaching method across the curriculum and across the primary and secondary age range. It produced teacher training materials which attempted to clarify the logic of inquiry- and discovery-based teaching and to support a programme of teacher self-development which set the acquisition of teaching skills within the critical framework of this logic. It has great potential as a basis for school-based in-service training and cooperative in-service training in groups which cross subject and age-range barriers. But it remains an enterprise for enthusiasts, people who tinker in their classrooms as motor-cycle enthusiasts tinker in their back yards: prepared to give a lot of time to increasing performance.

No doubt, curriculum research and development has many facets and can be seen in different lights. Indeed, this is evident from the contributions to this volume. A neglected emphasis which I wish to throw into relief here is its importance as a medium of teacher development. Schools will be improved, not by revamping content on a new-wine-in-old-bottles principle, but by the improvement of teaching. And only teachers can improve teaching.

The basis of the improvement of teaching is the teacher's developing his art under the impulse of ideas. In the past the most common expression of ideas has been through books. Some books, for example *How Gertrude Teaches her Children* (Pestalozzi 1894) tell stories of teaching; some like Dewey's *Democracy and Education* (1916) expound theories of education. Generally, the stories appear not to intersect with life in our own classrooms: the theories place the teacher in the power of the academic and fail to strengthen his hold on his own practice because they subordinate his judgement. But the expression in curricular form of ideas about knowledge or about teaching places the teacher in a powerful position to test them. Ideas give hostages to practice when they are expressed in curricula.

My own most ambitious claim for the curriculum movement is that no group of teachers who experiment seriously, cooperatively and doggedly with any of the curricula described in this book could fail to strengthen themselves as practitioners in the art of teaching.

It is rather the fashion at the moment to suggest that those involved in the Nuffield and Schools Council projects were naively optimistic about curriculum change as a means of improving schooling. Some may have been. But on the whole it was those in the system who were absurdly optimistic: especially perhaps local education authorities and some HMIs. In 1969 when I predicted at a conference that projects would fail in terms of the expectations being held of them because of lack of investment in dissemination and in-service training, I was attacked as absurdly pessimistic.

John Witherington, a former HMI, visited me within three months of the Humanities Curriculum Project being set up. After we had talked over its ideas and agreed that they were in accord with those that Morrell and he had set out in Schools Council Working Paper 2, he said: 'It will take fifty years to work them through, you know'. I would regard this estimate as that of an optimistic realist.

Yet the change in the conception of knowledge, of teaching and of the nature and basis of the authority of the school which is explored by the range of Nuffield and Schools Council Curriculum research and development is, I believe, the only likely road towards a solution of the problems of a common secondary education for all.

What structures were employed in the curriculum development movement, and what structures may be demanded if the challenge of the comprehensive secondary school is to be faced intelligently?

We are concerned with the improvement of schooling in the state educational system; and improvement is many-sided. It may be that the knowledge offered by the school is better warrantable, or that the process of teaching and learning is more humane and intelligent, or that students' attainment increases in the rather limited range of learning outcomes which are measured, or that students are given more choices. And much more.

In centralized systems the pursuit of improvement is generally through the regulation of schools throughout the system. Schools are the chain stores of education. The assumption is that there is some formula to be applied to each school alike throughout the system, irrespective of local conditions or the personalities involved in the educational transaction.

This assumption has not held in England, and in spite of some current trends towards centralisation, I think it is not likely to be embraced. Although the majority of English classrooms are run on lines so similar that one might think them centrally controlled, a substantial minority have an individuality which derives from the personality of the teacher, the background of the children, the opportunities of the locality or the impulse of the teacher towards experimental improvement. It is these, rather than the conformist classrooms, which have traditionally been quoted as examples of 'best practice'; and the Schools Council has often begun projects by surveys of such practice.

Given this way of looking at the system, the model of change is one in which a minority of able teachers explore and define a possibility, which in the course of time revivifies the tradition which sustains the majority in the system. But in fact the able minority are often isolated and relatively powerless in the system, while the belief that good ideas and practice will spread because of their quality is manifestly untrue. Teachers have relatively long careers and in most cases their practice changes little. Schools look different from those before the First World War: classrooms – especially at secondary level – much less so. The idea of a system led by the pioneer efforts of the leading edge of teachers seems more of an ideal than a reality.

When the Schools Council in its early days spoke of its task as 'to extend the range of choice open to teachers', it was acknowledging the ideal and perhaps even hoping that the minority of innovative teachers would become a majority. But its model was apparently a supermarket model in which curricula were created as products and teachers made a selection from them. Change would come through the exercise of choice among alternative curricular offerings, and perhaps imply an element of natural selection through the survival of the fittest.

But the Nuffield tradition, which the Schools Council inherited, was not cast in that mould. It traditionally offered teacher handbooks rather than finished curricular products and it stressed working through teacher groups. The English type of curriculum project must be seen against this background.

A project is a temporary institution existing for a defined and limited period of time. Although the Schools Council has weakened this pattern by funding follow-up work, it remains true. Projects, however much they may yearn towards perpetuity, are temporary task forces.

Like an army campaign or a civil engineering contract, they set up temporary offices from scratch, have staff posted to them or appointed on fixed-term contract, and then at the end of their term dismantle themselves. At their most serious they are like a commando raid, at their most lighthearted a truant escapade. What is the relation of these short-lived structures to the system?

There is no adequate study of this problem based on cases, though in their Ford SAFARI Project (Success and Failure and Recent Innovation), Barry MacDonald and Rob Walker have made a start by looking retrospectively at four projects, at their utilization in schools and at the biographies of individual teachers who have been involved in curriculum research and development. My account draws on their work but is not justified by it, since it is filled out by my own experience.

Most projects appear to relate to the system at four main points: they relate to teachers, they relate to examinations, they relate to teacher education and they relate to power in the system.

The most intimate of these relationships is that to teachers. This is founded in the intercourse between the members of the project team and the group of teachers in the original group of experimental or trial schools. Typically, a project breaks down the normal isolation of its teacher participants and through conferences and local groups creates the conditions for a collaborative exchange of ideas across classrooms. For the majority of teachers involved this is a positive, even a deeply satisfying, experience. A small minority, unable to establish a social or professional niche in the group become uninvolved, however, throughout the project.

Within the involved group, leadership figures arise. For them participation in the project is an important element in their professional and even personal identity. They are 'activists', keen to pass on their experience. The majority of participant teachers thoroughly enjoy the professional cooperation, apply much or some of what they have learned in their own classrooms, but do not wish to give much time to active dissemination of the ideas. A minority – perhaps a large minority in some cases – find the ideas either too difficult to embody in their practice, or unsatisfactory in themselves; and withdraw from the project at the earliest opportunity, often having to attack it in order to justify their position. (It is difficult to say to your head, 'It's really excellent, but not for me'.)

The project team, supported by – and under criticism from – this group of teachers ('our teachers', they often call them), produces a publishable corpus – teacher handbooks, curriculum materials, or the like. Usually the team – and to a lesser extent the teachers – see this as the medium for the dissemination of educational ideas; though their publisher sees it as a product to be marketed. The first thinks of dissemination, the second – quite properly – of sales.

Most projects are given some support for early dissemination and most attempt dissemination through conferences, often staffed by both activist teachers and project staff. At these early conferences a second wave of teachers meet the ideas of the project. And generally some of these become activists.

Thus, at the end of the dissemination phase supported by the sponsor, there remains as a resource the first-wave and second-wave activist teachers and the rump of the project team. At this point the remaining members of the project team terminate their contracts and return to the system.

This pattern is obviously by no means uniform, but it does provide a basis of comparison, and its weaknesses are obvious.

The second point of contact between project and system is external examination. In a country without central regulation of the curriculum by decree, it is the pressure of the O- and A-level requirements and to a lesser extent those of CSE which holds the curriculum in place and hence works against experiment and change from the fourth year of the secondary school onwards. For curriculum projects covering O- and A-level work, negotiation with the Boards – or at least with one board – is crucial: there is no hope of getting an examination course tried in schools if it does not lead to an examination! We do not know enough about these negotiations, nor has this book allowed space to report them in detail. There is some evidence that innovations with strong bases in the grammar school streams and in subject associations find it easier to evoke an examination response than do those which seek adaptation of subjects to a comprehensive intake; and there is clear evidence that some projects have had difficult negotiations with the O- and A-level boards. There are also cases where schools working with new curricular patterns have established Mode 3 O–levels, that is, a form of examination in which a school-based assessment, usually of both course work and examination, is validated by external moderation, and candidates do not sit a paper laid down centrally by the board.

This Mode 3 approach, rather rare at O-level, is much commoner in CSE, though not as widespread as the traditional (Mode 1) examination. This makes CSE a much more flexible instrument than GCE. Typically, however, it is responsive to schools rather than to projects: Mode 3 syllabuses are normally teacher initiatives, not project initiatives. Most projects however, give rise to networks of teachers with experience of Mode 3 examining, and hence provide a framework supportive of the teacher initiative needed.

A problem is that Mode 3 CSE is normally so much more responsive than O-level that many developments in the content of subjects are denied to the O-level group. More radical experiments may be confined to pupils not taking examinations: the time of the examination is counted too precious. For example, the Humanities Curriculum Project, though it is widely examined at CSE and occasionally at O-level, is all too often confined to lower streams, though it was intended for mixed ability groups (and need not demand more than a couple of periods a week). The other side of this is that a non-examinable constituency gives a project a great deal of freedom to be imaginative.

The relation between projects and teacher education is a fascinating one. To explore it I need to set down my own perspective on the issues.

The most important factor in the improvement of schooling is the improvement of teaching: and the art of teaching – like that of acting or playing music or painting – is not a mere skill or craft, but has a logic and a content of meaning. Good teaching expresses ideas about knowledge and about the relation of knowledge to life – the life of the learners themselves. Meretricious teaching – though it may have considerable charm – fails to affirm the importance of knowledge and of relationships.

In a broad sense this assumption underlies the work of 'the great educators' – Plato and Rousseau and Dewey and their like. But they wrote *books about education*. Such books lie outside the art of teaching as the philosophy of art lies outside the practice of art, and most teachers find themselves dependent on the exegesis provided by those who study education in libraries rather than in classrooms. This is a source of power and one basis of a claim to expertise for the teacher educator.

It is of very great importance that the curriculum research and development movement expresses ideas about education in teaching materials, in teachers' handbooks and in specifications and samples of teaching. In this it is continuous with a tradition of educational thought which goes back to Comenius. Its language is practice; and through it the teacher can learn his art as the actor learns about life and the theatre through playing Shakespeare or the musician learns about musical structure and ideas by playing Bach.

Now, this development is potentially threatening to the teacher educator because it gives the practitioner a power over ideas unattainable by the college or university tutor. Thus, although I was director of, and in many respects initiator of, the Humanities Curriculum Project, it is quite clear now that the teachers who have practised it self-critically in their classrooms over the years understand its ideas and strengths and shortcomings with a command that I shall never be able to attain. And in my experience most students in initial training who have attempted HCP in their teaching practice for a few hours, already understand it better than most college lecturers who are lecturing about it without doing it.

Only a few teachers have recognised the power that the curriculum movement has given them because they see curriculum innovation in terms of changing content and method without taking account of the extent to which this means changing themselves through the refinement of their practice of their art. Nor are the implications of this widely assimilated by teacher educators.

Curriculum development is about teacher self-development.

The implications of this position both for in-service and for initial teacher education are novel and formidable, though some people are beginning the task of thinking them across into practice.

Clearly, if teachers develop their art in the classroom, teacher educators cannot claim to be as good at teaching in schools as those who are so teaching. Experience and school-teaching skill are not acceptable bases for a claim to be qualified as a teacher educator. A much more complementary and consultant role is apparently appropriate, and this would probably best be founded in an ability to serve the needs of teachers and students who are trying to develop the capacity to monitor themselves in the performance of their art. This suggests inquiry and discovery as modes of learning; and at the level of higher education this is generally characterised as research-based teaching. This is a traditional profession of the university, though one not always well expressed in practice.

Thus, the idea of curriculum studies as a medium of teacher education may have very important implications for the role of the teacher educator. So also does the problem raised by the general emphasis laid by curriculum research and development on discovery- and inquiry-based teaching. Skill in such teaching is not easy to acquire, and is not generally possessed by teacher educators who for the most part were trained in and taught in an instructional style and have carried this into their present task. There seems to be a match between the teaching style built into the curriculum projects and the style appropriate to that study of teaching which uses curriculum studies as a medium. The Ford T project is an excellent focus for the study of these issues, as indeed are the materials for self-training in discussion work produced by a group of HCP teachers (Rudduck (ed) 1979).

The interaction between the curriculum development movement and power in the system is also a complicated one. The Schools Council has been supported by public funds, both by means of a levy on local education authorities and by grants from the central educational budget. But its constitution was intended to prevent its control by these sources of funds and in some sense to place it in the control of teachers. And its early assumptions were that it would increase the freedom of teachers rather than lead to direction.

The political history of the Schools Council is a complicated one, and too close in time to be easy to document. Two power struggles seem to be key to the lead-in to the reforms of 1978: that between programme committee and the joint secretaries, and that between the Department of Education and Science and the Council.

The constitution of the Council set up a programme committee which was the locus of policy and the executive committee, beneath which were three steering committees, A (pupils 2–13), B (pupils 11–16) and C (pupils 14–18). The subject committees were the lowest tier and fed proposals up through the steering committees to the programme committee. All these committees have a majority of teacher representatives who are nominated by the teacher unions (or *ex officio*) and not, for example, by HMI. In effect, the situation leads to the representatives on programme committee and the steering committees being for the most part teacher politicians, while the subject committees have teachers who are union members, but who are known for their curricular and teaching interests rather than their political influence. And the real power lies with the programme committee and the teacher politicians (see Corbett (1965), Manzer (1970) and Nisbet (1973) for an analysis).

On the permanent staff side were three joint secretaries who headed the administrative and salaried professional staff of the Council. They were short-term, not permanent and tenured, appointments. The Council also is served by a research team, headed by an academic, who has recently been a professor dividing his time between the Council and his university.

The chairman of the Schools Council chairs programme committee, is a ministerial appointment, but is part-time and generally holds another important post.

In the early days of the Council a series of able and politically skilled joint secretaries, notably, Derek Morrell, Geoffrey Caston and Joslyn Owen, working closely with the first chairman, Sir John Maud and Alan Bullock, were the centre of power and initiative in the Council. They inherited from their positions in the Civil Service and the world of the LEAs a network of contacts and a political sense which enabled them both to judge what could be done and to commend it to the establishment. They also inherited, perhaps from the Nuffield tradition, a tendency to 'find the right man and back him,' their criteria being creativeness and competence. The best of the work they sponsored was not based in, though it was answerable to, the teacher community and it was led by people who had neither written proposals to the Council nor answered advertisements by the Council. Nor did they set up a system for referring proposals coming to the Council analogous to that practised by the government research councils. They consulted with subject committees, they set up meetings at which they could look over likely people, they helped to design projects, they liaised with the research team; but in the end they were themselves the strongest influence.

The departure of Alan Bullock as chairman and of Geoffrey Caston in 1970 led to a palace revolution. The teacher unions on the programme committee had been slow to sense their power and mobilise it and now they and the local authority representatives moved to establish with firmness their ascendency over the administrative and professional staff, who were, of course, undoubtedly there to serve them. Now, the programme committee became master. The pattern and the problems changed.

The volume of business passing through programme committee is so heavy that it is not really possible for the members to make fully informed judgements based upon detailed study of documentation. Yet programme committee was disposed to be independent of the Council staff who had greater time to consider and evaluate proposals. And the lack of any referee system meant there was no real alternative source of advice except that of the subject committees who were competing for resources within the total Council programme.

The power of programme committee members had steadily increased over the professional and administrative staff in part because the leadership of the latter was not permanent but short-term, while the membership of programme committee had unusual stability by virtue of its being largely representative of unions and organisations. Hence individuals maintained their membership of the key committee over many years and were able to consolidate their personal power and influence. Moreover, the teachers on programme committee were successful teacher politicians – the people one wants at the top of one's union – rather than those teachers whose interests focussed on the day-to-day business of teaching.

The consequence of this change in the locus of power was an increase in politicking. To get through the business many of the matters coming before programme committee had to be settled beforehand by manoeuvring and bargaining. Members of the committee used informal contact as the joint secretaries had earlier done, but evaluation of the contacts was difficult in the time available to members.

A number of developments and circumstances made the Council vulnerable to attack. The powerful programme committee members acted in an authoritarian manner in a number of instances so that the question of their accountability arose. A number of their fundings were unfortunate; large projects produced little. Long term disappointments with enterprises started in the early years came home to roost in the period of the committee's power. The teachers' unions sometimes acted without taking the LEA and DES representatives with them. The Council became more conservative in its policy, losing radical support, without really commending itself to educational conservatives. Its examination proposals ran into difficulty.

Meanwhile, if I understand the situation aright, the DES and HMI began to hope for more influence over the curriculum and practice of the schools. The Council, half funded by the LEAs and dominated by the teacher unions, represented the powers which would be disposed to resist an extension of central influence. Corporate management in local government was challenging the power of the LEA *vis à vis* the rest of local government. A change in the teacher supply situation seemed likely to weaken teacher power. There was an almost world-wide disposition to question the heavy investment in education of the 1960s and early 1970s and to respond to a cry of 'back to basics', rejecting alike the knowledge-based curriculum movement and the earlier progressivism. And the Council's procedures appeared vulnerable to criticism.

An attack has been followed by a reform. The joint secretaries are to be replaced by a single tenured appointment. An able and experienced chairman has been appointed. New policies are being formulated. There seems hope that a balance between committees and secretariat will at last be found. The educational press seems confident that the Council has survived.

It seems to me of great importance that it should. For all its political difficulties, it has produced a very great volume of work supportive of teachers who are trying to improve their practice. No teacher and no person who cares about the quality of work in schools could see it go with equanimity. It is, paradoxically, the central support structure for decentralisation; and at a time when centralised systems are seeking to decentralise, it is essential to maintain the pull towards decentralisation in a decentralised system which is moving towards more centralisation. That move is desirable, I think, but plenty of decentralising inertia is needed to ensure that it does not go too far.

The local authorities, who contribute half the funds to the Schools Council, are perhaps the main loci of decentralised power. What power the teachers have comes largely from the balance of force between the DES and the LEAs. At the moment it is the LEA which has the greater power over curriculum on the ground, in spite of a widespread tendency for LEAs to deny that they control curriculum. They do not issue curriculum edicts; but their control of in-service opportunities, of promotion and of the crucial dispensation of the marginal funds which mean the difference between success and failure in the implementation of curriculum research and development places them in a key position. And generally speaking both curriculum workers and teachers recognise that they hold this pole position.

The significance of the local authorities' political power over the shaping of the school system is witnessed by the impact of reformist chief education officers such as Clegg and Mason in their areas.

Perhaps the DES is less concerned to capture this power for itself than to make its significance explicit and the local agencies accountable for it. Certainly, the fashion has swung from 'curriculum reform' to 'educational accountability.' But the roots of accountability lie in the curriculum movement; for accountability rests upon the concept of 'evaluation'.

Evaluation is a major area of educational research which has not so far been exploited in Britain as it has been in the United States, largely because the educational research establishment is so much weaker on this side of the Atlantic. In America evaluation can be taken to be the response of the research community to the opportunities provided by the curriculum movement. Initially, it was based upon the psycho-statistical model of research, which was familiar and current in educational research.

This style of research is designed to generalise from an experimental sample to a large target population a judgement which discriminates in terms of probability between hypotheses. It depends upon the possibility of making worthwhile discriminant judgements – preferring x to y – and on the possibility of adequately representing a large population by a relatively small sample.

The adaptation of this approach to curriculum development involved the attempt to discriminate between two or more experimental curricula by testing the hypotheses that a was better than b as compared with the hypothesis that b was better than a, the assumption being that the result on the experimental sample would generalise to the educational system as a whole.

Of course, a crucial difficulty in this approach is deciding what we mean by 'better'. Starting from a behaviourist and psychometric base, the educational researchers assumed that, since learning was defined by behaviourists as changes in behaviour, and since education was an intentional attempt to help people learn, then education must be concerned with intended changes in behaviour and the intention involved must be expressable in terms of the behaviour expected to emerge from the process. Specifications of such be- haviour were called 'intended learning outcomes' or 'behavioural objectives'. Because the researchers' instruments for quantitative observation were stan- dardised tests, they specified that such behavioural objectives should be expressed in testable form. They laid that obligation on the curriculum developers.

Thus, the doctrine became: test a new curriculum and an old curriculum (control group) in a sample situation by the criteria of objectives specified by the curriculum developers (or teachers). If one appears better than the other to an extent greater than the error factors in the sampling and measuring (which can be calculated mathematically) then that is the better curriculum.

It will be apparent that this procedure contains many questionable assump- tions (which cannot be pursued here, see Stenhouse (1975) Chapters 5 to 8). To what extent the Schools Council explored these when it rejected the bid to adopt the model in this country I do not know. But it was left to two of the Council's Working Party on curriculum evaluation to set forth the doctrine through the National Foundation for Educational Research (Wiseman and Pidgeon 1970).

Certainly, the assumption that one curriculum can be recommended rather than another irrespective of variation in the teachers, the pupils and the conditions across schools is not an assumption likely to be made in the English system. Even the present press towards a minimum common ground is ex- pressed in the much broader terms of syllabus and is far from curriculum specification.

The result was that, where objectives were adopted, they were used as tools of thinking rather than impositions upon thinking. Science 5–13 is a classic example. In Britain the curriculum developers were not dominated by the evaluators' demands.

The American reaction against the so-called 'agricultural model' of eva- luation, a reaction towards what was called by one of its leading exponents, Robert E. Stake, 'portrayal evaluation,' made a broader appeal in Britain than did the psychometric model. It appeared as Parlett and Hamilton's (1972) 'illuminative evaluation' and MacDonald's (1971) 'holistic evaluation', and it seems to have influenced most subsequent evaluation in this country.

Such evaluation concentrates on the descriptive portrayal of a curriculum in conception and in action and aims to brief those who will have to make decisions about the curriculum with data on which they can base judgement. Instead of discriminating between alternative courses of action, it seeks to make actors more discriminating. On the whole, such evaluation does not address the problem of a social or community assessment of curriculum in a direct way, but rather works through appeal to the judgement of individuals; whereas the psycho-statistical tradition appears to attempt to seek to override professional judgement with a technical decision-making procedure.

The British evaluation tradition is well-documented in two Schools Council publications, *Evaluation in Curriculum Development: Twelve Case Studies* (Schools Council 1973) and *Curriculum Evaluation Today: Trends and Implications* (Tawney 1976).

In the event the advocates of psychometric testing, baulked in imposing on curriculum research the objectives model in the form expressed above, have instead become involved in an attempt, not to evaluate alternatives, but rather to evaluate the educational system as a whole or units in it, such as schools or local authorities. The movement is that of accountability, and it is in many ways a development from curriculum evaluation. The failure of the objectives approach is signalled by the adoption of minimal standard criteria, objectives without aspiration. The failure to contribute to discriminating action has led to a documentation, through survey methods of testing, of the need for discriminate action! But that is another story, and another book.

What is worth raising in a context of accountability is the cost effectiveness of the curriculum movement. I cannot see how this could be measured, but I think one can say something about the nature of the judgement involved.

The most important line of development promoted by curriculum research is teacher development. Thus the achievements of curriculum projects might be compared for cost-effectiveness with other agencies of in-service education. The Humanities Curriculum Project, of which I had personal experience, cost about as much as running a small University Department or Institute of Education (of say eight staff) for five years. In these terms I think the majority of curriculum projects show up rather well. But unfortunately, they also show that curriculum research and in-service education in permanent institutions are complementary rather than alternative, so they point rather to the need for the utilisation of curriculum work by permanent agencies and vice versa than to backing one alternative at the expense of the other.

A second line of development is in the study of education. I think that the curriculum movement has revolutionised curriculum studies and has made possible an integration of theory and practice in educational thought which was lacking in the context of an emphasis on contributory disciplines. This influence has yet to be fully worked through.

Third, curriculum research and development has revolutionised teaching materials, created new and more flexible types of publishing, influenced the relationship between content and design.

Fourth, it has changed the conduct of schools. Many schools are now involved in conscious and self-critical curriculum planning, which hardly existed in 1960.

Finally, and most difficult to assess, it has affected students, because it has stressed the need to give them access to high-quality knowledge as a context for skills; and it has made war on *mere* exercises and the textbook rhetoric of falsely assertive conclusions.

The trouble is that it has not, of course, been fully successful. Like all human endeavours it has to be costed as an aspiration partly realised. However, with all these reserves, let me predict that its accounts will look better in terms of profit and loss than will those of its expensive successor, accountability. It has stored a lot of capital which will be invested in in-service education in the next decade.

Partly because a pattern of curriculum research and development which is expressed in fixed-term projects must hand over to the system the curatorship of its traditions, it is a good way of generating ideas and achievements which do not congeal.

I think a case could be made which amply justified curriculum research and development in terms of cost-effectiveness as compared with all other forms of research and support for the teaching profession and the practice of schooling. But that is scarcely a surprising conclusion from me!

Bibliography and Further Reading

Introduction Chapter 1

BIBLIOGRAPHY

Bruner, Jerome S. (1960), *The Process of Education*, Harvard University Press.
Bruner, Jerome S. (1966), *Toward a Theory of Instruction*, The Belknap Press of Harvard University Press.
Burstall, Clare, Jamieson, M., Cohen, S. and Hargreaves, M. (1974), *Primary French in the Balance*, National Foundation for Educational Research (NFER) Publishing Co.
Hamilton, David (1976), *Curriculum Evaluation*, Open Books.
Hamilton, David, Jenkins, David, King, Christine, MacDonald, Barry and Parlett, Malcolm (eds.) (1977), *Beyond the Numbers Game: A reader in Educational Evaluation*, Macmillan Education.
Schools Council (1973), *Evaluation in Curriculum Development: Twelve Case Studies*, Macmillan Education.
Stenhouse, Lawrence (1975), *An Introduction to Curriculum Research and Development*, Heinemann Educational Books.
Tawney, David (ed.) (1976), *Curriculum Evaluation Today: Trends and Implications* Macmillan Education.
Walker, Decker F. and Schaffarzick, Jon (1974), 'Comparing Curricula', *Review of Educational Research* 44, 1, 83–111.
Wastnedge, Ron (1972), 'Whatever happened to Nuffield Junior Science?' 35–40 in Hoyle, Eric (ed.), *Facing the Difficulties* Unit 13. Open University Second Level Course: The Curriculum: Context Design and Development. (*Problems of Curriculum Innovation*, I, Units 13–15), Open University Press.
Wiseman, Stephen and Pidgeon, Douglas (1970), *Curriculum Evaluation*, NFER Publishing Co.

Chapter 2 National Association for the Teaching of English

BIBLIOGRAPHY

Adams, Anthony (1976), *Teaching English*, The National Book League.
Barnes, D., Britton, J., and Rosen, H. (1971), *Language, the Learner and the School*, Penguin.

Barrs, H., Bryan, B., and Griffiths, P. (1971), *What Are We Doing Here?* One of a series of newsletters prepared at the international conference on English, University of York.

Boas, Guy (1956), 'The Association 1906–56', *English*, 62, Summer, 45–8.

Britton, J. (1970), *Language and Learning*. Penguin.

Britton, J. (1973), 'Ten Years of NATE'. *English in Education*, 7, 2, Summer, 5–9.

Dixon, J. (1972), 'Current concerns … and the future of NATE – a discussion document', *English in Education*, 6, 2, Summer, 71–82.

Dixon, J. (1975), *Growth Through English: Set in the Perspective of the Seventies*, OUP. (A revised version of the report on the Dartmouth seminar, first published in 1967.)

Hodgson, J. D. (1975), *Changes in English Teaching, Institutionalisation, Transmission and Ideology*, unpublished Ph.D. thesis, University of London.

A Language for Life (1975), The Report of the Bullock Committee, HMSO.

Moseley, C., and Moseley, D. (1977), *Language and Reading Among Under-Achievers*, National Foundation for Educational Research.

NATE (1975), *Language in Context*, evidence submitted to the Bullock Committee, NATE.

NATE (1976), *Language across the Curriculum: Guidelines for Schools*. Ward Lock Educational for NATE.

Owen, J. (1973), *The Management of Curriculum Development*, CUP.

Raleigh, W. (1906), quoted by Boas, op. cit.

Rosen, H. (1975), 'Out There or Where the Masons went', *English in Education*, 9, 1, Spring, 54–64.

Whitehead, F. (1967), 'The Next Stage', *English in Education*, vol. 2, no. 1, Summer, 4–6.

Whitehead, F. (1976), 'The Present State of English Teaching', *The Use of English*, Autumn, 11–17.

OTHER SOURCES

NATE archive

A collection of papers that document the setting up of NATE. These and other documents, including committee minutes, were made available to me by Mrs. Georgie Taylor, NATE office manager, at the Huddersfield office which I visited in December 1977. I am most grateful to Mrs. Taylor for her kindness and help.

Interviews

With Tony Adams, NATE secretary, and Brian Durrant, organiser of the 1977 annual conference. The interviews took place in December 1977. In addition, two teachers from a London Comprehensive School recorded their comments (January 1978). I am most grateful to all four for the time they gave.

PUBLISHED AND UNPUBLISHED MATERIAL RELATING TO THE
NATE PROJECTS SPONSORED BY THE CALOUSTE
GULBENKIAN FOUNDATION AND THE SCHOOLS COUNCIL

Adams, Anthony (ed.) (1970), *The Language of Failure*, vol. 4, no. 3 of *English in Education*, OUP for NATE.

Calthrop, K. (1973), *Reading Together*, Heinemann Educational Books for NATE.

Creber, J. W. Patrick (1972), *Lost for Words*, Penguin.

Richards Martyn (1969), 'Children as Readers', *The School Librarian*, vol. 17, no. 3, September.

Wigglesworth Colin (1973), 'Children as Readers: Project Work in Seven Schools', *Dialogue*, 15, September.

See also articles by teachers associated with the 'Children as Readers Project' in *English in Education* (1971), 5, 3.

The *Norwich Feasibility Study* is currently being written up by Ethel Seaman and John Nicholls. The Pre-school Committee of NATE is preparing a publication for parents and teachers to which Ethel Seaman and John Nicholls are contributing a chapter on home visiting. Other contributors will be Margaret Robinson, Sinclair Rogers, Maureen Shields and Gordon Wells.

OTHER PUBLICATIONS

Adams, Anthony and Pearce, John (1974), *Every English Teacher*, OUP.

Books for our Schools (1977), a joint statement by NATE and the Schools Library Association.

Britton, J. N. *et al.* (1966), *Multiple Marking of English Composition: An Account of an Experiment*, Schools Council Examination Bulletin 12, HMSO.

Britton, J. (ed.) (1974), *Talking and Writing*, Methuen.

Britton, J. *et al.* (1975), *The Development of Writing Abilities (11–18)*, Macmillan Education for the Schools Council.

Burgess, C. *et al.* (1973), *Understanding Children Writing*, Penguin Education. 'The work has developed largely out of the concern of the LATE for "Language across the curriculum".' (Adams (1976), op. cit., 24).

Clements, S. and Griffiths, P. (eds.) (1971), *Language across the Curriculum*. vol. 5, no. 2 of *English in Education*, Oxford University Press for NATE.

Jones, A. and Mulford, J. (1972), *Children Using Language*, OUP.

Jones, E. and Adams, A. (1969), *The World in Words: a Desk Book for Teachers of English and Humanities*, Pergamon.

LATE (1965), *Assessing Compositions: a Discussion Pamphlet*, Blackie.

LATE (1969), *Assessing Comprehensions: a Discussion Pamphlet*, Blackie.

Martin, N. *et al.* (1976), *Writing and Learning across the Curriculum (11–16)*, Ward Lock Educational for the Schools Council.

Mathieson, M. (1975), *The Preachers of Culture*, Allen and Unwin.

Mittins, W. H. (1970), *Attitudes to English Usage*, OUP.

NATE (1964), *English in the Primary School: the Evidence of the Association Presented to the Plowden Committee*, NATE.

NATE (1968), *English Examined: a Survey of 'O' Level Papers*, NATE.

Rosen, C. and Rosen H. (1973), *The Language of Primary School Children*. Penguin Education for the Schools Council.

Shayer, D. (1972), *The Teaching of English in Schools*, 1900–72. Routledge and Kegan Paul.

Thompson, D. (ed.) (1969), *Directions in the Teaching of English*, CUP.

Whitehead, F. (1966), *The Disappearing Dais: a Study of the Principles and Practice of English Teaching*, Chatto and Windus.

Wilkinson, A. (1971), *The Foundations of Language: Talking and Reading in Young Children*, OUP.

Wilkinson, A. *et al.* (1974), *The Quality of Listening*. Macmillan Education for the Schools Council.

Chapter 3 The School Mathematics Project

BIBLIOGRAPHY

Branford, Benchara (1908), *Study of Mathematical Education*, OUP.

Clarke, Norman (1973), 'SMP: the First Ten Years', (review) *IMA Bulletin*, 9, 3, March.

Coulson, C. A. (1973), Presidential Address, 'Mathematics and the Real World', *IMA Bulletin* 9, 1, January 2–7.

Duncan, E. *et al.* (1978), *Mathematics Grades K-12*; a series of school texts, Houghton Mifflin Co.

Entebbe Mathematics Series (1971), *Report to the Agency for International Development on the Activities of the African Mathematics Program*, July. *Final Report, The African Mathematics Program*, April, Educational Development Center, 55 Chapel Street, Newton, Mass.

Foster, Leslie (1977), review of SMP 7–13, *AMA Journal*, April.

Goodstein, R. L. (1962), 'New Thinking in School Mathematics' (review) and 'Synopses for Modern Secondary School Mathematics', OEEC, *Mathematical Gazette*, XLVI, February 355.

Griffiths, H. B. (1975), 'What is the reality for the universities?'; McLane, R. R. (1975), 'Where have all the students gone?' Proceedings of a Conference held in the University of Nottingham, 14–17 December, London Mathematical Society and others.

Hammersley, J. M. (1968), 'On the Enfeeblement of Mathematical Skills by "Modern Mathematics" and by Similar Soft Intellectual Trash in Schools and Universities'. *IMA Bulletin*, 4, 4 October.

Hilton, Peter (1976), 'Education in Mathematics and Science – The Spread of False Dichotomies', *Proceedings of the Third International Congress on Mathematical Education*. See also Shirley Hill's Short Communication.

Hodgkinson, John (1976), 'A Personal View on SMP', *Maths I.S.*, 5, 1, January.

HM Inspectorate (1977), *Report on Mathematics, Science and Modern Languages in Maintained Schools in England*, (private circulation).

Howson, A. G. (1974), Some Experiences of Educational Development in England, *Procceedings of the ICMI Conference, Tokyo*, 8–13.

Howson, A. G. (1975), 'Teacher Involvement in Curriculum Development', *Schriftenreihe des Institut fur Didaktik der Mathematik*, 6, 267–287.

Howson, A. G. (1978), 'Change in Mathematics Education Since the Late 1950s – Ideas and Realisation in Great Britain', *Educational Studies in Mathematics* 9, 183–223.

IAAM (1957), *Report: The Teaching of Mathematics*, CUP.

Institute of Mathematics and Its Applications (IMA) Bulletin (1969–76): Hammersley, J. M. (1973) 'Modern Mathematics: the Great Debate', 9, 8, August.

   Spohn, William G., Jr. (1971), 'Can Mathematics be Saved?' 7, 3, March.

   Stretch, K. L. (1976), 'Is Mathematical Education on the Right Track?' 12, 3, March.

   Thwaites, Bryan (1969), 'Ways Ahead in Secondary School Mathematics', 5, 3 July.

Kendall, P. C. (1977), 'Mathematics and the First Deadly Sin', *IMA Bulletin* 13, 5, May, 124–8.

Kerr, E. (1977), 'Some Thoughts on the Educational System and Mathematics Teaching' (Presidential Address), *Mathematical Gazette* 61, 417, October.

Kliebard, Herbert M. (1975), 'Persistent Curriculum Issues in Historical Perspective', in Pinar, W. (ed.), *Curriculum Theorizing: The Reconceptualists*, McCutchan, 39–88.

Kline, Morris (1966), 'Intellectuals and the Schools: A Case History', *Harvard Educational Review*, 36, 4, 505–11.

Lighthill, Sir James (1972), Presidential Address, Second International Congress on Mathematical Education, in Howson, A. G. (ed.), *Developments in Mathematical Education*, CUP, 88–100.

Lindsay, Robert (1975), 'Let the Dog See the Rabbit', Mathematical shortcomings at the school/employment interface, Shell Centre for Mathematical Education, University of Nottingham.

Lyness, R. C. (1969), 'Modern Maths Reconsidered', *Trends in Education*, DES, April.

McLane, R. R. (1975), see Griffiths (1975).

Malpas, Anthony J. (1974), Objectives and cognitive demands of the School Mathematics Project's main course:

'Objectives', *Mathematics in Schools*, 3, 5, 2–5.

'Cognitive demands', *Mathematics in Schools*, 3, 6, 20–21.

Mathematical Association (1968), *Mathematics Projects in British Secondary Schools*, G. Bell and Sons, revised edition 1976.

Mathematics in Schools (1975–76):

Editorial, 'SMP A-Level: A Worrying Situation', 4, 5, September 1975.

Burley, D. M. (1975), 'SMP: a disaster?' 4, 6, November 1975, 11–13.

Hersee, John (1976), 'SMP: a disaster averted', 5, 1 January, 1976, 2–3.

Harper, Ron (1976), 'SMP: the real issues', 5, 2, 9–10.

Meder, Albert E. Jr. (1957), 'Modern Mathematics and its Place in the Secondary School, *The Mathematics Teacher*, October, 418–23.

Moser, James M. (1970–76), *Developing Mathematical Processes, Grades K–6*, Rand McNally, Instructional materials for teachers and children; (a program devised from the Wisconsin Research and Development Centre for Cognitive Learning).

NACOME (1975), *Report: Overview and Analysis of School Mathematics Grades K–12*, Conference Board of the Mathematical Sciences National Committee on Mathematical Education, Washington D.C.

NCTM (1953), *The Learning of Mathematics* 21st Yearbook, Washington, National Council of Teachers of Mathematics, 323–27.

Niss, Mogens (1977), 'The "Crisis" in Mathematics Instruction and a New Teacher Education', *Int. J. Maths. Ed. Sc. Tech.*, 8, 3, August, 303–22.

OEEC (1961), *New Thinking in School Mathematics*, Organization for European Economic Co-operation.

Ollerenshaw, K. (1977), Mathematics and Education: A Plan for the 1980s, *IMA Bulletin*, 13, 6, June, 146–153.

Ormell, C. P. (1973a), Schools Council/University of Reading Sixth Form Mathematics Curriculum Project Paper, 15/73, 5.

Ormell, C. P. (1973b), 'The Problems of Curriculum Sequence in Mathematics', in Langford, G. and O'Connor, D. J. (eds.), *New Essays in the Philosophy of Education*, Routledge and Kegan Paul, 216–33.

Oxford Mathematical Conference (1951), *Report*, Times Publishing Company.

Parlett, M. and Hamilton, D. (1972), *Evaluation as Illumination: A New Approach to the Study of Innovatory Programmes*, Centre for Research in the Educational Sciences, University of Edinburgh.

Parliamentary Expenditure Committee (1978), *Tenth Report, The Attainment of the School Leaver*, HMSO.

Peters, R. S. (1963), *Education as Initiation: An Inaugural Address*, University of London Institute of Education, Evans Bros.

Pitt H. R. (1963), Priorities in the Reform of Mathematics Teaching, *Mathematical Gazette*, XLVII, 361, 288–332.

Preston, M. (1972), *The Measurement of Affective Behaviour in CSE Mathematics*, University of Leicester Ph.D. thesis.

Rogerson, Alan (1975), *The SMP A-Level and Mathematics 16–19*, SMP leaflet, July.

Rollett, A. P. (1963), 'A History of the Teaching of Modern Mathematics in England', *Mathematical Gazette*, XLVII, 362, December, 299–306. (This issue contains eight papers on modern mathematics and its teaching.)

Sherman, Helene (1977), *Common Elements in New Mathematics Programs: Origins and Evolution*, Columbia Teachers College Press.

Smithies, F. (1963), 'What is Modern Mathematics?', *Mathematical Gazette*, XLVII, 362, December, 278–98.

Sturgess, D. A. (1971), Review of SMP Books A-H, *Mathematics Teaching* No. 56, Autumn, 63–4.

Thom. René (1971), 'Modern Mathematics: An Educational and Philosophic Error?', *American Scientiest*, 59, 6, 695–99.

Thom, René (1973), 'Modern Mathematics: Does It Exist?' in Howson, A. G. (ed.), *Developments in Mathematical Education* (Proceedings of the Second International Congress on Mathematical Education), CUP, 1–196.

Thornton, E. B. C. (1963), 'The New "Maths" in American High School', *Math. Gazette*, XLVII, 360, May, 91–6.

Thwaites, Bryan (1961a), *On Teaching Mathematics: the Outcome of the Southampton Mathematics Conference*, Pergamon.

Thwaites, Bryan (1961b), *Mathematics: Divisible and Indivisible*, inaugural address, Southampton University.

Thwaites, Bryan (1972a), *The School Mathematics Project: the First Ten Years*, CUP.

Thwaites, Bryan (1972b), Summary paper, *modern mathematics in relation to the need of the profession*, Institute of Mathematics and its Applications, p. 37.

Times Educational Supplement (1974–76):

    Editorial (1976), 'Engineers with Chips on Their Shoulders', 3 September.

    Rogerson, Alan (1974), 'It's the Pupils that Count', 18 April.

    Thwaites, Bryan (1975), 'Red Herrings Served in Style', 3 January.

    Woodnough, Brian (1975), 'All at Sea Over New Mathematics', 24 January.

UNESCO (1969a), *School Mathematics in Arab Countries*.

UNESCO (1969b), *Mathematics Project for the Arab States, Regional Seminar in Cairo, 8–11 March 1969*.

UNESCO (1970–71), *Mathematics Materials for Grades 10, 11, and 12*.

Wooton, William (1965), *SMSG: The Making of a Curriculum*, Yale UP.

FURTHER READING

Brighouse, Alan (1977), 'SMP 7–13: the Primary School Background', *Maths in Schools* 6, 4, 35–6.

Kline, Morris (1970), 'Logic versus Pedagogy', *Amer. Math. Monthly*, 77, 264–82.

Kline, Morris (1973), *Why Johnny Can't Add: the Failure of the New Maths*, St. James' Press.

Kline, Morris (1966), A Proposal for the High School Mathematics Curriculum, *Maths Teacher*, 59, 322–30.

Rogerson, Alan (1975), 'The School Mathematics Project: A Case Study in the Implementation of Innovations', *J. App. Educ. Studies*, 3, 2, 9–11.

Rogerson, Alan (1975), 'The SMP; It's *raison d'être* and Future Plans', *Times Educational Supplement*, 8 October.

Rogerson, Alan (1976), 'One to one', *Teachers World*, 7 May.

Rogerson, Alan, (1976), 'Despite All the Excitement, Real Change Spreads Slowly', *The Teacher*, 9 April.

Rogerson, Alan (1976), 'Freedom to Experiment', *Teachers World*, 7 May.

Rogerson, Alan (1976), 'The aim's the same', *Teachers World*, 15 October.

Williams, Doug (ed.) (1975), *Recent Trends in British Mathematical Education*, Australia: the Mathematical Association of Victoria 8–9, 75–6.

Various journals carry reviews of the SMP texts, for example:
Mathematical Gazette: 49, 370, 441–42; 52, 382, 389–93; 53, 386, 428–31; 54, 387, 77–81; 55, 394, 462–65.
Mathematics Teaching: 50, 79–82; 53, 56; 54, 43; 55, 57; 56, 63–64.

Recent annual reports, the periodical newsletter *SMP News*, and other leaflets and booklets are available from the Executive Director at the SMP Office, for example:
The School Mathematics Project, 1976
The School Mathematics Project Report, 1977
The SMP A-Level and Mathematics 16–19 (1975)
Syllabuses for A-Level SMP Further Mathematics (1976)
The Syllabuses for the SMP GCE Examinations (1976)
SMP 7–13
SMP 7–13 Progress Reports
Manipulative Skills in Mathematics (1974), p. 21. (This important booklet sets out the position of the SMP on the place of manipulative skills in the learning of mathematics).
SMP Publications, CUP. (An annual prospectus of the student texts, teacher's guides, handbooks and other materials is issued.)

Chapter 4 Nuffield O-Level Chemistry

BIBLIOGRAPHY

Anderson, William (1966), 'Nuffield Chemistry Background Books', *Education in Chemistry*, 3, 6, 299–301.
Association for Science Education (1963), 'Science and Education: What's Going On?'. *ASE Bulletin*, 7, November, 22–24.
Association for Science Education (1966), 'Some Thoughts about Nuffield and the Approach of the Publication Date of the O-Level Texts'. *Education in Science*, 17, April, 11–12.
Booth, Norman (1975), 'The Impact of Science Teaching Projects on Secondary Education', *Trends in Education*, February, 25–32. Reprinted in *Education in Science*, 63, 27–30.
Bradley John (1967), 'How Not to Teach Chemistry'. *Education in Chemistry*, 4, 2, 58–64.
Bronowski, Jacob (1958), 'The Educated Man in 1984'. *Advancement of Science*, 306.
Chemical Society (1965a), 'The Nuffield Science Teaching Project', *Education in Chemistry*, 2, 2 March, 57.
Chemical Society (1965b), 'New Teachers' Guide Takes Shape', *Education in Chemistry*, 2,4, July, 159.
Chisman, D. G. (1964), 'The Nuffield Foundation Science Teaching Project', *Education in Chemistry*, 1, 1 January, 5–6.
Commonwealth Education Liaison Committee (CELC) (1964), *School Science Teaching*, Report of an Expert Conference held at the University of Ceylon, Peradeniya, December, 1963. HMSO.
Coulson, E. H. (1972), 'Some Recent Developments in Chemistry Teaching in Schools', *Chemical Society Reviews*, 1, 4, 495–521.
Eggleston, J. F., Galton, M. J., and Jones, M. E. (1976), *Processes and Products of Science Teaching*, Macmillan Education for Schools Council.

Farer-Brown, L. (1964), 'Address to Council of ASE, 31.12.1963', *ASE Bulletin*, 8, February, 15–18.

Flynn, H. E. and Monroe, R. G. (1970), 'Evaluation of a Curriculum', *British Journal of Educational Psychology*, 40, November, 271–82.

Fowles, G. (1968), 'Nuffield Chemistry: a Critical Commentary', *School Science Review*, XLIX, March, 561–68.

Gorbutt, D. (1970), *Subject Choice in Secondary Schools with Special Reference to the Swing from Science*, unpublished M.A. thesis, University of London.

Halliwell, H. F. (1964), 'The Nuffield Science Teaching Project', pp. 67–74 in CELC (1964), *op. cit.*

Halliwell, H. F. and Van Praagh, G. (1967), 'The Nuffield Project II: Chemistry, 11–16', *School Science Review*, XLVIII, 165, 332–36.

Halliwell, H. F. (1968), 'Chemical Education: Problems of Innovation', *RIC Reviews*, 1, 2 August.

Halliwell, H. F. (1972), 'Some Reflections on the Development of Science Education', *Pure and Applied Chemistry*, vol. 31, Butterworth.

Halliwell, H. F. (1974), 'Forward from Nyholm's Marchon Lecture', *Chemical Society Reviews*, 3, 3 (Reprint).

Hamilton, D. F. (1970), 'Nuffield O-Level Sciences: Sources or Courses', *School Science Review*, LI, 177, 905–6.

Harding, J. M. M. (1975), *Communication and Support for Change in School Science Education*, unpublished Ph.D. thesis, Chelsea College, University of London.

Hartwell, E. J. (1966), 'Education Through Chemistry', *Nature*, 5058, 8 October, 121–23 (Review).

Herron, Marshall D. (1971), 'The Nature of Scientific Enquiry', *School Review*, 79, February, 171–212.

Industrial Fund for the Advancement of Scientific Education in Schools (IFASES) (1963), Final Report by the Committee Established to Administer the Fund under its Trust Deed, IFASES.

Ingle, Richard and Coulson, Ernest (1975), 'The Revision of Nuffield O-Level Chemistry', *Education in Science*, 61, January, 15–17.

Ingle, R. B. and Shayer, M. (1971), 'Conceptual Demands in Nuffield O-Level Chemistry', *Education in Chemistry*, 8, 5, September, 182–83.

IUPAC Committee on the Teaching of Chemistry, (ed. Mathews, J. C.) (1966), *The Effect of Examinations in Determining the Chemistry Curriculum up to the Level of University Entrance*, Butterworth.

Jackson, A. (1966), 'Nuffield Under Trial', *Education in Chemistry*, 3, November, 280–84.

Jackson, A. (1967), 'Nuffield Chemistry: Two Views: In Defence of Nuffield', *Education in Chemistry*, 4, March, 58–67.

Kelly, P. J. (1975), *The Curriculum Diffusion Research Project: Outline Report*, Centre for Science Education, Chelsea College (mimeo).

Kempa, R. F. and Dubé, G. E. (1974), 'Science Interest and Attitude Traits in Students Subsequent to the Study of Chemistry at the Ordinary Level of the General Certificate of Education', *Journal of Research in Teaching*, 11, 4, 361–70.

Laughton, W. H. and Wilkinson, W. J. (1968), 'Pupils' Attitudes to Science Teaching', *Education in Science*, 26, February, 31–33.

McKinley, W. Lynn and Westbury, Ian (1975), 'Stability and Change: the Public Schools of Gary, Indiana, 1940–70', in Reid and Walker (1975), *op. cit.*

Maddox, John (1964), 'Livelier Science in Schools', *New Scientists*, 418, 17 November, 507–8.

Mathews, J. C. (1967), 'The Nuffield Project VII – O-Level Chemistry Examinations', *School Science Review*, XLIX, 167, 21–30.

Meyer, G. R. (1970), 'Reactions of Pupils to Nuffield Science Teaching Project Trial Materials in England at the Ordinary Level of the General Certificate of Education', *Journal of Research in Science Teaching*, 7, 4, 283–302.

New Scientist (1966), 'Nuffield Science', *New Scientist*, 7 July, 5–6.

Nicodemus, R. Ingle, R. B. and Jenkins, E. N. (1976), 'Adopting Nuffield O- and A-Level Chemistry', *Education in Chemistry*, 13, March, 46–48.

Nuffield Foundation Science Teaching Project (1963), *Progress Report*, Nuffield Foundation (mimeo).

Nuffield Foundation Science Teaching Project (1964), *Progress Report, 1964*, Longmans Green/Penguin.

Nuffield Foundation Science Teaching Project (1965), *Progress Report, 1965*, Longmans Green/Penguin.

Nuffield Foundation Science Teaching Project (1966), *Progress Report, 1966*, Longmans Green/Penguin.

Nunn, T. P. (1918), 'Science', 154–94, in Adams, John (ed.) (1918), *The New Teaching*, Hodder and Stoughton (1919, 1935).

Ormerod, M. B., and Duckworth, D. (1975), *Pupils' Attitudes to Science: a Review of Research*, NFER Publishing Co.

Platts, C. V. (1967), 'Attitudes towards Nuffield Chemistry', *Education in Science*, 24, June, 40–41.

Reid, W. A. and Walker, Decker F. (eds.) (1975), *Case Studies in Curriculum Change: Great Britain and the United States*, Routledge and Kegan Paul.

Robinson, Michael (1967), Reviews of Nuffield O-Level Chemistry and Physics, *Forum*, 9, Summer, 103–4.

Rogers, M. J. W. (1966), 'Books for the Nuffield Science Project: the Published Material', *Education in Chemistry*, 3, 6, 289–91.

Schools Council (1965), 'The Nuffield Foundation O-Level Science Teaching Materials', *ASE Bulletin*, 15, November, 23–27.

Schools Council (1969), 'The Nuffield Science Teaching Project', *Education in Science*, 32, April, 20–23.

Science Masters' Association (1957), *Science and Education: A Policy Statement by the Committee of the Science Masters' Association*, John Murray.

Science Masters' Association/Association of Women Science Teachers (1961), *Science and Education: A Policy Statement by the Committee of the SMA and AWST*, John Murray.

Snow, C. P. (1959), *The Two Cultures and the Scientific Revolution* (Rede Lecture, 1959), CUP.

Stokes, B. (1966), 'Nuffield Diffraction Grids and the Nuffield Periodic Table', *Education in Chemistry*, 3, November, 306–8.

Stokes, B. (1967), 'Nuffield Film Loops', *Education in Chemistry*, 4, January, 19–20.

Taylor, Nat (1968), 'Teaching Nuffield Chemistry: Origins of a TV Series', *Education in Chemistry*, 5, 5, 125–28.

Thorpe, C. W. (1970), *Nuffield O-Level Science in the South West*, Institute of Education, Exeter University (mimeo).

Times Educational Supplement (1964), 'Comment in Brief', *Times Educational Supplement* 9 October, 569. See too 'Private Party' (Astryx), 21 August, 249.

Tremlett, R. (1967), 'The Nuffield Project IV: Chemistry Apparatus and Laboratory Organization', *School Science Review*, XLVIII, 663–75.

Van Praagh, G. (1967), 'What it Costs to go Nuffield', *Times Educational Supplement*, 5 May, 1523.

Waring, M. R. H. (1975), *Aspects of the Dynamics of Curriculum Reform in Secondary School Science*, Ph.D. thesis, Chelsea College, University of London.

Waring, Mary (1979), *Social Pressures and Curriculum Innovation: Study of the Nuffield Foundation Science Teaching Project*, Methuen.

West, R. W. (1974), *An Evaluation of Nuffield Chemistry: Text, Performance, Context*, unpublished D.Phil. thesis, University of Sussex.

NUFFIELD O-LEVEL CHEMISTRY MATERIALS

Published by Longmans Group, Burnt Mills, Harlow, Essex and Penguin Education, Harmondsworth, Middlesex, from 1966.

For the teacher:	*Handbook for Teachers*
	The Sample Scheme: I: The Basic Course
	II: A course of Options
	Collected Experiments
For the pupil:	*Laboratory Investigations*
	Book of Data
	Background Books
Teaching Aids:	Nuffield Diffraction Grids
	A 'long' version of the Periodic Table
	Charts
	Series of 8mm film loops

Chapter 5 Primary French Project

BIBLIOGRAPHY

Annan Report (1960), *The Teaching of Russian*, Report of the Committee appointed by the Ministry of Education and the Secretary of State for Scotland, HMSO.

Burstall, Claire (1974), *Primary French in the Balance*, National Foundation for Educational Research.

Durette, R. (1972), 'A Five-Year FLES, Report', *Modern Language Journal*, 56, 23–24.

Handscombe, R. J. (1966), *Topics of Conversation and Centres of Interest in the Speech of Eleven and Twelve Year-old Children*, Nuffield Foundation Foreign Languages Teaching Materials Project. Occasional Paper 8.

Hoy, P. H. (1977), *The Early Teaching of Modern Languages*, Nuffield Foundation.

Kellermann, M. (1964), *Two Experiments in Language Teaching in Primary Schools in Leeds*, Nuffield Foundation.

Lazaro, C. M. (1963), *Report on Foreign Language Teaching in British Primary Schools*, Nuffield Foundation Foreign Languages Teaching Materials Project.

Rowlands, D. (1972), 'Towards FLES in Britain', *Modern Languages Journal*, January, 13–20.

Schools Council (1966), *French in the Primary School*, Working Paper 8, HMSO.

Stern, H. H. (1969), *Language and the Young School Child*, OUP.

UNESCO (1962), *Foreign Languages in Primary Education*, Report of an international meeting of experts, 9–14 April 1962, UNESCO Institute for Education.

MATERIALS PUBLISHED BY THE PRIMARY FRENCH PROJECT

Linguistic research

Published by the Nuffield Foundation Foreign Languages Teaching Materials Project, Micklegate House, York.

Hasan, R. (1965), *The Language of 8 Year-old Children*, Occasional paper 5.
Hasan, R. and Handscombe, R. (1965–66), *The Language of 9 Year-old Children*, Occasional papers 7, 9, 10, 13, 14.
Hasan R. and Handscombe, R. (1965–66), *The Language of 10 Year-old Children*, Occasional papers 15, 18, 19, 21, 22.
Handscombe, R. (1967), *The Written Language of 11 and 12 Year-old Children*, Occasional papers 25.
Handscombe, R. (1965), *Topics of Conversation and Centres of Interest in the Speech of 11 and 12 Year-old Children*, Occasional paper 8.
Hasan, R. (1964), *Grammatical Analysis Code*, Occasional paper 6.
Handscombe, R. (1966), *The First 1,000 Clauses*, Occasional paper 11.
Lecleroq, J. (1966), *Enquête sur le langage de l'enfant français*, Occasional paper 20.
Lazaro, C. M. (1963), *Report on Foreign Language Teaching in British Primary Schools*, Occasional paper 1.
Kellermann, M. (1964), *Two Experiments on Language Teaching in Primary Schools, Leeds.* (1965), *Audio-Visual Courses for Primary Schools*, Occasional paper 3.
Naylor, J. W. (1966), *French Readers for Primary Schools – A Bibliography*, Occasional paper 12.

Assessment tests

The Language Materials Development Unit of York University has produced a number of performance tests for each stage (1A, 1B, 2, 3 and 4a) of the *En Avant* materials. There are similar tests for the earlier stages of the Nuffield materials for the other three languages. Each kit contains a teacher's instruction booklet, a tape and a class set of non-expendable pupils' materials.

French language teaching materials

Nuffield Introductory French Course: En Avant Primary stages: Stage 1 (revised) and Stage 2. Mainly audio-visual with tapes and posters not filmstrips. There is a gradual introduction to reading and writing.
Transition stage: Stage 3.
Secondary stage: Stages 4a and 4b. Textbook-based stages with strips and tape aiming at extending and consolidating vocabulary and grammar.

Schools Council continuation materials: A votre avis

Stages 5 and 6 complete the course to O-level and CSE standard with emphasis on individual guided work. The latter is achieved with a wide range of separate pupils' books which treat specific areas of grammar (for example handling conditional tenses – 'If pigs could fly') and conversational areas (for example handling situations in which the traveller may find himself – 'What do I say now?'). There is also a stage 7 which may be categorised as enrichment material for the high flyers.

All materials are published, together with teachers' handbooks, by E. J. Arnold, Butterley Street, Leeds.

GERMAN

Nuffield introductory course: Vorwärts
Stages 1A, 1B, 2A and 2B. These stages have been abbreviated into a rapid introductory course called *Kurzfassung*. Published by E. J. Arnold.

Schools council continuation materials

Stages 3, 4 and 5 complete the course to O-level and CSE level.

SPANISH

Nuffield introductory course: Adelante

Stages 1, 2A and 2B, compressed additionally into a rapid introductory course entitled *Calatrava*. Published by Macmillan Education, Houndmills, Basingstoke, Hants.

Schools Council continuation materials

Stages 3 and 4 plus background film strips *Young People of Spain*. Published by E. J. Arnold.

RUSSIAN

Nuffield introductory course: Vperyod!

Stages 1, 2 and 3. Published by Macmillan Education.

Schools Council continuation materials

Stages 4 and 5 up to O-level and CSE level. Published by E. J. Arnold.

FILMS

Three 16mm colour films telling stories with puppet characters are available from the Language Materials Development Unit, York. There are French and Spanish versions.

TEACHING METHOD

Rowlands, D. G. (1972), *Group work in Modern Languages*. Language Materials Development Unit, York.
Robinson, J. A. (1976), *Teaching with En Avant*. Language Materials Development Unit, York.
Buckby, M. and Grant, D. (1971), *Faites vos Jeux*. Language Materials Development Unit, York.

OTHER RELEVANT PUBLICATIONS

Burstall, Clare (1970), *French in the Primary School: Attitudes and Achievements*, NFER.
Burstall Clare, Jamieson M., Cohen S., and Hargreaves M. (1974), *Primary French in the Balance*, NFER, (Statistical appendices also available).
Salter, Michael, (1973), *French from 13–16*, SCMLP Paper 62.
'French from 8–16', *Modern Languages Journal*, vol. III, 3. An account of a one-day conference organised by the MLA.
Schools Council (1966), *French in the Primary School* (Working Paper 8) HMSO.
Schools Council (1969), *Development of Modern Language Teaching in Secondary Schools* (Working Paper 19) HMSO.

Schools Council (1970), *Dialogue* 5, Modern Languages: Nuffield and Schools Council.

Chapter 6 Nuffield Secondary Science

BIBLIOGRAPHY

Alexander, D. (1973), 'Nuffield Secondary Science Project' in Tawney, D. (ed.), *Evaluation in Curriculum Development: Twelve Case Studies*, Schools Council Research Studies, Macmillan Education.
Alexander, D. (1974), *Evaluation of Nuffield Secondary Science*, Schools Council Research Studies, Macmillan Education.
Beard, E. G. (1974), *Nuffield Secondary Science: an Analysis*, Volkswagen Curriculum Analysis Project, University of Sussex (mimeo).
Central Advisory Council for Education (England) (1963), *Half our Future*, (The Newsom Report), HMSO.
MacDonald B. and Walker R. (1976), *Changing the Curriculum* (Ch. 4), Open Books.
Misselbrook, H. (1967–68), 'Nuffield Secondary Science', *School Science Review*, 49.
Misselbrook, H. (1969a), 'Nuffield Secondary Science' in *Education and Training*, vol. II, 12.
Misselbrook, H. (1969b), *Nuffield Secondary Science Teaching Project*, a paper written for Schools Council Conference, Scarborough.
Nuffield Foundation (1964), *Nineteenth Annual Report 1963–64*, OUP.
SAFARI Project (1973), *The Nuffield Approach* (mimeo), Centre for Applied Resarch in Education.
Schools Council (1965a), *Science for the Young School Leaver*, Working Paper No. 1, Schools Council.
Schools Council (1965b), *CSE Experimental Examinations: Science*, Examinations Bulletin 8 HMSO.
Schools Council (1971), *Choosing a curriculum for the young school leaver*, Working Paper 33, Evans/Methuen Educational.
Waring, Mary (1979), *Social Pressures and Curriculum Innovation: a Study of the Nuffield Foundation Science Teaching Project*, Methuen.

PUBLISHED MATERIAL

Published by the Longman Group Burnt Mill, Harlow, Essex.

Teachers guide

The essential introduction to the whole project, this contains a summary of objectives and approach, detailed descriptions of the content and arrangement of Themes, a full discussion of the appropriate teaching techniques, and advice on course construction with twelve examples as starting points.
Contents: An outline of Secondary Science; The aims of science teaching; How to use the books and materials; Safety; A brief history of the Project; Appendices; Extract from Schools Council *Working Paper 1*, Combined Science and Secondary Science.

Apparatus guide

This contains details of apparatus and materials required. Drawings and instructions are given for making about 160 pieces of apparatus.

Examining at CSE level

Written with the requirements of Mode 3 CSE in mind. It considers some practical aspects of assessment and evaluation and deals with the planning of a variety of tests on the Secondary Science material. Representative examples of different types of questions related to each Theme are included.

The themes

Theme 1 Interdependence of living things
Environment studies, classification and identification; 1.2 Basic exchanges; 1.3 Animal and plant growth; population studies; 1.4 Colonisation; disease, pest and weed control.

Theme 2 Continuity of life
2.1 Animal and plant reproduction and propagation; 2.2 The mechanism of inheritance; 2.3 The process of evolution.

Theme 3 Biology of man
3.1 Physical activity; 3.2 The human life cycle; reproduction, growth and development; 3.3 Health and hygiene; 3.4 Senses, behaviour and learning; 3.5 Men in the world: control of the environment.

Theme 4 Harnessing energy
4.1 Energy in action; 4.2 Man's energy, his physical limitations and the use of machines; 4.3 Electrical transmission of energy; 4.4 Problems of bringing energy to bear.

Theme 5 Extension of sense perception
5.1 Human limitations; extending the range of sense perception; 5.2 Hearing and the nature of sound; 5.3 Seeing and the behaviour of light; 5.4 Artificial aids to communications and recording.

Theme 6 Movement
6.1 Transport; 6.2 Natural movement of living things.

Theme 7 Using materials
7.1 Introduction; collecting, classification and preliminary investigations; 7.2 Metals and alloys; 7.3 Fuels; 7.4 Synthetic materials and natural products; building materials and modern plastics; cleaning and costing materials; fibres and fabrics; 7.5 Radioactive materials.

Theme 8 The earth and its place in the universe
8.1 Getting away from the Earth; 8.2 The solar system and beyond; 8.3 The weather; 8.4 The Earth's crust.

Pupils' books

Two pupils' background books have also been prepared by the project:
Britain's fuels
Rocks, minerals and fossils

Chapter 7 Science 5–13

FURTHER READING

Archives
The project archives are located at the University of Bristol School of Education, 19 Berkeley Square, Bristol. Permission to consult them can be obtained from Miss Sylvia Steventon, Librarian.

Evaluation report

The official evaluation report on the project is Wynne Harlen (1975), *Science 5–13: a Formative Evaluation*, Schools Council Research Studies, Macmillan Education.

Articles

Bradley, Howard (1976), *A Survey of Science Teaching in Primary Schools: Pointers for INSET*, University of Nottingham School of Education.

Ennever, Len (1970), 'The New Science' in Rodgers, Vincent (ed.) *Teaching in the British Primary School*, Collier-Macmillan.

Ennever, Len (1972), 'Science 5–13', *Dialogue* 11, Schools Council Newsletter, Summer.

Ennever, Len (1974), 'A Case Study of a Project', *Secondary Education*, 4, 2 March.

Ennever, Len (1975), 'Science' ch. 3 in Matthews, J. (ed.) *Trends in Primary Education*, Peter Owen.

Gammage, John (1976), *Science 5–13 Project*, Wollongong Institute of Education, P.O. Box 1496, Wollongong, 2500, NSW, Australia.

Richards, Colin and Abell, Barry (1973), Science 5–13: 'An Evaluation of an Evaluation', *School Science Review*, 54, 188, March.

Richards, Roy (1973), 'The Swinging of a Pendulum: Discovering Science with Young Children', *Education 3–13*, April.

Sockett, Hugh (1976), 'Approaches to Curriculum Planning II', in *Rationality and Artistry*, Course E203, Unit 17, Open University.

Toulson, Shirley (1974), 'The Influence of Science 5–13' *Dialogue* 18, Schools Council Newsletter, September 1974.

Wastnedge, Ron (1972), 'Whatever Happened to Nuffield Junior Science?', Supplementary Reading 1, in *Problems of Curriculum Innovation*, Course E283, Units 13–15, Open University Press, p. 35.

PUBLISHED MATERIALS

Published by Macdonald Educational, Holywell House, Worship Street, London EC2.

	With Objectives in Mind, Guide to Science 5–13.
First set:	*Metals*, Stages 1 and 2.
	Metals, Background Information.
	Working with Wood, Stages 1 and 2.
	Working with Wood, Background Information.
	Time, Stages 1 and 2 and Background.
	Trees, Stages 1 and 2.
Second set:	*Early Experiences*, Beginnings.
	Structures and Forces, Stages 1 and 2.
	Science from Toys, Stages 1 and 2 and Background.

Third set: *Change*, Stages 1 and 2 and Background.
                  Minibeasts, Stages 1 and 2.
                  Coloured Things, Stages 1 and 2.
                  Holes, Gaps and Cavities, Stages 1 and 2.
                  Structures and Forces, Stage 3.
                  Change, Stage 3.
Fourth set: *Children and Plastics*, Stages 1 and 2 and Background.
                  Ourselves, Stages 1 and 2.
                  Like and Unlike, Stages 1, 2 and 3.
                  Science, Models and Toys, Stage 3.

A resource unit *Using the Environment*, by Dr. Margaret Collis, has been produced in four parts and as a whole:
  Early Explorations
  Investigations Parts 1 and 2
  Tackling Problems
  Ways and means Parts 1 and 2
Understanding Science 5–13 is a unit which introduces the project's materials for those to whom the ideas are new. An index for the whole range of units is planned.

Chapter 8 Project Technology

BIBLIOGRAPHY

Becher, A. (1971), 'The Dissemination and Implementation of Educational Innovation', Annual Meeting of the British Association for the Advancement of Science, Section L, September.

Getzels, J. W. and Jackson, P. W. (1962), *Creativity and Intelligence*, Wiley.

Havelock, R. G. (1971), *Planning for Innovation through the Dissemination and Utilization of Knowledge*, Centre for Research and Utilization of Knowledge, Ann Arbor, Mich.

HMSO (1968), *Report of the Committee of enquiry into the Flow of Candidates in Science and Technology into Higher Education* (the Dainton Report).

Hutchings, D. W. and Heyworth, P. (1963), *Technology and the Sixth Form Boy*, Oxford University Department of Education.

MacDonald, B. and Walker, R. (1976), *Changing the Curriculum*, Open Books.

Page, G. T. (1965), *Engineering Among the Schools*, Institute of Mechanical Engineers, (out of print).

Pemberton, A. R. and Eggleston, S. J. (1973), *International Perspectives of Design Education*, Studies in Education, Driffield.

Schools Council (1967), *A School Approach to Technology* (Curriculum Bulletin 2), HMSO.

SCSST (1973), *School Technology Forum 1*, National Centre for School Technology, Nottingham.

Shipman, M. D. (1974), *Inside a Curriculum Project*, Methuen.

ADDITIONAL PAPERS AND PUBLICATIONS

Computer Education, termly, annual subscription £2 UK, £4 overseas. Available from Computer Education Group, North Staffordshire Polytechnic, Beaconside, Stafford.

Harrison, G. B. (1975), 'Project Technology', *Educational Development International*, 3, January.

Harrison, G. B. (1975), 'Schools technology centre', *Times Educational Supplement*, 10, October.

Kelly, P. J. (1976), *Curriculum Diffusion Research Project: Outline Report*. Centre for Science Education, Chelsea College, University of London, April.

Project, Technology (1969), *Science and Technology for Girls*, Occasional Paper 1 (out of print).

Project Technology (1970), *Local Science and Technology Centres*, 30p from the Centre for School Technology, Trent Polytechnic.

Project Technology (1970), *Young Technologist*. An account of an experiment by boys at Gateway School, Leicester, which won the second European Philips Contest for Young Scientists and Inventors. (out of print).

School Technology, formerly *Bulletin*. Quarterly from the Centre for School Technology, Trent Polytechnic. Annual subscription (cash with order) £3.

Schools Council (1968), *Technology and the Schools* (Working Paper 18), HMSO (out of print). An account of the feasibility stage of the project.

Schools Council (1968), 'Mind-making or Machine-Making?', *Dialogue* 1, September.

Schools Council (1971), *Support for School Science and Technology*, Working Paper 38, Evans/Metheun Educational.

Taylor, L. J. (1969), *Project Work in A-level Physics*, Occasional Paper 2; 25p from the Centre for School Technology, Trent Polytechnic.

Tawney, D. A. (1973), 'Project Technology' in Schools Council Research Studies, *Evaluation in Curriculum Development: Twelve Case Studies*, Macmillan Education.

PROJECT PUBLICATIONS

For teachers

1. *Project Technology Handbooks* to help fill gaps in the teacher's knowledge and experience, help him or her initiate and supervise technological activities, and give guidance on the availability, use and construction of apparatus.
   Published from September 1972 by Heinemann Educational Books, 22 Bedford Square, London WCIB 3HH.
   1. *Bernoulli's Principle and the Carburetter*
   2. *Simple Bridge Structures*
   3. *Simple Materials Testing Equipment*
   4. *Introducing Fluidics*
   5. *Engine Test Beds*
   6. *Muffle Furnaces*
   7. *The Ship and Her Environment*
   8. *Design with Plastics*
   9. *Simple Fluid Flow*
   10. *Industrial Archaeology for Schools Vo. 1*
   11. *Industrial Archaeology for Schools Vol. 2*
   12. *Food Science and Technology*
   13. *Basic Electrical and Electronic Construction Methods*
   14. *Simple Computer and Control Logic*
   In addition NCST has published the following titles:
   Equipment Guide for the Basic Electronics Course
   Equipment Guide for Control Technology
   NCST has also produced a set of technology modules, books, films and equipment.

2. *Review Material* Case studies and methods of operation which have helped schools in introducing and developing technological activities.

Published by Hodder and Stoughton Educational, St. Paul's House, Warwick Lane, London EC4P 4AH.

Schools Science and Technology 1: Applications of Science   Revised edition 1970. Selected descriptions and case histories of applied science projects and investigations.

Schools Science and Technology 2: Science Fairs, 1970   Selected descriptions and case histories from BBC TV's Science Fairs.

For teachers and pupils

3.   *Technology Briefs* aim to inspire and guide pupils in order to involve them personally and directly in the technological design process. The briefs therefore suggest fields of activity and identify some of the problems in these fields, but allow different interpretations. Each brief carries an indication of whether its principal purpose is constructional, e.g. vacuum-forming apparatus, or investigational, e.g. aircraft noise, although many are written with both purposes in mind. There are 77 briefs in A4 cards with teachers' notes. Heinemann Educational Books, 1975.

4.   *Course Material*
(a) *Complete courses*
Basic Electronics   A two- or three-year course for 13–14 year-old pupils of average ability, or to be used as a shorter, more intensive course by older pupils, and even by teachers themselves. Five books. An equipment package is also available. Hodder and Stoughton Educational.
Control Technology   A two- or three-year Mode 3 CSE course. The materials include pupils' assignments, pupil follow-up material and a teacher's handbook. The Meccano Project Technology Kit (code no. 12973) is also available as is a pneumatics kit and an electronics kit. Hodder and Stoughton Educational, 1975.

(b) *Course components and resource material*
Photocell Applications   Pupils' and teachers' guide for use with average and above-average pupils. Hodder and Stoughton Educational, 1973.
Fibres in Chemistry   A pupil/teacher handbook of background material and investigational briefs. Hodder and Stoughton Educational, 1974.

Chapter 9 The humanities curriculum project

BIBLIOGRAPHY

Central Advisory Council for Education (England) (CACE) (1963), *Half our Future* (the Newsom Report), HMSO.
The Humanities Project: an Introduction (1970), Heinemann Educational Books.
Rudduck, Jean (1973), 'Dissemination in Practice: an Account of the Dissemination Programme of the Humanities Curriculum Project', *Cambridge Journal of Education*, 3, 3, 156.
Schools Council (1965), *Raising the School-Leaving Age: a Co-operative Programme of Research and Development*, Working Paper 2, HMSO.
Schools Council (1967), *Society and the Young School Leaver: a Humanities Programme in Preparation for the Raising of the School-Leaving Age*, Working Paper 11, HMSO.
Schools Council (1976), *Dissemination of Innovation: the Humanities Curriculum Project*, Working Paper 56, Evans/Methuen Educational.
Stenhouse, Lawrence (1967), *Culture and Education*, Nelson.
Stenhouse, Lawrence (1973), 'The Humanities Curriculum Project' in Butcher, H. J. and Pont, H. B. (eds.), *Educational Research in Britain, 3*, University of London Press.

OTHER BOOKS AND ARTICLES

A fuller bibliography is available free from CARE, University of East Anglia, Norwich. Please send stamped addressed envelope or cost of postage. (Those articles marked with an asterisk have been duplicated and are available from the Centre for Applied Research in Education, University of East Anglia; price list will be sent on application.)

Adams, A. (1976), 'The Humanities Curriculum Project', *The Humanities Jungle*, Ward Lock Educational, 93–110.

*Aston, Alasdair (1971), 'The Humanities Curriculum Project', ILEAs *NEDAL*, 6, October. (An account of the project by an LEA officer with responsibility for its dissemination.)

Aston, Alasdair (1972), 'Consumer Report on Humanities Project', *The Teacher*, 19 May.

Bailey, C. (1971), 'Rationality, Democracy and the Neutral Teacher', *Cambridge Journal of Education*, Easter.

Bailey, C. (1973), 'Teaching by Discussion and the Neutral Teacher', *Proceedings of the Philosophy of Education Society of Great Britain*, VII, January, 38.

Bailey, C. (1975), 'Neutrality and Rationality in Teaching', in Bridges, D. and Scrimshaw, P. (eds.), *Values and Authority in Schools*, Hodder and Stoughton, 128.

Bethell, Andrew (1974), 'Have you Done Poverty this Term?' *Teaching London Kids*, 3, (see also a response by R. Exton in no. 4.)

Bone, James (1970) 'It Would Still be a Bloody School ...', *The New Schoolmaster*, 47, 1, January.

Bramwell, R. D. (1976), 'A Humanities Curriculum Project in English Secondary Schools', *Curriculum Theory Network*, 5, 4.

Chambers, J. (1972), 'Can a Teacher be Neutral about Mass Murder?' *The Teacher*, 4 February.

Cohen, Stephen (1971), 'Seven Years' Planning Bears Fruit', *The Teacher*, 15 October.

Department of Education and Science (1975), *A Language for Life*, (The Bullock Report) HMSO.

*Dhand, H. and Wilson, B. (1971), 'Handling of Controversial Issues in the Classroom', *Nova Scotia Social Studies Review*, May.

*Elliott, J. (1969), 'The Role of the Humanities in Vocational Education', *Studies in Education and Craft*, 2, 1, Autumn.

*Elliott, J. (1970), 'Learning through Discussion', *Times Educational Supplement*, 13 November.

Elliott, J. (1971), 'The Concept of the Neutral Teacher', *Cambridge Journal of Education*, 2, Easter, 60–67.

Elliott, J. (1973), 'Neutrality, Rationality and the Role of the Teacher', in *Proceedings of the Philosophy of Education Society of Great Britain*, viii, Blackwell, January, 39–65.

Elliott, J. (1973), 'The Humanities Project on "People and Work" and the Concept of Vocational Guidance', *The Careers Teacher*, Spring.

*Elliott, J. (1974), 'Sex Role Constraints on Freedom of Discussion: a Neglected Reality of the Classroom', *The New Era*, July.

Elliott, J. (1975), 'The Values of the Neutral Teacher', in Bridges, D. and Scrimshaw P. (eds.), *Values in Education*, University of London Press.

*Elliott, J. and MacDonald, B. (eds.) (1975), *People in Classrooms*, Occasional Publication 2, Centre for Applied Research in Education, University of East Anglia.

Exton, Richard (1971), 'Conference Course', *Times Educational Supplement*, 29 October.

Fordham, P. (1974), 'The Humanities Curriculum Project in an Adult Class', *Studies in Adult Education*, 6, 1.

*Hamingson, D. (ed.) (1973), *Towards Judgement*, the publications of the Evaluation Unit of the Humanities Curriculum Project 1970–72. Occasional Publication 1, Centre for Applied Research in Education, University of East Anglia.

Hare, R. M. (1976), 'Value Education in a Pluralist Society: a Philosophical Glance at the Humanities Curriculum Project', *Proceedings of the Philosophy of Education Society of Great Britain*, X, 7–23.

Haywood, R. (1970), 'Curriculum Project in Practice', *Forum*, Autumn.

Hipkin, John (1972), 'Neutrality as a Form of Commitment', *Trends in Education*, April.

Holly, D. (1974), *Beyond Curriculum*, Paladin, 48–59.

Hooton, Peggy (1973), 'Humanities Curriculum Project: Three Years On', *Dialogue*, 14, May.

The Humanities Project: An Introduction (1970), Heinemann Educational Books.

Humble, S. (1972). 'Curriculum Dissemination: the Art of the Impossible?', *Cambridge Journal of Education*, 2, 3, Michaelmas.

Humble, S. and Rudduck, J. (1972), 'Local Education Authorities and Curriculum Innovation', in *The Curriculum: Context, Design and Development*, Units 13–15, Open University.

Humble, S. and Simons, H. (1978), *From Council to Classroom: The Evaluation of the Humanities Curriculum Project Diffusion*, Schools Council Research Studies, Macmillan Education.

Hyland, J. T. (1977), 'Teaching and Legitimate Influence in Moral Education', *Journal of Further and Higher Education*, 2 (see also Stenhouse, 1977).

Leighton, Joan (1972), 'Home-Grown Humanities Curriculum Project . . . An Exercise in Self-Help', *Forum*, 15, 1, Autumn.

MacDonald, B. and Rudduck, J. (1971), 'Curriculum Research and Development Projects: Barriers to Success', *British Journal of Educational Psychology*, 41, 2, June, and in *The Curriculum: Context, and Design and Development*, Units 13–15, Open University.

MacDonald, B. (1971), 'The Evaluation of the Humanities Curriculum Project: A Holistic Approach', *Theory into Practice*, X, 3 June.

MacDonald, B. (1973), 'Rethinking Evaluation: Notes from the Cambridge Conference', *Cambridge Journal of Education*, 3, 2, Easter.

MacDonald, B. (1973), 'Briefing Decision Makers: an Evaluation of the Humanities Curriculum Project', in Schools Council, *Evaluation in Curriculum Development: Twelve Case Studies*, Macmillan Education.

OECD/CERI (1975), *Handbook on Curriculum Development*, 81–84.

*Rudduck, J. (1973), 'Dissemination in Practice', *Cambridge Journal of Education*, 3, 2, 143–58.

Rudduck, Jean (1976), 'The Humanities Curriculum Project', *Dialogue*, 22, Spring.

Rudduck, Jean (1976), *Dissemination of Innovation: the Humanities Curriculum Project*, Schools Council Working Paper 56, Evans/Methuen Educational.

Rudduck, Jean (with Peter Kelly) (1976), *The Dissemination of Curriculum Development*, A European Trend Report on Educational Research, National Foundation for Educational Research, 82–89.

Russell, John (1976), 'Russell Square Diary', *Teachers World*, 24 December. (Note: there was a reply by L. Stenhouse, the project director).

Schools Council (1973), *Pattern and Variation in Curriculum Development Projects*, Schools Council Research Studies, Macmillan Education, 53–76.

Schools Council (1975), *Teaching Materials for Disadvantaged Children*, Gulliford, R. and Widlake, P. Curriculum Bulletin 5, Evans/Methuen Educational, 63–73.

Simons, Helen (1971), 'Innovation and the Case Study of Schools', *Cambridge Journal of Education*, October.

Stenhouse, L. A (1968), 'The Humanities Curriculum Project', *Journal of Curriculum Studies*, 1, 26–33.

Stenhouse, L. A. (1969), 'The Nuffield Foundation – Schools Council Humanities Curriculum Project: An Experiment in the Interpretation of Evidence in Small Groups', *Report of the Claremont Reading Conference*, 33rd Yearbook, Claremont, California.

*Stenhouse, L. A. (1969), 'Open-Minded Teaching', *New Society*, 24 July.

*Stenhouse, L. A. (1969), 'Handling Controversial Issues in the Classroom', *Education Canada*, December.

Stenhouse, L. A. (1970), 'Controversial Issues in the Classroom', *Values and the Curriculum*, a report of the fourth International Curriculum Conference, Washington DC, National Education Association, Centre for the Study of Instruction, 103–15.

Stenhouse, L. A. (1970), 'Learning for Responsibility – the New Humanities', *The Teacher and the Needs of Society in Evolution*, Pergamon.

*Stenhouse, L. A. (1970), 'Pupils into Students', *Dialogue*, 5.

Stenhouse, L. A. (1970–71), 'Some Limitations of the Use of Objectives in Curriculum Research and Planning', *Pedagogica Europaea*.

Stenhouse, L. A. (1971), 'The Humanities Project: The Rationale', *Theory into Practice*, X, 3, June, 154–62.

Stenhouse, L. A. (1972), 'The Idea of Neutrality', *Times Educational Supplement*, 4 February.

Stenhouse, L. A. (1973), 'Innovation and Stress', *Times Educational Supplement*, 19 January.

Stenhouse, L. A. (1973), 'The Humanities Curriculum Project' in Butcher, H. J. and Pont, H. B. (eds.), *Educational Research in Britain*, 3, University of London Press, pp. 149–67.

Stenhouse, L. A. (1974), 'Relations Between the Sexes – a Reply', *The New Era*, 55, 6, July/August (see Margherita Rendel).

Stenhouse, L. A. (1975), 'Neutrality as a Criterion in Teaching: the Work of the Humanities Curriculum Project', in Taylor Monica J. (ed.), *Progress and Problems in Moral Education*, NFER Publishing Co., pp. 123–33.

Stenhouse, L. A. (1975), *An Introduction to Curriculum Research and Development*, Heinemann Educational Books (various references, see index).

Stenhouse, L. A. (1977), 'An Appeal for Evidence of the Effectiveness of an Alternative Role to that of Neutral Chairman in Promoting Rational Inquiry into Moral Issues: a Reply to John T. Hyland', *Journal of Further and Higher Education*, 2.

Thwaites, Bryan (1976/77), 'Visions of greatness or the defence of values in education', *Bulletin of the Institute of Mathematics and its Applications*, 12, 10, October 1976. Reply by Stenhouse, L. A., 'Humanities Curriculum Project: Comment on an Article by Dr. Thwaites', *Bulletin*, October 1976; and Dr. Bryan Thwaites replies *Bulletin of the Institute of Mathematics and its Applications*, March/April 1977.

Walker, Barbara (1972), 'Humanities Kits', *Times Educational Supplement*, 12 May.

Warnock, Mary (1975), in Brown, S. C. (ed.), *Philosophers Discuss Education*, Macmillan, p. 160 (see also Montefiore, Alan).

Watt, A. (1972), 'Can't Teachers be Trusted Any More?', *The Teacher*, 28 January.

Wenham, P. (1972), 'Humanities: Problems in the Package', *Resources*, February.

Wilby, Peter (1976), 'The Nuffield Way: Humanities', *The Sunday Times Magazine*, 21 November.

Wringe, S. (1974), 'Some Problems Raised by the Schools Council Humanities Project', *Journal of Curriculum Studies*, 6, May, p. 30.

Wynn, Barry (1971), 'Humanities Project', *Times Educational Supplement*, 28 August.

Chapter 10 The design and craft project

BIBLIOGRAPHY

Aylward, B. (ed.) (1973), *Design Education*, Evans Brothers.

Baynes, K. (1976), *About Design*, Design Council.

Board of Education (1913), *Report of the Consultative Committee on Practical Work in Secondary Schools*, HMSO.

Bruner, J. S. (1963), *The Process of Education*, Vintage Books.
Dodd, T. (1978), *Design and Technology in the School Curriculum*, Hodder and Stoughton.
Eggleston, J. (1971), 'Craft' in Whitefield R. C. (ed.), *Disciplines and the Curriculum*, McGraw Hill.
Eggleston, J. (1973), 'Focus on Creativity – New Perspectives in Design Education', *Times Educational Supplement*, 22 June.
Eggleston, J. (1974), letter to author.
Eggleston, J. (1976), *Developments in Design Education*, Open Books.
Ministry of Education (1959), *15–18* (Crowther Report), HMSO.
National Scheme for Handwork Committee (1922), *Report*.
Pemberton, A. R. (1973), 'In Perspective', *Craft Education Magazine* (Stanley Tools), 32, Autumn.
Schools Council (1969), *Education Through the Use of Materials*, (Working Paper 26) Evans/Methuen Educational.
Schools Council (1975), *Education Through Design and Craft*, Edward Arnold.

PROJECT MATERIALS

Published by Edward Arnold, Woodlands Park Avenue, Woodlands Park, Maidenhead.

Materials and Design: A Fresh Approach
A book for teachers in service and in training which deals with design practice and its development and implementation and introduces the design process which lies at the heart of the project's work.

Design for Today
A teachers' book, looking at four areas of design and development 'Materials and Domestic Life', 'Materials and Community Development', 'Materials and Leisure', and 'Materials and Work'. Includes commentary for Five Introductory Filmstrips.

Five Introductory Filmstrips stemming from topics in *Design for Today*:
Design in the Environment, Value for Money, Houses and Homes, Helping Out, Playthings.

Looking at Design
A book for teachers which introduces certain principles essential to design and craft work. It contains commentaries to the nine film-strips.

Filmstrips associated with *Looking at Design:*
Joining Materials Together, Selection and Use of Materials, Colour and Texture, Outline and Surfaces, Moulding and Casting, Materials and Tools, Shape, Form, Function.

You are a Designer
An introduction for pupils to the problem solving design approach.

Connections and Constructions
A pupil's resource book designed to assist the development of appropriate fabrication techniques when designing and making products in a wide range of hard and soft materials.

Education through Design and Craft
This book examines, for teachers and educationalists, the role the materials subjects have to play in education in a changing society, paying particular attention to aims and objectives, and examinations and assessment.

Design and Karting
An introduction to designing and building a kart, plus commentary and frame reproductions of accompanying filmstrip *Kart-Ways*.

Creative Use of Concrete
Practical and technical aspects of the use of concrete in schools, plus commentary on accompanying film strip *Designing with Concrete*.

Designing with Plastics
An examination of the role of plastics in design-based work.

Design with a Purpose
A 16 mm. film available from the National Audio-Visual Aids Library, Paxton Place, Gypsy Road, London SE279SR. Looks at the work of a group of 15-year old students involved in designing and making play equipment for infant-school children.

Chapter 11 Geography for the young school leaver

BIBLIOGRAPHY

Bloom, B. S. and Krathwohl, D. R. (1956 and 1964), *Taxonomy of Educational Objectives*, 2 vols., Longman.
Chorley, R. J. and Haggett, P. (1965), *Frontiers in Geographical Teaching*, Methuen.
Hebdon, R. *et al.* (1977), 'Changing the Geography Syllabus: What Do the Pupils Think?', *Teaching Geography* 3, 1.
James, Charity (1968), *Young Lives at Stake*, Collins.
Kerr, J. F. (1968), *Changing the Curriculum*, University of London Press.
MacDonald, Barry and Walker, Rob (1976), *Changing the Curriculum*, Open Books.
Stenhouse, L. A. (1975), *An Introduction to Curriculum Research and Development*, Heinemann Educational Books.
Taba, Hilda (1962), *Curriculum Development: Theory and Practice*, Harcourt, Brace and World.
Williams, M. (1976), *Geography and the Integrated Curriculum*, Heinemann Educational Books.
Young, M. F. D. (1972), 'On the Politics of Educational Knowledge', *Economy and Society*, 1, 2.

PERIODICALS PRODUCED BY THE PROJECT

The Project in Schools, Autumn 1972. A collection of experiences and reflections by teachers involved in the first term of the trial.
Bulletin for Environmental Education 49, May 1975. A GYSL special issue.
Teachers Talking, vol. 1–4. Available biannually from Nelson.

ARTICLES AND BOOKS ABOUT THE PROJECT

Graves, N. J. (1975), *Geography in Education*, Heinemann Educational Books.
Gulliford, R. and Wildlake, P. (1975), *Teaching Materials for Disadvantaged Children*, Schools Council Curriculum Bulletin 5, Evans/Methuen Educational.
Hall, P. and Roberts, M. (1975), Cities and People Reviews, *Teaching Geography*, 1, 2, November.
Hall, D. (1976), *Geography and the Geography Teacher*, Unwin Educational Books, Ch. 4.
Hebden, R. *et al.* (1977), Changing the Geography Syllabus: What Do the Pupils Think?', *Teaching Geography*, 3. 1.
Higginbottom, T. (1977), Managing Change in Geography Teaching', *Dialogue*, 24.
Humphrys, G. and Morgan, W. (1976), People, Place and Work Reviews, *Teaching Geography*, 2, 1, August 1976.

MacDonald, Barry and Walker, Rob (1976), *Changing the Curriculum*, Open Books.

Patmore, J. and Robson, S. (1975), Man, Land and Leisure Reviews, *Teaching Geography*, 1, 1, April.

Wheatley, A. (1976), Implementing a Resource Based Project in Boden P. (ed.), *Developments in Geography Teaching*. Open Books.

Chapter 12 History 13–16

BIBLIOGRAPHY

History 13–16 (n.d.) *A New Look at History* (mimeo) Schools Council Project History 13–16

Lamont, W. (1971), 'The Uses and Abuses of Examinations' in Ballard M. (ed.) *New Movements in the Study and Teaching of History*. Temple-Smith.

Price, M. (1968), History in Danger, *History*, 53, 342.

Shemilt (1977), *On Observing Experiments and Anticipating Reality: the Evaluation of History 13–16* (mimeo) Schools Council Project History 13–16.

Sylvester, David (1973), 'First Views from the Bridge', *Teaching History*, 3, 10, 443.

PROJECT MATERIALS

Published by Holmes Macdougall, 137–141 Leith Walk, Edinburgh EH6 8NS.

A new look at history

What is History? (3rd year course)
Teacher's Guide
3 Filmstrips and Notes
People in the Past
Mystery of Tollund Man
Mystery of Mark Pullen
Mystery of the Empty Grave
Looking at Evidence
Problems of Evidence
Asking Questions
Spiritmaster Report Sheets

Modern world studies

The Arab/Israeli Conflict
The Rise of Communist China
   Pupil books, teachers' guides, filmstrip notes, filmstrips, cassettes.

Enquiry in depth

Elizabethan England
The American West 1840–95
Britain 1815–51
   Pupil books, teachers' guides, filmstrip notes, filmstrip.

Chapter 13 The sixth form mathematics curriculum project

BIBLIOGRAPHY

Bentley, C. (1971), *Trials of Package 3, Phase 1. Results and Comments SFMCP.*

Bentley, C., Malvern, D. D., (1972), *Trials of Phase 2 Packages during School Year 1971–2: Results and Comments SFMCP.*

Bentley, C., Malvern, D. D. (1975), *Looking Back on the Applicable Mathematics Course SFMCP.*

Dainton (1968), *Enquiry into the Flow of Candidates in Science and Technology into Higher Education,* HMSO.

Flemming W. (1977), *Notes for Guidance on the Course Work Essay.*

Hartshorne, C. and Weiss, P. (eds.) (1931–35), *The Collected Papers of Charles Saunders Pierce,* vol. 1, para. 3, Harvard U.P.

Lambert, J. H. (1764), *Neues Organon II.*

Lickert, R. (1932), A Technique for the Measurement of Attitudes, *Archives Psychology,* 140.

Lockard, J. D. (ed.) (1972), *Eighth Report of the International Clearinghouse on Science and Mathematics Curricular Developments,* University of Maryland.

Ormell, C. P. (1971), 'Mathematics Through the Imagination', *Dialogue* 9, 10–11.

Ormell, C. P. (1972), *Computer Education and Mathematics,* Project Discussion Paper.

Pierce, C. S. (1878) in *Popular Science Monthly,* January, and (1901), *Baldwin's Dictionary of Philosophy.*

SFMCP (no date) *Applicable Mathematics at Alternative-Ordinary Level.*

SFMCP (no date) *Briefing Notes.*

SFMCP (no date) *Applicable Mathematics AO-level Examination Report.*

SFMCP (1972), *Local Feasibility Studies.*

SFMCP (1973), *Doing a Feasibility Study.*

SFMCP (1976a) *Teaching Notes,* pp. 2, 3, 5.

SFMCP (1976b), *Pilot Examination Syllabus,* Project Paper 21.

SFMCP (1978), *Maths Applicable News 3,* April.

PROJECT MATERIALS

These are published under the general title *Mathematics Applicable* by Heinemann Educational Books, 22 Bedfold Square, London WC1B 3HH.

Pupils' discussion unit: *Mathematics Changes Gear* (1975)

Starter units: *Understanding Indices* (1975)
  Geometry from Co-ordinates (1975)
  Introductory Probability (1975)
  Polynomial Models (1978)
  Vector Models (1978)

Continuation units: *Algebra with Applications* (1978)
  Calculus Applicable (1976)
  Logarithmic/Exponential (1975)

Teachers' guide: *Teaching Mathematics Applicable* (1978)

Chapter 14 Scottish integrated science

BIBLIOGRAPHY

Bernstein, B. (1971), 'On the Classification and Framing of Educational Knowledge' in Young, M. F. D., (ed.) *Knowledge and Control,* Collier-Macmillan.

Brown, S. A. (1974), Integrated Science – A Useful Innovation?' *Education in Science*, 59, 22–26.

Brown, S. A. (1975), *Affective Objectives in an Integrated Science Curriculum*, Ph.D. Thesis, University of Stirling.

Brown, S. A. (1976), *Attitude Goals in Secondary Schools Science*, Stirling Educational Monographs No. 1, University of Stirling: Department of Education.

Brown, S. A. (1977), 'Case Study B: Evaluation of Attitude Objectives' in Cohen, D. (ed.), *New Trends in Integrated Science, Volume IV*, UNESCO.

Brown, S. A., McIntyre, D. I., Drever, E. and Davies, J. K. (1976), *Innovations in Integrated Science in Scottish Secondary Schools*. Stirling Educational Monographs No. 2, University of Stirling: Department of Education.

Brown, S. A., and McIntyre, D. I. (1977), *Factors Influencing Teachers' Responses to Curricular Innovations*, Paper presented to the British Educational Research Association Annual Meeting, September, University of Nottingham.

Buckie, W., Sinton, R., and Young, L. (1978), *Everything, Everywhere, Everyone, Pupils' Books 1 and 2, Teacher's Book*, OUP.

Dahllöf, U. S. (1971), *Ability Grouping, Content Validity, and Curriculum Process Analysis*, New York: Teachers' College Press.

Doyle, W. and Ponder, G. A. (1977), 'The Practicality Ethic in Teacher Decision Making', *Merril-Palmer Quarterly*, April.

Hamilton, D. (1973), 'The Integration of Knowledge: Practice and Problems', *Journal of Curriculum Studies*, 5, 146–55.

Hamilton, D. (1975), 'Handling Innovation in the Classroom: Two Scottish Examples' in Reid, W. A. and Walker, D. F. *Curriculum Change*. Routledge and Kegan Paul.

Jeffrey, A. W. (1977), 'Case Study A: Evaluation of the Scottish Integrated Science Syllabus' in Cohen, D. (ed.), *New Trends in Integrated Science, Volume IV, Evaluation of Integrated Science Education*, UNESCO.

King, D. J. (1972), *Studies on Curriculum Paper 7, 'Science for General Education'*, M.Ed. thesis, University of Glasgow.

Mee, A. J., Boyd, P. and Ritchie, D. (1971), *Science for the Seventies*, Heinemann Educational Books. (Two textbooks and teachers' guides geared directly to the sections of work in the course.)

Nisbet, J. (1970), 'Curriculum Development in Scotland', *Journal of Curriculum Studies*, 2, 5–10.

Nisbet, J. (1975), 'Curriculum Development in Scotland and England', paper presented to the Annual Conference of the Scottish Educational Research Association, 2–4 October, St. Andrews University.

Roebuck, M., Bloomer, J. and Hamilton, D. (1974), *Project PHI: Independent Learning Materials and Science Teaching in Small Schools in the Highlands and Islands of Scotland*, University of Glasgow: Department of Education.

Scottish Central Committee on Science (1977a), *Scottish Integrated Science: New Science Worksheets Sections 1 to 8*, Heinemann Educational Books.

Scottish Central Committee on Science (1977b), *Scottish Integrated Science: New Science Worksheets Sections 9 to 15*, Heinemann Educational Books.

Scottish Central Committee on Science (1977c), *Scottish Integrated Science: Teachers' Guide Sections 1 to 8*, Heinemann Educational Books.

Scottish Central Committee on Science (1977d), *Scottish Integrated Science: Teachers' Guide Sections 9 to 15*, Heinemann Educational Books.

Scottish Education Department (1969a), *First Report of Consultative Committee on the Curriculum 1965–68*, HMSO.

Scottish Education Department (1969b), *Curriculum Paper 7: Science for General Education*. Consultative Committee on the Curriculum, HMSO.

Scottish Education Department (undated), *Integrated Science Course Memoranda for Teachers*, (prepared by a Working Party of practising teachers offering guidance on the teaching of each section).

Scottish Secondary Science Working Party (1969, 1974), *Science Worksheets*, Heinemann Educational Books.

OTHER PUBLICATIONS RELATING TO SCOTTISH INTEGRATED SCIENCE

Association for Science Education (1970), 'Science for General Education: for the First Two Years and the Early School Leaver', *School Science Review*, 176, pp. 692–99.

Jeffrey, A. W. (1971), 'Adapting a Syllabus to a New Environment', in Richmond, P. E. (ed.), *New Trends in Integrated Science Teaching, vol. 1*, 252–56, UNESCO. (An account of the adaptation of the scheme in a developing country – Malaysia).

Ritchie, D. (1969), 'Anticipating Going Comprehensive and Using the Scottish Integrated Science Course', *Education in Science*, April, 25, Association for Science Education.

Ritchie, W. R. (undated), 'Integrated Science in Scotland', *Integrated Science Bulletin 2*, Schools Council Integrated Science Project.

Schools Science Equipment Research Centre, *Apparatus List for Integrated Science*, 103 Broughton Street, Edinburgh.

Scottish Centre for Mathematics, Science and Technical Education (1976), *Occasional Paper No. 3: Science in S1 and S2*. A science course for pupils of all abilities in the first two years of Scottish secondary schools, Dundee College of Education.

Scottish Centre for Mathematics, Science and Technical Education (1977), *Memorandum No. 28: Science in S1 and S2. New Science Worksheets General Teachers' Guide*, Dundee College of Education.

Scottish Certificate of Education Examination Board (1974), *Biology: Ordinary and Higher Grade Syllabuses and Notes*, Edinburgh. (Latest edition of one of the three separate science courses that correspond to the integrated course.)

Scottish Certificate of Education Examination Board (1975), *Chemistry: Ordinary and Higher Grade Syllabuses and Notes*, Edinburgh. (Latest edition of one of the three separate science courses that correspond to the integrated course.)

Scottish Certificate of Education Examination Board (1976), *Physics: Ordinary and Higher Grade Syllabuses and Notes*, Edinburgh. (Latest edition of one of the three separate science courses that correspond to the integrated course.)

Chapter 15 Man: A course of study

BIBLIOGRAPHY

Bruner, J. (1966), *Toward a Theory of Instruction*, Cambridge, Mass., the Belknap Press of Harvard U.P. (1970).

Bruner, J. (1970), 'The Skill of Relevance and the Relevance of Skill' in *Education in the Seventies*, Encyclopaedia Brittanica International Ltd.

Bumstead, R. (1970), 'Man: a Course of Study', *Educate*, 3, 4.

Eiseley, L. (1972), 'The Winter of Man' in *New York Times*, 16 January.

Eisner, E. (1974), 'Applying five curricula orientations to Man: a Course of Study' in Eisner, E. and Vallance, E., *Conflicting Conceptions of Curriculum*.

Elliott, J. (1971), *The ideology of Man: a Course of Study*, a report to the Ford Foundation on the Summer Institute workshop at Miami, Florida (mimeo), University of East Anglia.

Ferber, Ellen (1970), 'What Makes Humans Human?', *American Education*, 6, 4.

Hanley, J., Whitla, D., Moo, E., and Walter, A. (1969–70), *Curiosity, Competence, Community: An evaluation of Man: a Course of Study*, Cambridge, Mass., Education Development Centre.

Hipkin, J. and Elliott, J. (1971), 'Man: a Course of Study', *Times Educational Supplement*, 30 April.

Inglis, F. (1975), 'Ideology and Curriculum: the Value Assumptions of the System Builders' in Golby, M., Greenwald, J. and West, R. (eds.), *Curriculum Design*, Croom Helm.

Jenkins, D. (1976a), 'Jerome Bruner', Radio Programme made for *Curriculum Design and Development*, Open University course E203.

Jenkins, D. (1976b), 'Man: A Course of Study' in *Design Issues*, units 14–15 of *Curriculum Design and Development*, Open University course E203.

Jones, R. (1968), *Fantasy and Feeling in Education*, New York University Press.

Link, F. (1972), *Seminars for Leadership Personnel*, Curriculum Development Associates.

Rudduck, J. (1972), 'Man: a Course of Study', *Cambridge Journal of Education*, 2, 2.

Stenhouse, L. (1975), *An Introduction to Curriculum Research and Development*, Heinemann Educational Books.

Totten, E. (1972), 'Man alive'. *The Guardian*, 27 June.

Tucker, R. (1972), 'Man: A Course of Study' in Rogers, V. and Weinland, T. (eds.), *Teaching Social Studies in the Urban Curriculum*, Addison-Wesley.

COURSE MATERIALS

Films
   'The Life Cycle of the Salmon' (10 mins)
   'Herring Gull Behaviour' (10 mins)
   'Animals in Amboseli' (20 mins)
   'The Younger Infant' (10 mins)
   'The Older Infant' (18 mins)
   'The Baboon Troop' (22 mins)
   'Miss Goodall and the Wild Chimpanzees' (30 mins)
   'Fishing at the Stone weir' (30 mins)
   'Life on the Tundra' (14 mins)
   'At the Caribou Crossing Place' (29 mins)
   'Autumn River Camp' (Parts 1 and 2) (26 and 32 mins)
   'Winter Sea-Ice Camp' (Parts 1 and 2) (32 and 30 mins)
   'The Legend of the Raven' (20 mins)
   Also available 'Knud' (31 mins)

Booklets
   Life Cycle
   Animal Adaptation
   Information and Behaviour
   Innate and Learned Behaviour
   Natural Selection
   Structure and Function
   Salmon
   Herring Gulls
   The Observer's Handbook
   Animals of the African Savanna

Baboons
The Baboon Troop
Baboon Communication
The Field Notes of Irven DeVore
A Journey to the Arctic
Songs and Stories of the Netsilik Eskimos
Antler and Fang
The Arctic
On Firm Ice
The Many Lives of Kiviok
This World We Know
The True Play
The Data Book
7 additional animal books

Other materials include records, five film strips, 23 maps and posters, three educational games and Eskimo cards. The *Teachers Guide* offers nine books of background information, bibliographies, suggested lesson plans, strategies for evaluation and a series of in-service seminars for teachers.

Chapter 16 The ford teaching project

BIBLIOGRAPHY

Adelman, C. (1973), *Recording, Interviews and Interpretations* (mimeo), University of East Anglia.
Adelman, C. (1976), *On First Hearing* (mimeo), University of East Anglia.
Adelman, C. and Elliott, J. (1973), *Meanings and a Derived Schema*, central team document H (mimeo), University of East Anglia.
Dearden R. S. (1972), 'Autonomy and Education' in Dearden R. S., Hirst P. H., Peters R. S. (eds.), *Education and the Development of Reason*, Routledge and Kegan Paul.
Elliott, J. (1973a), *Developing Awareness and Perception: the Methodology of Teacher Development*, Paper read to a Conference on the Study of the Curriculum, University of Sussex, July (mimeo), University of East Anglia.
Elliott, J. (1973b), *Three Points of View in the Classroom* (mimeo), University of East Anglia.
Elliott, J. (1975a), *Preparing Teachers for Classroom Accountability* (mimeo), Cambridge Institute of Education, published in *Education for Teaching*, Summer 1976.
Elliott, J. (1975b), *Classroom Accountability and the Self-Monitoring Teacher* (mimeo), Cambridge Institute of Education.
Elliott, J. (1976), *Developing Hypotheses About Classroom From Teachers' Practical Constructs* (mimeo), Cambridge Institute of Education.
Elliott, J. and Adelman, C. (1973a), *Towards a General Methodology of Inquiry/Discovery Teaching*, central team document I (mimeo), University of East Anglia.
Elliott, J. and Adelman, C. (1973b), 'Reflecting Where the Action Is: the Design of the Ford Teaching Project', *Education for Teaching*, November.
Ford Teaching Project (1973), *Reflections on the Easter Conference 1973*: A Look at the Problems and Principles of Inquiry/Discovery Teaching, central team document F (mimeo), University of East Anglia.
Ford Teaching Project (no date), *Implementing the Principles of Inquiry/Discovery Teaching: Some Hypotheses*, Unit 3. Cambridge Institute of Education.
Nisbet, John (1974), 'Bridging the Gap between Research and Practice', Address to National Foundation for Educational Research's Annual Conference.

Tizard, J. (1976), 'Psychology and Social Policy', *British Psychological Society Bulletin*, July.

Wrigley, J. (1976), 'How to Assess Innovation in Schools', *New Society*, 8 July.

FURTHER READING

Adelman, C. (1977) 'Sociological Constructions: Teachers' Categories' in Woods, P. and Hammersley, M. (eds.), *The Experience of Schooling*, Croom Helm.

Adelman, C. (1976), *On First Hearing* (mimeo), Paper to SSRC Conference 'Collecting, Using and Reporting Talk' in *Research in Education*.

Adelman, C. and Walker R. (1974), 'Stop Frame Cinematography with Synchronised Sound: a Technique for Recording in School Classrooms', *Journal of the Society of Motion Picture and Television Engineers*, 83, 3, Scarsdale, New York.

Adelman, C. and Walker R. (1975), 'Developing Pictures for Other Frames: Action Research and Case Study' in Chanan, G. and Delamont, S. (eds.), *Frontiers of Classroom Research*, NFER.

Almond, L. (1975), 'Ford Teaching Project', review in *Journal of Curriculum Studies*, November.

Bowen, R. B., Green, L. L. J., and Pols, R. (1975), 'The Ford Project – the Teacher as Researcher', *British Journal of In-Service Education*, Autumn.

Cook, M. (1975), 'Bridging the Gap between Theory and Practice,' a review of Ford Teaching Project publications, *Times Educational Supplement*, 18 July.

Cook, M. (1975), 'Where the Action–Research is – a Look at the Innovatory Work Arising out of the Ford Teaching Project', *Times Educational Supplement*, 11 July.

Cooper, D. and Ebbutt, D. (1974), 'Participation in Action–Research as an In-Service Experience', *Cambridge Journal of Educational*, Easter.

Elliott, J. (1974), 'Sex Role Constraints on Freedom of Discussion: a Neglected Reality of the Classroom', *The New Era*, July/August.

Elliott, J. (1975), *Classroom Accountability and Self-Monitoring Teacher*, Sept. (mimeo), Cambridge Institute of Education.

Elliott, J. (1975), *Preparing Teachers for Classroom Accountability*, Sept. (mimeo), Cambridge Institute of Education.

Elliott, J. (1976), 'Objectivity, Ideology and Teacher Participation in Educational Research'. *Research Intelligence*, BERA Bulletin.

Elliott, J. (1976), 'Developing Hypotheses about Classrooms from Teachers' Practical Constructs: an Account of the Work of the Ford Teaching Project', Paper read at a symposium on *Modes of Thought among Teachers* at the annual meeting of the American Educational Research Association, 1976.

Elliott, J. and Adelman, C. (1973), 'Reflecting Where the Action Is: the Design of the Ford Teaching Project', *Education for Teaching*, November.

Elliott, J. and Adelman, C. (1973), 'Inquiry and Discovery Teaching – a New Ford Teaching Project', *The New Era*, June.

Elliott, J. and Adelman, C. (1973), 'Supporting Teachers' Research in the Classroom'; Thurlow, J., 'Eliciting Pupils' Interpretations in the Primary School'; and Rowe, M., 'The Cyclical Structure of Evaluatory Schemes'; all from 'Teachers as Evaluators', *The New Era*, December.

Elliott, J. and Adelman, C. (1975), 'Teacher Education for Curriculum Reform: an Interim Report on the Work of the Ford Teaching Project', *British Journal of Teacher Education*, January.

Elliott, J. and Adelman C. (1975), 'Teachers Accounts and the Control of Classroom Research, *London Education Review*, Autumn.

Elliott, J. and Adelman, C. (1975), 'Aspirations into Reality: Approaches to Inquiry/Discovery Teaching', *Education 3–13*, October.

Maw, Janet (1976), 'The Ford Teaching Project: A Review of Published Documents in Relation to In-Service Education', *British Journal of In-Service Education*, Spring.
Munro, R. G. (1974), 'Self-Monitoring Teachers', *Times Educational Supplement*, 21 June.

PROJECT PUBLICATIONS

Available from the Project at Cambridge Institute of Education, Shaftesbury Road, Cambridge.

Unit 1 Patterns of teaching

The Language and Logic of Informal Teaching, John Elliott and Clem Adelman.
Primary School – *The Tins*.
Primary School Elective Tasks.
Primary School Science.
Paper Structures – Middle School.
Social Studies in a Secondary School.

Unit 2 Research Methods

Support for Research-Based Inquiry/Discovery Teaching by Ford Project Teachers.
Ways of Doing Research in One's Own Classroom by Ford Project Teachers.
Classroom Action Research by John Elliott and Clem Adelman.
The Stranger in the Classroom by John Elliott, Clem Adelman, Karen Sitte, and Ford Project Teachers.
Three Points of View in the Classroom – Generating Hypotheses from Classroom Observations, Recordings, and Interviews by John Elliott assisted by Ford Project Teacher.
Team Based Action Research by Ford Project Teachers.
Self-Monitoring Questioning Strategies by John Elliott assisted by Ford Project Teacher.
Eliciting Pupils' Accounts in the Classroom, by John Elliott, Clem Adelman, and Ford Project Teachers.

Unit 3 Hypotheses

The Innovation Process in the Classroom by John Elliott and Clem Adelman.
Implementing the Principles of Inquiry/Discovery Teaching: Some Hypotheses, by Ford Project Teachers.

Unit 4 Teacher case studies

A Third-Year Form Tries to Enter a Freer World – Research into Ways Towards Inquiry/Discovery Working, by Ford Project Teacher.
The Castles Group Ford Project Teacher *Inquiry/Discovery Learning in a Science* Classroom, and *The China Project* by Ford Project Teachers.
Question Strategies: A Self Analysis by Ford Project Teacher *Identifying Problems and Strategies in the Classroom*, by Ford Project Teachers.

Chapter 17 Reflections

BIBLIOGRAPHY

Bell, R. and Prescott, W. (eds.) (1975), *The Schools Council: A Second Look*, Ward Lock Educational.

Corbett, Anne (1975), 'Teachers and the Schools Council' in Bell and Prescott (1975).

Dewey, John (1916), *Democracy and Education*, Macmillan.

MacDonald, Barry (1973), 'Innovation and Incompetence' pp. 88–92 in Hamingson, Donald (ed.), *Towards Judgement: the Publications of the Evaluation unit of the Humanities Curriculum Project 1970–72*, Centre for Applied Research in Education, Occasional Publication 1.

Manzer, R. A. (1970), *Teachers and Politics*, Manchester U.P.

Nisbet, John (1973), The Schools Council, Unitied Kingdom, 7–76 in Centre for Educational Research and Innovation (CERI) *Case Studies of Educational Innovations: 1 At the Central Level*, Organization for Economic Co-operation and Development.

Parlett, Malcolm and Hamilton, David (1972), *Evaluation as Illumination: A New Approach to the Study of Innovatory Programmes*, Centre for Research in Educational Sciences, University of Edinburgh, Occasional Paper.

Pestalozzi, Joseph Heinrich (1894), *How Gertrude Teaches Her Children*, G. Allen and Unwin.

Rousseau, Jean-Jacques (1780), *Emile* (English translation, Dent).

Rudduck, Jean (ed.) (1979) *Learning to Teach through Discussion*. Centre for Applied Research in Education, UEA, Norwich.

Schools Council (1973), *Evaluation in Curriculum Development: Twelve Case Studies*, Macmillan Education.

Stenhouse, Lawrence (1975), *An Introduction to Curriculum Research and Development*, Heinemann Educational Books.

Tawney, David (ed.) (1976), *Curriculum Evaluation Today: Trends and implications*, Macmillan Education.

Wiseman, Stephen and Pidgeon, Douglas (1970), *Curriculum Evaluation*, NFER Publishing Co.

Index